PENGUIN BOOKS

GOD ON TRIAL

Peter Irons is a professor emeritus of political science at the University of California, San Diego, where he taught constitutional law from 1982 to 2004 and directed the Earl Warren Bill of Rights Project. A Harvard Law School graduate and civil liberties lawyer, he is a member of the Supreme Court bar. His previous books include *Justice at War, The Courage of Their Convictions, A People's History of the Supreme Court,* and *Jim Crow's Children,* all of which received Silver Gavel awards from the American Bar Association. He lives in Greenville, California.

GOD ON TRIAL

*Landmark Cases from America's
Religious Battlefields*

PETER IRONS

PENGUIN BOOKS

PENGUIN BOOKS

Published by the Penguin Group

Penguin Group (USA) Inc., 375 Hudson Street, New York, New York 10014, U.S.A.

Penguin Group (Canada), 90 Eglinton Avenue East, Suite 700, Toronto,
Ontario, Canada M4P 2Y3 (a division of Pearson Penguin Canada Inc.)

Penguin Books Ltd, 80 Strand, London WC2R 0RL, England

Penguin Ireland, 25 St Stephen's Green, Dublin 2, Ireland (a division of Penguin Books Ltd)

Penguin Group (Australia), 250 Camberwell Road, Camberwell,
Victoria 3124, Australia (a division of Pearson Australia Group Pty Ltd)

Penguin Books India Pvt Ltd, 11 Community Centre,
Panchsheel Park, New Delhi – 110 017, India

Penguin Group (NZ), 67 Apollo Drive, Rosedale, North Shore 0632,
New Zealand (a division of Pearson New Zealand Ltd)

Penguin Books (South Africa) (Pty) Ltd, 24 Sturdee Avenue,
Rosebank, Johannesburg 2196, South Africa

Penguin Books Ltd, Registered Offices:
80 Strand, London WC2R 0RL, England

First published in the United States of America by Viking Penguin,
a member of Penguin Group (USA) Inc. 2007
Published in Penguin Books 2008

10 9 8 7 6 5 4 3 2 1

THE LIBRARY OF CONGRESS HAS CATALOGED THE HARDCOVER EDITION AS FOLLOWS:
Irons, Peter H., 1940–
God on trial : dispatches from America's religious battlefields / Peter Irons.
p.   cm.
Includes bibliographical references and index.
ISBN 978-0-670-03851-0 (hc.)
ISBN 978-0-14-311375-1 (pbk.)
1. Freedom of religion—United States.   2. Church and state—United States.   I. Title.
KF4783.I76 2007
342.7308'52—dc22   2006052815

Printed in the United States of America
Designed by Carla Bolte • Set in Celeste

For my friends in the United Methodist Church
of Greenville, California, who really believe in
"Open Hearts, Open Minds, Open Doors"

And to the memory of Phil Paulson,
who never wavered in his indomitable
defense of church-state separation

CONTENTS

God on Trial tells the stories of recent conflicts over religion in six American communities: towns and cities that have become battlefields in America's growing religious wars. They are spread across the country, from Pennsylvania to California, and range in size from a rural town of barely a thousand people to the nation's seventh-largest city. Each conflict began with a decision by elected officials—school-board members, city councilors, county executives, or state legislators—to place a religious symbol on public property or to adopt a religious practice in public schools. Some of these symbols and practices went unchallenged for years, even decades, while others prompted an immediate objection by dissenting community residents. Each local conflict wound up in federal courtrooms, requiring judges—from the trial level to the Supreme Court's chamber—to interpret and apply the first clause of the First Amendment to the Constitution: "Congress shall make no law respecting an establishment of religion." The outcomes of these cases differed widely, reflecting long-standing judicial discord over the "original intent" of the clause's framers in 1789 and its current meaning, more than two centuries later. Similar cases have already divided local communities, and will soon be decided by judges and justices whose earlier rulings in Establishment Clause cases remain open for either reversal or reaffirmation.

The seeds of this book were planted some thirty years ago by a four-word sentence in a Supreme Court opinion that I read as a law student: "We live by symbols." Justice Oliver Wendell Holmes, who wrote these words, had in mind symbols that have long rallied their followers to heroic deeds, even to sacrifice their lives in wars to protect the values those symbols embody. One such symbol is the American flag, the defense of which against the Confederate insurrection in the Civil War spurred Holmes to enlist in the Union Army, in whose service he was twice gravely wounded in battle. An equally powerful symbol for many

Americans is the Christian cross, often linked to the flag in a merger of religious and patriotic zeal. The two tablets of the Ten Commandments symbolize for both Jews and Christians the moral foundation of God's rules for belief and behavior. Symbolic meaning can be expressed in words as well as objects. The first chapter of Genesis, read literally by many Christians, symbolizes their belief that God created all of Earth's living creatures, including humankind, in just six days. And spoken prayer at public events, from the first meeting of Congress in 1789 to the most recent presidential inauguration, has symbolized the dual commitment of elected officials to God and to the Constitution whose commands they swear to uphold.

Public-opinion polls going back more than four decades show that a strong majority of Americans supports the public display of religious symbols, prayer in public schools, and the teaching of "creationism" in high-school biology classes. But a minority—sometimes just one person in a community—objects to such displays and practices. Many dissenters—and we cannot know how many—simply hold their tongues and remain silent, fearful of provoking the hostility of their friends and neighbors. Others, however, voice their objections at school-board meetings, in city-council sessions, or in letters to their local papers. An even smaller number take the step of filing lawsuits, often with the aid of lawyers representing organizations committed to the separation of church and state, suits that are frequently opposed by lawyers from well-funded Religious Right groups. Only a tiny number of these suits reach the Supreme Court, but the decisions in such cases have ramifications far beyond the towns and cities in which they began.

Over the past three decades, both as a practicing lawyer and a constitutional-law professor, I have tracked hundreds of Supreme Court cases, and have written about dozens of them in several books, including *The Courage of Their Convictions*, which recounted sixteen cases—decided between 1940 and 1986—that raised issues of race, religion, protest, and privacy. For that book, I visited the communities in which the cases began, and interviewed the people who initiated legal challenges that resulted in landmark Supreme Court decisions. In a later book, *Jim Crow's Children: The Broken Promise of the Brown Decision,* I also visited the five communities—in Kansas, Delaware, Washington, D.C., Virginia, and South Carolina—from which challenges to school segregation all reached the Supreme Court and were jointly decided in 1954 in that historic decision. In both books, I recorded the first-person stories of people who were involved in those cases, recalling their experiences in words that expressed the range of emotions from pain to exultation. These stories, I felt, added human faces and voices to the dry words of judicial opinions.

When the seeds of Justice Holmes's observation finally sprouted in the idea for this book, I decided to follow the format of these earlier books, visiting the communities in which "symbol" cases began and recording the stories of people who played key roles in them. I also decided to include the stories of people on both sides of the cases, to understand better the differing values and beliefs that prompted them—some eagerly and others reluctantly—to stand on opposite sides of the "wall of separation" between church and state, an increasingly shaky wall in recent years. I faced the initial task of winnowing through dozens of possible cases. My final choice of the six that are recounted in five later chapters—two almost identical cases are joined in one chapter—reflects my judgment as to which cases were both significant and exciting, at least to me. I have placed these chapters in chronological order, based on the year the cases were filed and not on their final decision.

They begin in 1989 with a challenge in San Diego, California, to a forty-three-foot-high Latin cross in the middle of a 170-acre public park at the summit of Mount Soledad, the city's highest point and its most visible landmark. Next, I recount the challenge in 1995 to the recital of prayers at high-school football games in the Gulf Coast town of Santa Fe, Texas. Four years later, in 1999, separate lawsuits were filed against the display of the Ten Commandments in the courthouses of two rural Kentucky counties and on the grounds of the state capitol in Austin, Texas. The following year, in 2000, a parent with a first-grade student in Elk Grove, California, challenged the words "under God" in his daughter's daily recital of the Pledge of Allegiance to the American flag. Finally, in 2004, eleven parents of children in the public schools of Dover, Pennsylvania, challenged the school board's decision to require the reading in high-school biology classes of a statement supporting "intelligent design" as an alternative to the Darwinian theory of evolution.

——

All these cases share two features that influenced my decision to include them in this book. First, the judicial decisions they produced all provoked heated reactions from political leaders, including prominent members of Congress and President George W. Bush, most often in denunciation of "activist" judges whose decisions the politicians deplored. Some rulings even spurred campaigns for the impeachment of the offending judges; ironically, most had been named to the bench by Republican presidents. Second, each case drew the involvement of both Separationist and Religious Right groups and their legal teams, either as counsel or as "friends of the court" in filing supporting briefs. Many other groups, some with millions of members, like the American Legion and the National Education Association, also filed briefs in high-profile cases. For example, when the Pledge of Allegiance case reached the Supreme Court in 2004, the briefs of the parties were joined by more than fifty that expressed the views of almost one hundred interest groups on both sides.

These factors help to explain this book's admittedly provocative subtitle. It may seem hyperbolic to employ such a martial term as "battlefields" in recounting conflicts in which none of the combatants took up arms against one another. To be sure, in some cases tempers grew short, voices were raised, people were verbally abused, warned of eternal damnation, and even threatened with physical harm. But such expressions of anger and frustration are common when people clash over things in which they deeply believe, and few beliefs are more deeply held than religious convictions. Americans are fortunate—perhaps "blessed" is a better term—to have thus far been spared the bloody sectarian wars that have cost thousands of lives in other countries. In recent years, and even today, Catholics and Protestants in Northern Ireland, Muslims and Hindus in India, Jews and Palestinians in Israel, and Sunni and Shia Muslims in Iraq have killed one another in civil wars that have both religious roots and political aims. But even in America's history, lives have been lost in religious conflict. As we will see, the execution of "witches" in colonial Massachusetts, the hanging of Quakers in that colony, and the death of thirteen people in the "Bible Riots" that erupted in Philadelphia in the 1840s all stemmed from religious conflicts in which the executioners and rioters claimed divine sanction for their murderous acts.

We tend to look back on such events as aberrations from the tradition of religious tolerance that we like to think better reflects our nation's history. But this strain of religiously motivated violence is not ancient history. Over the past three decades, antiabortion militants have murdered doctors, nurses, and clinic patients in the name of God. Loosely tied under the banner of the "Army of God," these Christian extremists ironically share that name with a faction of Muslim extremists who have beheaded Americans in the name of Allah. Needless to say, the antiabortion movement should not be tarred with the brush of such domestic terrorists, any more than American Muslims should be charged with the crimes of their religion's terrorist fringe.

But the imagery of religious "warfare" remains in American society and politics, reflected in the titles of two recent books. David Limbaugh, a lawyer and brother of the better-known Rush Limbaugh, was the author in 2003 of *Persecution: How Liberals Are Waging War Against Christianity.* Journalist Clint Willis answered in 2005 with *Jesus Is Not a Republican: The Religious Right's War on America.* As these titles suggest, Limbaugh and Willis both blame their political adversaries for launching religious wars to achieve political goals. Behind their fevered rhetoric, both authors have correctly identified a long-standing feature of our nation's history, the close linkage of politics and religion. Back in the 1830s, Alexis de Tocqueville—a French Catholic visitor to America— noted that "religious zeal is perpetually stimulated in the United States by the duties of patriotism" and remarked that "you meet with a politician where you expected to find a priest."

Over the years since Tocqueville's perceptive observations, American politics has been infused with religious appeals for partisan support. The most notable recent example was voiced in the fiery speech by Pat Buchanan, the conservative writer and one-time presidential candidate, to the Republican national convention in 1992: "There is a religious war going on in this country, a cultural war as critical to the kind of nation we shall be as the Cold War itself, for this war is for the soul of America." Buchanan's linkage of religion to the broader American culture is telling, and reflects the fact that virtually every aspect of our culture—art, literature, television and film, family life, sexuality, and other elements of our society—has become a target of what I call the New Puritans. Those who campaign against pornography, abortion, and same-sex marriage are the same people who battle to protect such religious symbols and practices as the Ten Commandments, Christian crosses, and school prayer.

———

This book's structure reflects the intersection of American history, law, and politics as they jointly affect the religious battles that have been waged since our nation's earliest days. The first three chapters explore these factors in that order, providing the context for the cases recounted in the five that follow. Chapter One lays the historical foundation, beginning with the settlement of the New England colonies by English Puritans, determined to build a "New Jerusalem" in which church and state were linked with legal codes based explicitly on Old Testament proscriptions and punishments. Other colonies, such as New York, Pennsylvania, and Virginia, did not follow the model of the New England theocracies, but most taxed their residents to support established churches and punished religious dissenters, most notably Baptists, with fines and imprisonment for preaching without licenses. Two Virginia politicians, James Madison and Thomas Jefferson, were revolted by what Madison called in 1774 the "diabolical, hell-conceived principle of persecution" for religious beliefs, and responded with successful efforts to disestablish their state's Episcopal Church. Although Madison resisted calls at the Constitutional Convention in 1787 to add a bill of rights to the new nation's charter of government, he reluctantly bowed to pressure from opponents of its ratification, drafting in 1789, as a member of the First Congress, a bill of rights whose first two clauses provided that "Congress shall make no law respecting an establishment of religion, or prohibiting the free exercise thereof."

Chapter Two explains the seemingly puzzling fact that not until 1947 did the Supreme Court issue its first Establishment Clause ruling. Because the First Amendment, by its terms, applied only to congressional acts, the justices had consistently held that local and state laws were beyond their jurisdiction. Starting in 1925, however, the Court abruptly— and without explanation—began the process of "incorporating" First Amendment guarantees into the Fourteenth Amendment, which requires the states to provide their citizens with the same "due process" guarantees of the Fifth Amendment. One by one, beginning with the Free Speech and Free Press clauses, the Court protected First Amendment rights against state abridgment. A series of rulings between 1938 and 1943 extended that protection to the Free Exercise Clause, largely in cases brought by members of the Jehovah's Witnesses, who challenged laws that banned or restricted their practices of door-to-door and street-corner proselytizing. In 1947, the Court held that the Establishment Clause "requires the state to be a neutral in its relations with groups of religious believers and non-believers," in an opinion written by Justice Hugo Black. Over the next five decades, the Court applied the "neutrality" doctrine—with a few exceptions—in striking down state laws that allowed prayer and Bible-reading in public schools, the teaching of Biblical "creationism" in high-school biology classes, and the posting of the Ten Commandments in school classrooms. These decisions have all served as precedent in the cases recounted in this book, although the Court's divisions in recent Establishment Clause cases have exposed what Justice Clarence Thomas has aptly described as the "hopeless disarray" among his colleagues over that clause's interpretation and application.

Chapter Three examines the political factors in America's religious wars, first looking at the groups—most notably, the American Civil Liberties Union and Americans United for Separation of Church and State—that have long supported church-state separation. Beginning in the 1930s, ACLU lawyers racked up an impressive string of Supreme Court victories, largely in defending Jehovah's Witnesses. Founded in 1947, Americans United joined the ACLU in opposing laws that provided tax support for private religious schools, most of them Catholic. In these early Establishment Clause battles with local and state officials, ACLU and AU lawyers most often faced—and almost always defeated—

lawyers with little experience in First Amendment law. The emergence and rapid growth of the Religious Right during the Reagan years, however, prompted its leaders to establish legal arms for such groups as Pat Robertson's Christian Coalition and Jerry Falwell's Moral Majority. Robertson set up the American Center for Law and Justice in 1990, and Falwell soon followed by forming Liberty Counsel; more than a dozen other Religious Right groups now have their own legal arms. Lavishly funded by right-wing foundations, these organizations are staffed by skilled and media-savvy lawyers who have battled their ACLU and AU adversaries in dozens of religion cases over the past two decades.

With these first three chapters as background, Chapters Four through Eight take us into the six communities in which began the local battles over religious symbols and practices they recount. Each chapter ends with the first-person stories of people who played key roles on both sides of these battles. They include both evangelical and mainstream Christians, Jews, those with no religious ties, and atheists. They represent, in fact, people who live in almost every American town and city, distinguished only by taking a stand on issues that have divided their communities and the nation.

––––––

Let me, finally, explain the background and beliefs that impelled me to write this book. My longtime interest in religious disputes stems from those within my own family. One of my ancestors, the Reverend John Greenwood, ordained as an Anglican priest, broke with the Church of England and was among the first Puritan ministers in England. He was executed in 1593 for "writing against the Book of Common Prayer," spurring members of his church to seek sanctuary in Holland. My earliest American ancestor, William White, arrived with other Puritans from Holland and England on the *Mayflower* in 1620, and was a signer of the Mayflower Compact. The first generations of this family branch were staunch Puritans, several becoming Puritan ministers. More recently, my maternal grandparents were both religious apostates. My mother's father, whose parents were born in Ireland, was banished from his family in New Hampshire at the age of thirteen after refusing to attend daily

Catholic services. He and my maternal grandmother, raised as a Methodist in Nova Scotia, encouraged my mother to sample all the churches in Hudson, Massachusetts, where she grew up. She finally chose the Unitarian Church, which imposes no creedal affirmations on its members, as the most welcoming for a teen-ager with an inquiring mind.

My father's ancestors were Scots-Irish immigrants to western Pennsylvania in the 1780s, bringing with them the stern Calvinism of the Presbyterian Church and producing several noted ministers; the Irons Memorial Presbyterian Church in McDonald, Pennsylvania, bears the name of my great-great-grandfather. My father left the Presbyterian Church during his college years, and became a Unitarian when he married my mother. Along with my six brothers and sisters, I attended Unitarian churches from the age of seven through high school. During my years at Antioch College, whose first president in the 1850s was a noted Unitarian, Horace Mann, I attended Quaker meetings in the college chapel. Over the two decades after my graduation from Antioch in 1966, during which I obtained a doctorate in political science from Boston University and a J.D. from Harvard Law School, I rarely attended church, although I sometimes went to Quaker meetings and Buddhist services, relishing the focused spirituality they encouraged.

After I moved from Boston in 1982 to teach constitutional law at the University of California, San Diego, I returned to the Unitarian Church. Here I met my wife, whose parents are nonobservant Jews but insisted that she attend Hebrew school and go through the Bas Mitzvah ceremony. Our two daughters attended Unitarian Sunday school in San Diego, but after I retired from UCSD in 2004 and we moved to a very small town in northern California, far from the nearest Unitarian church, I began attending the local United Methodist church, whose members were delighted to finally have a bass in its seven-member choir. Greenville's Methodists have welcomed me into their church, although I do not recite the Lord's Prayer and sit quietly in my pew during the monthly Communion service. This family background of Puritans, Catholics, Methodists, Presbyterians, and Unitarians has shaped the perspective that I bring to this book.

During my legal career, I have been involved in several religion cases.

Between 1989 and 1998, I served as counsel for two San Diego atheists who filed a lawsuit to remove a Latin cross from the Mount Soledad Natural Park, arguing the case in the federal court of appeals and successfully opposing the city's petition for Supreme Court review of the lower-court order to remove the cross. My account of that case in Chapter Four includes my own participation in the ongoing legal battle. In 2004, I wrote and filed with the Supreme Court a "friend of the court" brief in the suit to block the recital of the words "under God" in the Pledge of Allegiance in public-school classrooms in Elk Grove, California. I filed the brief on behalf of nineteen eminent theologians and religious scholars—Christian, Jewish, Buddhist, and Hindu—who supported that challenge. That same year, I also represented Carrie Roat, a parent in the small Ozark mountain town of Humansville, Missouri, who challenged the display of the Ten Commandments and the recital of Christian prayers in her teen-aged son's school. Carrie filed her suit against Greg Thompson, the school superintendent, who had posted the Commandments and led the prayers, and who passionately defended his actions. That case ended with a settlement I negotiated with the school district's lawyer, in which the school board agreed to remove the Commandments and stop the prayers. Greg Thompson refused to sign the settlement and was fired for his recalcitrance. The story of Carrie's case, which provoked intense community hostility against her, could easily have been a chapter in this book, although it never reached trial.

It bears reflection that there are hundreds of towns like Humansville, in which religious symbols and practices in public places go unchallenged, but only a handful of people like Carrie, willing to take a stand against the majority of their fellow citizens. My own sympathies lie with the Carrie Roats in our nation's towns and cities, but we need also to understand the Greg Thompsons. Talking with people like them, in the six towns and cities I visited in recent months, has given me a deeper understanding of the differing beliefs and values that have sparked these local battles in America's growing religious wars. My hope in writing this book is that its readers will also deepen their understanding of the ongoing struggle for "the soul of America."

God on Trial

Chapter 1

"Respecting an Establishment of Religion"

The backdrop to America's growing religious wars lies in the dark underside of our nation's history. Before we visit the cities and towns in which recent battles over religious symbols and practices began, we need first to examine how that history shaped the current struggle between partisans on both sides of the national conflict over church-state separation. Those who debate the role of religion in the public square—preachers, politicians, and pundits among them—fire rhetorical volleys across the metaphorical "wall of separation" that divides the combatants, all claiming that history supports their side. Echoes of these noisy debates reverberate in the quiet chambers of the Supreme Court, which has the final word in deciding cases that begin with local disputes over religion and end with rulings that reflect the Court's reading of the historical record on which justices base their opinions. Over the past quarter-century, the Court's initial consensus in religion cases has dissolved into often bitter discord among the justices over the "intent" of the men who framed and adopted the Establishment of Religion Clause of the First Amendment.

Not surprisingly, the justices have differed sharply in their readings of America's religious history. On the rough spectrum from left to right, the more "liberal" justices have most often read that history as requiring "a wall between church and state" that "must be kept high and impregnable," as Justice Hugo Black stated in 1947. More "conservative" justices have generally dismissed the "misleading metaphor" of the church-state wall, as Justice William Rehnquist wrote in 1985. We will discuss those dueling opinions in the following chapter; my point here is that Black and Rehnquist both quoted extensively from the same historical record in reaching their opposite conclusions. Through Black's liberal eyes, this record supported his "separationist" position on church-state separation, while Rehnquist's conservative eyes found in it support for his "accommodationist" approach to Establishment Clause cases.

———

If justices like Black and Rehnquist have differed so sharply in their reading of America's religious history, it is fair to ask whether that history matters, or has simply become a convenient weapon for the combatants on both sides of our current religious wars. In my view, both propositions are true. The history of religious conflict that led to adoption of the Establishment Clause in 1791, as Black noted, clearly supports the contention of its primary author, James Madison, that the clause was intended to ensure "the total separation of the church from the state." It is equally clear, however, as Rehnquist pointed out, that Madison had initially proposed only that no "national religion be established," presumably leaving the states free from congressional regulation in religious matters. Which of Madison's words—and those of the other men who participated in framing the Establishment Clause— should we consider the best guide to its meaning and application? That question, I submit, makes little difference to the partisans on both sides of our current religious wars, who pick and choose from the framers' words only those that serve their political purposes.

There is, however, considerable irony in the complaints of today's Religious Right leaders that church-state separation is a "lie of the Left," propagated by "non-Christian people and atheistic people" who have conspired "to destroy the very foundation of our society," as Pat Robertson has charged. Many of today's evangelical Christians seem unaware that their colonial forebears were the very people that James Madison had labored for years to protect from the forced exactions of established churches. Those who denounce church-state separation as a "myth" have turned history on its head. Proclaiming that America was founded as a "Christian nation," and that its laws should reflect that heritage, they ignore the persecution of evangelicals and other religious dissenters who challenged the established churches of the colonial period. The earliest advocates of a "Christian nation" in the New World, in fact, persecuted adherents of nonconforming sects with an Old Testament vengeance. The real myth, taught to generations of schoolchildren, is that the Pilgrims who signed the Mayflower Compact in 1620 had left England to establish a colony in which all religions would be tolerated. It was, however, only the "Advancement of the Christian faith" the Compact's signers declared as their goal, and to whose adherents they promised "just and equal Laws" to which the colonists would owe "submission and obedience."

The Puritans who followed the first Pilgrims to Massachusetts in 1630 had even less regard for religious tolerance. As their name implies, they wanted to "purify" the Church of England, to which they still claimed allegiance, from doctrinal "corruption" and ecclesiastical domination. John Winthrop, the Massachusetts Bay Colony's first governor, famously depicted the Puritan vision of the "New Jerusalem" as a "city upon a hill," in which Christians would live by God's commandments, not the edicts of the Anglican hierarchy. American presidents from John Adams to Bill Clinton have invoked Winthrop's stirring imagery. Ronald Reagan, most notably, spoke of America as a "Shining City" that was "God-blessed, and teeming with people of all kinds living in harmony and peace," and whose "doors were open to anyone with the will and the heart to get here." What these presidents failed to note, however, was that Winthrop drew his image from the book of Matthew, recording the message of Jesus that only the "righteous" inhabitants of this holy city could "enter into the kingdom of heaven."

The doors of Puritan Massachusetts were definitely not open to the "unrighteous" who challenged its religious orthodoxy. Winthrop and his followers imposed a rigid theocracy on the colony, enforced by laws based on the Mosaic Code of the Old Testament. Nathaniel Ward, a former lawyer in the English courts and later a Puritan pastor, drafted in 1641 a "Body of Liberties" that heeded Winthrop's admonition to punish "anything that can be proved to be morally sinful by the word of God." In drafting the criminal code for the colony, Ward noted in the margin of each provision the book, chapter, and verse in the Bible that gave divine sanction to punishment of its transgression. Ward's listing of fifteen capital crimes began, not with murder, but with the most serious affront to Puritan orthodoxy, that of idolatry: "If any man after legal conviction shall have or worship any other god, but the lord god, he shall be put to death." Ward cited for this provision Chapter 17 of Deuteronomy, in which Moses told the Israelites that any person who has "served other gods, and worshipped them," shall be brought before the people, "and you shall stone them to death." Second on Ward's list of capital crimes was witchcraft, a law applied with a vengeance in the Puritan town of Salem in 1692, where nineteen women—most of them young household servants—were hanged and one man, Giles Corey, was pressed to death with heavy stones. "The Body of Liberties" also prescribed capital punishment for sexual practices that were condemned in the Mosaic Code, including homosexual sodomy and adultery. Executions for these crimes were infrequent; colonial records show that only two married persons were put to death for adultery. But having these crimes on the books served the purpose of social control, guided by the church and enforced by the state.

Today, most Americans are shocked and sickened by news accounts of public executions in countries like Saudi Arabia, often carried out by stoning or beheading, for crimes such as adultery and sodomy. We tend to forget that Islamic countries that have enacted the religious law of the Koran into their criminal codes are separated only by time and distance from the religious moralists of the New England colonies. Most Islamic regimes, including the Saudis, also prohibit—and often punish with fines and imprisonment—the practice of "heretical" religions such as Christianity. Baptists have been particularly subjected to persecution in Islamic countries, with Saudi Arabia a leading offender. The U.S. Commission on International Religious Freedom, established by Congress in 1998, reported in 2002 that foreign Christian workers in Saudi Arabia have been "detained, arrested, tortured, and subsequently deported." Richard Land, a prominent Southern Baptist and commission member, blasted the State Department for refusing to impose sanctions on the Saudi regime for such mistreatment. "It's unthinkable to me that our government is not pressing the Saudis on this," Land complained.

The established churches of colonial America also detained, arrested, tortured, and deported religious dissenters, especially Baptists and other evangelical Christians. Massachusetts townships levied a tax on all inhabitants for the support of "orthodox ministers." Many Baptists were arrested and fined for refusing to pay the tax. Four local assessors who considered the "clergy tax" unjust and failed to include it in their assessments were imprisoned. In the late seventeenth century, Baptists established a church in Kittery, Maine, then a part of Massachusetts, but faced relentless persecution. William Screven, pastor of the Kittery church, was repeatedly arrested for preaching the Baptist gospel, and members of his congregation were fined for attending his services. Threatened with banishment, Screven and his flock finally left Maine and settled in South Carolina. Another Baptist minister, Obadiah Holmes, was "well whipt" with thirty lashes in 1651 for baptizing followers in Lynn, Massachusetts.

Two more notable figures in Massachusetts were banished from the colony. Roger Williams, who arrived in Boston in 1631 as a Puritan pastor, became minister of the church in Salem, from whose pulpit he denounced the notion that civil authorities could enforce religious edicts. These views so offended his parishioners and the colony's political leaders that Williams left Salem after a few months for the relative tolerance of the church in Plymouth, where he continued his attacks on the Puritan theocracy. "Let any man show me a commission from the Son of God to civil powers in these spiritual affairs of His Christian kingdom and worship," he demanded in a pamphlet that enraged Puritan leaders. For this heresy, the General Court of Massachusetts expelled Williams from their midst in 1635. His establishment of a new colony in neighboring Rhode Island, in which all religions were tolerated, is celebrated today—especially by Baptists—as a landmark of religious freedom. But Rhode Island was a tiny vessel in a sea of intolerance.

Anne Hutchinson is an even more interesting figure than Williams, who in fact was orthodox in theology, disputing only the colony's power to enforce Puritan edicts through its laws. Hutchinson, in contrast, resisted Puritan worship altogether. She held services in her home—itself a violation of law—and preached to those who attended her "study" sessions the heretical doctrines that salvation comes through grace and not through "works," and that the Holy Spirit can dwell within every person through individual revelation. Although her husband was a close friend and ally of Governor Winthrop, Hutchinson so directly challenged Puritan orthodoxy that she found herself facing a trial before the General Court in 1637, with Winthrop as chief prosecutor and interrogator. Far more familiar with Biblical scripture, Hutchinson continually bested Winthrop in debates over theology, turning the tables with relentless questioning of her own. "How did Abraham know that it was God that bid him offer his son" for sacrifice, she demanded to know. "By an immediate voice," he replied. "So to me by an immediate revelation," Hutchinson said of her views on salvation by grace. "By the voice of his own spirit to my soul." Winthrop was so enraged at having fallen into Hutchinson's trap that he quickly called a vote on the heresy charges and secured a conviction with only three dissents. The penalty was banishment from the colony, and Hutchinson settled in Rhode Island, joining Roger Williams in exile.

One of Hutchinson's followers, Mary Dyer, suffered an even worse fate at Puritan hands. Banished with her husband to Rhode Island, she returned to England and joined the Society of Friends, or Quakers, whose teachings were similar to Hutchinson's. When she returned to Boston in 1657, Dyer was imprisoned for refusing to recant her Quaker beliefs, and was released only when her husband promised she would keep silent until she left the colony. Religious intolerance reached a new low in 1658, when the General Court passed a law banishing Quakers under "pain of death." When Dyer learned that two Quaker friends had been jailed, she returned to visit them and was herself imprisoned. Banished for a third time, she returned to Boston in less than a month, vowing to "look the bloody laws in the face," only to be jailed again. Sentenced to death, Dyer saw two Quakers hanged before her. Then, already bound and with a rope around her neck, she received a last-minute reprieve. She was again expelled to Rhode Island, but returned to Boston once again, determined to give up her life to gain the "repeal of that wicked law." On June 1, 1660, after refusing to repent her Quaker beliefs, Mary Dyer was executed by hanging on Boston Common.

Ironically, the Puritans who broke from the Church of England were equaled in their persecution of Baptists and other religious dissenters by the Virginians who had established that church as the colony's official religion. Baptists, in fact, were far more numerous in Virginia than in New England, and hundreds were fined or imprisoned for refusing to pay taxes that supported the Anglican Church. Others, many of them itinerant preachers, were jailed for violating the law that required a state license to conduct services. One Baptist preacher, John Weatherford, continued to preach to large crowds from his cell window in the Chesterfield County jail. So many people flocked to hear him that authorities erected a stone wall outside the jail, ten feet high and topped with jagged glass. Weatherford could not see those who came to hear him preach, but his followers would summon him to the cell window by waving a piece of cloth tied to a stick. When he saw this "call to worship," Weatherford began preaching. He was finally released in 1773, when Patrick Henry, a prominent lawyer and politician, came to his defense. Two years later, as every high-school student learns, Henry rallied his fellow Virginians to the growing revolutionary cause with his stirring challenge, "Give me liberty or give me death!" Lamentably, few of the students who read about John Winthrop and Patrick Henry in their textbooks learn anything about Mary Dyer or John Weatherford.

———

The revolutionary spirit that swept the colonies in the 1770s stemmed from long-standing grievances against British rule that were summarized in the popular slogan "No taxation without representation." The outbreak of armed rebellion in Massachusetts, beginning with the battles at Concord and Lexington in April 1775, spread throughout the colonies and spurred the patriots to adopt a Declaration of Independence at the State House in Philadelphia on July 4, 1776. In his final draft of the Declaration, Thomas Jefferson listed twenty-seven counts in his indictment of King

George; thirteen accused the king of violating British law in subjecting the colonies to "tyranny." Jefferson pointed to "the free system of English laws" as the foundation of governments that derive "their just powers from the consent of the governed." The men who signed the Declaration were schooled in English law and simply wanted to rid the colonies of arbitrary enforcement of laws they had no voice in shaping.

Significantly, the Declaration's signers voiced no objection to religious establishment, in England or the colonies. But the Declaration's statement, crafted by Jefferson, that "all men are created equal, that they are endowed by their Creator with certain unalienable Rights," contained the seeds of rejection of established religion, as incompatible with the "liberty of conscience" that Jefferson championed. The beleaguered revolutionaries had no time for debates over religion during the war that finally ended with the surrender of British General Charles Cornwallis at Yorktown, Virginia, on October 19, 1781. Nor did the representatives of the thirteen newly independent states make any reference to religion in the Articles of Confederation they adopted that same year. The Articles, in fact, did nothing more than establish "a firm league of friendship" among the states, with each retaining "its sovereignty, freedom and independence."

The fledgling Confederation of "sovereign" states was doomed to failure from the start, by a provision in the Articles giving each state a veto over amendments to the charter. Rhode Island, in fact, exercised an effective veto by refusing to send representatives to the Confederation Congress, which proved unable to resolve growing conflicts between the states over such contentious issues as uniform trade regulations. One conflict in particular, over fishing and navigation rights along the Potomac River, down to its outlet in Chesapeake Bay, created tensions between all four states—Maryland, Virginia, Pennsylvania, and Delaware—bordering those waterways. What became known as the Oyster War finally prompted delegates from these states to gather at the Mount Vernon estate of George Washington in 1785. But the meeting failed to settle the dispute, and those who attended resolved to invite delegates from all the other states to a convention at Annapolis, Maryland, in September 1786, to draft a "uniform system" of commercial regulations among the states.

Not enough delegates showed up in Annapolis to make a quorum, and nothing was done to end the Oyster War. But the delegates who did attend passed a resolution, urged by James Madison of Virginia and Alexander Hamilton of New York, calling upon all states to send delegates to another meeting, to consider "the situation of the United States" and to "devise such further provisions as shall appear to them necessary to render the constitution of the federal government adequate to the exigencies of the Union." The Annapolis delegates set the meeting time for the second Monday of May 1787 and the place in Philadelphia. Whether enough states would send delegates to yet another meeting was far from certain.

How does this capsule history of conflicts that led to the Constitutional Convention in 1787 relate to our current religious wars? There is, in fact, a direct link between James Madison's failed efforts to settle the Oyster War and his later role in drafting the Constitution and the Bill of Rights. Madison believed strongly in two principles. First, his experience as a Virginia representative to the ineffective Confederation Congress convinced Madison of the need for a strong "federal" government, with powers to enact uniform national laws in the areas of interstate commerce and foreign affairs. Second, and equally important, Madison opposed the taxation of his fellow Virginians to support the established Anglican Church. In 1785, two years before the Constitutional Convention, Madison had drafted and submitted a "Memorial and Remonstrance Against Religious Assessments" to the Virginia legislature.

In light of current debates over the "original intent" of the men who framed the Constitution and Bill of Rights, Madison's words in his "Remonstrance" deserve quotation. "It is proper to take alarm at the first experiment on our liberties," he began. "Who does not see that the same authority which can establish Christianity, in exclusion of all other Religions, may establish with the same ease any particular sect of Christians, in exclusion of all other Sects? That the same authority which can force a citizen to contribute three pence only of his property for the support of any one establishment, may force him to conform to any other establishment in all cases whatsoever?" Madison had no quarrel with religion in general, but he fiercely opposed its establishment. "During almost fifteen centuries has the legal establishment of Christianity been on trial," he wrote. "What have been its fruits? More or less in all places, pride and indolence in the Clergy, ignorance and servility in the laity, in both, superstition, bigotry and persecution."

Madison vehemently opposed state religious establishments, as his "Remonstrance" makes clear. But he left this battle in Virginia behind when he journeyed to Philadelphia for the Constitutional Convention in May 1787. Madison arrived at this meeting with a different goal, that of replacing the weak Articles of Confederation with a strong federal government. Before the delegates gathered, Madison explained to George Washington—who would preside over the convention's sessions—that he envisioned a federal government "with positive and complete authority in all cases which require uniformity; such as the regulation of trade, including the right of taxing both exports and imports." Madison also confided to Washington that his plan would place, "over and above this positive power, a negative in all cases whatsoever on the legislative acts of the states." This was a radical—even revolutionary—proposal that would in effect reduce the "sovereign" states to a subordinate role in the new federal system.

Over four hot summer months, delegates from twelve of the thirteen states—Rhode Island again refused to send delegates—hammered out a new Constitution. The debates were heated, and more than once threatened to scuttle the proceedings. Madison's plan for a new federal government envisioned three separate and coordinate branches: legislative, executive, and judicial. The delegates in Philadelphia devoted most of their debates to the Congress, granting its members broad authority to "make all laws which shall be necessary and proper for carrying into execution" the powers enumerated in Article I of the Constitution. The seventeen that were listed allowed Congress to regulate commerce with foreign nations and between the states, to borrow money on the credit of the United States, and to declare war against other nations. After much debate, the delegates also provided, in Article II, that "the executive power shall be vested in a President of the United States," elected for a term of four years. Along with his powers as "Commander-in-Chief of the Army and Navy of the United States," the president was directed to "take care that the laws be faithfully executed." Although some delegates fretted about the dangers of an "elected monarchy," most viewed the president as simply the executor of congressional directives, particularly in domestic affairs.

Surprisingly, the delegates spent little time debating the powers of the judicial branch, agreeing to vest "the judicial power of the United States" in a Supreme Court "and in such inferior courts" as Congress might create. Article III gave the federal courts jurisdiction over cases "arising under this Constitution" and "the laws of the United States." The delegates also provided, in Article VI—again with little debate— that "this Constitution, and the laws of the United States which shall be made in pursuance thereof . . . shall be the supreme law of the land; and the judges in every State shall be bound thereby, anything in the Constitution or laws of any State to the contrary notwithstanding." This rather convoluted provision, known as the Supremacy Clause, placed a veto power over all federal and state laws in the hands of unelected federal judges. But the Philadelphia delegates viewed the federal judiciary as the "least dangerous" branch, as Alexander Hamilton argued, with its jurisdiction limited to such issues as trade and taxation.

What transformed the "least dangerous" branch of the federal government into the "imperial judiciary" against which today's conservatives rail? None of the religion cases discussed in this book, in fact, would have come before federal judges had James Madison not been challenged at the Constitutional Convention by a fellow Virginia delegate. George Mason "wished the plan had been prefaced with a Bill of Rights," Madison recorded his colleague as saying. Such a provision "would give great quiet to the people," Mason argued. Another delegate, Elbridge Gerry of Massachusetts, "concurred in the idea and moved for a committee to prepare a Bill of Rights." Madison, however, strenuously opposed this proposal. In his view, the placement of a bill of rights in the Constitution—and its enforcement in the hands of federal judges—might undermine or even supersede the bills of rights that all but two state constitutions then contained. Madison's home state of Virginia had enshrined in its constitution in 1776 a Declaration of Rights, drafted by George Mason, protecting rights of religion, speech, and press. "All men are equally entitled to the free exercise of religion, according to the dictates of conscience," the Virginia constitution declared. Adding similar protections to the federal Constitution, Mason argued, would establish them as the "supreme law of the land" and prevent Congress from restricting such rights. Madison prevailed on this issue, however, and the state delegations in Philadelphia—with the abstention of Massachusetts—unanimously rejected Gerry's motion.

With this last obstacle removed, adoption of the new Constitution seemed assured. But three delegates resisted the rush to approve the document they had helped to draft. Hours before the final vote, on September 17, 1787, Virginia's influential governor, Edmund Randolph, proposed "a second general convention" at which "amendments to the plan might be offered" before the ratification process began. George Mason agreed that another convention was necessary, to add a bill of rights to the version before the Philadelphia delegates. "It was improper to say to the people, take this or nothing," he argued. Elbridge Gerry warned that he could not sign a document in which "the rights of the citizens" were not protected against congressional restriction. Madison recorded the verdict on Randolph's motion: "All the states answered—no." But after the state delegations unanimously voted to send the Constitution to the states for ratification, Randolph, Mason, and Gerry did not join the thirty-nine men who signed the new charter of national government.

———

The Constitution's fate rested on its ratification by conventions in at least nine of the thirteen "sovereign" states of the Confederation. Ironically, Edmund Randolph had proposed nine as "a respectable majority" of the states, and George Mason agreed this was the "preferable" number. They returned from Philadelphia to Virginia as opponents of ratification, placing their prestige behind the "Anti-Federalists," who feared the erosion—or perhaps the extinction—of their cherished rights at the hands of an all-powerful national government. James Madison, along with Alexander Hamilton of New York, headed the "Federalists," who attempted to quiet these fears with assurances that the "enumerated" powers of Congress in the Constitution were limited to "national" issues such as commerce and foreign affairs. But Madison was concerned about the Constitution's ratification. "The country must finally decide," he wrote to George Washington, "the sense of which is as yet wholly unknown."

It soon became known that ratification would not succeed without the addition of a bill of rights to the Constitution. Although four of the necessary nine states had given their assent by the end of 1787, ratification by three of the larger states—Massachusetts, New York, and Virginia—lay ahead. Without the approval of all three, the Constitution had little chance of success. The votes of five smaller states, of course, would satisfy the requirement that Randolph had secured in Philadelphia. Political reality, however, demanded that all the larger states ratify the Constitution. And the price of ratification, exacted by the Anti-Federalists in these crucial states, was agreement that the First Congress would adopt a bill of rights. Delegates to the Massachusetts convention, voting by the narrow margin of 187 to 168, directed their future congressmen to "exert all their influence" in pressing for a bill of rights. By the even narrower vote of thirty to twenty-seven, New York's convention agreed to ratification, also with a resolution demanding a bill of rights. Madison, who had compromised his principles in Philadelphia to secure the new Constitution, made a final compromise to secure its ratification in Virginia. To counter the heated objections of Patrick Henry that the Constitution "rendered insecure" the rights of Virginia's citizens, Madison promised Edmund Randolph that he would introduce a bill of rights in the First Congress. Randolph's acceptance of this assurance persuaded the Virginia convention to ratify the Constitution by a vote of eighty-nine to seventy-nine.

The Constitution's ratification became official with New Hampshire's vote, by the narrow margin of fifty-seven to forty-seven, on June 21, 1788. Few people today remember—or ever learned—that a shift of ten votes in Massachusetts, two in New York, or six in Virginia would most likely have doomed its adoption. Nor do they recall that only his promise to Randolph allowed Madison to gain later renown as the "Father of the Bill of Rights." Without this promise, in fact, Madison might well have lost his bid for election to the First Congress, in which he prevailed by a scant 366 votes over James Monroe, a young protégé of Patrick Henry and, like Madison, a future president.

Madison did carry out his promise, although he privately deplored "the nauseous project of amendments." He was prodded in a task he considered unnecessary by his friend and mentor Thomas Jefferson, who sent Madison a stream of letters from his diplomatic post in France. "I do not like," Jefferson wrote of the Constitution in December 1787, "the omission of a bill of rights providing clearly and without the aid of sophisms for freedom of religion, freedom of the press," and other guarantees against governmental oppression. Madison had doubted that Congress would restrict the rights of citizens, although Jefferson was less sanguine about this prospect, reminding Madison of "the tyranny of the legislatures." Jefferson looked to the federal judiciary to correct any such abuses. "The declaration of rights will be the text whereby they will try all the acts of the federal government; as by the same text they may try the opposition of subordinate governments." In other words, federal and state governments alike would be bound to enforce the provisions of a bill of rights as "the supreme law of the land." These were prophetic words, since more than a century would pass before the Supreme Court began to protect freedoms of religion, speech, and press against federal and state abridgment.

Madison spent months at the laborious task of sifting through some two hundred proposed amendments that eight of the state ratifying conventions had submitted. He finally imposed a rule of thumb, considering only those that had been proposed by at least four states, reducing the pile to seventeen proposed amendments. With this list in hand, Madison finally presented a resolution for debate in the House on August 24, 1789. For our purposes, the most important of the seventeen proposed amendments in his resolution was the third, stating that "Congress shall make no law establishing religion or prohibiting the free exercise thereof, nor shall the rights of conscience be infringed." Over the next month, both the House and Senate debated several different versions of this amendment. The Senate—which then conducted its deliberations behind closed doors, with only a bare record of motions and votes—considered three motions in its session on September 3. They all would have restricted the House ban on "establishing religion" to establishments that preferred one religious sect over others. The final Senate motion read: "Congress shall make no law establishing any particular denomination of religion in preference to another." However, all three motions were defeated, and the Senate finally adopted the language of the House version.

But, for reasons that went unrecorded, the Senate returned to the religion clause on September 9, changing the House amendment to read: "Congress shall make no law establishing articles of faith or a mode of worship, or prohibiting the free exercise of religion." The next day, the Senate included this version in the pared-down list of twelve amendments that it adopted and sent back to the House. Since it was clear the House would not accept the Senate version without further revision, the two bodies each named three members to a conference committee, which Madison chaired. Madison and his House colleagues adamantly refused to accept the Senate's version of the religion amendment. The senators backed down and agreed to a final version, which read: "Congress shall make no law respecting an establishment of religion, or prohibiting the free exercise thereof." These two clauses now begin the First Amendment, followed by guarantees of freedom of speech, press, assembly, and petition. The House approved the twelve proposed amendments on September 24, 1789, and the Senate followed suit the next day. State ratification of ten amendments—the first two were defeated—concluded on December 15, 1791, now celebrated as Bill of Rights Day. Had all twelve been ratified, of course, what is now the first amendment would be the third. It seems fitting, however, that primacy in the Bill of Rights should go to protection against the religious "establishment" that James Madison fought so tenaciously in Virginia, on behalf of Baptists and other dissenters.

Chapter 2

"A Wall Between Church and State"

It may seem puzzling that the Supreme Court did not decide a case involving the Establishment Clause until 1947, more than a century and a half after the First Amendment's ratification. The primary reason for this long delay stems from the clause's text, which limited its prohibition of religious establishments to congressional enactments. Without a challenge to a federal law before it, the Court would seemingly lack jurisdiction over any Establishment Clause case. That lack of jurisdiction, in fact, would extend to the other First Amendment guarantees of the freedoms of speech, press, assembly, and petition, all of which were protected only from congressional abridgment. State laws in these areas were shielded from federal judicial scrutiny. Had the Court adhered to this constitutional barrier, none of the cases recounted in later chapters—all of which challenged the actions of state and local lawmaking bodies—could have been decided by federal judges. But they all received hearings, and several reached the Supreme Court for final rulings. How this barrier was first breached, and finally toppled, is a story that needs a brief telling here.

The first shots in what ended with a judicial revolution in 1925 were fired in 1861 by the Confederate cannons that blasted the Union stronghold of Fort Sumter in the harbor of Charleston, South Carolina. Under the rhetorical banner of "states' rights," Southern politicians like Senator John Calhoun of South Carolina had fueled the flames of rebellion, echoing the demands of his state's delegates to the Constitutional Convention in 1787 that slavery be protected from federal regulation or abolition. It took a bloody Civil War to extinguish that national conflagration. To stamp out its remaining embers, Congress passed, and the states ratified in 1868, the Fourteenth Amendment, which imposed on the states the similar ban in the Fifth Amendment—which applied only to Congress—against laws depriving "any person of life, liberty or property, without due process of law." Over the next half-century, however, the conservative justices who dominated the Supreme Court recognized only the "liberty" of powerful corporations and sweat-shop owners, striking down dozens of state laws that set railroad rates and minimum wages. During this period, the justices turned deaf ears to the claims of political dissenters and religious minorities that the Fourteenth Amendment protected their liberty to speak their minds and spread their views, free from state punishment or regulation.

Remarkably, in a single sentence and without any citation to precedent, the Supreme Court in 1925 held that "freedom of speech and of the press—which are protected by the First Amendment from abridgment by Congress—are among the fundamental personal rights and 'liberties' protected by the due process clause of the Fourteenth Amendment from impairment by the states." Ironically, the Court's majority upheld in this case, *Gitlow v. New York*, the conviction of an avowed revolutionary under the state's "criminal anarchy" law, which punished any speech or writing that advocated the overthrow of government by force or violence. But the Court's ruling that Benjamin Gitlow could challenge the New York law under the First Amendment took the first step toward the "incorporation" of its provisions into the liberty guarantee of the Fourteenth Amendment. The *Gitlow* decision turned out to be more revolutionary in its impact on constitutional doctrine than Gitlow's own appeals to proletarian uprisings against capitalism. Having imposed the free-speech and free-press guarantees of the First Amendment on the states, the Court cleared the path to the incorporation of its remaining provisions—including the religion clauses—into the Fourteenth.

The Court, however, did not take its next judicial step toward full incorporation of the First Amendment until 1940, fifteen years after the

Gitlow decision. But this was a giant step toward the protection of religious minorities from the hostility of legislative majorities in the states and local communities. One religious minority in particular sought judicial protection against laws that hindered or even banned its distinctive brand of public evangelism. Members of the Watchtower Bible and Tract Society, better known as Jehovah's Witnesses, spread their apocalyptic message of an imminent War of Armageddon through door-to-door solicitation and street-corner preaching. Their denunciations of "false" religions, especially the Catholic Church, provoked a raft of state and local laws designed to prevent the Witnesses from knocking on doors and handing out "tracts" that portrayed the Pope as the Antichrist.

Beginning in 1938, the Supreme Court handed the Witnesses the first in a string of legal victories, first ruling that towns could not require permits to distribute literature in public places, and then holding, in 1939, that Witnesses could not be singled out in enforcing "anti-littering" laws. These early decisions, however, rested on the Free Speech and Free Press clauses of the First Amendment that *Gitlow* had imposed on the states. But in 1940, the Court formally incorporated the religion clauses into the Fourteenth Amendment. Newton Cantwell and his sons, Jesse and Russell, had been arrested for distributing pamphlets attacking the Pope in a heavily Catholic neighborhood in New Haven, Connecticut. The Cantwells requested donations from those who took their literature, but did not insist on payment. Responding to complaints by outraged Catholics, the police charged the Witnesses with violating a state law barring the solicitation of money "for any cause" without a "certificate of approval" from the state's Public Welfare Council, whose secretary was required to determine whether "the cause is a religious one" or a "bona fide object of charity."

Justice Owen Roberts spoke for all nine justices in striking down the Connecticut law. Giving a public official the power to decide which causes are religious deprived the Cantwells of "their liberty without due process of law in contravention of the Fourteenth Amendment," Roberts stated. That amendment, he added, "has rendered the legislatures of the states as incompetent as Congress" to pass laws "respecting an establishment of religion or prohibiting the free exercise thereof." Although Roberts based his opinion in *Cantwell v. Connecticut* on the Free Exercise Clause, the Court's ruling effectively incorporated both religion clauses into the Fourteenth Amendment. It bears mention that no religious group has done more than the Witnesses in protecting the rights of every other denomination, including Catholics, to preach and proselytize without fear of official restriction. Between 1938 and 1955, often assisted by ACLU lawyers, the Witnesses took forty-five cases to the Supreme Court and won thirty-six; not even the NAACP—victorious in twenty-nine cases during those years—matched this record.

———

The Supreme Court's first application of the Free Exercise Clause to the states in the *Cantwell* case began with a street-corner clash between members of a small and unpopular religious minority, the Jehovah's Witnesses, and those who belonged to a much larger and more influential denomination, the Roman Catholic Church. The divergent histories of these mutually hostile religions help to shape our understanding of the Court's later rulings in Establishment Clause cases. The Witnesses, of course, were not among the dissenting sects the First Amendment's framers intended to protect from being taxed, as Madison said, even "three pence" to support the established churches of his time. Catholics, however, along with more numerous and more resistant Baptists, were taxed to pay the salaries of ministers who denounced their "popish" beliefs.

When the Constitution was ratified in 1789, Catholics numbered less than 1 percent of the nation's four million inhabitants. The first report on the church's membership, in 1785, estimated the Catholic population as twenty-five thousand, of whom sixteen thousand resided in Maryland and seven thousand in Pennsylvania. Outside these more tolerant states, Catholics were not only few in number but also generally barred from voting; even Maryland denied the ballot to Catholics. Before and after the American Revolution, noted politicians voiced the prevalent anti-Catholic sentiment. Samuel Adams said in 1768, "Much more is to be dreaded from the growth of popery in America, than from the Stamp

Act, or any other acts destructive of civil rights"; John Jay—later the nation's first chief justice—proposed in New York a prohibition against Catholic office-holding. In 1788, the New York legislature approved a law requiring public officials to renounce foreign authorities "in all matters ecclesiastical as well as civil," effectively barring Catholics from holding office.

The early ripples of Catholic immigration to the American colonies became a tidal wave in the nineteenth century. Driven from their homes by the Great Famine in the 1840s, more than a million Irish peasants—most of them illiterate and unskilled—crossed the Atlantic and crowded into the urban slums of Boston, New York, Philadelphia, and other Eastern cities. To say the least, these Irish Catholics were not welcomed by the "native" Protestants with whom they competed for low-wage jobs and shoddy housing. Today's religious wars, and even those of the colonial era, pale in comparison with the violence that erupted in 1844 over the issue of Bible-reading in Philadelphia's public schools. The story of this bloody episode in America's religious history—one example of many others during the nineteenth century—deserves a brief recounting here, for the light it sheds on more recent conflicts over religion in public schools.

Two factors lay behind the "Bible Riots" in Philadelphia. First, virtually all public schools at that time began the day with recitation of the Lord's Prayer and readings from the King James Version of the Bible. In this respect, tax-supported public schools simply continued the practices of the church-run private schools they supplanted. Second, few Catholic schools then existed, largely because few parishes could afford to support a separate parochial-school system. As a result, most Catholic children attended public schools and were subjected to daily doses of teaching from a Bible whose introduction disparaged the Pope as "that man of sin." Not surprisingly, many Catholics resented this slur on their church, and their bishop in Philadelphia petitioned the Board of Controllers of the Public Schools to grant Catholic students the right to have their Douay Version of the Bible read to them in place of the King James Version. When the board granted this request in May 1844, members of the American Protestant Association responded with fiery oratory and even more fiery actions, burning two Catholic churches and a convent to the ground while Protestant firefighters stood by. After three days of rioting in May and another in July, thirteen people had died in a war over Bible-reading in the schools.

————

Over the century that followed the "Bible Riots" in 1844, the American Catholic population mushroomed by more than seventy-fold, from three hundred thousand to some twenty-three million in 1944. The first wave of Irish emigrants had been joined by Catholics from Italy, Poland, and other European countries. Catholics had gained considerable political power, winning mayoral elections in Boston and New York City. In 1928, New York's Catholic governor Al Smith had run for president as the Democratic candidate, although anti-Catholic prejudice contributed to his defeat. Two Catholics—Roger Taney and Edward White—had served as chief justice, and another Catholic, Frank Murphy, sat on the Supreme Court in 1947, when the justices decided a lawsuit brought by Arch Everson against local officials in Ewing Township, New Jersey, a suburb of the state's capital, Trenton.

In this case, Catholics in Ewing Township were not singled out for discrimination, but were instead the beneficiaries of tax-funded support for their children who attended parochial schools. Ewing Township then had no high school, and the town reimbursed the parents of all high-school students for their bus transportation to schools in Trenton, both public and parochial. The yearly amount of this subsidy was small, just over a thousand dollars, but Everson argued that any tax support for religious schools violated the Establishment Clause. After the New Jersey Supreme Court ruled against Everson, two prominent lawyers—Edward Burke and E. Hilton Jackson—agreed to bring his appeal to the U.S. Supreme Court. Burke, a former Democratic senator from Nebraska, and Jackson, who worked closely with Baptist groups, had been recruited by a newly formed organization, Protestants and Other Americans United for Separation of Church and State, which later dropped the first three words of its unwieldy name to appear more inclusive.

Burke and Jackson had the advantage of arguing the *Everson* case before a decidedly liberal Supreme Court. Seven of its members, beginning with Hugo Black in 1937, had been named by President Franklin D. Roosevelt, and two—including Chief Justice Fred Vinson—by Harry Truman. There were judicial lightweights on the Court in 1947—most notably Vinson and Stanley Reed—and some whose service was distinguished but relatively brief, including Frank Murphy, Robert Jackson, Wiley Rutledge, and Harold Burton. But the Court has rarely seen the combined talent of justices like Black, Felix Frankfurter, and William O. Douglas, who between them served for ninety-three years and left an indelible mark on constitutional law, one their conservative successors have not yet erased.

The Court handed down its decision in *Everson v. Ewing Township* on February 10, 1947. Remarkably, all nine justices agreed with every part of Hugo Black's majority opinion—joined by four other justices—except its conclusion, upholding the reimbursement for bus transportation to parochial schools. In the Court's first interpretation of the Establishment of Religion Clause, Black wanted to "vividly remind present-day Americans of the evils, fears, and political problems that caused that expression to be written into our Bill of Rights." Sounding like a schoolmaster, he began his history lesson with the experiences of colonial settlers who "came here to escape the bondage of laws which compelled them to support and attend government favored churches." Those who resisted the exactions of established churches, Black wrote, "had been fined, cast in jail, cruelly tortured, and killed." More to the point, "these practices of the old world were transplanted to and began to thrive in the soil of the new America." The colonial settlers, Black noted, were no more tolerant of religious dissenters. "Catholics found themselves hounded and proscribed because of their faith; Quakers who followed their conscience went to jail; Baptists were particularly obnoxious to certain dominant Protestant sects; men and women of varied faiths who happened to be in a minority in a particular locality were persecuted because they steadfastly persisted in worshipping God only as their own consciences dictated." This "burning hatred of dissenters" shocked "freedom-loving colonials into a feeling of abhorrence" toward established religions.

Black turned from this colonial history to the work of James Madison and Thomas Jefferson in Virginia, quoting from Madison's "Memorial and Remonstrance" against tax levies to support the established Anglican Church, and Jefferson's "Bill for Religious Liberty." Both men, he noted, had been instrumental in the drafting and adoption of the First Amendment and its religion clauses. Black also quoted approvingly from Jefferson's 1802 letter to the Baptists of Danbury, Connecticut, who had written him to complain about their taxation to support that state's established Congregational Church, which was not disestablished until 1818. Jefferson, then serving his first term as president, knew he had no power over state laws, but he pointed in his reply to "that act of the whole American people which declared that their legislature should 'make no law respecting an establishment of religion, or prohibiting the free exercise thereof,' thus building a wall of separation between Church & State."

Black built on Jefferson's wall in constructing his "broad interpretation" of the Establishment Clause, in eight sentences that remain standing as the foundation—however shaky in recent years—of the Court's reading of the framers' intent. "The 'establishment of religion' clause of the First Amendment means at least this: Neither a state nor the Federal Government can set up a church. Neither can pass laws which aid one religion, aid all religions, or prefer one religion over another. Neither can force nor influence a person to go to or to remain away from church against his will or force him to profess a belief or disbelief in any religion. No person can be punished for entertaining or professing religious beliefs or disbeliefs, for church attendance or non-attendance. No tax in any amount, large or small, can be levied to support any religious activities or institutions, whatever they may be called, or whatever form they may adopt to teach or practice religion. Neither a state nor the Federal Government can, openly or secretly, participate in the affairs of any religious organizations or groups and vice versa."

Black summarized his reading of the First Amendment's religion clauses in these words: "That Amendment requires the state to be a neutral in its relations with groups of religious believers and non-believers; it does not require the state to be their adversary. State power is no more to be used so as to handicap religions, than it is to favor them."

In his *Everson* opinion, Black had seemingly nailed shut the door to any governmental support for religion. Returning to Jefferson's letter to the Danbury Baptists, he wrote that the First Amendment "has erected a wall between church and state. That wall must be kept high and impregnable. We could not approve the slightest breach." But the final sentence of his opinion opened a door wide enough for a bus to drive through: "New Jersey has not breached it here." Getting children safely to and from schools, Black argued, was a proper function of government, similar to police and fire protection. Besides, the bus subsidies went directly to parents and did not aid the parochial schools in their religious mission.

Four of Black's colleagues could hardly believe the sharp turn at the end of his opinion. Writing for these dissenters, who included Frankfurter, Jackson, and Burton, Justice Wiley Rutledge suggested that Madison and Jefferson would be shocked by the majority's ruling. This was not "just a little case about bus fares," Rutledge said, or a dispute over "three pence" of Arch Everson's taxes, but the very "kind of evil at which Madison and Jefferson struck." Subsidizing "the transportation of Catholic children to receive Catholic religious instruction," Rutledge added, exacted from taxpayers like Everson funds that supported "the propagation of opinions which he disbelieves," quoting from Madison's "Memorial and Remonstrance."

Whatever their destination, the buses in New Jersey did no more than deliver students to their schoolhouse doors. What happened inside those doors, particularly those of public schools, raised a question the justices confronted in a case that stepped on the heels of their *Everson* decision. Vashti McCollum, a parent in Champaign, Illinois, and a professed "humanist," challenged the "released time" program of religious instruction in her town's schools. Under this program, children whose parents consented would be released from regular classes to receive weekly religious instruction in the schools' classrooms from Protestant, Catholic, or Jewish clergy. Students whose parents did not consent were sent to "secular" classes, although these were apparently little more than study-hall sessions. The program was sponsored by a private group, the Champaign Council on Religious Education, but the school superintendent was required to approve the participating clergy.

When the *McCollum* case reached the Supreme Court in 1948, after the Illinois Supreme Court upheld the released-time program, the advocates of church-state separation filed a half-dozen "friend of the court" briefs urging the justices to reverse that decision. Recruited by the POAU, the groups supporting Vashti McCollum included the Synagogue Council of America, the American Ethical Union, the Unitarian Church, the ACLU, and the Seventh-day Adventists. Edward Burke returned to the Supreme Court to argue for McCollum, while his colleague, E. Hilton Jackson, filed a supporting brief for several Baptist groups.

With the scales weighted so heavily on McCollum's side, the Supreme Court firmly closed the door in the "wall of separation" that Hugo Black had opened in his *Everson* opinion. Perhaps chastened by the chiding of the *Everson* dissenters, Black wrote for the Court in the *McCollum* case, repeating his statement that the Establishment Clause "erected a wall between Church and State which must be kept high and impregnable." What distinguished buses from classroom religious instruction, Black said, was that Champaign's released-time program "affords sectarian groups an invaluable aid in that it helps to provide pupils for their religious classes through use of the state's compulsory public school machinery. This is not separation of Church and State."

The POAU and its Separationist allies viewed the *McCollum* decision as a welcome correction of their setback in the *Everson* case. Overlooked in their jubilation, however, was the "danger signal" that Justice Robert Jackson waved in his concurring opinion in *McCollum*. The "sweeping constitutional doctrine" that Hugo Black had enunciated, Jackson warned, threatened to transform the Court into "a super board of education for every school board in the nation" and subject the justices to "constant law suits" over the allowable role of religion in public schools.

It was "idle to pretend," Jackson added, that "we can find in the Constitution one word to help us as judges to decide where the secular ends and the sectarian begins in education." In deciding the flood of school cases that he predicted, Jackson could discern "no law but our own prepossessions." The sole *McCollum* dissenter, Justice Stanley Reed, waved another danger signal, decrying a "rigid interpretation" of the Establishment Clause that "conflicts with the accepted habits of our people" in allowing religious instruction and exercises in the nation's public schools.

To his later chagrin, Justice Jackson had correctly predicted that the Court would become, in effect, a nine-member national school board, imposing the "prepossessions" of shifting majorities in religion cases. Four years after the *McCollum* decision, Jackson was among the three dissenters in another released-time case, this one from New York. Under this statewide program, students were excused from regular classes to receive religious instruction in churches or synagogues. Perhaps sensing defeat, the POAU and its allies stayed out of this case. Writing for the Court in *Zorach v. Clausen*, Justice William O. Douglas—who had voted with the *McCollum* majority—explained how, in his view, the two programs differed. "In the *McCollum* case the classrooms were used for religious instruction and the force of the public school was used to promote that instruction," he said. "We follow the *McCollum* case. But we cannot expand it to cover the present released-time program unless separation of Church and State means that public institutions can make no adjustments of their schedules to accommodate the religious needs of the people."

Justice Black heaped scorn in his *Zorach* dissent on what he saw as Douglas's apostasy in the *McCollum* case. "I see no significant difference between the invalid Illinois system and that of New York here sustained," he wrote. "Except for the use of the school buildings in Illinois, there is no difference between the systems which I consider even worthy of mention." In both programs, Black noted, "school authorities release some of the children on the condition that they attend the religious classes, get reports on whether they attend, and hold the other children in the school building until the religious hour is over." Douglas wrote in *Zorach* that failure to "accommodate" the wishes of parents who desired religious instruction for their children during school hours would give preference to "those who believe in no religion over those who do believe." Black found this statement incredible. "The First Amendment has lost much," he replied, "if the religious follower and the atheist are no longer to be judicially regarded as entitled to equal justice under law."

There is particular irony in the fact that Douglas added this sentence in his *Zorach* opinion: "We are a religious people whose institutions presuppose a Supreme Being." We can only speculate about why Douglas felt compelled to make this statement. Perhaps the timing of the *Zorach* case—decided in 1952, during the hottest period of the Cold War against "godless" communism—prompted his bow to American religiosity. It is additionally ironic that today's conservative justices and Religious Right lawyers repeatedly quote this one sentence, written by a justice who professed no religion and rarely attended church, in their assault on the "wall of separation" between church and state. Another aspect of Douglas's opinion deserves mention here. For the first time, the notion of "accommodation" emerged as an alternative—and potential rival—to the principle of strict separation in the *Everson* and *McCollum* opinions. Much like a swinging door, the accommodation of religion in schools and other public places has offered passage through the church-state wall to justices who move from one side to the other, depending on the "prepossessions" they all deny having.

––––

The Court's decisions in the *Everson*, *McCollum*, and *Zorach* cases, although differing in their outcomes, had one thing in common: they all stemmed from conflicts over religion in public schools. Over the past six decades, in fact, a considerable majority of the Court's Establishment Clause rulings have involved religion in schools. The reasons are obvious, although the judicial resolution of these conflicts has proved difficult, as these early cases demonstrate. In his *McCollum* concurrence, Justice Felix Frankfurter explained that conflicts within local communities "are most easily and most bitterly engendered" by disputes over religion in the schools. "Designed to serve as perhaps the most powerful agency for promoting cohesion among a heterogeneous democratic people," he wrote, "the public school must keep scrupulously free from entanglement in the strife of sects." Frankfurter knew that efforts to inject religion into schools could split communities into warring factions, pitting Catholics against Protestants, Christians against Jews, and believers against nonbelievers. "But the inevitability of such attempts," he argued, "is the very reason for Constitutional provisions primarily concerned with the protection of minority groups."

Justice Frankfurter's advocacy of purely "secular" public schools, however, conflicted with both historical practice and political reality. Justice Stanley Reed's reference to "the accepted habits of our people" in his *McCollum* dissent, and his rejection of any "rigid interpretation" of the Establishment Clause, foreshadowed later divisions within the Court over one of these habits, prayer in public schools. During the past six decades, the Court's rulings on this divisive issue have provoked vociferous dissent, reflecting the overwhelming public support for school prayer—roughly 70 percent in repeated polls. Nonetheless, the Court has not yet backed down from its first prayer decisions in the early 1960s. This consistent stance, at odds with the Court's shifting positions in other Establishment Clause cases, stems from judicial recognition that schoolchildren—unlike adults—face greater pressure to conform when their teachers and fellow students bow their heads in prayer.

Objections to the coercion of religious conformity, including the prayers of the established churches, had prompted James Madison to draft the First Amendment's religion clauses. Similar objections prompted Steven Engel and four other parents in North Hempstead, a suburb of New York City, to challenge the prayer recited each day in their children's classrooms: "Almighty God, we acknowledge our dependence upon Thee, and we beg Thy blessings upon us, our parents, our teachers and our Country." The Board of Regents, which governed the state's public schools, had adopted this prayer in 1951, but the North Hempstead school board did not require its daily recital until 1958. Engel objected to what he called "this one-size-fits-all prayer that doesn't fit the religious faiths of all people," and sought legal support from the ACLU, which filed suit in state court against William Vitale, who chaired the town's school board. News reports of the lawsuit provoked a community reaction that shocked Engel. "We received midnight calls, obscene calls and letters," he later said. "Someone burned a cross under the gas tank of the car of my neighbor, Larry Ross," a fellow plaintiff, and Engel's children endured taunting in their schools. After New York's highest court upheld the prayer, the Supreme Court took the case of *Engel v. Vitale* for review. Having passed on the *Zorach* case, Separationist groups—including the POAU and the American Jewish Committee— filed briefs supporting the plaintiffs, countered by the attorneys general of twenty-two states in which classroom prayer was a cherished tradition.

Ten years after its *Zorach* decision, the Supreme Court had six new members when the justices heard arguments in *Engel v. Vitale* in April 1962. Justices Frankfurter and Reed had both retired, and Earl Warren now headed the Court after Chief Justice Fred Vinson's death in 1953. Warren's 1954 opinion for a unanimous Court in *Brown v. Board of Education*, striking down racial segregation in public schools, had launched the Court into an unparalleled era—spanning the next fifteen years—of judicial concern for minorities. Steven Engel and his fellow plaintiffs could not have picked a better time for their challenge to school prayer.

Hugo Black, now in his twenty-fifth year on the Court, dusted off his *Everson* opinion in writing for the *Engel* majority, again quoting Madison and Jefferson on the evils of religious compulsion. To Black, the Regents' prayer was just as offensive to the Establishment Clause as the Anglican Book of Common Prayer had been to the clause's framers. "When the power, prestige, and financial support of government is placed behind a particular religious belief," Black wrote, "the indirect coercive pressure upon religious minorities to conform to the prevailing officially approved religion is plain." In his solitary *Engel* dissent, Justice Potter Stewart—placed on the Court by President Dwight Eisenhower— dusted off Stanley Reed's solitary dissent in the *McCollum* case. "What is relevant to the issue here," Stewart wrote, "is not the history of an established church in sixteenth century England or in eighteenth century America, but the history of the religious traditions of our people, reflected in countless practices of the institutions and officials of our government." To Stewart, prayers in public schools were among the practices the Court should not discard.

Steven Engel was delighted with the Court's ruling. "Hugo Black really hit the nail on the head," he later said. But the rejection of school prayer brought howls of outrage from religious and political figures. Francis Cardinal Spellman of New York was "shocked and frightened"; evangelist Billy Graham was "shocked and disappointed." Alabama Representative George Andrews complained that the Court had "put the Negroes in the schools, and now they've driven God out." Seventy-five congressmen of both parties introduced bills to return prayer to classrooms through a constitutional amendment.

The justices could easily have denied review the next year in *Abington Township v. Schempp*, citing *Engel* as recent and binding precedent. Most likely, they had two reasons for driving another nail into the coffin of school prayer. First, the devotional rituals in this Philadelphia suburb were far more sectarian than the Regents' prayer in New York. In fact, classes in the Abington schools began with virtually the same practices—recital of the Lord's Prayer and readings from the Bible— that had sparked the nineteenth-century "Bible Riots" in nearby Philadelphia. Second, the justices wanted to remind those who demanded a constitutional amendment to reverse *Engel* that the Court stood firm in the face of political pressure.

Ellery Schempp was a sixteen-year-old junior at Abington High School in 1956. His family belonged to the Unitarian Church, whose members reject the Christian Trinity and are not bound to any religious creed. When Ellery decided to remain seated while his classmates stood for their homeroom "morning devotionals," he remembers his teacher saying, "You're supposed to follow the rules," and his reply: "In good conscience, I cannot do that any longer." Ellery later said of his refusal to stand, "I was terribly, terribly nervous, nervous as a cat." But his parents were supportive and contacted the Pennsylvania ACLU, which filed suit for the Schempps in federal court to halt the religious practices in Abington's schools.

Much like Steven Engel and his fellow plaintiffs, the Schempps faced community hostility for challenging school prayer, including dog feces smeared on their porch and late-night calls. "I learned that if people were mad at us," Ellery recalled, "they would call us 'Communists.' If they were really, really mad, they would call us 'atheists.' When they called us 'commie atheists' they had exhausted their vocabulary—that was the worst they could think of!" Unlike their New York counterparts, however, the Schempps prevailed in the lower courts, and the Supreme Court agreed to hear the school board's appeal from these decisions. Lawyers for Separationist groups and the attorneys general of nineteen states dusted off their dueling briefs from the *Engel* case for this second round of school-prayer arguments, in February 1963.

Given the Court's ruling in the *Engel* case, the practice of reciting the Lord's Prayer in the Abington schools was unlikely to survive judicial scrutiny. The school board's lawyer, Philip Ward, hoped to rescue Bible-reading from a similar fate at the hands of skeptical justices. Pennsylvania's schools, he asserted, used the Bible "to bring lessons in morality to the children." Ward conceded that the Bible was a religious book, but claimed the state was "teaching morality, cut adrift from theology." The state's lawmakers, he said, wanted to find the best source for teaching morality. "So what did they do? They picked a common source of morality, the Bible." Ward appealed to tradition: "Must the government rip out that document, that tradition, simply because it involves a religious book?"

The Schempps' lawyer, Henry Sawyer, scoffed at Ward's argument. "I think it is the final arrogance to talk constantly about 'our religious tradition' and equate it with the Bible," Sawyer responded. "Sure, religious tradition. *Whose* religious tradition? It isn't any part of the religious tradition of a substantial number of Americans." He pointed the justices to the lower-court testimony of Dr. Solomon Grayzel, a noted Jewish scholar, who had said that passages in the New Testament could be offensive to Jewish students. Sawyer concluded by suggesting that Pennsylvania's schools "are a kind of Protestant institution to which others are cordially invited," so long as they stand in the hallways during morning devotions.

Hugo Black took a break from writing opinions in religion cases. Chief Justice Warren assigned the *Schempp* case to Justice Tom Clark, the first Texan to serve on the Court, perhaps thinking that an opinion by a conservative Southerner might not spark the heated reaction that followed the *Engel* decision. Ruling that classroom Bible-reading violated the Establishment Clause, Clark muted the sharp tone of Black's opinions. "The place of religion in our society is an exalted one," he wrote, "achieved through a long tradition of reliance on the home, the church, and the inviolable citadel of the individual heart and mind." Americans "have come to realize through bitter experience that it is not within the power of government to invade that citadel," he added. "In the relationship between man and religion, the State is firmly committed to a position of neutrality." Arguments that Bible-reading and prayer were only "minor encroachments on the First Amendment" did not convert Clark. "The breach of neutrality that is today a trickling stream may all too soon become a raging torrent," he replied. In another solitary dissent, Justice Potter Stewart argued that Ellery Schempp had infringed the "free exercise" rights of his classmates to pray, and that his judicial colleagues had established a "religion of secularism" in place of Christianity.

Having seen the handwriting on the wall in the *Engel* case, few people were surprised by the *Schempp* ruling, and criticism was also muted in tone, although a solid majority of the public still backed efforts to restore prayer in the schools. One aspect of Clark's opinion drew little notice at the time, but later formed the basis of the Court's approach to Establishment Clause cases. Clark proposed a judicial test of laws in this area: "What are the purpose and primary effect of the enactment? If either is the advancement or inhibition of religion then the enactment exceeds the scope of legislative power as circumscribed by the Constitution."

———

After the *Engel* and *Schempp* decisions, courtroom battles over religion shifted from public-school prayer to church-run schools. The Court's next round of Establishment Clause cases reflected the growing political influence of Catholic voters, who persuaded lawmakers in several states to provide subsidies to parochial schools. In 1971, the justices heard arguments in two cases that challenged tax-funded payments to religious schools. A Pennsylvania law authorized the purchase of "secular educational services" from private schools, including teachers' salaries and textbooks, but also prohibited payment for courses that contained "any subject matter expressing religious teaching, or the morals or forms of worship of any sect." Under a Rhode Island law, the state paid a 15-percent salary supplement for teachers in private schools who agreed not to offer courses in religion. Over 90 percent of Pennsylvania's tax-subsidized teachers, and all those in Rhode Island, taught in Catholic parochial schools.

The Supreme Court had also shifted after the school-prayer cases, following the retirement of Chief Justice Earl Warren in 1969 and his replacement by Warren Burger, placed on the bench by President Richard Nixon. Picked for his conservative "law and order" opinions as a federal appellate judge, Burger headed a Court on which Hugo Black—then in his thirty-fourth and final year of service—still wielded influence over his colleagues. Nixon must have been surprised when Burger wrote for the Court in the salary-subsidy cases, striking down both the Pennsylvania and Rhode Island laws, under the caption of *Lemon v. Kurtzman*. Burger's first citation, in fact, was to Black's opinion in the *Everson* case, mapping the "forbidden territory" into which states must not trespass under the Establishment Clause. Expanding the boundaries that Justice Clark had drawn in his *Schempp* opinion, Burger outlined a new judicial test in such cases: "First, the statute must have a secular legislative purpose; second, its principal or primary effect must be one that neither advances nor inhibits religion; finally the statute must not foster an ex-cessive government entanglement with religion." Deciding how much—if any—religious content parochial-school teachers inserted into their courses, Burger reasoned, would entangle state officials in theological briars they should better avoid.

Perhaps because it came with the imprimatur of a supposedly con-servative chief justice, the *Lemon* decision sparked little protest at the time; even President Nixon—who had assiduously courted Catholic voters—held his tongue. Over succeeding years, however, what became known as the *"Lemon* test" drew the ire of more conservative justices who became soured on the notion of church-state separation. But, much as Winston Churchill once said of democracy that it was the worst form of government except for all the others, judicial critics of the *Lemon* test have thus far been unable to displace it with a better one.

The Court's difficulties in applying the *Lemon* test are well illustrated by three pairs of Establishment Clause decisions, which served as prece-dent in one or more of the later cases this book recounts. In each of these areas—the public display of religious symbols, conflicts over teach-ing evolution in public schools, and prayer at school events—the Court wrestled with questions of "purpose" and "effect," reaching consensus only in one case decided before *Lemon* became the judicial standard.

For most Americans, Christmas is a holiday with both sacred and secular meaning. Christians celebrate the birth of Jesus, and even non-Christians cannot avoid exposure to such trappings of the Christmas season as department-store Santas and Salvation Army bell-ringers. The central symbol of Christmas, of course, is the Nativity crèche, depicting the manger in which Jesus was born. Many Christians place crèches in their homes or yards, and merchants display them in store windows, sometimes flanked by a Jewish menorah. Such private displays do not offend the Constitution, but their placement in public places has of-fended some people enough for them to file lawsuits seeking their re-moval. However Grinch-like these suits must seem to others, they nonetheless have forced judges to rule on cases they would have un-doubtedly preferred to avoid.

The first challenge to Nativity displays reached the Supreme Court in 1984, from the city of Pawtucket, Rhode Island. For some forty years, city workers had erected a city-owned crèche as part of a Christmas-season display in a downtown park. Surrounding the crèche were such traditional items as candy-striped poles, a Christmas tree, a giant teddy bear, hundreds of colored lights, and a large banner that offered "Seasons Greetings" to all who viewed the display. Ruling on a suit filed by local ACLU members, with supporting briefs from Jewish groups, the Court upheld the Pawtucket display by a five-to-four margin. Chief Justice Burger, who personally oversaw the Court's annual Christmas display, and led his colleagues in caroling around the tree, wrote for the majority in *Lynch v. Donnelly.* Conceding that "the creche is identified with one religious faith," Burger shied from banning its display "at the very time people are taking note of the season with Christmas hymns and carols in public schools and other public places." Christmas, he suggested, was so embedded in the nation's heritage that it had become more of a secular than a religious holiday.

The author of the *Lemon* test backed away from his own creation in his *Lynch* opinion. "We have repeatedly emphasized our unwillingness to be confined to any single test," Burger wrote. Justice William J. Brennan, speaking for the four dissenters, chided the majority. "The Court's less-than-vigorous application of the *Lemon* test suggests that its commitment to those standards may be only superficial," he countered. The Court could hardly ignore the "Christian religious meaning" of the crèche, Brennan said, and the message it conveyed to nonbelievers "as a dramatic reminder of their differences with Christian faith."

Standing uncomfortably between Burger and Brennan, Justice Sandra Day O'Connor sought to harmonize their judicial discord. President Ronald Reagan had made history with her appointment in 1981 as the first female justice. In a separate concurring opinion, O'Connor proposed looking at governmental "endorsement" of religious messages, viewed in their overall context. The "holiday setting" of the Pawtucket display, O'Connor concluded, "negates any message of endorsement" of the "religious and indeed sectarian significance of the crèche" that was surrounded by "purely secular symbols" of the Christmas season. Although she did not suggest abandoning the *Lemon* test, what became known as the "endorsement test" emerged from O'Connor's opinion as a new verse in the Court's hymnal.

The Court's next "display" case actually involved two separate displays, and produced two separate majority opinions, with only two justices joining both. The two Christmas-season displays, both in downtown Pittsburgh, Pennsylvania, were erected in adjacent parts of the city's government center. The first, an ornate Nativity crèche, was placed on the Grand Staircase of the Allegheny County Courthouse. The crèche had been donated to the county by the Holy Name Society, a Catholic group, and bore a sign acknowledging the gift. Its manger was topped by an angel holding a banner proclaiming "Gloria in Excelsis Deo." The second display, outside the nearby City-County Building, consisted of an eighteen-foot Jewish menorah, standing next to a forty-five-foot Christmas tree, at the base of which was a sign declaring the city's "salute to liberty." The menorah was owned by Chabad, a Jewish group, but was erected and removed each year by city workers. The Greater Pittsburgh ACLU chapter sued the joint city-county government and won a federal appellate-court ruling that both the crèche and menorah constituted governmental endorsement of religion, one of Christianity and the other of Judaism.

The Supreme Court, however, ruling on the city's appeal in 1989, ordered the crèche removed and allowed the menorah to remain. So what's the difference? one might ask. The difference seemed to be the Christmas tree, and the somewhat less sectarian nature of the menorah. Candy canes and teddy bears might have saved the crèche, but its placement as "the single element" of the courthouse display made its "religious meaning unmistakably clear" to Justice Harry Blackmun, who wrote for the five-justice majority in the crèche case. In contrast, he said in a separate opinion for six justices, the effect of "placing a menorah next to a Christmas tree is to create an 'overall holiday setting' that represents both Christmas and Chanukah—two holidays, not one." Justice

O'Connor joined both opinions, with three of her colleagues voting to strike down both displays and another four voting to uphold both.

Chief Justice Burger had retired in 1986, and President Reagan had chosen Justice William Rehnquist, named to the Court by President Nixon in 1972, to replace him. Reagan had also added Justices Antonin Scalia and Anthony Kennedy to the Court, tilting the bench sharply to the right. Rehnquist and Scalia joined Kennedy's separate opinion in *Allegheny County v. ACLU*, supporting both the crèche and the menorah displays. Blasting O'Connor's endorsement test as "an unwelcome addition to our tangled Establishment Clause jurisprudence," Kennedy proposed its replacement with his own "coercion" test. Under this standard, governments could not "coerce anyone to support or participate" in religious activities. Passive displays such as the Pittsburgh crèche and menorah, Kennedy argued, did not coerce anyone to affirm the religious beliefs they symbolized. Considering that the placement of a Christmas tree might have been the deciding factor in the divergent *Allegheny County* decisions, Justice O'Connor's appeal for an Establishment Clause test "capable of consistent application to the relevant problems" seems, in retrospect, both naïve and futile.

―――――

Since the *Everson* decision in 1947, the justices have been asked to review hundreds of cases involving some aspect of religion in public schools. They have declined most of these invitations, but the sheer volume of such cases illustrates the emergence of schools as lightning rods for local conflicts over religion. Children who attend different churches, or belong to none, sit together in classrooms into which disputes between adults over what is taught often spill. The Court's reluctance to expose students to the cross-fire of religious battles helps to explain why the justices—thus far, at least—have come closer to agreement on the "consistent application" of the Establishment Clause to schools than to other areas of the public square.

The longest-running battle over what is taught in public schools began in 1925, in the small town of Dayton, Tennessee. John Scopes, a young high-school biology teacher who had been recruited by ACLU lawyers, challenged a state law that forbade teachers to present "any theory that denies the story of the divine creation of man as taught in the Bible, and to teach instead that man has descended from a lower order of animals." The Supreme Court never ruled in the Scopes case, because state judges reversed his conviction by a local jury on procedural grounds. But in 1968—three years before the *Lemon* decision—the justices unanimously struck down a similar Arkansas law, enacted in 1928. Susan Epperson, who taught biology at Little Rock's Central High School, was again represented by ACLU lawyers in challenging this law. Writing for the Court in *Epperson v. Arkansas*, Justice Abe Fortas characterized the state's attack on Darwin's theory of evolution as "a product of the upsurge of 'fundamentalist' religious fervor" that viewed evolution as an "atheist" assault on the Bible. Efforts to "blot out a particular theory because of its supposed conflict with the Biblical account" of creation, Fortas wrote, violated the neutrality principle of the *Everson* case.

This firm judicial rebuff in *Epperson* prompted fundamentalists to shift their tactics. Unable to dislodge Darwin from public-school biology classes, they demanded "equal time" for a revised version of Genesis, dubbed "creation science" by its advocates. The new breed of Biblical creationists pointed to "gaps" in the fossil record of evolution in arguing that humans did not share a common ancestor with other species. They also dropped references to God in their literature, positing instead an unnamed "creator" of the universe and everything it contains. Waving the banner of "academic freedom," creationists persuaded Louisiana lawmakers in 1981 to require "Balanced Treatment for Creation-Science and Evolution-Science" in the state's public schools. Once again, ACLU lawyers challenged the law on behalf of another high-school biology teacher, Don Aguillard, filing suit against Louisiana governor Edwin Edwards.

The Supreme Court was not persuaded that "creation science" deserved any time in biology classes. Ruling in 1987, a seven-justice majority struck down the law as an impermissible effort to "restructure the science curriculum to conform with a particular religious viewpoint."

Writing for the Court in *Edwards v. Aguillard*, Justice William Brennan applied the first "prong" of the three-part *Lemon* test, finding no secular purpose behind the law. Brennan quoted the statements of its primary sponsor, State Senator Bill Keith, who did not conceal his "religious belief that a supernatural creator was responsible for the creation of humankind." Brennan's reliance on *Lemon* drew a sour retort from Justice Scalia, joined in dissent by Justice Rehnquist. "Our cases interpreting and applying the purpose test have made such a maze of the Establishment Clause that even the most conscientious government officials can only guess what motives will be held unconstitutional," Scalia wrote. "Abandoning *Lemon*'s purpose test," he added, "would be a good place to start" in finding a path out of this judicial maze.

Senator Bill Keith had made the mistake in 1981 of voicing his religious objections to evolution, allowing Justice Brennan to find "no clear secular purpose" behind the Creationism Act the Court struck down. That same year, Alabama State Senator Donald Holmes made a similar mistake, urging his colleagues to adopt a law that would "return voluntary prayer" to public-school classrooms. His later admission that he had "no other purpose in mind" allowed Justice John Paul Stevens to find no "clearly secular purpose" behind Alabama's prayer law. Both state lawmakers, in truth, were penalized for their honesty in expressing the religious motivations that prompted the laws they sponsored.

The Alabama law that Senator Holmes had sponsored authorized a period of silence in public schools "for meditation or voluntary prayer." Ishmael Jaffree, a Mobile lawyer with three elementary-school children, filed suit in federal court against the law. Angered by Jaffree's challenge, state lawmakers responded with their own challenge to Supreme Court precedent, passing a statute that allowed teachers to lead "willing students" in prayer to "Almighty God, the Creator and Supreme Judge of the world." The justices summarily affirmed a ruling by federal appellate judges against the second law, but accepted Governor George Wallace's appeal from the lower court's invalidation of the first statute. Writing for the Court in *Wallace v. Jaffree*, Justice Stevens noted that an earlier Alabama law, adopted in 1978, provided for a minute of silence "for meditation." Nothing prohibited students from praying during this silent period. Adding the words "or voluntary prayer" to this law, Stevens wrote, "indicates that the State intended to characterize prayer as a favored practice. Such an endorsement is not consistent with the established principle that the government must pursue a course of complete neutrality toward religion."

The whole notion of governmental neutrality in religious disputes irked Justice Rehnquist, a self-described "partisan" for the conservative political views he brought to the bench. Among the three *Edwards* dissenters, Rehnquist launched the most blistering attack on the neutrality doctrine, arguing that "nothing in the Establishment Clause requires government to be strictly neutral between religion and irreligion, nor does that Clause prohibit Congress or the States from pursuing legitimate secular ends through nondiscriminatory sectarian means." Dismissing Jefferson's "wall of separation" between church and state as "a metaphor based on bad history," he urged that it "should be frankly and explicitly abandoned." From his reading of history, Rehnquist concluded that the Establishment Clause's framers intended simply "to prevent the establishment of a national religion or the governmental preference of one religious sect over another." For good measure, he blasted the *Lemon* test for producing "unprincipled results" since its inception. Chief Justice Burger, the test's author, also dissented in the *Edwards* case, decrying the majority's reliance on *Lemon* as a "naïve preoccupation with an easy, bright-line approach for addressing constitutional issues."

As Burger had predicted, judicial agreement on a bright-line standard in religion cases proved futile in the Court's next significant school-prayer case, decided in 1992. In fact, the justices were even more divided in *Lee v. Weisman*, which involved prayers at the Nathan Bishop Middle School in Providence, Rhode Island. At the school's graduation ceremonies in 1986, a Baptist minister had delivered the invocation and benediction "in the name of our Lord and Savior, Jesus Christ." Daniel and Vivian Weisman, whose daughter Merith was among the graduates, had protested the Christian prayers, but they continued for the next two years. When Merith's sister, Deborah, graduated in 1989, Principal Robert E. Lee invited Rabbi Leslie Gutterman to deliver the prayers, assuming this would satisfy the Jewish parents. Tucked into what one commentator later called "a typical Jewish prayer," the rabbi's invocation thanked God for the nation's "court system where all may seek justice." Objecting to any prayers at school events, the Weismans turned to the federal courts and sued Principal Lee and the Providence school board, winning lower-court rulings that relied on the *Lemon* test in striking down the graduation prayers.

In their appeal to the Supreme Court, the board's lawyers—joined by the administration of President George H. W. Bush—asked the justices to "reconsider" the *Lemon* test. Writing for the five-justice majority that rejected this request, Justice Anthony Kennedy sidestepped *Lemon* and applied the "coercion" test he had proposed in his *Allegheny County* opinion. Unlike the passive displays in that case, which did not coerce anyone to view them or affirm their religious meaning, Kennedy said, students like Deborah Weisman faced "subtle coercive pressure" to attend their graduation ceremonies and bow their heads during clergy-led prayers. Much like Chief Justice Warren, whose 1954 opinion in *Brown v. Board of Education* cited psychological studies indicating that racial segregation created "feelings of inferiority" in black children, Kennedy cited research showing that "adolescents are often susceptible to pressure from their peers toward conformity, and that the influence is strongest in matters of social convention."

Kennedy's reliance on academic studies of adolescent behavior drew a scornful reply from Justice Scalia, speaking for the four *Weisman* dissenters. Scalia noted that President Bush had "asked those attending his inauguration to bow their heads" in prayer. Why, then, should Deborah Weisman and her family decline to do the same and "to thank God, as Americans have always done, for the blessings He has generously bestowed on them and on their country." After this judicial invocation, Scalia allied himself with "the disciples of Blackstone rather than of Freud," denouncing Kennedy's "psycho-coercion test, which suffers the double disability of having no roots whatever in our people's historic practice, and being as infinitely expandable as the reasons for psycho-therapy itself."

———

What can we conclude from this chapter's review of the Court's most significant Establishment Clause cases over the six decades since Justice Black proclaimed the "neutrality" doctrine in his *Everson* opinion? None of Black's colleagues took issue with that standard, or with the "wall of separation" that decision erected between church and state. But even in the *Everson* case, the Court was divided over the application of the neutrality principle, and the thirty-two justices who have voted in subsequent Establishment Clause cases remained divided on virtually all, with *Epperson* a notable exception during the Warren Court years. Judicial unanimity in this contentious area has never occurred in the past, and will probably never emerge in the future, at least as long as the Court's ideological balance is not radically shifted by one president's, or one party's, domination of the political process through which empty seats on the bench are filled. Not even President Franklin D. Roosevelt, who placed nine justices on the Court, picked men who agreed in every religion case.

In my view, the Court's continuing divisions over the Establishment Clause reflect the inability of any single "test" of its application to satisfy justices who are themselves divided into opposing philosophical and ideological camps. However simplistic the "liberal" and "conservative" labels may seem, they do roughly predict—with notable exceptions, to be sure—positions on many issues, religion among them. Liberal justices have generally sided with the challengers in Establishment Clause cases, with conservatives backing state and local officials. The wide spectrum of judicial positions in religion cases helps to explain the failure of any Establishment Clause test to provide the "consistency" that Justice O'Connor urged with no success. The oldest of these tests, offered by Chief Justice Burger in his *Lemon* opinion, did not even satisfy its author. However, despite repeated efforts to drive a judicial stake through its heart, the *Lemon* test remains barely alive, "like some ghoul in a late-night horror movie that repeatedly sits up in its grave and shuffles abroad," as Justice Scalia has ruefully noted. Recent variants of the *Lemon* test, most notably O'Connor's "endorsement" test and Kennedy's "coercion" test, have failed to replace it.

Perhaps the most perceptive assessment of the current Establishment Clause morass came from Justice Clarence Thomas, four years after he joined the Court in 1991. Thomas has a unique perspective on these issues, rejecting the clause's incorporation into the Fourteenth Amendment and its application to the states, which he asserts are free to establish religions and promote sectarian practices. From his solitary perch above the fray, Thomas observed that "our Establishment Clause jurisprudence is in hopeless disarray." This judicial disarray, as the following chapter will discuss, has provided the lawyers on both sides of America's religious wars with ammunition for courtroom battles that begin in the nation's schools, parks, and public buildings.

Chapter 3

"We Can Never Give Up"

Barry Lynn and Jay Sekulow have a lot in common. Both are lawyers, both are Christians, and both direct organizations whose offices are within easy walking distance from the Supreme Court's chambers. Whenever the justices hear arguments in religion cases, television crews and newspaper reporters cluster around Lynn and Sekulow on the Court's marble steps, knowing they will provide good sound bites and snappy quotes. When the Court hands down its decisions in these cases, the two men sit side by side in network studios, trading friendly banter as each puts his group's spin on the ruling. Beneath their mutual cordiality, however, they are fierce combatants for their causes, one leading the Separationist forces and the other heading those on the Religious Right, Lynn as executive director of Americans United for Separation of Church and State and Sekulow as chief counsel of the American Center for Law and Justice. These two organizations, joined in many legal and political battles by allies with common goals, operate in effect as the command posts for the opposing troops in America's religious wars.

Lynn and Sekulow have something else in common. There is a significant—but little-noticed—parallel in the separate histories of AU and the ACLJ, and within the broader constituencies from which both groups emerged. The gradual widening of this parallel, and its eventual disappearance, reflect the shifting currents of American politics over the past four decades. Both the Separationist and Religious Right groups that now battle over the "wall of separation" between church and state once stood together, arrayed as fellow Protestants against the Catholics whose Vatican-led hierarchy they equally viewed as bent on breaching that wall. One Protestant denomination in particular, the Baptist Church, had long warned that Catholics were not committed to American values and institutions. Back in 1888, Thomas J. Morgan, a prominent Baptist preacher, voiced these fears: "We will be asked at no distant day to recognize that there is no religion except Catholicism; that there is no worship except that of the Cathedral; that the state has no right to exist except as a servant of the church."

As we have seen, their colonial-era persecution by fellow Protestants cemented the Baptist commitment to church-state separation. The rapid growth of the Catholic Church during the first half of the twentieth century, and its campaigns for state aid to parochial schools, prompted Baptist leaders to join with mainstream Protestants who shared their fears of growing Catholic influence. In 1947, Louie D. Newton, then serving as president of the Southern Baptist Convention, was among the five signatories of the "Manifesto" of the newly formed organization Protestants and Other Americans United for Separation of Church and State. In an unstated but clear reference to the Catholic Church, that document included this warning to American Protestants: "A powerful church, unaccustomed in its own history and tradition to the American ideal of separation of church and state, but flourishing under the religious liberty provided by our form of government, and emboldened by the wide diffusion of a false conception of tolerance, has committed itself in authoritative declarations and by positive acts to a policy plainly subversive of religious liberty as guaranteed by the Constitution." Predictably, American Catholics were affronted by this attack on their commitment to the Constitution. John Courtney Murray, a Jesuit priest and his church's most articulate defender, replied that "we are the friends of its liberties" and that "no man has to fear from us infringement of any of his rights." Murray expressed his hope that Catholics and Protestants "could agree to be American citizens, divided in religious faith, but united in our loyalty to the First Amendment."

Baptist leaders, however, continued to view the Catholic Church with suspicion. The 1960 presidential candidacy of John F. Kennedy, the first Catholic since Al Smith in 1928 to seek the White House, prompted one of Newton's successors as president of the Southern Baptist Convention, W. A. Criswell, to warn that Kennedy's election would "spell the death of a free church in a free state." To be sure, Criswell was not the only Protestant leader who appealed to anti-Catholic sentiment among his followers; the Reverend Norman Vincent Peale and the evangelist Billy Graham also gave their tacit support to Kennedy's Republican opponent, Richard Nixon.

The significance of Criswell's foray into partisan politics, and its relevance to this book, lie in his own election in 1968 to head the Southern Baptist Convention, the first step in the gradual—and by now complete—capture of the nation's largest Protestant denomination by the advocates of Biblical inerrancy, a doctrine that is fundamental to most evangelical Christians. Criswell himself became a leading figure in both the Religious Right and the Republican Party; in 1984, he gave the benediction at the GOP national convention, asking God to "bless us as we march to victory and a greater destiny." In Criswell's view, God was a Republican, and the Southern Baptist Convention has followed him into the party's fold, joining forces with evangelical Christians in other denominations in building the Religious Right into a powerful force in American politics. Along the way, Louie Newton's role in founding Americans United, and its branding of the Catholic Church as "subversive of religious liberty," have been replaced by the current alliance between Southern Baptists and conservative Catholics in their joint campaigns against abortion and gay rights, and their efforts to secure government funding for "faith-based" social programs.

My purpose in noting the anti-Catholic roots of both Separationist and Religious Right groups is not to suggest that either remains infected with that old hostility. Americans United now welcomes Catholics into its fold, and has filed briefs supporting the church's exemption from restrictive zoning laws. The ACLJ's first executive director was a Catholic deacon, Keith Fournier, and the group works closely with Catholic-led organizations like the Thomas More Law Center in many cases, most recently the battle to "save" the Mount Soledad cross in San Diego. What is remarkable, in looking at the contending sides in today's religious wars, is the radical shift that has broken apart the Protestant camp over the past three decades. Once united in supporting church-state separation, and in viewing the Catholic Church as the major threat to that principle, liberal and conservative Protestants now stand on opposite sides of the "wall of separation." In this realignment of forces, "mainstream" Protestants work closely with Jewish and even atheist groups in promoting the Separationist cause. Evangelical Protestants, meanwhile, have been joined on the Religious Right by conservative Catholics and Orthodox Jews who share their concern that "secular humanists" pose the greatest threat to "traditional" American values and institutions. In the broader "cultural war" in which Pat Buchanan—himself a Catholic—sounded the tocsin, former allies have become adversaries, and former enemies have embraced one another.

The factors that have produced this realignment are varied and complex, and do not yield to easy analysis. In my view, they are rooted in theological debates within American Protestantism that go back more than a century, and that came to a head in 1919, with the founding of the World's Christian Fundamentals Association in Philadelphia, at a meeting attended by six thousand delegates. Their common enemy was the "modernism" that had infected Protestant seminaries, whose professors—and the students they sent into thousands of church pulpits—viewed the Bible, not as the revealed word of God, to be accepted as literally true, but as a collection of stories that had been inspired by God but were shaped by human hands. The "higher criticism" of Biblical scholars, the growing acceptance of Darwin's theory of evolution, the Bolshevik Revolution of "godless" communists in Russia and the agitation of their American supporters, and the carnage of the First World War all combined to shake the faith of many Protestants. The self-styled "fundamentalists" of the WCFA fought back with the distribution of millions of copies of a twelve-pamphlet series that outlined the "Fundamentals of the Faith." Pocket-sized and easy to read, they probably convinced few "modernists" to fall on their knees and beg for God's forgiveness, but their circulation to the "doubting Thomases" in small-town churches most likely produced many conversions to their Sunday-school certitudes.

It is tempting to dismiss the old-style fundamentalists as unlettered and credulous Bible-thumpers, able to believe that the world was created in six days, some eight thousand years ago. Despite the inroads of science, however, this bedrock of fundamentalism has not eroded over time. A national poll, conducted by NBC in 2005, showed that 44 percent of the public, including one-third of those with college degrees, accept the six-day Genesis account of creation. Belief in Biblical inerrancy, the bedrock of evangelical faith, is even greater. George Barna, a respected religious pollster, reported in 2006 that 61 percent of Americans profess their belief that "every word in the Bible is true and can be trusted." Among those who identify themselves as evangelical Christians, this figure rises to 89 percent. The depth of these convictions is hard to gauge, since 41 percent of those polled by Barna confess that they rarely or never read the Bible. Nonetheless, the breadth of public support today for the fundamentalist doctrines proclaimed by the WCFA in 1919 is striking.

The relevance to this book of these recent surveys lies in the substantial base of evangelical Christians who form the core constituency of the Religious Right. Barna puts their number at some fifteen million, about 9 percent of the adult population. What distinguishes evangelicals from the larger groups of "born-again" and "notional" Christians—equally balanced at 36 percent in Barna's latest polling—is their commitment to religious and political activism. According to Barna, evangelicals feel a "personal responsibility to share their religious beliefs about Christ" in more ways than personal devotion and church attendance. Virtually all evangelicals cast their ballots on Election Day, but many take a more active role in politics, from the precinct level to involvement in congressional and presidential campaigns. Not surprisingly, considering their conservative political and religious views, evangelicals are overwhelmingly Republican; in the 2004 presidential election, 84 percent of them—the largest segment of the voting population—supported President George W. Bush over Senator John Kerry. Among the "values voters" credited by pollsters with providing Bush's three-million-vote margin over Kerry, evangelical Christians made up a significant chunk.

Lumped together from Barna's polling data, evangelical Christians and their "born-again" brethren fall just short of a majority among the American public, at 45 percent of the nation's population. Combining the 36 percent who fit within Barna's category of "notional" Christians—a group that includes many Catholics and members of mainstream Protestant churches—with the 10 percent who are not Christian, we find a slightly larger group of 46 percent, leaving 9 percent who decline to identify themselves with any religious label. In short, although 80 percent of Americans label themselves as Christians in the Barna surveys, closely matching the numbers in other polls, neither side in this religious divide commands a majority.

What matters more than professed beliefs, however, is the commitment that believers bring to their causes. In this respect, the evangelicals who form the base of the Religious Right wield an influence far beyond their numbers. They join organizations like the Christian Coalition, they run for offices from local school boards to Congress, and they donate money to groups like the American Center for Law and Justice. And they are motivated by deep convictions that God has called them to reclaim the nation from the "secular humanists" who have replaced the "godless communists" as the main threat to their values. In each of the communities I visited in writing this book, evangelicals led the battles to defend the religious symbols and practices they cherish.

The ultimate goal of many evangelicals is to restore America as the "Christian nation" they believe the Founding Fathers intended to establish. In 2004, Barna asked a national sample of members of different religious groups whether they favored or opposed "a constitutional amendment to establish Christianity as the official religion of the United States." Only 32 percent supported this proposal; even a 53-percent majority of self-identified "born-again" Christians rejected it, along with

72 percent of "notional" Christians and 77 percent among those of non-Christian faiths. But a strong majority—66 percent—of evangelicals endorsed the "Christian nation" amendment. There are tiny groups devoted to pushing this cause, but even its most fervent advocates know that its chances of success are close to zero.

Nonetheless, the support for such an amendment by one-third of the public, and two-thirds of evangelicals, reveals the attraction of an official declaration that America remains, as the Supreme Court stated in 1892, "a Christian nation." These words had no legal force then, nor did their more recent echo in the 2004 platform of the Texas Republican Party, proclaiming that "the United States of America is a Christian Nation." The evangelicals whose literature often quotes the Supreme Court's words, and who now dominate more than a third of Republican state committees, pursue their goal of a Christian nation with religious zeal and political fervor, determined to exercise the "dominion" over the nation's laws and institutions they believe God has commanded them to secure.

_____

People like Jay Sekulow, and his colleagues in other Religious Right organizations, rally their troops with dire warnings that "secular humanists" threaten the "traditional" Christian values they hold dear. In a recent fund-raising appeal, Sekulow looked forward to "the day that children are allowed to pray in schools again, the Bible is once again honored as the basis for morality and law, secular humanism no longer reigns supreme in our public institutions, and hostility toward religion in the public square is eliminated." From his nearby office on Capitol Hill, Barry Lynn issued his own jeremiad against the Religious Right, warning that its leaders "want their world view to be the world view imposed on everyone else in the country. Pat Robertson, Jerry Falwell, and others like them do not respect individual freedom. They want an officially Christian nation, and they want their interpretation of the Bible to be written into law."

Sekulow and Lynn are equally skilled in the rough-and-tumble of issue politics, and they both know that soothing words do not persuade people to open their checkbooks. Behind their rhetoric, they also recognize that neither side in their legal and political battles commands a majority of the American people. In fact, a recent poll showed an even split on the question of whether the United States was a "Christian" or a "secular" nation, with 45 percent on each side, and the remaining 10 percent scratching their heads in the "don't know" category. With public opinion up for grabs, it makes sense for activists like Sekulow and Lynn to portray their adversaries as dangerous radicals, bent on undermining the values they both profess to share.

The growing intensity of America's religious wars, in my view, stems from recent shifts within the nation's composition that have given both the Religious Right and Separationists greater numbers of potential supporters. Over the past few decades, the increasing polarization of American politics has divided the major parties into fiercely opposed ideological camps on the left and right, with a shrinking number of "moderate" voters to swing close elections. During this same period, there has been a corresponding religious polarization, matching—and in many ways reflecting—this partisan division.

Judged simply by numbers, America remains—as it has always been—an overwhelmingly Christian nation. In recent polls, four out of five adults identify themselves as Christians. Significantly, however, fewer than half—just 47 percent—are now members of Christian churches, the lowest number in our history. Equally notable is the fact that more than a third of those who claim to be Christians rarely or never attend church services. Over the past decade, both the Roman Catholic Church and most of the "mainstream" Protestant denominations—Presbyterian, Methodist, Episcopal, United Church of Christ, and Lutheran among them—have lost ground in their proportions of the total population. During this same period, membership in evangelical Christian churches has grown rapidly. The largest evangelical denomination, the Assemblies of God, almost doubled its membership between 1990 and 2001, to more than two million, while "nondenominational" Christian churches, most of them fundamentalist in belief, increased more than tenfold in size, to a total membership of more than three million.

At the same time, the number of non-Christians has risen sharply. Between 1990 and 2001, according to the American Religious Identification Survey of the City University of New York, the American Hindu population rose from 227,000 to 766,000, while the number of Buddhists increased from 401,000 to 1.1 million. The Muslim population also more than doubled, from 527,000 to 1.1 million. The most dramatic increase, however, came in the numbers of Americans who profess no religious beliefs or church affiliation. As the CUNY study reported, "The greatest increase in absolute as well as percentage terms has been among those adults who do not subscribe to any religious identification; their number has more than doubled from 14.3 million in 1990 to 29.4 million in 2001; their proportion has grown from just eight percent of the total in 1990 to over fourteen percent in 2001." Adding together the members of non-Christian religions, including some three million Jews, with those who profess no religious belief, roughly one-fifth of Americans now stand outside the Christian majority. And within that majority, those whose faith is based on the doctrine of Biblical inerrancy, the foundation of evangelical Christianity, constitute a roughly equal one-fifth of the population. These are admittedly imprecise calculations; people who sit beside one another in the same church pew may hold very different beliefs, and divergent views on church-state separation.

By themselves, the numbers of potential supporters of Separationist and Religious Right groups, however substantial, are less important than the numbers of those who back them with membership, contributions, and active participation. In this respect, the Separationists are out-manned, out-funded, and out-worked by their Religious Right adversaries. A rough calculation puts the total of committed Separationists at a half-million, with the combined annual budgets of the organizations they support at ten million dollars. Somewhere between three million and four million people belong to Religious Right groups with legal arms, controlling yearly budgets devoted to church-state litigation of close to fifty million dollars.

The biggest reward for these expenditures, of course, is a Supreme

Court victory that sets a precedent for future Establishment Clause cases. These are the cases—two or three in most years—that draw national media coverage and give Barry Lynn and Jay Sekulow the opportunity to reach millions of television viewers and newspaper readers. For example, when the Court ruled in 2000 against officially sponsored prayer at high-school football games, Lynn exulted to reporters. "The court has reaffirmed the principle that prayer cannot be imposed on young people against their will," he said. "Mob rule on religion has no place in our public schools." Sekulow, who argued and lost the case, sounded recalcitrant in defeat. "The court has drawn the line," he responded. "I'm disappointed at the hostility the court showed toward student speech."

———

Jay Sekulow did not lose the football-game prayer case because he made a bad argument in the Supreme Court chamber, or lacked experience before the justices. In fact, he enjoyed several advantages over his opponent, Anthony Griffin. Over the past decade, Sekulow had argued a dozen religion cases in the Court, and had won several landmark decisions. He had the assistance of a dozen lawyers on his staff in preparing a polished and persuasive brief, with more than fifty citations to Supreme Court precedent. He had the backing of the Texas attorney general and the state's governor, George W. Bush. And he had overwhelming public opinion on his side. In contrast, Griffin was making his first Supreme Court argument, ran his law practice from a one-man office, and was opposing the historic practice of seeking God's blessing at a public event, a tradition that had opened every session of the Supreme Court for more than two centuries.

Despite his advantages over Griffin, Sekulow actually lost this case— and most likely had anticipated his defeat—even before he began his argument. The reasons have nothing to do with his considerable legal skills; they reflect, instead, the advantages that Separationist groups had built up over the Religious Right during the five decades since the Supreme Court's first Establishment Clause ruling in 1947. Sekulow faced in the football-game prayer case a body of precedent that groups like the American Civil Liberties Union and Americans United had won from a generally liberal Court, and which only the most conservative justices—just three in that case—were willing to overturn. I have singled out this prayer case to illustrate the importance of the head start that Separationist groups enjoyed in their courtroom battles with the Religious Right.

The ACLU is by far the oldest and largest member of the Separationist camp, although church-state cases make up a small part of its litigation docket, which includes cases that range from abortion rights to capital punishment. With four hundred thousand members, and affiliates in all fifty states, the ACLU draws on the services of some two thousand volunteer lawyers who take on pro-bono cases out of conviction. Some are solo practitioners in small towns; others are senior partners in some of the nation's largest and most prestigious big-city firms. It is not coincidental that ACLU lawyers were involved in all the cases recounted in this book, either as counsel for the plaintiffs or as authors of "friend of the court" briefs on their behalf.

Anthony Griffin, a solo practitioner in Galveston, Texas, was one of these volunteer lawyers, recruited by the director of the ACLU's Texas affiliate and backed by the resources of its national staff. David Friedman, a partner in a five-member law firm in Louisville, Kentucky, argued and won a Supreme Court ruling in the Ten Commandments cases from two rural counties in his state. Jim McElroy, whose 160-lawyer firm in San Diego specializes in securities litigation on behalf of corporate shareholders, has handled the ongoing challenge to the Mount Soledad cross since 1998, assisted by the ACLU's staff lawyer in San Diego. Eric Rothschild, whose firm in Philadelphia has more than four hundred lawyers, headed the ACLU's legal team in the "intelligent design" case from Dover, Pennsylvania. And David Remes, partner in the 520-lawyer powerhouse firm of Covington & Burling in Washington, D.C., prepared the ACLU and AU's "friend of the court" brief to the Supreme Court in the Pledge of Allegiance case from Elk Grove, California.

Counting all of its volunteer lawyers, the ACLU is America's biggest private law firm, second only to the federal government in appearances before the Supreme Court. Although its leaders profess that "the Bill of Rights is our only client," and its lawyers have defended such unpopular groups as the Ku Klux Klan and the American Nazi Party, the ACLU is widely perceived to have a liberal bias. Not surprisingly, Religious Right leaders have lambasted the ACLU as "anti-Christian" for its long-standing defense of church-state separation. Shortly after the 9/11 terrorist attacks on the World Trade Center and the Pentagon, Jerry Falwell and Pat Robertson launched their own attack from Falwell's television studio. "The ACLU's got to take a lot of blame for this," Falwell charged, "throwing God out of the public square, out of the schools. I point the finger in their face and say, 'You helped this happen.'" Robertson added his emphatic "Amen" to Falwell's blast at the "Christ-haters" in the ACLU and its Separationist allies "who have tried to secularize America."

It would be difficult to stick the label of "Christ-hater" on Barry Lynn, since the director of Americans United for Separation of Church and State is also an ordained minister in the United Church of Christ. That fact, known to both Falwell and Robertson, has not dissuaded them from hurling other epithets at Lynn. "Some of the greatest opponents we have to honoring Christ in this country are guys like Reverend Barry Lynn," Falwell huffed, adding that he "is about as reverend as an oak tree." Not to be outdone, Robertson derided Lynn as "lower than a child molester" for urging the Internal Revenue Service to lift the tax-exempt status of Robertson's Christian Coalition for its partisan political activities. "He just seems to have a particular distaste for me personally," Lynn replied in brushing aside Robertson's low blow. In a sense, the attacks on Lynn can be viewed as backhanded compliments on his success in defending the Separationist cause against what Lynn calls "the moral myopia of the so-called religious right," charging that its leaders "want to turn America into a theocracy along their narrow religious lines."

With just sixty thousand dues-paying members, a yearly budget of five million dollars, and seven staff lawyers, Americans United cannot match the membership or budgets of Religious Right groups and their legal arms. But what makes Barry Lynn a thorn in the sides of Falwell and Robertson, and provokes their ire against him, is his unmatched skill in presenting the Separationist case to the media—and through it to the broader public—as the embodiment of the American ideals of religious tolerance and pluralism.

Falwell and Robertson, however, view Lynn as an apostle of intolerance toward the Christian majority, and a front man for the "secular humanists" and atheists who hide behind his ministerial respectability. The Separationist camp does include members of these groups, although neither is a major force in American society. The most recent national survey of religious identification found just over a million Americans who identified themselves as agnostic or humanist, and just under a million who labeled themselves as atheists, roughly 1 percent of the adult population between them. Few in either group, however, belong to organizations with any substantial membership. The American Humanist Association, founded in 1941, claims 110 local chapters in thirty-six states, and its monthly publication, *The Humanist*, has just fifteen thousand subscribers. Humanists have joined forces with Americans United and other Separationist groups on church-state issues; Edd Doerr, a former AHA president and the most prominent humanist leader, stresses the need for coalitions "with moderate to liberal people and leaders in the Catholic, Protestant, and Jewish communities." In contrast to this ecumenical approach, atheists seem to relish their role as outsiders in American society, and keep their distance from fellow Separationists. American Atheists, the largest organization in that splintered movement, has fewer than five thousand members, and no leader with any national visibility. What they lack in numbers and influence, however, has not prevented humanists and atheists from becoming targets of the Religious Right, whose leaders blame these marginal groups for leading the attack on Christian values and traditions. Pat Robertson, for example, has urged his evangelical followers to "drive the gods of secular humanism" from their supposed dominance of American society.

Pat Robertson was not the first Religious Right leader to denounce "secular humanists" and their Separationist allies. But he was the first to recognize that courtrooms had become crucial battlegrounds in America's religious wars, and to commit massive resources to his movement's legal campaigns. No other person on either side of the church-state divide has matched Robertson's ability to mix religion, politics, and law. The nation's most prominent televangelist and founder of the Christian Coalition is also a graduate of Yale Law School, although he failed the New York bar exam and never practiced law. Nonetheless, Robertson boasts of his legal training and regularly issues his own verdicts—usually critical—on Supreme Court rulings. In his view, "The Supreme Court of the supposedly Christian United States guaranteed the moral collapse of this nation when it forbade children in the public schools to pray to the God of Jacob, to learn of His moral law or even to view in their classrooms the heart of the law, the Ten Commandments." Robertson warns: "The Christians of America are in bondage to nine old men in black robes of the Supreme Court. It's time to declare ourselves free from judicial tyranny." Like many on the Religious Right, Robertson harks back to the theocratic legal codes of colonial New England, praising them as "steeped with biblical principles of the Old and New Testaments."

Long a critic of the ACLU, whose leaders he likened to "termites" in gnawing away at "Christian institutions," Robertson decided in 1990 to found the American Center for Law and Justice as a counterweight to the ACLU. He picked Jay Sekulow, then a thirty-three-year-old lawyer, to head the new group. A self-proclaimed "messianic Jew" who converted to evangelical Christianity in college, Sekulow had attracted Robertson's attention by arguing and winning two Supreme Court cases. In 1987, Sekulow won a unanimous ruling that Los Angeles airport officials could not bar members of a group called Jews for Jesus from distributing literature in the airport's public spaces. Three years later, Sekulow won a five-to-four decision that upheld the right of high-school students to hold Bible-club meetings on school premises, but outside of classroom time.

Armed with several hundred thousand dollars in seed money from Robertson's Christian Broadcasting Network, Sekulow accepted his offer to head the ACLJ, beginning with a modest office in Virginia Beach, Virginia, and a small cadre of lawyers, several of them fellow Jewish converts to Christianity. Now housed in a five-million-dollar townhouse on Capitol Hill in Washington, D.C., the ACLJ employs thirty-five full-time lawyers and five lobbyists, with an annual budget of sixteen million dollars. Sekulow has a daily radio show, aired by nearly six hundred stations, a weekly television program, and an e-mail bank of some eight hundred thousand supporters, who sign online petitions and flood congressional offices with mail and phone calls on a range of issues, from banning "partial-birth" abortion to "saving" the Mount Soledad cross in San Diego. For his efforts, Sekulow earns more than six hundred thousand dollars each year, less than senior partners in Washington's powerhouse law firms, but far more than the heads of any other nonprofit legal group.

With a dozen Supreme Court arguments under his belt, Sekulow is now the most experienced lawyer on the Religious Right, earning him *Time* magazine's designation in 2005 as one of America's twenty-five most influential evangelicals. Sekulow's clout in Republican circles has also given him a powerful voice in advising President George W. Bush on Supreme Court nominations; he played a key—and perhaps decisive—role in persuading Bush to name John Roberts as chief justice in 2005, and he pushed hard for Samuel Alito's nomination to replace Justice Sandra Day O'Connor in 2006.

Although the ACLJ clearly heads the Religious Right's legal forces, largely a result of Sekulow's national prominence and media visibility, more than a dozen Christian groups have thrown lawyers into battle against their Separationist adversaries. Some are little more than letterhead operations, run from one-man law offices. Others are adjuncts of larger and often well-funded organizations, such as the Eagle Forum, founded by Phyllis Schlafly, the veteran antifeminist crusader, and Concerned Women for America, headed by Beverly LaHaye, whose husband, Tim, has earned millions from his series of "Left Behind" novels, based on his apocalyptic reading of the book of Revelation. Most of these groups, however, confine their legal efforts to filing "friend of the court" briefs in cases that reach the Supreme Court, a relatively cheap way to fly the flag in support of Religious Right positions. Both the Eagle Forum and the CWA, for example, filed such briefs in three cases recounted in this book, involving challenges to football-game prayers, courthouse display of the Ten Commandments, and the words "under God" in the Pledge of Allegiance.

Three of the Religious Right legal groups, however, have both the staffing and funding to join the ACLJ as major players in religion cases. Liberty Counsel, headed by Mathew Staver and based in Orlando, Florida, has the backing of televangelist Jerry Falwell, founder of the now-defunct Moral Majority, which he reconstituted in 2004 as the Faith and Values Coalition. Staver, a former Seventh-day Adventist minister who later became a Southern Baptist, switched careers to law after viewing a video on abortion that featured photos of a fetus developing in the womb. "That was when I realized that the law could either help us or hinder us in the expression of our faith," Staver said. Plunging into antiabortion cases after his graduation from the University of Kentucky law school in 1987, Staver branched out into school-prayer cases and joined forces with Falwell in 1994. Staver had the fire-in-the-belly commitment, Falwell said, "to do war with the ACLU, with the secularists, with Americans United, and all who hate Christ and want to drive God from the public square."

In contrast to Jay Sekulow, whose ACLJ perks include a chauffeur, a private jet, and houses in three states, Staver runs Liberty Counsel on a relatively modest annual budget of $1.4 million and pays himself a seventy-thousand-dollar salary. And, unlike Sekulow, who never castigates his opponents, Staver has gained a reputation for abrasive behavior and below-the-belt tactics. Shannon Minter, a lawyer who represented a Florida transsexual in a child-custody case, accused Staver of "ruthlessly" attacking her client. "We can have disagreements," Minter said, "but saying deliberately humiliating and painful things is morally wrong." Staver makes no apologies for his admittedly zealous advocacy.

"We are in a cultural war," he says. "As it intensifies, we will, too." Staver's most notable case, defending the Kentucky county officials who posted the Ten Commandments in their courthouses, ended in 2005 with a five-to-four defeat. But Staver remains convinced that God is on his side. "Our head coach has called us onto the field and placed us right in the middle of the game," says the former high-school football player. "We can never give up."

Mat Staver has a fellow culture warrior in Richard Thompson, a former Michigan county prosecutor who heads the Thomas More Law Center in Ann Arbor. Staver and Thompson have joined forces in legal battles to display the Ten Commandments in public places and to "save" the Mount Soledad cross in San Diego. "It's an important part of the culture war," Thompson says of these campaigns. "Symbols mean something to people." What makes this alliance remarkable is that Thompson is Catholic, a religion whose seat of authority, the Vatican, had long symbolized to evangelical Protestants the "Popery" against which their forebears rebelled. The close working relationship between groups like Liberty Counsel and the More Center has significance as a symbolic measure of the political realignment that has turned former enemies into allies in America's religious wars.

Richard Thompson founded the More Center in 1999 with $1.5 million in seed money from Tom Monaghan, who sold his Domino's Pizza chain in 1998 for one billion dollars and devoted his fortune to Catholic causes. The two men had worked together in antiabortion campaigns, and agreed on the need for a Catholic-led law firm to serve as "the sword and shield for people of faith." They chose the name of the sixteenth-century Catholic lawyer who was beheaded for refusing to acknowledge King Henry VIII as head of England's Catholic Church, and whose last words were "The King's good servant, but God's first." There is a whiff of self-conscious martyrdom in Thompson's penchant for charging headlong into seemingly unwinnable legal battles. He lost his re-election bid in 1996 after repeatedly failing to secure the conviction of Jack Kevorkian, the notorious "assisted-suicide" doctor, a task his successor later accomplished.

More recently, after confidently predicting victory, Thompson lost the "intelligent design" case in Dover, Pennsylvania, drawing criticism from other Religious Right groups for taking on a lost cause. Smarting from that defeat, the More Center has removed all references to the Dover case from its Internet Web site. Thompson brushes off those who decry his "opportunistic" tactics, painting the More Center as a bastion of resistance to the nation's transformation into "a secular, atheist society." With a staff of five full-time lawyers and an annual budget of $2.4 million, the More Center, despite its legal setbacks, has established itself as the leading Catholic force in the Religious Right's legal battalions.

Based in the Phoenix suburb of Scottsdale, Arizona, the Alliance Defense Fund rounds out the four most active and well-heeled legal groups on the Religious Right. The ADF was created in 1994 by a coalition of influential evangelical leaders, led by Dr. James Dobson and the Reverend D. James Kennedy, who now rival—and perhaps eclipse—Pat Robertson and Jerry Falwell in their clout on the Religious Right. Dobson's organization, Focus on the Family, reported a 2004 income of $136 million, while Kennedy's Coral Ridge Ministries took in thirty-nine million dollars. Originally designed to provide legal support and advice to some 125 cooperating evangelical groups, the ADF stayed out of courtroom battles until 2004, when its director, Alan E. Sears, began hiring lawyers to combat the advocates of same-sex marriage, backed by a seventeen-million-dollar annual budget. A former Reagan-administration lawyer, who directed the Attorney General's Commission on Pornography, Sears has turned the ADF into the legal vanguard of the antigay movement.

Like his compatriots in the ACLJ, Liberty Counsel, and More Center, Sears has blasted the ACLU and its Separationist allies for waging "war on America" and seeking to "eliminate Christian and historic faith symbols from government documents, buildings, and monuments." His 2005 book, *The ACLU v. America*, accused the ACLU of employing "fear, intimidation, disinformation, and the filing of lawsuits to limit the spread and influence of the Gospel in the United States." Unlike its fellow Religious Right legal groups, however, the ADF has confined its efforts to preserve Christian symbols and practices to "friend of the court" briefs in Supreme Court cases. Nonetheless, the ADF's influence on the Religious Right has prompted Americans United to denounce its "radical agenda to destroy the wall of separation between church and state" and to warn that its goal is "to create a harsh fundamentalist Christian theocracy in America."

Before we begin our journey to the towns and cities in which recent battles over religious symbols and practices have erupted, and hear the voices of people on both sides of those conflicts, we will first sit down with Barry Lynn and Jay Sekulow in their Washington offices and learn more about the different backgrounds, values, and experiences that shaped their roles as commanders of the opposing forces in America's growing religious wars.

BARRY LYNN

I was born in 1948 in Harrisburg, Pennsylvania, and lived there for about five years, and then moved to Bethlehem, Pennsylvania, where my dad worked as a salesman for the Bethlehem Steel Company. I spent all my years there up until going to high school. My mother and father were both Republicans, and I was one of those kids for Goldwater. They were moderate Republicans, and cared very much about the party until the last decade or so of my father's life, when he turned on the party because he felt the party had turned on him. He felt they had become subsumed by the Right, over issues like abortion, which he felt was nobody's business in the government.

During my high-school years, I gradually moved from my parents' conservative views to becoming a liberal. I think my religious upbringing in the United Church of Christ had a lot to do with this; because I was a dedicated Sunday-school scholar, I read all the books you're supposed to read and did all the homework and prepared every Sunday morning. And this simply was incompatible with the conservative ideology that I was reading about in *National Review* and Ayn Rand's novels. I was reading Ayn Rand at probably an earlier than necessary age.

By the end of my high-school years, the very beginning of college, I'd kind of rejected all of that. I'd like to think I've moved nothing but further into progressive politics since that time. My parents were not particularly happy with some of my activities in high school, like refusing to march with the band, which was going to play at a kind of pro–Vietnam War event back in 1966. And we did have a lot of debates through the next four years, about civil rights and my opposition to the war in Vietnam. I marched with Martin Luther King, and I was very excited when King merged the civil-rights issues with a call for peace in Vietnam.

I remember vividly the specific event that changed my political life, and that was a debate held while I was probably a junior in high school, between William F. Buckley, who was at that time still a hero, and Norman Thomas, the Socialist leader. This was at Lehigh University, in the basketball gymnasium, and I went to hear it because my father was a huge Buckley fan, and I was, and I thought, This is great. And here's this very aging, frail man—it was a few years before Thomas died—he was clearly having a lot of trouble, but he still had a powerful voice and a powerful message. And I remember to this minute, sitting there at the end of this debate that probably lasted for two hours and realizing there is no moral content to anything Bill Buckley says. It's just about gimme, gimme, gimme. There's no sense of community, and that's what Norman Thomas was talking about. I was thinking that I am fundamentally wrong, and I've got to find a new way to think about politics. And that night, it's as clear now as it was then, in 1964 or '65.

I went to Dickinson College, in Carlisle, Pennsylvania, which was at the time, in 1966 to 1970, a pretty progressive school. It was the kind of place where poets and folksingers came, and people who might not have been appearing on too many college campuses. There was a tremendous liberal atmosphere, in the best sense, and also a lot of progressive politics, and it enabled me to meet people who thought as I did. I wasn't sure that anybody believed the things I did for sure until I left Bethlehem and went on to college. But it was a very important place. I met the woman I ended up marrying there, Joann Harley. And I also learned you could get really excited about learning, you could get excited about listening to different sides of issues. I resisted having a major until they told me they'd throw me out of school unless I got one, so I became an English major, with a minor in psychology. To this day I don't understand most of what Shakespeare wrote. I tried toward the end of my English-literature career to read contemporary American Southern literature, and I enjoyed that far more than Shakespeare, and I still do.

When I graduated from Dickinson in 1970, I had every intention of becoming a pastoral minister in the United Church of Christ. I was very much a part of that church. I took, and I continue to take, religion very seriously, but this was my original plan. That's not completely accurate. I was torn in the early years of going to college about my ministerial interests and my legal interests. I got that interest simply out of my fascination with the resolution of disputes, the idea that we had a constitution that guaranteed all of these rights of people, and that you could vindicate those rights in a court. So that was very appealing. It was important, as you thought about antiwar protests, to see that protesters could raise First Amendment issues, they could make claims, they could find ways to avoid the clutches of the Selective Service System by having lawyers who understood what the law was, and could use it, in the best sense of the word, for its intended purpose, which was to let people be as free as they could be, including free of government efforts to seize them and force them into wars with which they did not agree. Unfortunately, I didn't see much activity on the part of the legal profession, particularly in antiwar activities; that seemed to be coming predominantly from the churches. The American Bar Association would not get into it, but churches were in the vanguard. Every time I went to a protest in New York, for example, religious leaders were the people who were leading the moral campaign against what I considered to be an immoral military intervention.

By the end of college, I had flunked my Army physical with a heart condition I didn't know I had at the time. So going to Vietnam, or going to Canada or anywhere else, was not really on my mind anymore; it was, What's the vocation that will take me closest to being able to do the good work that I wanted to do? And it became clear to me that it was the seminary, not law school. I went to Boston University School of Theology, after a year of taking classes and doing regular things, becoming an experimental subject for new drugs to earn money to buy a camera. My last year in seminary, I was doing what I thought would be very exciting, an internship at the Massachusetts General Hospital in the chaplaincy department. It was a horrific experience, another mind-changing and career-changing experience, because it was so bad. One of the first clues I had was when I was told that one of my new patients was a woman who had become just so acclimated to the hospital that, although she was perfectly fine and she could go home, she didn't want to. I should deal with this, I should explore this with her. So, for a couple of weeks, under that presumption, I explored with her, was she one of those people who like being in the hospital? The third week, I decided to just bluntly approach the question, since she appeared to be in relatively good health, why she hadn't gone home? And she said, How would I get up to my third-floor apartment? I said, Well, the cab driver will take your bags up. She said, No one would do that. I said, Oh yes, they would, and I could help you get that, or go with you and we could just do it. And then I thought to myself, Wait a minute, in the midst of psychologizing this woman's life, what she needed was one piece of data from the system, and that was a way physically to get home and to get to the third floor. Maybe that's the kind of stuff—you keep the religious impulse going, but maybe I could find a way to go to law school somehow, and then I'd be able to help people: Hey, here's how you work the system; it's there for you. There was a series of other unpleasant events at the hospital, but all of them led me in the direction of saying, Sometimes it's a good thing to know what people's psychological and spiritual condition is, but they still need something else. They need an advocate. Maybe I could find a way to get a law degree. But that wasn't something I made any plans to do then.

I was not ordained right after I finished seminary. I waited a year; I taught school in Boston, and then became ordained, and spent what was my only time in the parish ministry. That was North Barnstead, New Hampshire, one of these churches that could only stay open part of the year. Summer people would come up, they'd go to church, then they'd go home; the church didn't have enough other people living up there to maintain itself, so that was my only pastoral experience. It had always been my intention to be in the pastoral ministry; I thought, You have to do the counseling and you have to do the pastoral work, and then you can talk in a more prophetic way about the rest of the culture.

After that year in New Hampshire, I came to Washington, worked for the United Church of Christ's lobbying office on the Hill, the Office for Church and Society, and at the same time, at night, went to Georgetown law school, and after about four years and a couple of summers I did get that law degree. What I was doing for the church was mostly advocacy on behalf of Vietnam veterans, particularly those with other-than-honorable discharges, a major administrative and constitutional scandal. People could be scarred for life with administrative discharges, for which there had been nothing remotely looking like a trial. And then also amnesty for war resisters. And I worked very hard, with a small handful of people—Louise Ransom, whose son had been killed in Vietnam, started Gold Star Mothers for Amnesty, and worked with Henry Schwarzschild of the ACLU, just a small cadre of people who kept this issue alive. Even before the Carter pardons, Henry Schwarzschild and I had gotten Senator Kennedy to insist that the Justice Department produce a list of all the people who were still in legal jeopardy, and we found tens of thousands who had left the country under the assumption they had been indicted, who in fact were never indicted, so they'd been living in exile for years, for no legal reason. So we got these lists, we set up phone banks in several cities, and then people would call in and find out if they could just come back across the border. It cleared the way for thousands of people to come back. This was the first significant achievement of my professional career.

Those years with the UCC trained me to do a lot of things. I was given enormous flexibility to work legislatively, to go to conferences, to put together a bigger, broader religious response to what was essentially a moral question, of what do you do to the people who were right from the beginning, the Vietnam resisters. There were so few people working on those issues all the time, that I learned to do television and things that a lot of people who might be in a comparable position would simply not have been able to do. They wouldn't have had the opportunities. And as I say to young activists, you don't get good at this stuff unless you practice it. You get stale. If I'm not on television with some right-wing character for a month, you forget how wacky the conversation is likely to turn.

When I left the UCC, we had a daughter, Christina; I liked her a lot, and I told my wife that I wanted to hang around more with her. So I edited a magazine called the *Military Law Reporter* for about a year and a half, because I could do a lot of it at home, and I liked it. This was very much a magazine oriented toward defense lawyers, but, ironically, it was sold mainly to the military, because there was nothing like it at the time. They may not have liked the editorializing, but they had to get the record of the cases. So that gave me a lot of free time with my daughter, who was then three or four years old. I'd take her to day care, we'd go on picnics, we had a great time. My wife was, and still is, a physician; she wasn't making a lot of money, but it made it possible to be a little more flexible.

Then I worked in the Washington office of the ACLU after obtaining my law degree and passing the bar exam. I joined the ACLU in 1984, when the person they had working on religion and free speech left, and they offered me a position as legislative counsel. This allowed me to take issues very close to my heart. I'll never forget my first day at the ACLU, which was also the first day of the great debate on the Senate's proposal to amend the Constitution to have school prayers. John Shattuck, who directed the office, said, "Barry, would you go over and do CNN?" They're over at the "swamp," the area where a lot of the media is done outside of the Capitol. I said yeah, and then I noticed it was really raining, I mean torrential rain. So I went over there, I'm under an umbrella, and as I'm doing this live feed I'm thinking to myself, There are a lot of people in America who are saying, There's one more nitwit from the ACLU who doesn't know enough to come in out of the rain. That was literally my first day at the ACLU. And I continued with them, working on free-speech and religious-liberty issues during my tenure there, from 1984 to 1991.

After I left the ACLU, my wife and I left Washington and moved to New Hampshire, where she worked at the Dartmouth Medical Center. But it was very cold and gray, and I didn't really enjoy the work I was doing up there, a project that was supposed to teach doctors how to communicate with patients. In 1992, I got a call from the search committee for Americans United for Separation of Church and State. The gentleman who preceded me here had left to go back into the parish ministry, and they said, Might you be interested? And I said, When do I get on the airplane to come down and talk? So I came down, we had a series of two or three interviews, and it seemed to be a way out of New Hampshire and a way into the thing I loved the best. During the time I was at the ACLU, I would frequently be invited to participate in Americans United events—do a debate, attend their national convention, do an interview for their magazine—so I was very familiar with the organization and had a lot of respect for its focus. This was more important than anything I did at the ACLU, the work I'd done on religious freedom, and here was a golden opportunity. So we decided to move back here to Washington.

There was a little bit of squabble on the Americans United board of directors about whether I was the right candidate, did I have enough administrative experience, and my background with the ACLU, was that too out there, too edgy, and I said, No, we need to grow. This is an organization that, at that time, had eleven people on the staff. I said, There's no reason that AU can't be three times as big. We don't have a development department—how are you getting any money at all? These are the things I want to do, and collateral to that, something I think was very important that I had done off and on, talk radio. I love talk radio, I like going back and forth with people who are actually smart. Pat Buchanan had put together a show at NBC; they were looking for people who could sit together with Pat for three hours in a small room, three days a week. That show turned out to be on about 120 stations. All of a sudden, I had a national reputation as being the anti-Buchanan, and that was very helpful in terms of people saying, What else does that guy do? He runs this group? Hey, that's a good group. That was a good kind of cross-promotional opportunity. It lasted for about a year and a half, before Pat went on to run for president.

So I started to build up the organization. Now we have thirty-six full-time employees, we have lots of interns, we have seven lawyers on the staff, we do trials as well as friend-of-the-court briefs that are so important in all these constitutional areas. And I worked to build up a development department, getting the big grants necessary for big new projects, and to become what I hope Americans United is, the pre-eminent voice for the core issues of church-state separation: government-funded religion, religion in schools, religiously based censorship. These are all issues that AU has been fighting since it was founded in 1948.

During the early years of AU, the biggest threat to church-state separation came from the Catholic Church. This was pre–Vatican II, and the church was using its influence to get nuns into public schools and to censor movies the church considered blasphemous. Today, I think, the Religious Right poses the real threat, mostly evangelical Protestants who want to write their theology into law. I believe that what the Religious Right wants for America is a theocracy, a government run along their sectarian religious lines. Sometimes I refer to it as "theocracy light," because I don't honestly think that if they took over all branches of government, and they're very close to that in some sad ways now, they're not going to pull out the tongue of someone who states an Islamic prayer, but they're going to make that person feel like a second-class citizen in his or her school or business, and that's bad enough from my perspective. They have very few principles. Hypocrisy is a very well-defined New Testament sin; the New Testament doesn't talk about homosexuality, it doesn't talk about abortion, the whole Bible doesn't talk about abortion. But there's a lot of this "Oh, you hypocrites" stuff in the Bible. And I think the amount of hypocrisy on the Religious Right is truly staggering.

When I point out some of this hypocrisy, people get mad and call me names. And you just have to get used to that kind of stuff. You know, I think I really do tick off people sometimes. Pat Buchanan once said, halfway through one of our radio shows, Barry, you have an extraordinary ability to tick people off when you want to do that. And I said, Yes, but sometimes I don't want to do that, and they just get mad anyway. Jerry Falwell, I think, genuinely does not like me. He says things like, You're not a real minister, you're just a left-wing thug. We were on CNN one night, on the *Crossfire* program, and he said, Barry, if you read your Bible you'd be a conservative. And I said, Actually, I do read my Bible, and that's why I'm a liberal. And I have some messages you might be interested in hearing, and I'll tell you, right here on the air, I know you do five services every Sunday in Lynchburg, at the Thomas Road Baptist Church. I'd be happy to preach every one of those sermons, good Gospel lessons, any day you want. And he said, I wouldn't have you down here to preach in a corner.

Pat Robertson is a different kind of person than Falwell. Certainly with Robertson, I think he genuinely has an acceptance-hate relationship with me. For example, when AU filed a lawsuit against Robertson for using tax-exempt funds to finance his private business ventures, he called me "lower than a child molester." But I was invited down once to his university in Virginia, and they really wanted me to come—money was no object, "We'll drive you down." He knows that I'm right about some things, and he's occasionally right about things. Once I saw him somewhere and he said, Barry, how are we going stop the State Department from helping Afghanistan write an Islamic constitution? And I said, Pat, you're right, I don't know what in the world we're doing over there. But you've got to tell me why you're still trying to write a Christian constitution. And he said, Well, Barry, it's different. And I said, It's not different, it's just a different religion. And so we argued about that, but it was a civilized argument.

I think these guys know that I didn't get my degree by mail order, that I've thought about these issues and take them seriously, and there's a certain amount of grudging acceptance. And with people like Jay Sekulow, we've always had a very good relationship, we've talked about issues, what his family does and my family does. I'm still friends with

Pat Buchanan, with Ollie North. I like people who are principled; it's too bad they have the wrong principles in 95 percent of the cases. But when Ollie North, who I also did a radio show with, opposes the death penalty, he does something about it. So when he gets documents about somebody who's about to be executed, in a state where the governor is not going to listen to me if I call him, he'll listen to Ollie and say, Yeah, I'll do that. And that, to me, is a person that deserves credit. He'll say, It's part of the pro-life agenda. But once you stake out a position on a part of that agenda and say, I mean this, and I'm going to put my time where my mouth is, that's really good.

One of the first things I ask people who want to be lawyers for this organization is, How are you going to feel, practicing in a much more conservative judicial system? Almost every circuit now has primarily appointees from Republican administrations, although not every judge is from the Religious Right. But we do have to be careful, within the constraints of how much is possible, filing cases that are not the first one you think of, but the best ones we can develop on areas like government funding of religion. The issue of faith-based initiative could still be in litigation ten years from now. I don't think it's going to be disposed of by the first case that gets to the Supreme Court. You know, my office here at AU is just a five-minute walk from the Supreme Court, and a couple of minutes more to the Capitol. We used to look first to the Court as our last line of defense against the Religious Right. But now, with Chief Justice Roberts and Justice Alito on the Court, I think we have to shift our efforts from the judicial branch to Congress, especially the Senate, to block laws and constitutional amendments that would erode church-state separation. My old friend Lowell Weicker—who was a Republican senator from Connecticut back in the 1970s and '80s, and one of the great defenders of church-state separation in Congress— used to say, Barry, the Senate is the last great protector of the rights of the people, not the Supreme Court. And that's absolutely the case today.

One thing I've learned in fourteen years with AU is that we can appeal to people, even to evangelical Protestants, who see the dangers of imposing the religious beliefs of one group onto those who differ with them. But you still have to say to groups that are sure they have all the answers, the best ideas, that the way you convert people to those ideas, theological or political, is to persuade people to change their mind, not have government become the tool for forcing people to change their mind. And that's really what the debate is today, it's about autonomy, it's about whether the Constitution really does protect and preserve the right of Americans, at least in certain spheres of their life, to make their own moral choices, based on their own conscience. It's a tough job, but I wouldn't trade it for anything else. ❖

JAY SEKULOW

I was born on June 10, 1956, in Brooklyn, but we moved to Long Island just after I was born and lived there until I was into my teens. My family was Jewish, and we attended a Reform synagogue in Long Island. Religion was not a big topic of discussion in our home. Sometimes my father referred to "the Supreme Being," but he usually reserved such references for the holidays. I didn't think much about God either. I was pretty secure in my Jewish identity, which, as far as I knew, included not believing in Jesus. Although we weren't "religious," we did many things to reinforce our culture and our heritage. I especially enjoyed the many Jewish celebrations—my Bar Mitzvah, for example. That was a red-letter day. Instead of my usual blue yarmulka with the white lining, I wore a white satin yarmulka with gold embroidery, and a tallis to match. Maybe my performance was leaning toward mediocre, but, still, to be Bar Mitzvah signaled the end of Hebrew school and the thrill of "growing up."

Two years later, my family left New York and moved to Atlanta, Georgia. We joined a synagogue which I would describe as "very Reform." My high-school grades were pretty much like my Bar Mitzvah Torah-reading—mediocre. It wasn't dull wits or laziness, just a short supply of motivation. After a short stint at the local junior college, I developed an appetite for learning and decided to enroll in a four-year school. My desire to stay in Atlanta was probably the main reason I looked into Atlanta Baptist College, later known as Mercer University. I visited the school and found the friendly, small-campus atmosphere appealing. To add to the appeal, the campus was only a five-minute drive from our house. I enrolled in Atlanta Baptist College with a competitive determination to out-study and outsmart all the Christians.

I did well in my pre-law studies, and attacked the mandatory Bible classes with a cynical confidence, certain that it would not be difficult to disprove the idea that Jesus was the Messiah. I met a guy named Glenn Borders, whom I immediately labeled a "Jesus freak." Glenn took his religion seriously. There could be no doubt of that; he wore a big wooden cross around his neck. I knew of Jewish people who wore a rather large *chai,* but I'd never seen anything the size of Glenn's cross. When we talked, I forgot about the big wood cross—maybe because Glenn wasn't trying to shove it down my throat. It was partly due to our friendship that my competitive attitude toward the Bible courses I was taking changed to an attitude of genuine curiosity.

Glenn suggested I read Isaiah 53. My mind was boggled by the description of the "suffering servant" who sounded so much like Jesus. I had to be misreading the text. I kept looking for a traditional Jewish explanation that would satisfy, but found none. The only plausible explanation seemed to be Jesus. My Christian friends were suggesting other passages for me to read, such as Daniel 9. As I read, my suspicion that Jesus might really be the Messiah was confirmed. That decision, however, was strictly intellectual. I'd been struggling to resolve this question for about a year, and I was glad to have finally arrived at a decision.

How did I feel about believing that Jesus was the Messiah? Actually, I was half relieved. Once I'd gotten past the point of not wanting to know, I realized something. I had never felt the need for a Messiah before, but now that I was studying the prophecies and reading about what the Messiah was supposed to do, it sounded pretty good. I'd always thought my cultural Judaism was sufficient, but in the course of studying about the Messiah who would die as a sin-bearer, I realized that I needed a Messiah to do that for me. When I concluded that Jesus was that Messiah, I was grateful. It didn't occur to me that I needed to do anything about it.

A few days later, one of my Christian friends invited me to hear the Jews for Jesus singing group, The Liberated Wailing Wall. You have no idea what a relief it was to see other Jews who believed that Jesus is the Messiah. Their presentation of "Jewish gospel music" and some of the things they said helped me realize that if I really believed in Jesus, I needed to make a commitment to him. At the end of the program, they invited people who wanted to commit their life to Jesus to come up the aisle to meet with them at the front of the church. I responded to that invitation. It was February 1976. I wasn't concerned about how my parents would respond. It didn't enter my mind that they might be upset. After all, Jesus was a Jew. I knew that much. I didn't see what the big deal would be about my believing he was the Jewish Messiah. He was Jewish, I was Jewish, I didn't see that there was any reason for us not to believe in him.

As it turned out, my parents did not react the way I know that some families of Jewish believers have. They knew I believed in Jesus; they knew I was getting literature from Jews for Jesus, because I was living at home and they saw it. Our relationship didn't change, and I have always been grateful that, whatever my parents might think of my beliefs, they love and respect me enough to prevent any disagreement from tearing us apart.

I went on to law school at Mercer after I completed my undergraduate degree, and I graduated in the top 5 percent of my class. I began my career in law as a tax prosecutor for the IRS. It was the best experience I could have had. In one sense it's a miserable job: prosecuting people for fraud and tax evasion never won anybody a popularity contest. I even had a few death threats from time to time. What made it worthwhile was the fact that I was trying as many as twelve cases per week. It was phenomenal. I stayed with the IRS for about eighteen months; then my name came up for a transfer which I didn't want to take.

At that point, I figured, If I'm going to set up private practice, now is the time to do it. So I rented space with a friend from law school. Our monthly overhead was about sixteen hundred dollars. I thought that was a fortune! I didn't have a client, not one, but I did have some good contacts. In less than eight months, my firm was up to nine lawyers. We were the fastest-growing firm in Atlanta. How did we do it? We took on some pretty controversial cases and won. We were known as very tough litigators, and we developed a rapport and a good client base. When people were in trouble, they went to Sekulow and Roth.

Yet there was something else I wanted to do. I thought more and more about using my legal skills to serve God. In 1986, I became the Jews for Jesus general legal counsel. That's how I got my first Supreme Court case, Los Angeles *Board of Airport Commissioners versus Jews for Jesus*, in 1987. That case involved a challenge to a regulation banning any group—religious, political, or whatever—from distributing literature in the airport, which was a public facility. Whether or not one appreciates seeing individuals clad in Jews for Jesus T-shirts handing out literature at the airport was immaterial. If their rights of free speech are denied in the airport, who knows when and where you may eventually be denied your freedom of speech?

I'll never forget my first Supreme Court argument, even though I've argued there twelve times now. I came to the courtroom early, before the proceedings began. The podium was adjustable, right? I lowered it. I'm five feet seven and a half inches tall, and the last thing I needed was to be standing up on the tips of my toes to reach the podium. My parents were right in there. Whatever their feelings may be about my beliefs, they were there to support me. And I felt God's presence in that courtroom. It was clear. Even my parents, who don't believe like I do, said, "The calmness was eerie."

Our case was the first to be heard that day. I could hardly believe it when I heard Chief Justice Rehnquist say, "Now we'll hear case number 86-104, *Board of Airport Commissioners versus Jews for Jesus*." While the justices were busy raking the opposing counsel over the coals, I was changing the strategy of our case. I saw where the judges were headed, and I knew I'd have to reply to what was being said. Half an hour later,

I heard a voice call out, "Mr. Sekulow?" And I went up there. Me, a short Jewish guy from Brooklyn, New York, went before the justices of the Supreme Court of the United States to defend the constitutional right to stand in an airport and hand out tracts about Jesus. I'd prepared my first sentence carefully, because I knew it might be my only opportunity to make a statement. I said: "Mr. Chief Justice, may it please the court, local governments have important interests to protect concerning the efficient operation of the airports under their jurisdiction; however, the facts in this case do not justify the repression of cherished First Amendment freedoms based on a broad ban prohibiting all First Amendment activities to take place." That's all I got to say. Because, for the next half-hour, they grilled me. Justice Scalia and I got into a dialogue that reminded me of the teacher-student interactions from my days back in law school. He'd say, "What if this-and-this?" And I'd have to answer him. There were times when I had to say, "Your Honor, that's exactly what I did not say. You left out such-and-such." And so it went for the next thirty minutes of what was probably the most intense experience of my life. I had walked into the courtroom thinking about Jesus and how he overturned the moneychangers' tables at the Temple. Jesus was an activist; he stood up for what he knew was right. I drew strength from his example.

We won that case with a unanimous decision, and from there I started working on evangelism cases, even though I had a pretty significant private practice going on at the same time. Then, in 1990, the *Mergens* case, the Bible-club case, came up. What happened was that another legal group had it, but they wanted somebody that had experience in the Supreme Court on our side. The head of that group asked me to take the case up—it was already granted review. So I came in, put the brief together for the Supreme Court, and argued the case.

And from that case is when we formed the American Center for Law and Justice. This was Pat Robertson's idea. Pat called me after the decision came out in *Mergens*. I had known him casually, at a meeting or a dinner, not well. But Pat called me and said, Come on up to Norfolk and let's meet. He wanted to put together a large ACLU counterpoint, basically. At that time, in 1990, there was not an organized effort on our side, where on the other side you had the ACLU and People for the American Way; they were pretty coordinated and organized. We didn't have that. I thought it was high time that we did. So we put the ACLJ together, we got an executive director, I handled the legal work, and it grew very quickly.

When we started out in the ACLJ, there was this trend where any religion case was always argued as a free-exercise case, and they just weren't doing very well; the courts were not hospitable to free-exercise cases, they're still not. I proposed what was then a radical idea, of turning the argument from free exercise to free speech. And there was a howl of protest from people on our side, who thought that was heretical— you're abandoning the Free Exercise Clause for free speech. There was not a free-speech approach to it, and what happened when I made this argument was that groups like the ACLU and People for the American Way suddenly had to change their entire defense tactic, because now I put the Establishment Clause burden on them. As a defense, I'm arguing speech—who's the censor?—and it worked, initially very well. For the first couple of cases in the Supreme Court, we had two unanimous decisions, one was eight to one, one was six to three, it was clearly going our way.

For the first ten years of the ACLJ, we had two big things on our agenda. We had major legal action against pro-life protesters—I mean, it was gigantic. Everything from criminal investigations to big RICO suits to the Free Access to Clinic Entrances Act. I was going town to town, litigating in federal courts literally coast to coast. I represented Randall Terry, I represented Operation Rescue, and it was ugly. So my goal there was to keep my clients out of jail; it was pretty straightforward. So we had that agenda going on. And, at the same time, the religion-in-the-schools cases were percolating along pretty well. We had *Mergens* already, we were getting ready for *Lamb's Chapel*, a couple of the "See you at the flagpole" cases. So you had a convergence of the pro-life activity, which was getting much more of a higher profile than the religion cases, but they were going on at the same time. I had one term at the Supreme Court, I think we filed six briefs in different cases, I argued two, and we almost had a third. Those were busy times. What we were trying to do is even out the playing field for religious speech. We just wanted equal access, we weren't entitled to any more.

When we started out, we didn't have a proactive strategy, it was defensive. That changed in 1993. Once we had *Mergens* and *Lamb's Chapel* under our belt, that gave us the ability to go out and be a lot more aggressive, to make sure things were being done properly. Schools would get letters from the ACLU, they'd get a response from us. We'd send out a letter to every school district in the country at Christmastime, saying, "Don't overreact at Christmas when the school musical has a Christmas song in it, or a song about Hanukkah, don't overreact to this." And when cities and towns had problems about Nativity displays or menorahs that were being put up, every mayor got a letter from us, every city council, every town lawyer. You had this at election time too, we'd send out a letter saying, Pastors have free-speech rights, you don't have the right to endorse a candidate but you can speak about the moral issues of the day, right up to the election. Americans United would send out a counter-letter, You'd better not cross that line—it was sort of dueling letters. I got the letters stopped in the late 1990s, because I think we'd succeeded. If you want to have the Bible club, the kid can have the Bible club; if you want to have the Nativity scene, there are ways to do it.

Let me give you an example of how we try to work these things out. We got a call last year from a woman who was in charge of the PTA in her town. She's doing the teacher-appreciation dinner, before the schools go on Christmas break. They were going to decorate the room and the tables in red and green, and the school district said, You can't do that, those colors are representative of Christmas. But I didn't file a federal lawsuit to get that resolved. One of our lawyers spoke to the school-board lawyer and said, This is an overreaction here. Walked through it, no problem. You know, some groups will advertise, they've got seven hundred lawyers on standby, ready to clamp down. I think it's great, but there's not seven hundred problems. And if you have to go to court over the problem, something in the process went wrong, because most of these things get worked out. There are exceptions, but for the most part you can get it resolved.

Most people on the other side think religious conservatives all think alike and agree on everything, which isn't true. For example, I don't like school-organized prayer. I never did. I think a school policy that requires the recitation of a prayer at the beginning of the school day, like you had in New York and Pennsylvania in the *Engel* and *Schempp* cases, is unconstitutional. And I use those cases to distinguish the cases I have. But I'm in the minority on my side in this; it's probably about five to one against me. If you talk to most of the other Christian legal groups, I think they would say mandatory prayer at the beginning of the school day is fine. The problem is, as I remind people, when the prayer is not "our Father," "our King," instead it's in Arabic, and it's a Muslim prayer, are you going to be okay with it then? And you get this, Well, no, that's not the way the country was founded. And it's true. The Judeo-Christian influence on the country was much more significant than any other religious influence, but the First Amendment doesn't work that way. I like the student-led, student-initiated prayer. I think that the debate on prayer in the schools was handled appropriately in the Equal Access Act. That is the best answer. I think if religious students want to evangelize, if they want to talk to their friends about their faith, they have a right to do it. And school districts should realize that that's a protected right.

I had the case on the margins, which was Santa Fe, the football-game prayer case. And the background didn't help me: stormy facts make for rough law. The lawyer on the other side, Anthony Griffin, made an effective point that the kids who challenged the prayers had been pushed around and called names, which didn't help my argument. And the Supreme Court said the school district was too involved in the prayer policy, and that's because they previously had a student chaplain, and they tried to correct themselves, and there was not enough time between their initial actions and what actually happened. And what happened in Santa Fe was, of course you want to win the case for the client, but I wanted to make sure *Lamb's Chapel* and *Mergens* weren't hurt. And Justice Stevens in the opinion pointed out that, look, there's nothing in the Constitution or in the Court's precedents that prohibit students from praying before, after, or during the school day, they have the right to do that; he cited *Mergens*, he cited *Lamb's Chapel*. So in that sense it was Mission Accomplished.

Do I ever feel pressure from my friends on the right? Sure. Look, you're a human being, and these are friends, and sometimes you disagree. I get accused of being the moderate middle of the Religious Right, the mushy middle, Sekulow's too pragmatic. But I'm a litigator. It's one thing to be the activist on the corner, or the activist of an organization—you're mobilizing the troops. I have to do that, and walk across that street and argue a case at the Supreme Court. So I'm not calling the justices names. I don't think you gain anything by going after the individual justices or the Court as an institution. I was on a major network program once, the host will be nameless, and he said, Those liberal justices are a bunch of pinheads, and why don't you just say it? I said, I'm an officer of the court, and I'm not going to say that. You have to be pragmatic, and I've got to litigate there. Some of the other groups have the luxury and the ability to just be out there, but I don't think that would help me when I stand up before the justices.

If I'm going to be effective in what I do, it's also important to get along with people on the other side. The best example is Barry Lynn of Americans United. We're friends. Do I think there's anything dangerous or disturbing about what he does? No, I think this is America. This is a country where you can say, I don't think the Pledge of Allegiance is constitutional, because of "under God." And somebody else can say, I think the Pledge is constitutional because it says "under God." And you can duke it out in the courtroom and still have dinner afterward. My view is, you can agree to disagree in the public discourse. We get on the air—I'll never forget this—Barry and I were at the Supreme Court, waiting for a decision to come out. So we're both there, and we had breakfast together. We were supposed to be on CNN that afternoon, on the *Lou Dobbs* program. And I got a call from a CNN producer saying, We're a little bit concerned, because we saw you and Barry together, and we want to be sure this is going to be a real joust of a fight on TV. And I said, Don't worry about that, but we're friends. We may disagree completely with each other's view on a particular topic, but that doesn't mean we don't respect each other. He's a bright guy, and very pleasant. We just disagree on these topics.

Mike Newdow and I are good friends. I was there for the arguments in his Pledge of Allegiance case. I told him before the arguments, I'll give you two pieces of advice: don't talk so quickly, and don't talk with your hands. He said, How do you not talk with your hands? And I said, Just don't talk with your hands. I keep one hand behind my back. I think he did great, he got an A-plus. His answers were good; I think he handled himself professionally. I like Mike a lot. He got a bad rap, because he did a bold thing. People didn't like it, and I didn't like it. I told him, Watch yourself on this. And, having said that, I didn't think he'd get a vote. You can sometimes have a great argument and not win; that happens more times than not.

I don't like the demonization of the left. And I don't like the demonization of the right. It works both ways. And when we think they've crossed the line, or they think we've crossed the line, we talk about it. I make sure we don't personalize it. I refuse, refuse, refuse. Yea, though they speak ill of you, just grin and bear it. My point is, there's no point in demonizing the other side. Most people, if you talk to them about me personally, Barry, Mike, they're going to say, We like him. Sometimes the next in line—the deputy crowd, as I call it—they'll personalize it. And when they do it, I just ignore it.

I know there are fringes on both sides of these religion issues, very passionate in their views, who think the other side is dangerous, but I don't think they're going to carry the day. I'll tell you why. Because you have voices, and I'm not patting myself on the back, and others as well, who can go out there and explain that that's not the way to approach things. You don't go to a debate or a discussion and start vilifying the person on the other side. I've seen it happen. I've had it. I went down to a school district in Mississippi to tell the principal, You can't have a prayer over the intercom system. The school superintendent was a Christian guy, trying to do the right thing, and he said, How do I draw this line? I took a lot of flak from my side on that. But when that case, and a lot of cases, started going to the Supreme Court in the nineties, judges and justices knew I did that, so I was an honest broker. And I think those situations are not good for religion, it's not good for America. Having said that, it's a free country, and people are going to disagree, it's as old as the Republic. ❖

Chapter 4

"With the Cross of Jesus"

The Mount Soledad Cross Case from San Diego, California

San Diego proudly bills itself as "America's Finest City." The second-largest city in California, after Los Angeles, and the seventh-largest in the United States, it is home to more than 1.3 million people, having doubled in population since 1970. San Diego is also the home of the nation's longest-running battle over religious symbols in public places, a lawsuit that was filed in 1989 and was still unresolved in 2007, after dozens of courtroom hearings, city-council debates, and judicial rulings in state and federal courts.

The seemingly unending conflict in San Diego over the Mount Soledad cross—erected in 1954 in the center of a public park, at the summit of the city's highest peak—offers an instructive example of the power of religious symbols, both to inspire their adherents and to incite their antagonists. And the longevity of *Paulson v. San Diego*, the case that sought to remove the cross from the park, illustrates the difficulty of ending a legal struggle between a stubborn plaintiff on one side, with a handful of supporters, and equally stubborn city officials on the other, backed by overwhelming majorities of the city's voters. The Mount Soledad case also demonstrates how the Religious Right can turn a local conflict into a national crusade to defend "the cross of Christ" against its "atheist" opponents.

On the surface, San Diego seems an unlikely setting for conflicts over religion. The city's last four mayors have been Catholic, Jewish, and Protestant, and election campaigns have never focused on a candidate's religious affiliation or beliefs. San Diego is a laid-back city, attracting more than thirty million visitors each year, drawn by the year-round temperate climate, seventy miles of Pacific Ocean beaches, and a raft of tourist attractions, including the world-famous San Diego Zoo, Sea-World, and the newly renovated Gaslamp Quarter in the city's downtown center. But, along with its palm trees and sandy beaches, San Diego has long been a military center, and is now the home port of the world's largest naval fleet. A huge Marine Corps base, Camp Pendleton, lies just north of the city. Since World War II, several million Navy and Marine troops have been stationed in San Diego, and thousands have returned to the city to work or enjoy their retirement. Military veterans make up a substantial part of the city's residents, and most are conservative in politics. However, San Diego is no longer the safe Republican city it was for many years. Partisan gerrymandering has given both Democrats and the GOP two safe congressional seats that include parts of the city, and several city-council members in recent years have been notably liberal.

San Diego is justly proud of its many public parks, especially the fourteen-hundred-acre Balboa Park, whose Spanish-style buildings were constructed to host a world's fair in 1915, and which shares its space with the zoo. Another park, some ten miles north of the city center, offers visitors a panoramic view of the city from the summit of Mount Soledad, jutting 820 feet above the ocean at its foot. To the south, the view from the 170-acre park stretches to the border with Mexico and the adjoining city of Tijuana, another popular tourist attraction. And to the north, visitors can see the campus of the University of California, San Diego, established in 1962 as an outgrowth of the Scripps Institution of Oceanography. The Mount Soledad Natural Park, which the city dedicated as a public park in 1916, is located in La Jolla, one of the wealthiest of San Diego's disparate neighborhoods.

Among La Jolla's most influential families are the Kelloggs, who own the La Jolla Beach and Tennis Club. In 1952, during the Korean War, they were instrumental in founding the Mount Soledad Memorial Committee. This organization's well-connected leaders persuaded the San

Diego city council to allow the construction, at the summit of the Mount Soledad park, of a forty-three-foot-tall Latin cross as a memorial to Korean veterans. City officials granted permission to erect the cross, but retained ownership of the cross site. Significantly, the cross was dedicated on April 18, 1954, an Easter Sunday, at a religious service that featured Bible readings and prayers, and the singing of "Onward, Christian Soldiers." Over the next forty years, in fact, the Memorial Committee conducted services every Easter Sunday, but never on Veterans Day. Also significantly, the city's official maps and tourist brochures identified the site as the "Easter Cross."

Not until 1989, thirty-five years after the cross was erected, did anyone question the city's legal authority to allow a private group to place a Christian symbol on its property. Early that year, I wrote a letter to the San Diego city attorney, John Witt, asking for a legal opinion on whether the cross's location in a public park violated the Establishment of Religion Clause of the First Amendment. I had joined the UCSD faculty in 1982, teaching constitutional law in the political-science department, and drove past the Mount Soledad cross on my way to the campus. At the same time, two other San Diego residents, Philip Paulson and Howard Kreisner, also informed Witt that they were preparing a lawsuit to challenge the Easter Cross. The two men were professed atheists, and Paulson, who first proposed the lawsuit to remove the Easter Cross, was a Vietnam veteran who objected to a war memorial that was solely a Christian symbol. I had not met Paulson and Kreisner, but learned of their efforts through an article in the *San Diego Union*, the city's morning newspaper, and contacted them with an offer to work together on the lawsuit. At our first meeting, they showed me the draft of a lawsuit they had prepared to file in the San Diego federal court as *pro se* plaintiffs, without legal counsel. Kreisner, who had done the legal research for the lawsuit, was determined to argue the case himself, and I agreed to assist him and Paulson on a pro-bono basis.

In response to my letter, and the threatened lawsuit by Paulson and Kreisner, John Witt instructed one of his deputies, Mary Kay Jackson, to draft a memorandum on the legal issues raised by the Mount Soledad cross. Her memo, submitted on April 28, 1989, cited both the federal Constitution's ban of any "establishment of religion" and two provisions of the California constitution. The first barred any governmental "preference" to religion, while the second prohibited state or local bodies from granting "anything to or in aid of any religious sect, church, creed, or sectarian purpose." Noting that the Supreme Court had never decided a case "dealing specifically with the question of crosses on public lands," Jackson canvassed the decisions of lower federal courts on this issue, finding seven earlier cases, none of which, she admitted, "allowed the cross to remain" on public property. However, Jackson argued in her memo to Witt that each of these cases could be distinguished from the Mount Soledad cross, because of its "secular purpose" as a war memorial. Therefore, she concluded, "the City is not violating either the Federal or California Constitutions" by allowing the cross to remain in the park.

Jackson's memo, which I shared with Paulson and Kreisner, did not deter them from filing their lawsuit in federal district court on May 31, 1989. In fact, the memo only strengthened their belief that any judge, conservative or liberal, would rule in their favor. As it turned out, the case of *Paulson v. San Diego* was assigned to one of the most conservative judges on the federal bench. Gordon Thompson was a native San Diegan, born in 1929, who grew up and still lived in the affluent Point Loma neighborhood, where he had attended the Presbyterian church since childhood. Thompson began his legal career as a prosecutor in the district attorney's office, leaving after three years to join a law firm whose clients included many of San Diego's banks and businesses. He also became active in Republican politics, and was rewarded by President Richard Nixon in 1970 with a seat on the district court, where he served as chief judge from 1984 to 1991. Thompson was certainly not the judge that Paulson and Kreisner would have picked for their case, but they hoped he would defer to the decisions of fellow judges.

During the first hearing on the Mount Soledad case, in 1991, Thompson made clear his personal view that the Easter Cross should remain in the park. But he also made clear his commitment to precedent established in similar cases by the Ninth Circuit Court of Appeals, which bound district judges to its rulings. In the most recent case, decided just a few months earlier, the Ninth Circuit had invoked the "no preference" clause of the California constitution to order the removal of Christian religious statuary from a San Bernardino county park. Howard Kreisner, who argued for himself and Phil Paulson, cited this case and other judicial rulings that Mary Kay Jackson had "distinguished" in her memo to Witt. It was undeniable, Kreisner told Judge Thompson, that the Easter Cross was a sectarian religious symbol, despite the city's efforts to portray it as a secular war memorial with no sectarian meaning. Appearing for the city, Jackson argued that the cross had "lost its religious symbolization" and had become "resymbolized" into a secular object.

Jackson's effort to strip the cross of religious meaning clearly offended Judge Thompson, for whom the cross was the central symbol of his religious beliefs. In his ruling, issued on December 3, 1991, Thompson stressed that "the Latin cross is a powerful religious symbol" and represents "the Christian message of the crucifixion and resurrection of Jesus Christ, a doctrine at the heart of Christianity." He also cited the Memorial Association's use of the cross site only for Easter services, noting that nothing in the park indicated to visitors "that the cross was intended to commemorate our country's war dead." Given this history, Thompson concluded, "the city's purported commemorative objective is a pretext" for its sectarian "preference" for Christianity. He concluded his opinion by ordering the city to remove the Easter Cross within thirty days.

————

In fact, more than five thousand days passed before the city took the first step toward complying with Judge Thompson's order. Over the next fourteen years, San Diego officials refused to abandon their efforts to "Save the Cross" on Mount Soledad. Several factors affected the city's initial response to Thompson's ruling. First, the city attorney had assured the city council that the cross would survive judicial scrutiny, and urged an appeal to the Ninth Circuit. Second, most council members sincerely believed that a Christian symbol could properly serve as a memorial to

San Diegans who had given their lives to defend the nation. Third, Judge Thompson had suggested in his opinion that the Easter Cross might remain on Mount Soledad if the site was no longer public property, a broad hint that the city might legally "transfer" a portion of land around the cross to a private group. Fourth, and perhaps most important, public reaction to Thompson's ruling was overwhelmingly critical. By a margin of ten to one, letters to the city's newspapers denounced the decision, and calls to council members demanded action to save the cross.

Responding to this pressure, the council adopted two measures by unanimous vote. The first authorized Witt to file an appeal with the Ninth Circuit; the second placed a proposition on the ballot for the next election, in June 1992. Proposition F asked voters to approve "the removal from dedicated park status of that portion of Mt. Soledad Natural Park necessary to maintain the property as an historic war memorial," and to transfer that parcel "to a private non-profit corporation for not less than fair market value." Under the city charter, approval of Proposition F required a two-thirds vote in favor. That hurdle was easily overcome. Mayor Maureen O'Connor headed the list of city officials who urged voters in the official ballot pamphlet to "Save the Cross." Not surprisingly, 76 percent of the voters supported the proposition.

Armed with voter approval to sell a portion of the Mount Soledad park, including the Easter Cross itself, city officials decided to hold off until the Ninth Circuit ruled on their appeal of Judge Thompson's order, just in case it was reversed. In this second judicial round, Phil Paulson and Howard Kreisner asked me to brief and argue the case for them, since I was admitted to practice before the Ninth Circuit and had argued other appellate cases. The hearing took place in 1993 at the court's picturesque Spanish-style chambers in Pasadena, California, before a three-judge panel, with Mary Kay Jackson leading off for the city. It was clear from the outset that none of the judges had much sympathy with Jackson's argument. She had tried to buttress her case by attaching to her brief a batch of newspaper articles reporting that veterans' groups, including the American Legion, had taken part in Easter services sponsored by the Mount Soledad Memorial Association. I had objected in my brief that none of this material had been considered by Judge Thompson, and that Jackson was improperly bringing it before the appellate panel. Jackson became flustered as the judges grilled her on this issue, and I took just fifteen minutes in reply, pointing the panel to the Ninth Circuit case on which Thompson had relied for precedent.

In their unanimous ruling, written by Judge Thomas Tang, the appellate panel chastised Jackson's effort to introduce documents that "were not before the district court and therefore cannot be considered part of the record on appeal." But this made no difference in their decision. "Even if we were to agree that the cross has always been explicitly recognized and referred to as a war memorial," Tang wrote, "that would not obviate the appearance of preference" for the Christian religion. "A sectarian war memorial carries an inherently religious message and creates an appearance of honoring only those servicemen of that particular religion," he concluded.

Defeated in the first two rounds of the Mount Soledad case, San Diego officials decided to keep up their fight to "Save the Cross," approving John Witt's request to seek an *en banc* review of Judge Tang's ruling by a larger panel of Ninth Circuit judges. This was a long shot, for three reasons. First, a majority vote of the twenty-eight Ninth Circuit judges was necessary to secure *en banc* review of any three-judge panel decision. Second, Witt would have to argue that Tang's opinion was "clearly erroneous" in its reasoning. Lastly, the Ninth Circuit—along with other circuits—rarely granted *en banc* review of its panel decisions. But this effort, however unlikely to succeed, would at least buy time while city officials pondered their next move to block the enforcement of Judge Thompson's order to remove the Easter Cross from the Mount Soledad park. Despite these long odds, Witt filed his request in early 1994, only to be rebuffed by the unanimous vote of the Ninth Circuit judges to deny *en banc* review.

Down by three rounds after this defeat, the San Diego council sent Witt back from his corner for a fourth round, granting his request to seek review of the Ninth Circuit ruling by the U.S. Supreme Court. This was an even longer shot, since the Court regularly voted to hear fewer than 2 percent of appeals from lower-court decisions. Witt knew, however, that Paulson and Kreisner were preparing to ask Judge Thompson to enforce his order. And, once again, the city would buy time while the Supreme Court considered Witt's petition. Witt pinned his hopes on two slim reeds. First, under the Court's unwritten rules, it would require the votes of only four justices to hear the case. Back in 1989, four conservative justices—three still on the Court in 1994—had dissented in a case that challenged the display of a Christian Nativity crèche in a county courthouse during the Christmas season. With the addition of Justice Clarence Thomas to the Court in 1991, Witt might pick up the four votes he needed to have the Mount Soledad case heard. Second, the Court had reversed more than 80 percent of the Ninth Circuit rulings that it had reviewed in recent years, the lowest batting average of any appellate court.

Witt filed his Supreme Court petition and a supporting brief in September 1994, and I answered with a brief asking the justices to deny the city's request. Confined by the Court's rules to ten pages, both briefs did little more than review the Ninth Circuit's ruling, reaching opposite conclusions on its reasoning. I considered Witt's petition an exercise in futility, and was not surprised when the Court denied it on October 10, without any recorded dissent. I was also not surprised when San Diego officials announced, shortly after their defeat in the fourth round of the Mount Soledad case, that they had sold 222 square feet of the park, including the concrete base on which the Easter Cross rested and the iron fence surrounding it, about fifteen feet on each side, to the Mount Soledad Memorial Association for the "fair market value" of $14,500. This figure had been determined by the city's property appraiser, who based his calculations on prior sales of "undeveloped" land in La Jolla. This sale, arranged in advance, and without any opportunity for other groups to bid for the property, allowed city officials to claim they had complied with Judge Thompson's hint that selling the Easter Cross site to a private group might cure its constitutional violations.

Following the sale, the Mount Soledad case returned to Thompson for round five in this protracted litigation, with a new party in the case.

Thompson granted a motion by the Memorial Association to recognize the group as an "intervenor" and to assert its ownership of the Easter Cross and the portion of the park the city had sold to it. Paulson and Kreisner responded with a motion to void what they called the "sweetheart deal" to sell the "postage stamp" plot around the cross, arguing that the city had violated its own regulations in failing to allow other groups to bid for the site. In addition, they claimed, the small plaque the Memorial Association had attached to the fence around the cross, declaring the area within the fence as private property, did not remedy the constitutional violation.

During 1995, while these motions were pending, the case slowed to a crawl. Judge Thompson had allowed the plaintiffs to obtain documents from the city and the Memorial Association about the sale of the cross site, and assigned a federal magistrate to supervise the discovery process, in preparation for a hearing on the legality of the transaction. Thompson also postponed the hearing indefinitely, because of serious health problems, but declined to refer the case to another judge during his absence from the bench. He had assumed "senior" status in 1994, relieving him from regular case assignments and allowing him to choose the cases he would hear. Thompson seemed determined, however, to hang on to the Mount Soledad case, in no hurry to move it along. During this lengthy hiatus, newspaper coverage of the case dwindled and then disappeared.

That changed abruptly in March 1996. More from curiosity than design, I visited the city's park office in La Jolla and asked whether anyone had reserved the Mount Soledad park for Easter Sunday, on April 7. Permits to use park facilities for any event were required in advance, and were issued on a "first-come-first-served" basis. To my surprise, I was informed that the Memorial Association, which had conducted Easter services at the cross site every year since 1954, had not obtained a permit for 1996. On the spur of the moment, I requested an application to hold a gathering on Easter Sunday, between six and eight in the morning. Obviously surprised, the park office's manager handed me the form and then went into his office, presumably to alert city officials—and perhaps Bill

Kellogg of the Memorial Association—of my request. Because events required an organizational sponsor, and suspicious that the park manager might suddenly "discover" a permit to the Association, I promptly called Phil Paulson from a nearby pay phone and got his approval to reserve the site for the Atheist Coalition of San Diego, to which he belonged; by this time, Howard Kreisner had moved to Texas and was no longer a plaintiff in the suit. Had I planned my visit to the park office in advance, I might have asked Tom Owen-Towle, minister of the First Unitarian Church in San Diego, of which I was a member, to sponsor the Easter service. But time was short, and I listed the Atheist Coalition as the event's sponsor and handed the completed form to the park manager.

Within hours of leaving the office, I received a call from a reporter for the *San Diego Union-Tribune*, who had obviously been tipped off by city officials to this surprise development. The next day, a banner headline alerted readers, "Atheists Take Over Easter Cross." I was quoted as saying the Easter service would be an ecumenical, nonsectarian gathering, to which Christians and non-Christians were invited, with the theme "The Park Belongs to Everyone." But the participation of several ministers, including Tom Owen-Towle, did not dampen the instant outrage. The words "Atheist Coalition" on the permit inflamed the public, and the *Union-Tribune* was flooded with letters denouncing the event as a "publicity stunt" and an affront to Christians. Bill Kellogg was quoted as saying he simply "forgot" to obtain a permit for the Memorial Association.

Before sunrise on Easter Sunday, several hundred people gathered around the Mount Soledad cross. Tom Owen-Towle and I spoke at the service, along with a Presbyterian minister and the pastor of the San Diego Community Church, which has a largely gay-and-lesbian congregation. David Noelle, speaking for the San Diego Humanist Association, noted: "It didn't seem very polite for us to gather here this morning. After all, we had good reason to suspect that our celebration would interfere with the plans of others who hoped to worship here." He turned to the cross looming over the gathering. "This large cross in a public park, still standing despite court orders for its removal, is a clear message that, in the eyes of the City of San Diego, Christians are to be preferred and others are to be, at best, merely tolerated." As Noelle was speaking, a group of Bible-waving protesters pushed their way through the crowd, loudly singing hymns to drown him out. Even the Christian ministers who spoke faced taunts. Predictably, the newspaper and television coverage of the event focused on the sideshow of the protesters. As the *Union-Tribune* reported: "There were hell-fire shouters and serious doubters, men in white robes carrying staffs and women wearing T-shirts that said, 'Beware of God.' A man, naked except for a loincloth, carried a cross. Another man stood guard at the railing circling the cross and said he was willing to die to keep the cross standing. 'It's a symbol of purity rising above the scum. They have no right to be here on Easter or any time else if they are only here to broadcast sin,' he said." Perhaps most ominously, among the crowd was Tom Metzger, national leader of the White Aryan Resistance and San Diego's most notorious racist and anti-Semite, who remained quiet and simply glared at the speakers.

———

After tempers had cooled from the "atheist invasion" of the cross site, more than a year passed before round six in the Mount Soledad case, a delay caused largely by Judge Thompson's lengthy absence from the bench. After reviewing the briefs and records submitted on the city's sale of the plot underneath the cross, he issued his ruling on September 18, 1997. His opinion found "most telling" the city's appeal to "Save the Cross on Mount Soledad" in campaigning for voter approval of Proposition F in 1992. "For the city to take the position of trying to 'save' such a preeminent Christian symbol," Thompson wrote, "clearly shows a governmental preference for the Christian religion." Thompson also faulted the city's "no bid" sale of the cross site to the Memorial Association. "The exclusion of any other purchasers of or bidders for the land," he stated, "gives the appearance of preferring the Christian religion over all others." Finally, "the city's attempt to comply with this Court's order by selling only a small portion of the land underneath the Mt. Soledad cross still shows a preference or aid to the Christian religion," in violation of the California constitution's "no preference" clause. Six years after city officials had disregarded his initial order to remove the cross,

Thompson once again gave them thirty days to comply with his latest order.

Before this ruling, Phil Paulson and I had explored the prospect of moving the cross to the nearby Mount Soledad Presbyterian Church, about half a mile down the hill from the park. The church had plenty of outdoor space to accommodate the cross, and its pastor, the Reverend Mark Slomka, had indicated his receptiveness to this idea. Despite this possible way to comply with Judge Thompson's order, there was a new obstacle to resolving the case, now in its eighth year of litigation. John Witt, the elected city attorney, had left office in 1996 and was replaced by one of his former deputies, Casey Gwinn. Unlike Witt, who delegated the case to his staff and never appeared at the courtroom hearings, Gwinn viewed the cross challenge as an affront to his evangelical Christian faith and handled the case himself. He regularly preached at local evangelical churches; in one sermon at the Mission Valley Christian Fellowship, Gwinn said, "I'm just here as a follower of Jesus. The way that we experience everlasting life is to accept a personal relationship with Jesus and to say I claim him as my way to eternal life. There's no other way to get there."

Following Judge Thompson's third order to remove the cross, the San Diego city council met on September 30, 1997, to consider its next move. Casey Gwinn urged the council to authorize a second sale of the cross site, this time with a larger portion of land and an open bidding process. During the public-comment period, Phil Paulson stated, "I do not want to see the cross on Mt. Soledad defaced, demolished, or desecrated. But rather I want the cross moved from the Mt. Soledad public park to the Mt. Soledad Presbyterian Church." The council, however, approved Gwinn's proposal to conduct a "restructured" sale of the cross site.

Twice in the next month, Paulson and I met with Gwinn to press our proposal to move the cross to the nearby church. The discussions were friendly, but Gwinn made clear he had no desire to relocate the cross. When the second meeting ended, Paulson reminded Gwinn of the city's unbroken string of judicial defeats in the case. "If I placed a turtle on top of this conference table and hit it behind the head forty-four times," Paulson said, "would you suspect that the turtle would stick his head inside the shell? The city of San Diego had forty-four federal judges unanimously rule against them. Count them! Add them up! Are they going to stick their heads out of the shell again?" Gwinn laughed, but told Paulson he was preparing for a new sale of the cross site.

Between these two meetings, Gwinn had filed an appeal of Judge Thompson's latest order with the Ninth Circuit, which set a deadline for filing the city's brief on February 4, 1998. Round seven in the case, however, was not fought before the appellate court. A few days before Gwinn's brief was due, he abruptly withdrew the appeal. Judge Thompson had scheduled a hearing for March 9, 1998, to consider Paulson's motion for a "more definite order" to set a final deadline for removing the cross from the park. At this hearing, Thompson gave the city its first courtroom victory, telling Gwinn the city could proceed with the "restructured" sale, but reserving judgment on its legality until it was completed. At a press conference outside the courthouse, Gwinn predicted that Thompson would approve the sale and finally end the case, but I expressed doubt that any sale allowing the cross to remain in the park would pass judicial muster. Still, the city had definitely bought more time, and Thompson seemed receptive to the "open bidding" process that Gwinn proposed.

Shortly after this hearing, I told Phil Paulson of my decision to drop out of the case, which had taken a toll on my family. After the "atheist" service at the cross site on Easter Sunday in 1996, I received several threats on my telephone answering machine: "We know where you live and we're going to get you," one said. Over the next two years, newspaper and television coverage of the case prompted more calls. Concerned for the safety of our two young daughters, my wife convinced me to turn the case over to another lawyer. Paulson then recruited James McElroy, a prominent San Diego lawyer and also the national board chairman of the Southern Poverty Law Center, to represent him in further proceedings. McElroy had long been active in civil-rights litigation and had assisted Morris Dees, the SPLC director, in winning a

$12.5-million judgment against Tom Metzger for having instigated racist skinheads to attack and stomp to death an Ethiopian man in Portland, Oregon. Meticulous in his legal preparation, but also brash and outspoken, McElroy was more than willing to take on the city in the Mount Soledad case.

When city officials, responding to Judge Thompson's latest order, prepared their instructions to prospective bidders for the cross site, they extended its boundary to include the circular area around the cross, up to the sidewalk around it, an area just over half an acre in size. The city's invitation for bids noted that the property was "presently the site of a large, concrete, Latin cross." Bidders would not be required to retain the cross, but were required to submit evidence of their "experience and qualifications to maintain the property as an historic war memorial." This, of course, had long been the city's description of the Easter Cross. Five organizations submitted bids, three proposing to retain the cross and two—the National League for the Separation of Church and State, and the Freedom From Religion Foundation—proposing to replace it with secular war memorials. The Mount Soledad Memorial Association's bid of $106,000 topped the list, six thousand dollars above the next-highest bid. There was no evidence that city officials had tipped off the Association to the competing bids, but the odd figure did raise skeptical eyebrows. Significantly, the city's review committee gave the Association extra points for having shown "a very strong track record over 46 years of being involved in the existing memorial." Predictably, the city council voted unanimously to approve the sale to the Memorial Association.

Round eight of the Mount Soledad case was fought, once again, in Judge Thompson's courtroom. Jim McElroy filed a motion in August 1999 to void the second sale, arguing that requiring bidders to demonstrate prior experience in maintaining "an historic war memorial" gave the Memorial Association an advantage that other bidders could not match, and that the half-acre plot was still too small to distinguish the cross site from the surrounding park. Ruling on February 3, 2000, Thompson gave the city its second judicial victory, upholding the sale as a "neutral" process that had not favored any of the bidding groups. His brief opinion made clear Thompson's view that San Diego officials had now complied with his earlier orders and that the Easter Cross could remain in the park. As far as he was concerned, the ten-year-old case was now over.

Jim McElroy, however, was not about to throw his towel into the judicial ring. He promptly filed an appeal to the Ninth Circuit, ringing the bell for the ninth round in the Mount Soledad case. McElroy faced off with Casey Gwinn, who claimed that San Diego was now a spectator in the case, having sold the cross site to comply with Judge Thompson's orders. But a third lawyer now joined the fight. The Memorial Association had retained Charles Berwanger, an experienced property lawyer with a big San Diego firm, to argue its claim as the legal owner of the half-acre plot on which the Easter Cross sat. Berwanger told the three-judge panel that any order to remove the cross from "private property" would violate the Association's rights under the "free exercise of religion" and "freedom of speech" clauses of the First Amendment. McElroy replied to this Alphonse-and-Gaston routine by arguing that Berwanger was in fact the real spectator in the courtroom. By requiring prior experience in maintaining a war memorial on the cross site, McElroy argued, the city had given an unfair advantage to the Memorial Association. But he lost the ninth round on August 22, 2001. The three-judge panel, headed by Chief Judge Procter Hug, Jr., unanimously upheld Judge Thompson's approval of the "restructured" sale.

Hug made three points in his opinion. First, he said, the city's requirement that bidders demonstrate prior experience in maintaining "an historic war memorial" was "not only logical and reasonable, but indeed prudent considering the intended and required function of the property." Second, however small the half-acre plot within the 170-acre park, visitors would see the Memorial Association's plaques around the site and "quickly recognize that the cross sits on private property." And, third, echoing Berwanger's First Amendment argument, Hug agreed that "requiring the removal of the cross from private property would infringe upon the Association's fundamental constitutional rights."

Despite this judicial blow, McElroy still led in rounds by a six-to-three margin. He opened the tenth round with a counter-punch, asking the Ninth Circuit judges to grant an *en banc* review of Hug's ruling. Casey Gwinn's predecessor as city attorney, John Witt, had failed in 1994 to gain a single vote for Ninth Circuit review of its decision to uphold Judge Thompson's first order to remove the Mount Soledad cross. McElroy, however, won the majority he needed, and the court set a hearing for March 21, 2002, before an eleven-judge panel at its courtroom in Phoenix, Arizona. He was also lucky in drawing a panel that was heavily weighted in his favor. Eight of its members had been placed on the bench by presidents Jimmy Carter and Bill Clinton, including Chief Judge Mary Schroeder, who had replaced Procter Hug in that post after he moved to senior status in January 2002.

The same three lawyers who had argued the year before in Pasadena—McElroy, Gwinn, and Berwanger—largely restated their positions in Phoenix. In this round, however, McElroy won on points by a seven-to-four margin, in a ruling handed down on June 26, 2002. Writing for the majority, Judge Susan Graber, named to the bench by President Clinton, held that the city's sale of the cross site to the Memorial Association "granted a direct, immediate, and substantial benefit in aid of a Christian message." Graber based her opinion on what seemed a trivial issue. In selling the site to the Association, she wrote, "the City gave away for free an economically valuable means of fulfilling the main condition of the sale." In contrast, Graber said, bidders who wanted to replace the cross "would be saddled with the costs of removing the cross and of constructing an alternative war memorial." In his brief opinion for the four dissenters, Judge Ferdinand Fernandez, placed on the bench by President George H. W. Bush, simply asserted that San Diego officials "did not stray from the path of neutrality" in selling the Easter Cross site to the Memorial Association.

Judge Graber's opinion returned the Mount Soledad case to Judge Thompson, with instructions to "devise a remedy for the constitutional violation" he had found in 1991, eleven years earlier. Before any further proceedings, however, Casey Gwinn bought time for another year, fighting rounds eleven and twelve in this marathon battle. He first asked the Ninth Circuit judges to reconsider their ruling, which the court denied in October 2002. Gwinn then filed the city's second petition for review by the Supreme Court, losing again in April 2003. He tried to put a good face on his defeat, telling reporters he was "not terribly surprised" by the Supreme Court's ruling, but "felt we had to go through the process." On a conciliatory note, Gwinn suggested that he could sit down with McElroy and Berwanger and "try to find common ground" in resolving the case. McElroy sounded less conciliatory. "The city has been rather strident in their approach in the past," he said. But he did not reject the city's olive branch: "I'm hoping they now might come to the table with more of an open mind and a willingness to entertain the fact that we need to do more to make this work constitutionally."

The third lawyer in the case, Charles Berwanger, knew that Judge Thompson could hardly approve a third sale of the cross site, and had little choice but to enforce his original order to remove the cross. He also realized that the Memorial Association had the most to lose in the case. Over the past four years, the Association had spent more than a million dollars to construct granite walls around the cross site, collecting much of this money from the families of veterans who paid the Association to place plaques with their names and pictures on the walls. If Thompson voided the second sale, ownership of the cross and the memorial walls around it would revert to the city. Faced with this prospect, Berwanger signaled his willingness to work out a settlement with McElroy, under which the cross would be relocated to the Mount Soledad Presbyterian Church, as Phil Paulson and I had proposed in 1997. Presumably, the city would allow the Association to maintain the memorial walls in the park.

———

Over the next year, McElroy and Berwanger, along with Mark Slomka, pastor of the Presbyterian church, worked out a settlement that satisfied them all. Slomka told reporters in July 2004 that his church's elders had voted unanimously to accept the cross if the city council approved the deal. Carl Dustin, the Memorial Association's vice president and former commander of the American Legion post that had raised funds in 1954 to erect the Easter Cross, said the post's members had also voted unanimously to support moving the cross. Jim McElroy joined the chorus, stating that the Mount Soledad case would finally end if the cross was relocated to the church's grounds. All that remained was approval from the city council and Judge Thompson, who was unlikely to object to the settlement.

The council met on July 19 to discuss the proposed settlement. But a wrench suddenly hit this well-greased machinery. Casey Gwinn urged the council to authorize a third sale of the cross site, and to put another proposition in the ballot to secure voter approval. "The voters and taxpayers of San Diego have a right to weigh in on the future of this cross," he said. "Whether the cross comes or goes should be decided by a private property owner, not by the City of San Diego." Gwinn's proposal, if successful, would unravel the settlement that McElroy and Berwanger had worked out, and which they planned to submit to Judge Thompson, expecting his approval to end the fifteen-year-old lawsuit. Gwinn, however, was determined to keep the Easter Cross on Mount Soledad, counting on public support to back him.

With Gwinn's proposal on the agenda, the council meeting on July 27 drew a large crowd and unleashed a flood of heated rhetoric on both sides. Jim McElroy called on the council to "be a gracious loser" and bow to court rulings against the city. Bill Kellogg, who headed the Memorial Association, called the proposed sale "fraught with problems." Moving the cross, he said, "will allow us to return the focus to honoring our veterans, instead of debating the issues of separation of church and state." Cross supporters dominated the microphone during the public-comment period. "The courts have been wrong," argued a Baptist minister, James Gilbert. "Stand up for what is right." On the other side, Vietnam veteran Bill Paul told the council, "The cross may represent some people, but it doesn't represent me nor many of my fellow Marines." The prospect of further litigation obviously concerned some council members, but they approved Gwinn's ballot proposal by a five-to-three vote. Councillor

Scott Peters, whose district included the Mount Soledad park, acknowledged the competing pressures. "There will be a lot of hard feelings if the cross is moved," he said, "but there will be harder feelings if people don't get to weigh in on that." The council added to its approval of what became Proposition K a statement that, if the measure failed, the city would honor the agreement between McElroy and Berwanger to remove and relocate the Easter Cross, setting the vote for the election on November 2, 2004.

Hardly anyone expected the measure to fail, but the latest effort to "Save the Cross" would be overshadowed on the November ballot by other campaigns, including the battle for the White House between President George W. Bush and Senator John Kerry. As the election neared, the low-key debate over Proposition K suddenly hit the headlines. Charles LiMandri, a San Diego lawyer whose practice centered on personal-injury and medical-malpractice cases, announced that the Thomas More Law Center would lead the fight to save the Easter Cross. Lavishly funded by Thomas Monaghan, of the Domino's Pizza chain, the More Center was based in Ann Arbor, Michigan, and described itself as "dedicated to the defense and promotion of the religious freedom of Christians, time-honored family values, and the sanctity of human life." Led and staffed by Catholic lawyers, the More Center focused most of its efforts on such issues as abortion and same-sex marriage. Early in 2004, LiMandri became director of the Center's West Coast office, located in his law firm, and jumped into the Mount Soledad case shortly after the city council placed Proposition K on the ballot.

LiMandri feared that the divided city-council vote on the ballot measure, and the active opposition to its passage by Bill Kellogg of the Memorial Association, might sway voters who were concerned about the prospect of further, and costly, litigation over the Easter Cross. Kellogg, in fact, along with the commander of the La Jolla American Legion Post, had signed the ballot-pamphlet argument against Proposition K, urging a "no" vote "to preserve the Mt. Soledad cross and save our tax dollars!" LiMandri countered with a ballot argument, which he signed along with three retired Navy officers, warning voters that the cross was "threatened by special interests trying to strip San Diego of its historical identity." He also wrote an op-ed article in the *San Diego Union-Tribune* denouncing the "current leadership of the Mt. Soledad Memorial Association" for its "shameless betrayal" of veterans who had "sacrificed their lives" in the nation's wars.

LiMandri's criticism of the Memorial Association and its American Legion supporters, in a city with many veterans, may have backfired. When the ballots were counted, 59 percent of San Diego's voters rejected Proposition K. They also elected a new city attorney to replace Casey Gwinn, barred by a term-limit law from a third term. His successor, Michael Aguirre, had squeaked by one of Gwinn's deputies by a 1-percent margin. A Democrat and self-professed advocate for "underdogs," Aguirre had ducked questions about Proposition K during his campaign, but he now faced decisions about the city's position in the Mount Soledad case, which had returned to Judge Thompson for approval of the settlement that Jim McElroy and Charles Berwanger had fashioned.

Even before the voters rejected Proposition K, however, LiMandri had filed a brief with Thompson on behalf of Richard Steel, a former Navy pilot who had signed the ballot-pamphlet argument against the proposition. LiMandri asked Thompson to rule that San Diego retained "title to the land" on which the Easter Cross sat, and to "completely remove any power of the Association to remove the cross." In a press release, he also urged Thompson not to "surrender to the demands of a hypersensitive atheist who is set on destroying one of San Diego's most treasured landmarks." LiMandri sounded less optimistic after the defeat of Proposition K. "At this point, we do not anticipate bringing a legal challenge, but we're still reviewing that," he said. He faced another legal obstacle, since the Thomas More Law Center was not a party to the Mount Soledad case, and Judge Thompson could simply ignore his brief.

LiMandri had another card up his sleeve, however, which he pulled out shortly after voters rejected Proposition K. On November 10, 2004, he sent a letter to Congressman Duncan Hunter, who represented a suburban San Diego district and chaired the powerful House Armed Services Committee. LiMandri told Hunter, "Our best hope to preserve the Mt. Soledad Cross is to have it declared a Federal National Memorial Park," and urged him to join "the fight to save the Cross." Along with Congressman Randy "Duke" Cunningham, whose district included the Mount Soledad park and who served on the Defense Appropriations Subcommittee, Hunter slipped an amendment into a three-hundred-billion-dollar military appropriations bill. Adopted without any committee hearing or floor debate, the measure authorized the San Diego city council to transfer the cross site to the National Park Service as a veterans' memorial. President Bush signed the bill on December 8, 2004, two days after Mike Aguirre took office as San Diego's city attorney.

One of Aguirre's first decisions was to abandon Casey Gwinn's fervent defense of the Easter Cross. With a council meeting set for March 8, 2005, Aguirre sent its members a legal opinion on February 24, stating flatly that the cross was unconstitutional and that transferring the site to the Park Service would simply invite further litigation. Aguirre noted that the Park Service might not even accept the transfer, since a federal judge had recently ruled against a cross in the Mojave National Preserve, a decision the Ninth Circuit had upheld in June 2004. Aguirre's memo now placed both the city attorney and Charles Berwanger on Jim McElroy's side, with no party in the Mount Soledad case still defending the cross's continued presence in the park.

More than 350 people, dominated by cross supporters, crowded the city's municipal auditorium for the council meeting on March 8. During an emotional six-hour hearing, sixty speakers implored the council to "Save the Cross" by giving the site to the Park Service, while fifteen others, mainly veterans, argued for moving the cross to the nearby Presbyterian church. Bill Kellogg of the Memorial Association warned the council that Park Service officials might not allow his group to continue maintaining the site and selling plaques to veterans' families. "Moving the cross to private land will save the cross," he said, "and will allow the association to operate the memorial walls and honor veterans for posterity." The deciding vote on the issue was cast by Councillor Scott Peters, who had supported Proposition K the year before, predicting "a lot of hard feelings if the cross is moved." But he also voted to move the cross if that measure failed. "As a public official," Peters now told the audience, "I promised with my hand on the Bible, so help me God, to uphold the Constitution, and I can't ignore what the Ninth Circuit Court of Appeals is doing." When the council finally voted, the motion to transfer the Easter Cross to the Park Service lost by a five-to-three margin, and council members left the auditorium to a chorus of boos. Mayor Dick Murphy vowed to continue the fight. "It's not over until it's over," he said.

Murphy was right: the cross fight was not over. Public reaction to the council's vote was immediate and emphatic, spearheaded by one of San Diego's former mayors, Roger Hedgecock. Back in 1985, Hedgecock had resigned his post after being convicted on twelve counts of perjury, stemming from illegal contributions to his 1983 election campaign. He escaped a one-year jail sentence, however, after the California Supreme Court reversed his perjury convictions and Hedgecock cut a deal with prosecutors, pleading guilty to a felony conspiracy charge that was reduced to a misdemeanor and later dismissed. Proclaiming his vindication, Hedgecock began a new career as a radio talk-show host, billing himself as "Southern California's Radio Mayor." Shedding his previous image as a "moderate" Republican, he moved sharply to the right, lambasting "liberals" and skewering the "spineless" city officials who had voted to move the Mount Soledad cross. "We're done with judges and lawyers and lawmakers," he told his listeners. "The council folks may march up the hill with axes or drive a bulldozer up the mount intent upon destruction. There they will find the townsfolk. And this time the vote will be simple. Take down our cross after you take us down!"

Behind his fiery rhetoric, Hedgecock had a plan to block the council. He and Rick Roberts, a fellow right-wing radio voice, called together a group of cross supporters to plot their strategy. Roberts invited a longtime friend, Phil Thalheimer, to attend the meeting. Thalheimer, who owned a pilot-training school, had lost a council race against Scott Peters and was eager to punish him for voting to remove the Easter Cross. Before the meeting ended, Thalheimer agreed to chair a new organization, San Diegans for the Mt. Soledad National War Memorial. On

March 13, 2005, Thalheimer announced a petition drive to overturn the council decision through a ballot referendum in the July 26 primary election for mayoral and council candidates. The council vote to remove the cross, Thalheimer said, "means that this symbol, both an indelible part of San Diego's landscape and a salute to our veterans, will be torn down and carted off without a fight." Many observers found it odd that the latest drive to save the Easter Cross was headed by Thalheimer, who is Jewish. "I know that a lot of people have questioned why a practicing Jew would chair a committee to preserve a war memorial that includes a Christian cross," he later said. "But for me, it's a free speech issue. Once you start knocking off symbols, a cross or a Star of David, it's a very slippery slope."

Under the city's election rules, Thalheimer's group needed to collect thirty-four thousand signatures of registered voters to place their proposition on the ballot. This proved to be an easy task. Approached at shopping centers and Sunday church services, more than seventy-three thousand voters signed petitions to reverse the city council's vote to remove the Easter Cross, filling thirteen boxes that Thalheimer and Mayor Murphy carried into the city clerk's office on the filing date of April 7, 2005. "It's a clear and absolute demand by the citizens of San Diego that they want this war memorial to stay where it is," Thalheimer said of the petition campaign. "It can't be clearer." It was not so clear, however, to Jim McElroy, who told reporters he would file a lawsuit to block a vote on the proposed referendum. But Thalheimer's group found an unlikely ally in city attorney Mike Aguirre. "The voters have a right to review all major decisions by their elected officials," he told reporters, though he repeated his opinion that voter approval of the referendum would most likely fail to survive judicial scrutiny. "The court can still decide it is unconstitutional," he added, "especially if it is done to send a religious message."

———

Two months after voting to remove the Easter Cross, San Diego's city councillors met once more in the municipal auditorium on May 17, 2005, for another emotional six-hour marathon, at which nearly a hundred people spoke. Some cross supporters broke down in tears, and one called any effort to move the cross a "hate crime" against Christians. Phil Thalheimer urged the council to place a third proposition on the July ballot, authorizing transfer of the cross site to the National Park Service. "Please, transfer it today," he implored. "Listen to the city of San Diego." The council listened, and six members—including two who had voted in March to remove the cross—placed Proposition A before the voters, directing the city to "donate to the federal government all of the city's rights, title, and interests in the Mt. Soledad Veterans Memorial property." The councillors left the meeting as cross supporters sang "Onward, Christian Soldiers."

Phil Thalheimer headed the five citizens who signed the ballot-pamphlet argument supporting Proposition A, along with Congressman "Duke" Cunningham and talk-show hosts Roger Hedgecock and Rick Roberts. They urged voters to "Honor our Veterans! Protect our Memorial! Transfer the Land!" The countering argument, signed by Jim McElroy and the minister of San Diego's Unitarian Universalist church, warned, "The land transfer would be illegal and will cost taxpayers more money in lawsuits." Thalheimer's group had raised almost $150,000 to promote the proposition with radio and newspaper advertisements, but McElroy dismissed this effort as futile. "I think it would be like burning dollar bills to win a popularity contest," he said, vowing to challenge Proposition A in court.

Cross supporters did win the popularity contest on July 26, with the same 76 percent that voters had given Proposition F in 1992, thirteen years earlier. "It still doesn't mean a damn thing," McElroy responded. "Voters should have never voted on it. And when the court tells them this is not going to work, what else have they got?" Charles LiMandri of the Thomas More Law Center, who stayed on the sidelines during the Proposition A campaign, strapped on his group's "sword and shield for people of faith" and vowed to fight McElroy for years to come. "This is going to be going on past our lifetimes," he said. "This culture war isn't going to end. We see this as a bigger battle. We're fighting for the minds, hearts and souls of America."

LiMandri faced two problems, however, in challenging McElroy to more courtroom battles. McElroy had already beaten him to the punch before the July election, filing a lawsuit in San Diego Superior Court that sought to block the vote and declare Proposition A unconstitutional. McElroy took the unusual step of switching from federal to state court because Judge Thompson, after presiding over the case for sixteen years, had shown no inclination to enforce his 1991 order to remove the cross. Although Judge Patricia Yim Cowett allowed the vote to proceed, she gave McElroy a victory in round eleven of the legal battle, handing down a thirty-four-page "tentative" opinion on September 2. Noting that Thalheimer's ballot argument for Proposition A had urged voters to "save" the cross, Cowett also quoted statements of council members who had voted to transfer the cross site to the National Park Service. Councillor Tony Young said that he voted to place Proposition A on the ballot to ensure that "the cross is going to stay up there," with Brian Maienshein agreeing that he wanted "to preserve the cross on Mt. Soledad." The "consistent, repeated, and numerous references to saving the cross," Cowett wrote, showed "an unconstitutional preference of the Christian religion to the exclusion of other religious and non-religious beliefs in violation of the No Preference Clause of the California Constitution." Before she issued her final ruling, Cowett said, she would hear arguments from the parties on October 3, making clear that she would be unlikely to change her mind.

LiMandri's second problem was that he did not represent any party in the Mount Soledad case, and would be unable to argue before Judge Cowett at the October 3 hearing. All the lawyers in the case—Mike Aguirre, Jim McElroy, and Charles Berwanger—agreed with Cowett's tentative ruling and would certainly not oppose her final decision. That lineup changed, however, with Aguirre's sudden and unexpected announcement, on September 7, that he was hiring LiMandri to represent the voters who had adopted Proposition A. "My job is to in a good-faith way try to vindicate their vote even though I disagree with it," Aguirre explained, adding, "Voters deserve their day in court." LiMandri agreed that cross supporters deserved a lawyer "who passionately believes in them."

On his part, Jim McElroy greeted the news with scorn. "This is like hiring the Ku Klux Klan to represent you in a desegregation case," he fumed.

As it turned out, McElroy had no cause for concern in round twelve of the courtroom battles over the Easter Cross. The hearing before Judge Cowett was heated, to say the least. Charles Berwanger, appearing for the Memorial Association, set off sparks by charging that LiMandri did not care about the veterans' aspect of the memorial and was simply determined to save the Easter Cross to further his Christian agenda. "Mr. Berwanger has his own agenda," replied LiMandri. "He only cares about the association owning the land" around the cross. LiMandri set off his own sparks by attacking the "anti-Christian motives" of Phil Paulson in challenging the cross. His brief included quotes from an atheist Web site in which Paulson had supposedly written, "Jesus Christ was a bastard and a rape baby." Such "hateful statements" revealed Paulson's "deep hostility towards Christianity," LiMandri said. Paulson later claimed the offending quote came from an 1811 blasphemy case, but his penchant for hyperbole gave LiMandri an opening to claim the case began with people "who hate God."

LiMandri's presence at the hearing, in fact, gave Judge Cowett another reason to confirm her tentative ruling with a final decision on October 7, 2005. Quoting from the More Center's Web site, she noted its goal of "providing legal representation to defend and protect Christians and their religious beliefs." Hiring LiMandri to represent the city, Cowett wrote, "gives the clear appearance of fostering an excessive government entanglement with religion." She took pains to assure readers that her opinion "does not attempt to, nor does it actually, demonstrate hostility to religion."

Cowett's assurance did not mollify Phil Thalheimer, who denounced her ruling as "a fundamental attack on the expression of religion" and "the very kind of radical activism from the bench that risks turning democracies into dictatorships." Roger Hedgecock, with his trademark hyperbole, told his radio listeners, "Attempts to remove our cross will be met with citizens who literally will be armed with torches and pitchforks." On his part, Jim McElroy expressed his satisfaction with Cowett's decision. "I'm hopeful that our very ugly, very divisive, very expensive, very shameful episode of trying to buck the law and court decisions is now over," he said. "This was a foolish waste of taxpayers' money."

Judge Cowett left one crucial question unanswered: in which courtroom would round thirteen in the case be fought? Her decision was limited to the constitutional issues raised by the Mount Soledad cross, and had not included any order directing its removal from the park. "The city is the only party that can appeal," Jim McElroy noted. "I don't think the city is going to want to appeal. It's going to cost them a ton of money for their time and effort." Aguirre had until December 6, sixty days from Cowett's ruling, to file an appeal with the state appellate court, and he took a wait-and-see position, suggesting in the interim that cross supporters and opponents settle the case through mediation. McElroy dismissed this idea, saying the city council should honor the settlement agreement with the Memorial Association and prepare to move the cross. If the council balked, McElroy would ask Judge Thompson, who had postponed hearings in his courtroom to wait for Cowett's decision, to enforce his 1991 cross-removal order. Thompson had also, however, suggested that he might put off any further proceedings until the Ninth Circuit ruled on a pending appeal by the Memorial Association, disputing the city's claim to ownership of the entire cross site, including the granite walls and plaques the Association had erected. McElroy and Berwanger had written a letter to Thompson, which Mike Aguirre also signed, noting that all parties had agreed to the cross's removal. Resolution of the land-ownership issue, they argued, should not delay Thompson's approval of the settlement agreement, which would not disturb the memorial walls. Obviously waiting for Aguirre's decision on appealing Cowett's ruling, Thompson did not respond and left the lawyers hanging.

Widely known as a quick-draw lawyer, Aguirre had a reason to keep his gun holstered while the sixty-day clock ran on filing an appeal of Cowett's decision. San Diego politics had been in an uproar ever since Mayor Dick Murphy, buffeted by charges of mismanaging the city's billion-dollar pension fund, had abruptly resigned and left office on

July 15, 2005. Aguirre, whose relentless criticism of Murphy had prompted his resignation, had not formally backed either of the two candidates who vied for Murphy's office in an election set for November 8. But he clearly favored Donna Frye, a city councillor who had voted to remove the Easter Cross, while her opponent, former San Diego police chief Jerry Sanders, had pledged to continue the legal battle to keep it on Mount Soledad. Frye had bested Sanders in the crowded July primary, but he prevailed in the November runoff by a ten-point margin.

The morning after his victory celebration, Sanders called Roger Hedgecock, who had boosted his campaign, with a surprise announcement on the air. Mike Aguirre, Sanders said, had agreed to appeal Judge Cowett's ruling against the Easter Cross to the state appellate court. Aguirre then called Hedgecock to confirm the news. "I'm not going to insist that everything I want goes through," he said. "I still think it's unconstitutional. But I'm going to try to work collaboratively with him," Aguirre said of the mayor-elect. Despite his personal opinion that efforts to overturn Judge Cowett's ruling would prove futile, Aguirre went ahead and filed an appeal with the state's Fourth Circuit Court of Appeals. Charles LiMandri of the Thomas More Law Center, whose participation in the case had irked Cowett, predicted victory for cross supporters. "We need two out of three judges" on the appellate court, he said, "and I think it's unlikely we'll get three judges as liberal as she is."

Angered that Aguirre had bowed to Mayor Sanders in filing the appeal, Jim McElroy promptly went back to Judge Thompson in the federal court, seeking a ruling to enforce the original injunction to remove the cross from Mount Soledad. Although Thompson had indicated that he would defer any decision until the state judges had ruled on the city's appeal, he changed his mind after a hearing in December 2005. Thompson read the newspapers, and was likely annoyed by Aguirre's capitulation to Sanders. On March 3, 2006, Thompson ended the fourteenth round in this judicial slug-fest. "It is now time, and perhaps long overdue," he said firmly, "for this Court to enforce its initial permanent injunction forbidding the presence of the Mount Soledad Cross on City property." Thompson noted that he had spent years hearing arguments over the cross, as had the Ninth Circuit judges who had twice upheld his orders to remove the cross, in rulings the Supreme Court had twice declined to review. "Consistently, every court that has addressed the issue has ruled that the presence of the Latin cross on Mount Soledad," Thompson said, violated the No Preference Clause of the California constitution. He gave the city ninety days to remove the cross, a deadline of August 1, 2006, threatening to impose a daily fine of five thousand dollars if the city did not comply with this final ruling. As far as Thompson was concerned, the fight was over.

Jim McElroy raised his arms in victory. "I don't think the city has its heart in taking more action," he told reporters. "It's time to end 17 years of litigation and it's time for the taxpayers to end footing the bill for futile litigation." Mike Aguirre conceded defeat. "We're free to disagree with the court's ruling but not to disobey it," he said. "It's very disappointing, I know, for the religious community. My hope is that we'll be able to use the next ninety days to find a resolution that allows us to come together to solve this problem." He agreed to sit down with McElroy and Bill Kellogg of the Mount Soledad Memorial Association to work out arrangements for moving the cross to private property before Thompson's deadline. The only questions were where to move the cross and when it would come down.

———

But the cross did not come down. Amazingly, the fight resumed after Judge Thompson had seemingly rung the final bell. Rising from the judicial canvas, Mayor Sanders began swinging with an appeal to President Bush to seize the cross site under the federal government's "eminent domain" powers. Cheered on by local cross supporters and Religious Right groups across the country, Sanders also pressed the city council to authorize an appeal to the Ninth Circuit, along with a request for a judicial stay of Thompson's order. On May 22, 2006, Sanders flew to Washington and met with White House officials and lawyers to seek Bush's intervention. He returned empty-handed to San Diego. "They indicated it's going to be tough to get this done," he told reporters. Bush's press secretary, Tony Snow, issued the lukewarm statement that "the president and the administration are actively reviewing both administrative and legislative options for preserving that veterans' war memorial." Most likely, the president's lawyers were wary of inheriting a lawsuit that might expose the federal government to heavy legal fees and payment of the five-thousand-dollars-per-day fines that Judge Thompson had threatened if the cross remained on Mount Soledad after his August 1 deadline.

Despite his cool White House reception, Sanders asked the San Diego city council to instruct Mike Aguirre to file an appeal and a stay request with the Ninth Circuit. With the votes of two recently elected members and three longtime cross supporters, the council approved this measure by a five-to-three margin on May 23, disregarding Aguirre's warning that its chances of success were "remote." Four weeks later, on June 21, the Ninth Circuit denied—without comment—the stay request, although it also docketed the city's appeal for argument in October 2006. By that time, of course, the case might have been mooted, since denial of the stay request kept the clock running on Judge Thompson's August deadline for the cross's removal from Mount Soledad.

Reeling on the judicial ropes from the Ninth Circuit's blow, San Diego officials launched a final, desperate counter-punch. By another five-to-three vote, the city council directed Mike Aguirre to seek a stay of Thompson's order from the Supreme Court. Under the Court's rules, this request would be decided by Justice Anthony Kennedy, who handled "emergency" appeals from Ninth Circuit rulings. Although he dutifully complied with the council's order, Aguirre expressed his doubt that it would succeed. "It is unusual for the Supreme Court in a case this far advanced to issue a stay order," he told reporters. But he was wrong in this prediction. On July 3, 2006, in a fifty-three-word order, Kennedy granted a "temporary" stay in the Mount Soledad case, "pending further order" by himself or the full Court. On his part, Jim McElroy downplayed the significance of Kennedy's order, predicting that he would rescind it within the next week or ten days. "Its practical effect is not much," McElroy told reporters. "It's like he's saying, 'We got your briefs, you will be hearing from us.' "

Kennedy had, in fact, a stack of briefs on his desk, including McElroy's twenty-two-page argument that there "is not one single Federal or California case involving the permanent placement of a Latin cross that supports the City's position" and that "no important federal question exists for this Court to address." The stack also included friend-of-the-court briefs supporting the city from the American Center for Law and Justice, the Religious Right legal group headed by Jay Sekulow, and from the American Legion.

Much to McElroy's dismay, Kennedy waited only four days before he finished plowing through the briefs and issued his "further order" on June 8, extending the stay of Judge Thompson's order, at least until the California appellate judges and the Ninth Circuit had ruled on the city's appeals from Judge Cowett's and the Ninth Circuit's rulings. Conceding that "a stay application to a Circuit Justice on a matter before a court of appeals is rarely granted," Kennedy cited three factors behind his ruling. First, he wrote in a four-page opinion, "the harm in a brief delay pending the Court of Appeals' expedited consideration of the case seems slight." In other words, allowing the cross to remain on Mount Soledad until the appeals were finally decided would be less burdensome than returning or reconstructing it should the city finally win the case. Second, Kennedy cited the congressional measure that President Bush had signed in December 2004, directing city officials to transfer the cross site to the federal government. "San Diego voters," he wrote, "have approved a ballot proposition authorizing donation of the monument to the United States." Third, and most significant, Kennedy wrote, "Congress' evident desire to preserve the memorial makes it substantially more likely that four Justices will agree to review the case in the event the Court of Appeals affirms the District Court's order." Under the Supreme Court's unwritten but long-standing "rule of four," it takes just four votes to review a state or federal court ruling.

What Kennedy did not say, in granting the city's stay request, was that he knew there were at least four votes—perhaps five, counting his own—to review any lower-court ruling in the Mount Soledad case, regardless of which side appealed from an adverse holding. What he also did not say was that, assuming the Court agreed to hear the case, his vote would most likely prove decisive. That prospect sent shudders through Phil Paulson and Jim McElroy, and elated cross supporters. In 1989, Kennedy had voted to uphold the display of a Christmas-season Nativity crèche in the rotunda of the Pittsburgh, Pennsylvania, city hall; more recently, in 2005, he voted to allow the permanent display of the Ten Commandments in Kentucky courthouses and the Texas State Capitol grounds. However, in the Pittsburgh case, dissenting from the majority's ruling against the crèche, Kennedy had cautioned that the Establishment Clause "forbids a city to permit the permanent erection of a large Latin cross on the roof of city hall." The roof of San Diego's city hall is not visible from the street, but the Mount Soledad cross can be seen from miles away. Jim McElroy had overlooked Kennedy's comment in his hastily prepared brief on the stay issue, but it would probably not have affected Kennedy's calculation that at least four of his fellow justices would vote to review any lower-court decision in the case.

McElroy's response to Kennedy's extension of his initial stay order was uncharacteristically muted. "I certainly understand the Court's logic, but I disagree with it," he told reporters. Phil Paulson, whose earlier reference to Jesus as a "rape baby" had inflamed his detractors, followed McElroy's advice to refrain from public comment on the case. Cross supporters were predictably jubilant over the judicial reprieve; Mayor Jerry Sanders called it "validation that this was the right course of action," and Phil Thalheimer, who headed the drive to "save" the cross by donating it to the federal government, predicted that "the Supreme Court will take this case."

The city's legal reprieve gave cross supporters time to plot their next effort to circumvent Judge Thompson's removal order and its review by the Ninth Circuit. Once again, Representative Duncan Hunter wielded his clout as chairman of the House Armed Services Committee. In June 2006, he introduced a bill to exercise the federal government's power of eminent domain and transfer the cross site to the Defense Department, providing for a "memorandum of understanding" with the Mount Soledad Memorial Association to maintain the site. On July 19, the House adopted Hunter's bill by a vote of 349 to 74, with his fellow Republicans all behind him. Even a majority of House Democrats, perhaps aware that this was a "throw-away" vote in an election year, cast "yea" votes for the bill. By a unanimous voice vote on July 31, the Senate followed suit, sending Hunter's bill to the White House for President Bush's signature. Flanked at his Oval Office desk by cross supporters, including Bill Kellogg, Phil Thalheimer, and Charles LiMandri, Bush signed the transfer bill on August 14. In a backhanded slap at Judge Thompson, Bush's press secretary issued a statement expressing the president's view that "judicial activism should not stand in the way of the people."

Jim McElroy, however, stood in the way of this latest effort to "federalize" the Mount Soledad cross. The week before Hunter's bill reached Bush's desk, McElroy had filed a new lawsuit in San Diego's federal court, seeking an injunction to block the president from signing it. This suit, which named Defense Secretary Donald Rumsfeld as the lead defendant, added a new plaintiff to the case, since Phil Paulson had recently been diagnosed with inoperable and terminal liver cancer, following an unsuccessful operation to remove the tumor. "I fully expect someone to say it's God's revenge," Paulson said when he told reporters of his condition. The new plaintiff, Steve Trunk, was also a Vietnam War veteran and a professed atheist. From a legal perspective, McElroy's preemptive move was premature, since Bush had not yet signed the bill, although everyone knew that he would; the White House had already announced the signing ceremony. Much like chess players who anticipate their opponent's next move, McElroy countered with the claim that the impending transfer of the cross site to the Defense Department would violate the Establishment Clause of the First Amendment. His motion came before Judge Barry Ted Moskowitz, placed on the bench by President Bill Clinton in 1995. After a brief hearing on August 11, 2006, Moskowitz denied the motion to block the transfer, but said that he would hear further arguments within the next two months. "This is a matter of public concern so it should get priority," he said.

Moving quickly, McElroy followed with a second new lawsuit, filed on August 22 on behalf of the Jewish War Veterans and three San Diego residents: Richard Smith, a Navy veteran and physician, who is Jewish; Smith's wife, Mina Sagheb, who is Muslim; and Judith Copeland, a San Diego attorney. Judge Moskowitz consolidated both cases on his docket, taking the issue—for the first time since 1989—away from Judge Thompson. Although federal cases have long been randomly assigned to judges by computers, Charles LiMandri of the Thomas More Law Center nonetheless suggested that McElroy had somehow arranged to bring the suits before a "practicing Jew" who would supposedly be prejudiced against the cross as a Christian symbol. On his part, McElroy accused cross supporters of "venue shopping" in transferring the cross site to the federal government. "It's just like saying pinto beans and baked beans are different," he said. "They're still beans."

These new developments placed the city's pending appeals to the Ninth Circuit of Judge Thompson's removal order, and to the California appellate court of Judge Cowett's invalidation of Proposition A, in a state of legal limbo. President Bush's signature on the transfer bill had turned the Mount Soledad cross site into federal property, removing the city of San Diego from its ownership and as a party to new lawsuits. Whether these cases would moot these appeals, however, depends on Judge Moscowitz's rulings, which have not been issued at this writing, on the constitutionality of the transfer under the Establishment Clause. And however he rules, the Mount Soledad case will certainly return to the Ninth Circuit, since the losing party will undoubtedly appeal from that decision. It is also likely that the losing party in the Ninth Circuit will ask the Supreme Court to review that decision. Whatever the outcome, the Mount Soledad case will go down in history as the longest-running Establishment Clause case in American legal history.

Seventeen years after he initiated this challenge to "the cross of Jesus" on public property, and facing his likely death before its final decision, Phil Paulson reflected on his efforts. "I'm not concerned about the end result," he said. "I'm more concerned about the trying. It's all in the trying. I measure success based on my own efforts. People who know me know that Philip Paulson has perseverance, persistence, ceaseless determined energy. I never give up."

On October 25, 2006, Phil Paulson died, having never given up in his seventeen-year battle to remove the cross from the summit of Mount Soledad.

PHIL PAULSON

I was born on July 13, 1947, and raised in Clayton, Wisconsin, in the northwestern part of the state. It's a small town, about five hundred people, in the St. Croix River Valley, right on the border of Minnesota. When I was a kid, I knew everybody in town, including the names of the dogs and cats. I could walk down the street and walk into anybody's home and have cookies and milk. When you're in a real small town, everybody eyes you up, and everybody knows everybody's personal business.

My ancestors came from Sweden, on my father's side, in the nineteenth century. They were all war protesters, and they were trying to flee from King Oscar of Sweden. They were also religious protesters. They didn't like the Lutheran priests coming down from Uppsala, in the north; they wanted the priests from Lund, in the south of Sweden, across from Denmark, where they spoke a sort of Danish-and-Swedish dialect.

My grandfather started up the telephone company in my hometown, and he also had a farm-implement business. My father was a manufacturer, and my older twin brothers invented a mechanical string-bean picker. They are now kind of like right-wing militia people; they manufacture Civil War ordnance, exact replicas from the original blueprints, and they do Civil War re-enactments.

In Clayton, we had two Lutheran churches, a Norwegian church and a German church. My maternal grandfather started up the Lutheran church in my hometown; he was a Lutheran evangelist, and he started up many Lutheran churches in Wisconsin and Minnesota. I was brought up in a very strict Lutheran tradition. My mother named me P. K. Paulson, and I asked her once why P.K., and she said, It stands for Preacher's Kid, and I always wanted you to become a preacher.

A very traumatic thing happened to me in Sunday school, just before confirmation class. I was about ten or eleven years old. Our minister was a very strict Lutheran, and we had a Sunday-school class, and he asked a question about God: What is God? And I asked a question that brought up a doubt about God. Who created God? I was sort of a smart-aleck kid, and I thought it was kind of funny—who created God?—I thought it was a good question. But the minister didn't think so, he thought it was blasphemy, I was questioning the entity of God. And he slapped me across the face, grabbed my ear, took me to his office, called my mother, said that I had blasphemed God, and told her to come down and get me. He told her I wasn't coming back to church until you get him back on the right track. So I was grounded for a week in my room, and my mother would make me pray all this time. Well, that had an impression on me, and I started questioning, and I thought that blasphemy was just honest thought; there is nothing wrong with blasphemy. But to them, it was the unpardonable sin, because it was going against the Holy Spirit.

My mother sent me back to Sunday school, and I finally made it through confirmation. I had to memorize the catechism, and then I became a full-fledged member of the Lutheran Church, and I could take the sacraments of the church, meaning I could eat the body of Jesus and drink his blood. I had to stand up before the whole congregation, and the minister said, Do you renounce the Devil and all his works and all his ways, and believe in the Lord Jesus Christ with all your soul and all your heart and all your might? And I started thinking, What is all this about Jesus partnering up with the Father, and this Holy Spirit, and the Devil? Why did God create the Devil? This started percolating in my mind, and creating more doubt. That was the start.

I loved my father, but he and I constantly argued. I disagreed strongly with his right-wing views. He was an active member of the Republican Party; he was chairman of the Polk County Republican Party. When I was a kid, I remember sitting at the kitchen table, and Senator Joe McCarthy was sitting right across the table from me. My father didn't like him, because Joe McCarthy smelled of whiskey on his breath, plus he was Catholic. So I came from a very right-wing, religiously oriented family life, and I felt constrained in my freedom of expression, but my father allowed me to express my thoughts, up to a point. He told me there are two discussions that are off limits: politics and religion.

Well, I rebelled against that, and I became very liberal and very atheistic. It wasn't so much a rebellion against him, it was a battle for the mind, to bring about intellectual emancipation, from ancestral tradition, ritualistic creed, that I could just discard on the ash heap of history and become a freethinker. It was a great feeling. Some people like to call the Holy Spirit a great thing; I like the "ah-ha" feeling, solving problems. I'm a systems thinker. I don't care how hard you believe—if the system doesn't work, it doesn't work. The scientific approach to thinking became a way of life to me, the humanistic approach to life.

After I finished high school, I went into the Army on April 8, 1966, when I was eighteen. What happened was that my two older twin brothers had gotten their draft notices. My father knew everybody on the local draft board, and he told them, If you take them off the draft list, Philip will volunteer in their place. So they did that, and I volunteered for the draft, which made me number one on the list.

When I went to Vietnam, I extended my tour of duty over there for another six months. So I spent eighteen months in Vietnam, with an honorable discharge. I was in every major battle in Vietnam—the Iron Triangle, Bien Hoa, Junction City—because I was a paratrooper in the 173rd Airborne. We were the first ones out in battle. General Westmoreland loved us so much that he put us out there in front. I was with a rifle company, and served as a point man for a whole year. That was all jungle warfare. The big, huge battle was the battle for Dac Tho, up on the Ho Chi Minh Trail. One time, I was out on patrol, on guard duty, and there was a big clump of bamboo, with two trails coming out, and a bunch of Viet Cong came up, and one peeked in from the bamboo, about six inches from my face. Needless to say, I almost filled my pants. I hollered to everybody, and started shooting at them, and we got several of them before they disappeared into the bamboo.

Another important event that changed my mind is that I was an atheist in a foxhole. There was a chaplain there who always said, Why don't you go to church? He was a Southern Baptist and I didn't want to tell him I was an atheist. But I didn't go to church, and I know he kept me from getting promoted. Every time we had a firefight, it confirmed to me that the concept of the all-loving God just doesn't hold water. Who'd pray to that guy who caused this in the first place? This whole thing was just a myth to me. I like to be helpful to people, and I think that's what really weighs in, what the Jewish people call a mitzvah, when we look back on our own life. As far as the reward-and-punishment thing, I just threw that out the window. At one time, I even gave God the finger. This was after a firefight, and I had to carry my own friends in my arms to the dust-off helicopter. One guy had been covered with white phosphorus, and his arm was covered with fire, lit up like a candle going up in the helicopter, and I gave God the finger as they lifted off. I saw thousands of North Vietnamese dead, I've seen my whole platoon killed, when I was the only one who survived. I don't like talking about this; some of these things do weigh on my brain, and I still get these thoughts, I get dreams, and I wake up about this. It's not something that just goes away.

I went to college after I came back from Vietnam, at the University of Wisconsin in River Falls, and I had a triple major: journalism, political science, and sociology. I was still a Republican, on the conservative side. I've always enjoyed debating, ever since our kitchen-table debates when I was a kid, so I joined the debate team. My partner was a communist, and we won every debate, all the way up. He also studied humanism, and that got me going. My father later said, I should never have allowed you to go to college, because they taught you to become an atheist, and that was not right.

After I finished college, I worked on a newspaper in Wisconsin, covering local news and taking pictures. I moved to San Diego in 1979 because my older brother Eugene served in the Marine Corps here and told me that the weather was great, the same temperature all year. When I first got here, I tried to get any kind of job I could, temporary jobs, teaching GED classes on Navy ships and teaching photography. Then I decided to go back to school, and I graduated from National University in San Diego with a master's degree in public administration, and I later got a master's in management of information systems. After that, I started teaching adjunct, which I've been doing ever since, computer information systems.

Here's how I got involved in the Mount Soledad case. Howard Kreisner was a friend of mine who filed a lawsuit against the city of San Diego over the Christmas display in Balboa Park, where they put up a Nativity crèche every year from Thanksgiving through Christmas, with a manger and the Baby Jesus and Mary and Joseph and donkeys. That didn't really bother me, since it wasn't a permanent display. That case was finally settled when the city agreed that other groups, like the ACLU, could put up displays about the Bill of Rights.

But Howard wanted to go after other religious displays on public land. In 1989, Howard, myself, and Steve Thorne got together. Steve was the American Atheists director for San Diego; this was the group that was headed by Madalyn Murray O'Hair, who had won a school-prayer case in the Supreme Court in the early 1960s and became the most hated woman in the United States. At this meeting with Howard and Steve, I told them, Every time I go up to Mount Soledad I have two questions: what is it, and where is it? What is it? It's the unmistakable symbol of the Christian religion. And where is it? It's in the middle of a public park. I go around town and see all the graffiti that gangs spray on walls and bridges. To me, the cross on Mount Soledad is graffiti; the Christians are marking out their turf, and the public park is everybody's turf. They have no right to mark out their turf. So it became a real issue with me. The people who put up the cross in 1954 claimed it was a war memorial. I'm not offended by a cross. I was offended by making myself a second-class citizen, because I'm a veteran and I served in Vietnam, and that cross up there does not represent all veterans. I'm an atheist, and it doesn't represent me or other veterans who are not Christians, who are Jewish or agnostics or atheists.

We filed the case in federal court in San Diego on May 30, 1989, with me and Howard as the plaintiffs. Steve Thorne lived outside the city, so he couldn't be a plaintiff. So Howard and I agreed to do this ourselves. Howard was a control freak, and he did most of the work himself, doing the legal research and writing the complaint, and I stayed out of his way. But I think the most powerful argument we had in the case was what I did. I went down to the public library and said, Give me all the Thomas maps from 1952 to 1989. And, lo and behold, I discovered that in 1954 they changed the name from Mount Soledad park to the Mount Soledad Easter Cross. And we filed those maps as exhibits. It was a great graphic; Thomas maps serve as legal documents, because they go to the city and say, What do you want to call this? And Judge Thompson was a lifelong resident of San Diego, and he knew that the cross site was strictly for Easter sunrise services. The other good exhibit in the case was the program from the dedication of the cross in 1954, when they gave the invocation to Jesus Christ and sang a bunch of Christian hymns, like "Onward, Christian Soldiers." That's what the cross was about from the time they put it up, a memorial to Jesus, not to veterans like me, who aren't Christians.

We filed the case *pro se* because we didn't trust the ACLU, we didn't trust anybody, because most people hate atheists. They don't admit to hating them, but they do. But I raised the money for the case. I'm the most hated person in San Diego, and I know it. When I first started this, there were a lot of death threats, so I called the FBI, and they put agents in front of my house for a while. One guy used to call me and make threats, and I used the Star 69 on my phone to get his number. So I called him and I said, I know who you are and where you live, and I've got a machete right by my front door. And that stopped him.

My mother named me Philip Paulson. But after I became a plaintiff against the city, the *Union-Tribune* renamed me "Atheist Philip Paulson." So I acquired a new name here in San Diego. That's what they call me in every story about the cross case. When we had city attorney Casey Gwinn defending the cross, they never called him "Bible-thumping, Southern Baptist Casey Gwinn." Here's a funny story. We've had three hearings before the Ninth Circuit Court of Appeals, and they've ruled in our favor every time. The last hearing, after the city appealed from Judge Thompson's second ruling that the city's sale of the cross site to the Mount Soledad Memorial Association was rigged, was an *en banc* hearing, which people tell me is about as rare as being struck by lightning. I flew out to Phoenix, Arizona, and here you have this panel of about thirteen judges up there, and it's like cross-examination, rat-a-tat-a-tat with questions. Casey Gwinn gets up and he said, The statute of limitations has run out on this case, because it's gone on this many years. Old Judge Pregerson sat up, and he said, Excuse me, Mr. Gwinn, but there is no statute of limitations on the Constitution. I had to get up and walk out the door, because I didn't want to be laughing in court. But it was just so hilarious. Casey Gwinn was undoubtedly the best lawyer we ever had.

This case has been in the courts for seventeen years, and the cross is still up there on Mount Soledad. The city has lost every ruling, all the way up to the Supreme Court. I think the reason they've never given up is that politicians in San Diego have been intimidated by the cross crusaders, who believe that this is a Christian nation. I'm convinced they think if that cross comes down they will lose their privilege of exercising their freedom of religion. They believe you need to merge the state with religion in order to protect their religious freedom. The reason the political leaders, the city-council members, won't give up is what I call the bandwagon. You don't want to be on the losing side of the issue, you want to be on the winning side. They got three-quarters of the vote last time, in a special election that not very many people turned out for. And they got Roger Hedgecock and Rick Roberts, right-wing radio talk-show hosts, and they really cranked out the sound bites, and they were constantly ranting against "Atheist Philip Paulson." I was the Devil Incarnate in San Diego, and this atheist was going to take away their freedom of religion. There was a constant ranting of lies that I was going to destroy the war memorial. No, that's not true. I like the war memorial up there, it can stay. I just don't want the cross up there; put a first-class war memorial in its place.

Back in 1997 or '98, I recommended to city attorney Casey Gwinn that he talk to the Presbyterian church board in La Jolla, just down the hill from Mount Soledad, about taking the cross. And he did that, and the church agreed to it. But Casey Gwinn came back and told us he didn't want to move the cross to the church. And the reason he wouldn't go along with the church, I'm convinced, is that he was a born-again Christian and wanted the cross to stay where it was.

One of the weirdest things in this case is what happened with the Mount Soledad Memorial Association. They weren't in this case at the beginning; it was just a lawsuit against the city of San Diego, which owned the park, including the cross. But Judge Thompson allowed them to intervene in the case on the city's side, since they claimed to own the cross. But after they lost the last ruling in the Ninth Circuit, they agreed to a settlement with me and the city in which the cross would be relocated to another location on church property.

But then, out of nowhere, comes the Thomas More Law Center, from Ann Arbor, Michigan, which is a right-wing Christian legal group. They persuaded Judge Thompson to let them intervene in the case, even though they didn't represent any of the parties on either side. Their lawyer in San Diego, Charles LiMandri, got together with Roger Hedge-cock and Rick Roberts and decided that, Hey, we're going to lose this thing unless we nationalize the cross. So they went to Congressmen Randy "Duke" Cunningham and Duncan Hunter, with a proposal to turn the Mount Soledad park over to the federal government as a national war memorial. They slipped this into an omnibus spending bill at eleven o'clock at night, with the help of Majority Leader Tom DeLay. No discussion, nobody even knew it was in there. But it passed the House and went to the Senate, and then President Bush signed it.

It went to the National Park Service, and they told the Mount Soledad Memorial Association, If we take this, you'll be out as the keeper of the cross. The reason the Mount Soledad Memorial Association sat down with the Devil, me, was they figured out if they were going to lose this piece of property they have over a million dollars of improvements up there, with people buying plaques, big lawsuit, breach of contract. To me, it wasn't "We've seen the light"—it breaches the separation of church and state. But they saw the writing on the wall, they saw lawsuit time. When they joined me, Atheist Phil Paulson, as plaintiffs, their funding sources dried up. I asked Bill Kellogg, who runs the Memorial Association, why he didn't just remove the cross and avoid all the lawsuits, and he told me, if I did that, I would have been murdered.

Even after the settlement with the city and the Mount Soledad Memorial Association, nobody in the city attorney's office or the mayor's office wants to move this forward. They could get it over right now. Take it down and move it to church property—the whole issue is resolved. But they won't do it. This is outrageous behavior.

My position has always been: I don't want to destroy that cross. I want them to take a carbon-tungsten saw blade and cut it at the base, with a sufficient number of straps that you can raise it up, put it on a house-moving truck, and move it to a church that wants it. I think it's inevitable that the cross is going to be moved to a church property. A lot of people don't understand that. But it's like, it's done, get over it. Roger Hedgecock has a lot of people believing that it's going to be destroyed and moved to a landfill, and he's going to stand in front of the bulldozer when it comes in. But all this drama-queen stuff is not going to go anywhere. I really think we are going to win in the end.

People are not going to calm down right away, they're going to say, It's the anti-God judges, this sort of thing. Because they want to make this a Christian nation, get down on their knees and pray to the Baby Jesus, who has a deadbeat father who left him behind. This is the craziness they believe in, not worthy of any reasonable person's sense of worship. But they want everybody else to worship that crazy God concept. We are led to believe by them that this is a Christian nation, all knees will bow. They're doing this for Jesus, and failure to do so means you're going to burn in the lake of fire. They're absolutely frightened.

LiMandri even said on his Web site, If there's a conflict between the Constitution of the United States and the Bible, I will go with the Bible, and I will go with God first. The new city attorney, Mike Aguirre, agrees that the cross is unconstitutional and has to be moved to private property. He even asked a question in public comment before the city council: If you knew that the cross was unconstitutional, would you still be for keeping the cross on Mount Soledad? Let me see a raise of hands. All the cross crusaders raised their hands. It was a frightening experience. And I spoke out loud and I said, You are all traitors to the U.S. Constitution!

To be honest, I wasn't at all surprised when the cross crusaders got President Bush to sign a bill that took the cross from the city under eminent domain. That's not going to work, either. It doesn't matter who owns the cross, it's still on public property and it violates the Constitution. It's going to come down, sooner or later. But I might not be around to watch them put the cross on a flat-bed truck and move it to private property, whether it's on church grounds or someplace else. I now have what the doctors tell me is terminal liver cancer, with a prognosis of six to twelve months if the chemotherapy works, maybe longer, maybe shorter. But I want people to understand how an atheist dies. I don't have any problem with death. When it's time to go, it's time to go. When you die, you're in a total unconscious state. I'm not into that wishful thinking. There's no by-and-by in the sky when you die.

Sure, I'd like to live long enough to see the cross come down. But if I don't, I have every confidence that Jim McElroy and Steve Trunk will keep this case going, and that we will ultimately win. This has never been a Phil Paulson case. I started it for all the veterans—whether they're Christian, Jewish, Buddhist, Muslim, or atheist—who don't think a war memorial should have the cross of Jesus to represent them all. I'm proud to be a veteran, and I'm proud to be an atheist. When I die, and I'm buried in a veterans' cemetery, there's going to be an atheist symbol on my gravestone. And I don't care what symbol is on the gravestones next to mine. We all served our country, and we have the right to choose our own symbol. But not the cross of Jesus for all of us. ❖

PHIL THALHEIMER

I'm a first-generation American. I was born in Philadelphia in 1958, and I grew up in a Conservative Jewish home. My parents are both Holocaust survivors, my father was actually a member of the American armed forces during World War II, that's how he got his citizenship. My mother was rescued as part of the eleven hundred people that Roosevelt took off a quota, that were captured in Italy and brought into the United States through Canada, so they were off-quota.

I've always been interested personally in issues of religion in the public square, and I have a unique perspective on this, through my father's experience. Religious symbols, primarily Jewish, were a constant problem in Germany when he was growing up. I heard some about that, but my parents didn't really talk much about it, and there was a general sense of, Don't make waves. When you make waves, you get yourself in trouble. Didn't stick well with me. I just really believed from the beginning, my understanding of the Constitution is that the state, whatever it is, cannot tell me what to practice, cannot ask me for tithing, cannot say to me, I can practice my Judaism but I also must be part of the Anglican Church.

I went to Abington Township High School, outside Philadelphia, which is the school where they had this Supreme Court decision in the 1960s that you can't read from the Bible and say the Lord's Prayer in school. I don't have any problem with a school prayer if you say "God bless." But if you say "in the name of Jesus Christ," then you have excluded me. It's a public school, it's public money, it forces the student to do some affirmative action to avoid it. From a peer point of view, it's very difficult. So I'm aware of these issues.

I did my undergraduate work all on the East Coast, mostly at Temple University in Philadelphia. It's a fascinating school, being urban the way it is. When I was there, if you were between eighteen and twenty-five, you could pretty much get in no matter what—they understood that secondary education was crap in Philadelphia, but once you were there, you had to perform. So they had an unbelievable attrition rate. By second semester of sophomore year, you either got it or you didn't. I came in a little bit later; I transferred from a small liberal-arts college, Drew University in New Jersey, which I hated. I went from this huge high school to this little college, thinking, This is good—but it wasn't. I like Temple for that: it was urban, and it had every stripe of religion and protest. I remember distinctly one time I was getting a Philly cheese steak for lunch, and on one side of the street were the Jewish Defense League and some very right-wing Zionist organizations, and across the street were the PLO. And they were yammering at each other in a way that was fascinating to me, and it was very vocal, and people were very passionate, but there was no fisticuffs, no interaction, no need for police. It wasn't racial or prejudicial; it was, You're wrong and I'm going to tell you why, and I liked that, I just found that fascinating.

My degree from Temple was in psychology, and I worked for a while in Philadelphia as a clinical psychologist. But I discovered that I hated it, because my clients were just whining about their problems. I'd end up telling them to get a life. Finally, my supervisor came up to me and said, Phil, this might not be the best choice of career for you. You really like business, you dabble here, you dabble there. There's something called industrial psychology you might be much better at. I'd always been interested in business. I started my first business when I was thirteen. My parents bought me a lawn mower for my birthday—that's what I wanted—and pretty soon I had two hundred lawns, and half a dozen kids working for me. I paid them twice the minimum wage. I later sold the business and invested in the stock market.

So I took my supervisor's advice. I came to San Diego for grad school in 1983, and got a master's degree at the California School of Professional Psychology. In the city of San Diego, I came in with my industrial-psychology background to the organizational-development wing. I started in the city government in 1986 as a paid intern, and left ten years later as a deputy director; I was basically the chief information officer for the city. I wrote the city's Information Master Plan, and part of it was to eliminate my own position in the reorganization of information systems. Then I spent four years with the San Diego Data Processing Corporation, from 1996 to 2000. I came in there as senior management and rose to be one of the top executives in the company, handling training, customer service, human relations, and what became known as client relationships, a kooky kind of touchy-feely term that means you answer the phone, say hello, and ask, How can I help you? We were providing data systems for the city, which had really archaic and inefficient technology, and I proposed a lot of reforms. Unfortunately, the company's management opposed my reforms, and so I resigned to work full-time on my flight school, San Diego Flight Training International.

I'd always loved flying. I was the kid staring through the fence at the airport, dragging my parents to every air show. I opened my flight school while I was still working for the city. I'd leave the house at four in the morning, work out, get here about five-thirty, work here to about seven, get downtown by seven-thirty, came back here at five, stay here until nine, ten at night. Now we own nineteen aircraft, and we train 350 to 400 pilots every year. We basically take a person from McDonald's, flipping hamburgers, to the airlines in roughly three years, and they get a college degree along the way. I'm really proud of that.

I've been aware of the issues around Mount Soledad since its inception. I was working for the city when the case began in 1989, but I didn't get involved until I was running for city council in 2004, in the district that includes the Mount Soledad park and the war memorial, which surrounds the cross. How I got into Mount Soledad is interesting. Rick Roberts, the talk-show host, and I are very close friends. We met through my flight school—he trained here, and we just hit it off. He was one of the first people I announced I was going to be a candidate for city council, and he thought at that point that I'd lost my mind completely. Since I lost the election, running against an incumbent, although it was very close, he was probably right.

The cross issue was not a big focus in my campaign, which was more about the city's incredibly corrupt and mismanaged government, making San Diego a national laughing stock. During my campaign, when it did come up, what I said was: I personally believe the cross should stay where it is. However, if it is shown to be illegal, then it needs to come down. If there were a legal avenue to exercise to keep it there, let's use them. I don't know if it's right or wrong. The federal government steps in, Congressmen Hunter and Cunningham, and they push through this bill, and they come up with what appears to be an option, transfer the war memorial and the cross to the National Park Service. I don't know if it's a good option or a bad option, but it's an option. And the city council says no. And that just made me unhappy, because I think, for a symbol like that, it's part of San Diego history, they should have absolutely explored all options available to them. And I don't believe they did.

What got me involved in the Mount Soledad issue was when the city council decided not to transfer the land, not even to go down that path. What happened is that this thing happened in the council on a Tuesday, and on Wednesday morning I called Rick Roberts's show and said, I don't agree with this, I wish the city of San Diego had exercised this option. I was actually in the gym, on the machine. And Rick said, I haven't asked Phil about this, but I'm going to ask right now if you'd be willing to take the point on this—that was his term—and to see if we can find a way for the city and the citizens to get involved and maybe ask the city to make a different decision. And that's how I got involved.

A couple of days later, we had a meeting which brought together a plethora of people with different stakes in this, political, religious, business people, crossing gender lines, crossing religious lines, also crossing political lines. There was a significant number of Democrats who were comfortable with this particular symbol. Rick's station provided the space, and word got out that we're going to do this. And there were people there who'd been in this fight for a long time, but there were others who had not been involved that much before. It just got out by word of mouth, and there were thirty-five to forty people there. I said to Rick, I will chair this meeting, but whatever the group wants to do, from that point forward, I'm willing to be supportive, and it was during that meeting they asked if I would be willing to chair it ongoing, and I did.

This was a Friday, and by Monday we had a petition to overturn the city council's vote not to transfer the war memorial to the federal government. Interesting enough, Mike Aguirre's office was very helpful in putting the wording together. He's been a real enigma through this whole thing. I like the man, even though I don't agree with him on everything, but he was very helpful. So, by Monday that week, we had a document we could run with, and we did. Then we got a working committee together. The Republican Party sort of stayed on the fringes, but certainly let people know, provided their mailing lists, and we got volunteers. Just off the Web, we picked up four or five hundred volunteers, who carried the petition around, went to churches, went to synagogues. We also had a contract with some paid petitioners, who were just wacky people. But for every three petitions we got signed, they only got one for us. Our volunteers got all the rest, which I thought was very impressive. We had twenty-three days, we got about 107,000 signatures, and we only needed thirty-six thousand. And we got the proposition on the ballot, and it was approved by 76 percent of the voters.

Now, I know that a lot of people have questioned why a practicing Jew would chair a committee to preserve a war memorial that includes a Christian cross. For the supporters, they could say, See, it's not a religious thing; he's Jewish. And for the Jews, it's like, Oh God, we don't need this. Both communities were like, Who is this guy? I don't see any contradiction, it really comes out of my family's experiences. My parents are slightly to the left of Hillary Clinton, and that's the environment I grew up in. My family are staunch, staunch Democrats. They have a visceral hatred of Bush, and they loved Clinton, they loved Carter, and they loved Roosevelt. They were all mad at me when I got into this; they all think of California as being a great liberal state. These are all Holocaust survivors. My father, who was born in 1921, said, Look, let's see what our son is doing. And he came out to San Diego, and I took him up to the Mount Soledad park. He looked at the plaques that are memorials to veterans, and saw the Stars of David on some of them, and he said to me, I get it, I understand why you're doing this. And he also said he would be proud of having a plaque with the Star of David on this memorial. And I was very proud of my father. Even my aunt, who would make Hillary look Republican, said, You know what, I understand this one. Because they watched what happened when religious symbols in their own communities were being knocked down, and that's where they're coming from.

The Jewish response to my involvement with the cross issue was fascinating. The Jewish community is divided into levels of practice from very conservative to very liberal. The so-called Orthodox or Hasidim on one side, and the Reform Jews and even the agnostics and atheists on the other. The more conservative you were, the more the synagogue stepped up. The local Hasidic rabbi stepped in and said, We certainly had a lot of issues with the cross, but the freedom-of-speech issue is important, the idea of having a faith-based symbol in the public square, a menorah or a cross or a crescent. Their position was, you start down this path and we might not have a menorah on Hanukkah. The further you got out to the more liberal side, the more uncomfortable and ambivalent the community became.

My own congregation—I belong to a Reform synagogue—there was one synagogue meeting that was interesting. I was getting personally blasted over this issue, and the people who were blasting me didn't even know I was there. They were just expounding over this—you know, He can't be Jewish. And the rabbi got up and she said, You know, I think we ought to let Phil speak, because you're talking about a member of this congregation, and before you blast him, at least let him talk. And she said, I'm not personally taking a position, but these are the issues. And she articulated them really well, from a Judaic point of view. And then she turned to me and said, Phil, do you want to say anything? And I said, just for the congregation: I was born of Jewish parents, I have a Jewish wife, I'm raising my children Jewish, they are in religious school at this synagogue. I think I pass the litmus test of being Jewish. Politically, you may not agree with me, but let's put that argument to rest. It's very funny, there were a couple of people who were making the biggest complaints about me, and the color was just draining from their faces.

The traditional view of the Jewish community is to stay as far away as they can from these issues, for fear of two things. One is, it goes both ways. Once you start knocking off symbols, it's a very slippery slope.

There are a lot of Jewish organizations that are on public land, going all the way back to the first synagogue here in the United States, the Touro Synagogue in Rhode Island, all the way up to the Larry Lawrence Center in San Diego, which is on city land. So that's one. The other issue is, Jews traditionally have taken a position of live and let live.

I know on a national level there's a kind of coalition of Zionist Jews and evangelical Christians on support for Israel and religious issues in this country. I worry about that coalition sometimes, because where the Christians are coming from is very uncomfortable for me as a Jew. Their position goes back to an interpretation of Revelations that a certain number of Jews need to convert for the final return of the Messiah. Kind of problematic, from Jewish theology, number one, and, number two, it has kind of a tone of, You know, you guys are okay, you didn't really get it right, but some of you will see the light and come around. That's not where I'm coming from at all. And while a number of them were involved with this cross petition, the point for me was the ability to express a position that I'm not uncomfortable with you being uncomfortable with a particular position.

This may sound surprising, but I agree with the judges who ruled that the cross violates the California constitution. I believe it does. I think the issue comes down to whether it violates the federal Constitution, and I think, today, there's no debate that it's a war memorial, it has all the accoutrements that would make it that. I also think that, looking at other war memorials around the country, there are symbols of faith, primarily crosses, and they've never come down. I think this cross now does represent a memorial to veterans of all wars, it has that potential of being a national monument, and that's what we want to make it into. But the final decision on the cross will be up to the courts, and that's fine with me.

Assuming some court says you have to remove the cross, some people say they won't let the cross come down. I won't be one of them. I will not chain myself to the cross. So, unlike a Roger Hedgecock or a Rick Roberts, who would ultimately turn it into civil disobedience, I won't have anything to do with that. I'm not Christian, and I don't have that kind of faith-based position. I have always stated that this is a country of law, and if we have exhausted our legal options, whatever they may be, and the court says, Sorry, good try, great effort, but it's not going to happen—the only reason I stepped into this was my belief that there may be a legal remedy. Hey, there isn't. I didn't know. But I knew that if I didn't step in it would have been over. And I wanted to be absolutely certain in my core that all available legal remedies had been tried. I understand that it's a burden on the taxpayers, potentially. I also understand there are some things worth fighting for. Ultimately, it may turn out that there is no legal option. And at that point, I wouldn't be happy about it, but that's what it is.

To me, this is a free-speech issue, and at some point you've got to say, I did all that I could do, and at that point you step aside. I'm not going to like it, but there are other rulings that I don't particularly like. It's reminiscent, at a much lower level, of what happened in Gaza. The Israeli government says, We're done. And the Jewish settlers say, We're not moving. Yes, you are. You can walk out, or be carried out. But you are moving. And if it gets to that point, my argument to my supporters would be, Look, I don't agree with this ruling, I think personally it's wrong; however, for me, it should not result in city of San Diego or federal law-enforcement personnel being in danger of getting hurt. I can't support that. We did everything humanly possible to keep the cross, but at that point you've got to accept it. This is not like putting Rosa Parks at the back of the bus. If there were a situation like that—say, Jews were being marched off to camps, or Christians—at that point I would stand up. There's a higher-level issue here. Even if it were a synagogue, I'm not going to stand in front of a synagogue if they say it's on public land and has to go. But if they're bulldozing all synagogues, you've got a whole different situation.

Philip Paulson said to me at one of the city-council meetings that it was people like me who created the Nazis in Germany. I think Paulson has every right to express his opinion, and if he calls me a Nazi sympathizer, he is well within his rights. What I'm not sure in my mind that he's right to do is to say that I can't express my faith or my position in the public square. In my mind, that creates a preference for a very different kind of religion. His abhorrence to having a cross in the war memorial is in many ways as radical and divisive as saying you can only have a cross there. From my own background, knowing what happened in Germany, you start down a path; at least for Jews, the end result was not too good.

I never understood the Constitution to say you can't have anything of a faith-based symbol anywhere in the public square. I've always believed the cross had the right to be there as long as I can come up to it, or not come up to it, and if I wasn't required in any way, shape, or form to participate, if I chose to or chose not to. To me, this is different than Christian prayers in schools. I had an interesting debate once with a Jewish attorney, highly regarded, clerked with the Supreme Court, who said, When I was in school, we had prayer, we had a Christmas tree, and I didn't have a problem with that. And I said, I do. Here's what's wrong. Students in that class are not there voluntarily, it's a captive audience. They are stuck there, under authority, and they have no control over it. That child has no choice. Now government has made a choice. I don't see that relating to the cross. This cross is up there as a symbol, and it's been part of this city's history for a long time, and I've never thought of it as causing any problem for me or any other individual.

Mr. Paulson, I remember him saying every time he went down Interstate 5, past the cross, he was offended. My response to that was, Look to the left going south, look to the right going north. I even understand why he was offended. But I don't think you have a constitutional right not to be offended, and I use that in a broad sense. That's what this country, in a lot of ways, is about. I worry about an America where people cannot express their faith-based opinion. I really want to get back to a place that's inclusive. ❖

Chapter 5

"No Pray, No Play"

The Football-Game Prayer Case from Santa Fe, Texas

Santa Fe is one of many towns in Texas where Friday-night football games and Sunday-morning sermons are both part of a shared culture and tradition. Many Texans say, only half in jest, that high-school football is the state's official religion. Just a few years ago, calling on Jesus to bless those who cheered for the Santa Fe Indians, in prayers delivered by Baptist ministers before each home game, was a ritual that few of the town's residents questioned. Before 1995, none of Santa Fe's residents had publicly objected to the football-game prayers, or those recited every morning in school classrooms and at high-school graduation ceremonies. "We're all Christians here," one resident explained, overlooking Santa Fe's only Jewish family.

But not all of the town's Christians supported the prayers that ran from Monday-morning bells to Friday-night kickoff. After two families sued in federal court to end these long-standing practices, Santa Fe was roiled with conflict. Bowing to lower-court decisions, school officials reluctantly ended the classroom and graduation prayers, but defended the football-game "invocations" up to the Supreme Court, which ruled against the prayers in June 2000. Tommie Weaver, who runs an old-fashioned barbershop on Warpath Avenue in Santa Fe, spoke for most of the town's outraged citizens. "The government is trying to take the Lord out of our hearts and minds, and it's going to be the downfall of this country," he said. "The Devil is getting too much say here."

Understanding why Santa Fe became a battleground in the "cultural war" that has raged across the nation for the past three decades, and why the conflict over football-game prayer turned ugly and even violent, requires a look at the town's history and location. Santa Fe, with a population of just over ten thousand, is thirty miles south of Houston and twenty miles north of Galveston, which sits on the Gulf of Mexico. Named for the railroad whose tracks run beside the town's main street, Santa Fe is a patchwork mixture of rural and suburban areas. West of the tracks, there are still dairy farms, on which the town's economy was first based. Most of the people on this side of town live in older homes, with pickup trucks in their gravel driveways. On the east side of the tracks, newly constructed homes, some fronted with plantation-style white columns, house the more affluent residents of Santa Fe, who commute to offices in Houston or the petrochemical industries that surround Galveston.

Whether old or new, however, most of Santa Fe's residents share a common attachment to conservative religious and political views. John Couch, who played a central role in the football-game prayer case when he chaired the Santa Fe district's school board, spoke for both of the town's groups in explaining what differentiated his community from its urban neighbors to the north and south. Born in Galveston and raised in Santa Fe, Couch is a chemical-plant engineer who relishes the town's insulation from the corrupting influences of big-city culture. "There are a lot of good values from the 1950s," he says. "We had a quieter, gentler society back then. There are a lot of people here who wouldn't mind taking a step backward."

In one respect, Santa Fe remains a step backward from the past half-century. To say the least, the town is not hospitable to African Americans. Although the neighboring towns of Hitchcock, La Marque, and Texas City are roughly one-third black in population, Santa Fe is 95 percent white, with only twenty-four black residents, and Santa Fe High School has just two black students. "Everybody knows about Santa Fe," said Anthony Ross, a black laborer who lives in nearby Dickinson. "They just don't care about anybody that's not white. You're not wanted there, and you'll be threatened." As recently as 2003, the Ku Klux Klan held a rally in Santa Fe, although some one hundred people gathered to protest the racist event. "A lot of people in this town don't want this here," said Annette Anderson, one of the protesters. "They are just not strong enough to say it." But other Santa Fe residents expressed sympathy with the Klan's message. "I do believe that people have their place," David Shouse said. "I don't think it's that whites are better than blacks, but whites have their place and blacks have theirs." And that place, for people like Shouse, is not in Santa Fe.

Blacks are not the only minority that feels threatened in Santa Fe. During the height of the football-game prayer conflict, thirteen-year-old Philip Nevelow, the town's only Jewish student, complained that schoolmates had taunted him for two years with anti-Semitic slurs. Philip's father, Eric, described his son's ordeal. "It started when he was in seventh grade," he said. Students would surround Philip and yell, "Hitler missed one. He should have killed you too." Eric Nevelow complained to school officials, but said they did nothing to stop the harassment, which culminated in threats to hang Philip. Fearing for their son's safety, the Nevelows filed a federal lawsuit against the school district, charging that the prayer dispute had contributed to a climate of intolerance in the schools. To protect Philip from further harassment, the Nevelows finally left Santa Fe and moved to a more welcoming town near Dallas.

Santa Fe is certainly not the most racist or religiously intolerant town in Texas, but community leaders were sufficiently concerned about the passions stirred by the prayer case to erect a billboard that read: "Santa Fe is no place for hate." However sincere the message, it did little to erase almost ten years of harassment of Santa Fe students who did not belong to the town's Southern Baptist majority. Not all Baptists, to be sure, look upon members of other religions as sinners who must be "born again" to be saved from hell. But some allow their evangelical zeal to affect their behavior toward those who cling to "evil" doctrines.

If one incident can be seen as precipitating the Santa Fe prayer case, it happened in April 1993, in the seventh-grade Texas-history class taught by David Wilson. When he handed out fliers advertising a Baptist revival meeting, one student asked if non-Baptists were invited, prompting Wilson to ask what church she attended. Her reply that she was a Mormon triggered a ten-minute diatribe from Wilson about the "non-Christian, cult-like nature of Mormonism, and its general evils," as a federal judge later wrote of this incident. Wilson's remarks, in front of the girl's class-mates, prompted fellow students to say things like "He sure does make it sound evil," and "Gee, it's kind of like the KKK, isn't it?" Understandably upset, the Mormon girl told her parents about Wilson's attack on her re-ligion, and they complained to school officials. The Santa Fe schools had policies that barred distribution of religious literature in class or the verbal abuse of students, and Wilson was given a written reprimand and directed to apologize to the girl and her parents, and to his class.

————

David Wilson's apology to his Mormon student did not end the abuse to which she had been subjected. The girl's friends also became targets of taunts and even physical attacks. Three girls, the teen-aged daughters of Dan and Debbie Mason, stood up for their friends and their own belief that religion did not belong in their schools. Dan was a self-employed contractor in Santa Fe, and Debbie had volunteered in her daughters' schools for many years. Debbie grew up in Flint, Michigan, and was raised in the Baptist Church. "I found out that Jesus loved everybody," she later said of her childhood religious upbringing. When she and Dan moved to Santa Fe in 1978, as refugees from the Rust Belt, Debbie brought with her a firm belief in church-state separation, which she passed on to her daughters. The oldest of the Mason's four girls, Jessica, had graduated from high school before the prayer conflict erupted, but her next-younger sister, Jennifer, began attending Santa Fe school-board meetings with her mother when she was twelve. "Ever since I was young," she recalls, "I was the one to speak out on things that didn't seem right." Jennifer, known as Jenni, was not afraid to speak up at board meetings. "At first I fought on student issues such as the quality of food in the lunch room, funding for academics, and the fact that the schools regularly ran out of toilet paper and had only a handful of working toilets for a school with more than six hundred students," she says. "As I got older, I began speaking on more important topics."

Religion in the schools soon became the most important topic for Jenni, her sisters, and her mother. Jenni's sister Tiffany recalls having a Mormon friend in grade school who broke into tears when she was taunted on the playground. "They'd say she was in a cult," Tiffany said. "They'd say she was going to hell." The youngest of the Mason sisters, Danielle, suffered more than taunts for her beliefs. She recalls what happened in the sixth grade, when she declined to accept a Gideon Bible in her classroom. "Teachers got after me, students got after me," she says. "I was pushed into lockers. I was called a devil worshipper. Emotionally it hurt me." Danielle suffered physically as well. She came down with shingles, a painful nerve inflammation, and Debbie Mason finally took Danielle out of school and began home-schooling her.

The Masons were upset by more than hallway and playground harassment. In addition to Bible distribution, school officials had also allowed teachers to lead classroom and lunchtime prayers, and continued the long-standing practices of graduation and football-game prayers. Debbie and Jenni were frustrated in their first efforts to voice their concerns. "We started out by going to the principals at the school, which got you nowhere," Jenni recalls. "We then went to the superintendent— same outcome. We then brought in a roomful of people to ask the school board to stop allowing religion in the schools—they refused."

By the fall of 1994, the Masons had run into a stone wall of official resistance to their complaints. "With no one else to appeal to," Jenni says, "we sought help from the American Civil Liberties Union." Debbie called the ACLU office in Houston, and its director, Debbie Perkey, agreed to visit Santa Fe and explain to the school board that Supreme Court rulings had banned prayer in public schools and at officially sponsored school events. On their part, Santa Fe's school-board members dug in their heels. John Couch, the board's most vocal and recalcitrant member, vowed that he would willingly face a lawsuit and even go to jail to keep prayer in the schools. "This isn't a matter of win or lose," he said. "It's a matter of right or wrong."

After several heated board meetings failed to resolve the prayer issue, Debbie Perkey referred the Masons and other frustrated parents to

Anthony Griffin, an ACLU volunteer lawyer in Galveston. Griffin, who also served as counsel for the NAACP, is African American, and had attracted national media attention in 1993 by defending leaders of the Texas Knights of the Ku Klux Klan. Protesting the court-ordered integration of an all-white housing project in Vidor, a small town near Beaumont, Klan members had allegedly threatened to burn down the project if blacks moved in. After the Texas Commission on Human Rights ordered Klan officers to turn over the group's membership files, they sought legal help from the ACLU, which sent them to Griffin. When the Klansmen first met with Griffin, they were surprised to find that he was black, but he took their case and won a reversal of the Commission's order. Griffin later explained his decision to defend his unpopular clients: "If I don't stand up and defend the Klan's right to free speech, my right to free speech will be gone." Griffin's stand drew praise, and national awards, from the ACLU and other civil-liberties groups, but also prompted NAACP officials to announce that he was "relieved of his duties because of his decision to represent the Ku Klux Klan."

Along with the parents of other Santa Fe students who had been subjected to taunts and bullying, Debbie Mason met with Griffin to discuss a possible lawsuit against school officials. He drafted a complaint that sought a judicial order to end the classroom, graduation, and football-game prayers in Santa Fe's schools. Equally important, Griffin detailed the history of abuse suffered by students who objected to these practices, including the classroom diatribe leveled by David Wilson at his Mormon student in 1993. Considering the certainty that a lawsuit would provoke anger in Santa Fe, and perhaps even retaliation against the complaining families and their children, Griffin offered to protect his new clients by labeling them as "Does" in the complaint. Conscious that her vocal protests had already made her notorious in Santa Fe, Debbie Mason decided not to join the suit as a plaintiff. The complaint was brought in the name of two "Doe" families, one Mormon and the other Catholic, whose names have never been revealed or published. In April 1995, Griffin filed the complaint in *Doe v. Santa Fe Independent School District* in Galveston's federal district court.

Anthony Griffin was right about the anger the lawsuit would provoke in Santa Fe. Jenni Mason recalls what happened in the Baptist church she had attended from the age of three. "It was a rarity for me to miss a single Sunday," she says. "Not only did I attend, but I volunteered with the younger kids in the afternoon, worked Bible School during the summer, and helped with outreach events." Just before Easter in 1995, only days after Griffin filed the *Doe* complaint, Jenni sat in the pews and listened to her pastor, whom she had known for years, criticize the suit. The pastor then called Mike Lopez, a member of Santa Fe's school board, to the pulpit. Lopez was not full of Christian charity that morning. He painted the people behind the suit as "dim-witted" and "bored" housewives with a "void" in their lives. "While names were not mentioned," Jenni says, "he described the family he felt was responsible so well that there was no doubt who was being spoken of—it was my family. I was in shock. I started to cry. I could not believe they were actually being allowed to say such hateful things about a family from up there at the pulpit. I got up from the pew, left the sanctuary, and went home."

Recalling this incident, Lopez offered no apologies. "I'll stand by that statement," he said. The Masons and other families who challenged the prayers, he added, had blown up their complaints about religious coercion and abuse in the schools. "I can't understand how a thirty-second prayer offered up in the name of Jesus Christ can so traumatize a child beyond repair, yet that same child can go see graphic violence in R-rated movies and be okay," he said. On her part, Debbie Mason replied that her husband, Dan, could no longer get work in Santa Fe, and that she received threatening calls, warning her to "watch your back." "I thought I was going to have a nervous breakdown," she said of the harassment. "And it's all in the name of Jesus Christ."

―――

The Santa Fe case was assigned to District Judge Samuel B. Kent, who had been placed on the bench in 1990 by President George H. W. Bush, and who was known by local lawyers as "Rocket Docket Sam Kent" because he dispatched cases as quickly as possible. Kent was also known for his folksy humor and irascible temper. He displayed flashes of both when lawyers for an insurance company asked him to transfer a hearing to Houston, suggesting that Galveston was too remote. Kent replied that "regular limousine service is available from Hobby Airport, even to the steps of this humble courthouse, which has got lights, indoor plummin', 'lectric doors, and all sorts of new stuff, almost like them big courthouses back East."

Kent's first ruling in the Santa Fe case came just weeks after Anthony Griffin filed the complaint. Griffin had asked for an order that school officials not allow prayers at the high-school graduation in late May 1995. The Supreme Court had ruled in 1992, in *Lee v. Weisman*, that schools could not select clergy members to deliver graduation prayers. The Fifth Circuit federal appellate court, however, whose decisions were binding on Kent, had interpreted *Lee* to permit student-led prayers that were "nonsectarian and non-proselytizing" in content, in the case of *Jones v. Clear Creek School District*. Santa Fe school officials had adopted a policy on graduation prayers after the *Clear Creek* decision, providing that students could "elect to choose student volunteers to deliver nonsectarian, non-proselytizing invocations and benedictions for the purpose of solemnizing their graduation ceremonies." Ruling on May 10, Judge Kent cited the *Clear Creek* decision in permitting a student-led "invocation" at the Santa Fe graduation. Kent explained that "generic prayers to the 'Almighty', or to 'God', or to 'Our Heavenly Father (or Mother)', or the like, will of course be permitted. Reference to any particular deity, by name, such as Mohammed, Jesus, Buddha, or the like, will likewise be permitted, as long as the general thrust of the prayer is non-proselytizing."

Underscoring his written opinion, Kent added remarks from the bench that sent shock waves through Santa Fe. "Make no mistake," he said, "the court is going to have a United States marshal in attendance at the graduation. If any student offends this court, that student will be summarily arrested and will face up to six months incarceration in the Galveston County Jail for contempt of court. Anyone who violates these orders, no kidding, is going to wish that he or she had died as a child when this court gets through with it." The marshal did not show up at the graduation, but the student who delivered the opening prayer—and who must have been nervous—carefully avoided any mention of Jesus.

At a later hearing in the case, Judge Kent again lost his temper when Anthony Griffin informed him that Santa Fe school officials were trying to discover the names of the "Doe" plaintiffs. Kent filed an order that said any further efforts "overtly or covertly to ferret out the identities of the plaintiffs by means of bogus petitions, questionnaires, individual interrogation, or downright 'snooping' " would result in "THE HARSHEST POSSIBLE CONTEMPT CITATIONS AND/OR CRIMINAL LIABILITY," capitalizing the consequences to make his point clear. Kent balanced these rulings—after a hearing at which Debbie and Jenni Mason and the "Doe" parents testified about the harassment they had endured—with a finding that Santa Fe school officials had acted in good faith and were not liable for damages, prompting John Couch to proclaim the school board's vindication in the lawsuit. "Most of the complaints in the suit were absurd," he said. "The people who filed this suit, like many left-wing organizations in this country, wanted to make the word 'Jesus' taboo and take away our children's right to pray. And we refused to stand for that."

However, Kent's initial rulings on the graduation and football-game prayers remained in force, ordering the school board "to establish or to clarify existing policies to deal with either banning all prayer, or firmly establishing reasonable guidelines to allow nonsectarian and non-proselytizing prayer at all relevant school functions." Confronted with this order, the board held several meetings to frame a response, finally adopting two policy statements, one dealing with graduation ceremonies and the other with football games. Both provided for student elections to choose speakers to "deliver invocations and benedictions" at these events. Presumably, these students could offer prayers that were sectarian and even proselytizing, which both the Fifth Circuit court and Kent had proscribed. But the new policies each contained a fallback provision. "If the District is enjoined by court order from the enforcement of this policy," they read, "then and only then" would "nonsectarian, non-proselytizing" prayers be allowed at graduations and football games.

———

Anthony Griffin promptly challenged the new policies, arguing that prayer at *any* school events violated the Supreme Court's ruling in *Lee v. Weisman.* The board's lawyers, headed by Lisa Brown of the prestigious Houston firm of Bracewell and Patterson, countered that student-led prayers, even those with sectarian content, did not fall within *Lee*'s proscription. In June 1996, after that year's high-school graduation but shortly before the football season began, Judge Kent issued a two-part ruling in the Santa Fe case. He first held that the policies allowing graduation and football-game prayers, without limits on their religious content, violated the Fifth Circuit's *Clear Creek* decision and were unconstitutional. However, because the board's "fall-back" provisions had not been implemented, Kent ruled that any decision about their legality would be premature. In effect, he gave both the school officials and the "Does" half a loaf. Unsatisfied with the slices Kent had offered them, both sides filed appeals with the Fifth Circuit, whose *Clear Creek* decision had been anything but clear on these issues.

Arguing before a panel of three Fifth Circuit judges, Lisa Brown claimed that Judge Kent had erred in holding that student-led prayers must be "nonsectarian and non-proselytizing," adding that such prayers were "private speech" and that school officials could not censor their content. Anthony Griffin countered for the "Does" that Kent had wrongly construed the *Clear Creek* decision by defining "nonsectarian" to permit references to Jesus and other "deities" in graduation prayers, and that no prayers should be allowed at football games.

Santa Fe's schools conducted two more graduations, and the Indians played another two football seasons, before the Fifth Circuit panel handed down its ruling on February 26, 1999. The judges faced a difficult task in navigating murky judicial waters, since the Supreme Court had declined to review the *Clear Creek* decision that allowed students to deliver "nonsectarian" graduation prayers, but had earlier ruled against similar clergy-led prayers in *Lee v. Weisman.* Two of the Fifth Circuit judges clearly felt that *Lee* had banned prayers at any school functions, whether delivered by clergy or students. But they also felt bound to apply *Clear Creek* as controlling precedent in their circuit. Judge Jacques Wiener, joined by Judge Carl Stewart, wrote the majority opinion in *Doe v. Santa Fe*. Like Judge Kent, Wiener ducked the question of the board's "fall-back" provisions, but he struck down the policies that permitted sectarian prayers at graduations and football games, dismissing the claim that graduation ceremonies were "public forums" in which the content of speech could not be dictated or censored. A true public forum, he wrote, involved a setting in which speakers would have "free rein to address issues, or even a particular issue, of political and social significance." High-school graduations were not such settings, Wiener said. "The limited number of speakers, the monolithically non-controversial nature of graduation ceremonies, and the tightly restricted and highly controlled form of 'speech' involved," he wrote, "all militate against labeling such ceremonies as public forums of any type. Absent feathers, webbed feet, a bill, and a quack, this bird just ain't a duck!"

Wiener made two more points on graduation prayers. First, he wrote, sectarian prayers would "dramatically alter" the secular nature of ceremonies designed to recognize the graduates' academic achievements. "Rather than solemnize a graduation, sectarian and proselytizing prayers would transform the character of the ceremony and conceivably even disrupt it." Second, prayers would be "delivered to a government-organized audience, by means of government-owned appliances and equipment, on government-controlled property, at a government-sponsored event, thereby clearly raising substantial Establishment Clause concerns." Surprisingly, Wiener devoted just two paragraphs of his lengthy opinion to football-game prayers. In fact, his analysis of this issue fit into one sentence, in which he described football games as "hardly the sober type of annual event that can be appropriately solemnized with prayer."

The sole dissenter on the panel, Judge E. Grady Jolly, heaped scorn on Wiener's opinion. "Today, for the first time in our court's history," he wrote, "the majority expressly exerts control over the content of its citizens' prayers." In this respect, Jolly made a compelling point. By following the *Clear Creek* precedent, Wiener had, in effect, required school officials to ensure that graduation prayers would be "nonsectarian and non-proselytizing." How could that be done without reviewing their content, and possibly censoring those prayers that crossed the sectarian line? Jolly, however, in defending even sectarian prayer at school functions, undermined his argument by citing *Lee v. Weisman* as the "most recent and relevant" Supreme Court precedent. The *Lee* decision, he noted, "refutes the notion that a government-sponsored, 'nonsectarian, non-proselytizing' prayer might be any less constitutionally deficient than a sectarian, proselytizing one." Jolly stepped around *Lee* by arguing that the Santa Fe graduation prayers were not government-sponsored and were simply "private" speech. "The state is not involved," he wrote. "The school board has neither scripted, supervised, endorsed, suggested, nor edited these personal viewpoints."

Jolly devoted one more paragraph than Wiener to football-game prayers, but his analysis was equally lacking in substance. "Of course, football games lack the solemnity of a graduation ceremony," he conceded. "It may be headline news to the majority," Jolly wrote, "but a 'solemn' ceremony is not the only occasion when many citizens feel the need for serious thoughts and words." However, in stressing the "secular" reasons for allowing students to deliver a "brief, serious message" at football games, Jolly ignored the fact that school officials had expected—as everyone in Santa Fe knew—that such messages would be religious in content.

Shortly after Judge Wiener issued the panel's ruling, Lisa Brown filed a motion for an *en banc* review by the Fifth Circuit, which required a majority vote of all fifteen judges. Her motion was denied in April 1999 by a one-vote margin, prompting a second dissent from Judge Jolly in the Santa Fe case. Seven of the circuit's most conservative judges, all named to the bench by Republican presidents, signed the dissent, an unusual step in denials of *en banc* review. Still upset by Wiener's opinion, Jolly blasted it as "surely, surely wrong in fundamental ways." Wiener had been most clearly wrong, in Jolly's view, in ruling that "sectarian" prayers could not be delivered at school functions, although "nonsectarian" prayers were allowed. The Supreme Court had struck down this kind of "viewpoint discrimination," Jolly argued, in recent decisions that Wiener had ignored. Jolly ended his dissent by accusing Wiener of committing a grave judicial sin, by writing an opinion "that has all the appearance of simply advancing personal philosophy."

———

Coaches know that one-point losses are harder on their players than blowouts, and Santa Fe school officials reacted to their one-vote judicial defeat by authorizing Lisa Brown to ask for Supreme Court review of the Fifth Circuit's ruling. Even before she filed a petition for certiorari on July 2, 1999, another game had begun. Before the school year ended in May, members of Santa Fe High School's senior class voted to begin their graduation ceremony with prayer. And in August, shortly after classes began, that year's seniors took part in two separate elections, conducted under the school board's policy that allowed student-led prayers at football games. In the first election, a majority voted to begin football games that fall with a prayer; a week later, they chose Stephanie Vega, a sixteen-year-old junior and a Catholic, to deliver those prayers.

Over that summer, while members of the football team practiced for their opening game on September 3, Santa Fe's school superintendent, Richard Ownby, wrestled with a dilemma. Ownby fervently supported football-game prayers, but he also knew that federal judges had ruled them unconstitutional. After talking with the school district's lawyers, he reluctantly issued a statement on August 19, two weeks before the first game. Ownby did not mention Stephanie Vega, but warned that any student who delivered a prayer over the stadium's public-address system "would be disciplined just as if they had cursed." Ownby quickly repented his words, but they terrified Vega, who promptly relinquished her elected position. "I do not want to be expelled from school for using the word 'God' in a reverent manner," she told reporters who had jumped on Ownby's statement as hot news in a hot summer. "When a student is told by the government that she may say anything except a prayer, and if she does pray, she will be disciplined as if she had cursed, it is just too much pressure," Vega said.

The runner-up in the May election, however, was willing to face the pressure. Marian Ward, the seventeen-year-old daughter of a Southern Baptist minister, was determined to offer a prayer at the opening game. She found an advocate in Kelly Coghlan, a Houston lawyer who read the news reports of Marian's decision to face Ownby's threat of discipline. Coghlan, whose Web site tells prospective clients, "Kelly considers the Bible his most resourceful book of law," called Marian's parents and offered his services without charge, which they eagerly accepted. The day before the game, Coghlan rushed to the federal courthouse in Houston and filed a lawsuit on Marian's behalf, seeking a judicial order to prevent Santa Fe officials from censoring the prayer she had prepared for the opening game. Coghlan found a sympathetic judge, willing to disregard the rulings of Judge Kent and the Fifth Circuit. Just hours before kickoff in Santa Fe, Judge Simeon Lake granted a temporary restraining order, stating in a brief opinion that the bans on sectarian prayer "clearly prefer atheism over any religious faith."

Armed with Lake's order, Coghlan rushed back to Santa Fe and handed it to Ownby. He also alerted the media, and reporters and television crews rushed to the Santa Fe football stadium, jammed with some four thousand spectators. Joined by her parents, Marian stood in the announcer's booth, dressed in her green marching-band uniform. She was introduced by Superintendent Ownby, who told the crowd that Marian "has been selected by her peers to deliver a message of her own choice." He added, "Santa Fe Independent School District does not require, suggest, or endorse the contents of her choice of a pre-game message."

Marian then took the microphone. She began with these words: "Since a very good judge that was using a lot of wisdom this afternoon ruled that I have freedom of speech tonight, I'm going to take it." With her voice cracking, Marian said, "God, thank you for this evening. Thank you for all the prayers that were lifted up this week for me. I pray that you'll bless each and every person here tonight." She then asked God to keep the players on both teams safe and prayed that everyone in the stadium would show good sportsmanship. She ended with these words: "In Jesus' name I pray. Amen." For almost two minutes, the stadium erupted with thunderous applause. Marian Ward had suddenly become a national figure in the battle over school prayer. "This is a battle that needs to be fought," she told reporters. "I've gotten the opportunity to do it."

Not everyone in Santa Fe joined the applause for Marian Ward. Amanda Bruce, a Catholic and one of her classmates, said that Marian's prayer was an affront to "every other faith that does not pray to Jesus or God. People need to think about the person sitting next to them who may not be a Christian." Along with Debbie Mason and her daughters, Amanda helped to organize a protest outside the Santa Fe stadium at the school's homecoming game on October 8. When the group's leaders met with Richard Ownby to inform him of their plans, he said he would first check with local ministers to "get a feel" for how the community might react. "I cannot guarantee that they won't take your signs and burn them," Ownby warned.

Santa Fe police beefed up security around the stadium entrance, as forty protesters held up signs that read "Prayer Is Private" and "Just Because I Don't Pray Baptist Does Not Mean I Don't Pray." Jenni Mason recalls that night. "People who walked into the stadium called us names, cursed at teens, told us we were going to hell," she says. "When people pushed teens and other protesters, the police officers told them to 'push them back.' They were no help at all." Marian Ward again delivered a pre-game prayer, after Judge Lake extended his order allowing prayers for the entire football season. The fans who cheered before kickoff left the stadium silently, however, as the Santa Fe Indians fell to their Texas City rivals in a fifty-to-nothing blowout.

———

Santa Fe's football season was just ending in 1999 when the Supreme Court granted, on November 15, the school board's petition to review the Fifth Circuit ruling, with oral arguments set for March 29, 2000. Surprisingly, the justices ducked the issue of graduation prayers, instructing the lawyers on both sides to address the single question of whether "permitting student-led, student-initiated prayer at football games violates the Establishment Clause." The Court did not explain why it would not rule on graduation prayers; perhaps the justices felt that a decision on football-game prayers would extend to those at all school functions.

The Santa Fe school board found a new head coach for its legal team at the Supreme Court. Marian Ward's pre-game prayers drew national media coverage, and Religious Right groups rallied to her support. The board's chairman, John Couch, was a longtime fan of Jay Sekulow, the chief counsel of the American Center for Law and Justice. Sekulow quickly accepted Couch's offer to argue the board's case before the justices. Articulate and media-savvy, Sekulow had won several religion cases in the Court. His most important victory came in 1993, in *Westside School District v. Mergens*, in which the Court upheld the right of high-school students to hold meetings of a Bible club after school hours. Sekulow had based his *Mergens* argument on free-speech grounds, claiming that schools could not open their facilities to student groups with secular purposes—such as chess clubs—but engage in "viewpoint discrimination" against those with religious aims. The Santa Fe case, Sekulow felt, involved a similar kind of discrimination against religious speech, and would allow him to point to *Mergens* for precedent.

Not surprisingly, in his Supreme Court brief for the Santa Fe school board, Sekulow cited and quoted from the *Mergens* decision sixteen times. His biggest challenge was to lead the justices away from the *Lee* case, which had struck down graduation prayers delivered by clergy members. In that case, Sekulow argued, school officials had chosen the rabbi who offered the prayers, and had provided written guidelines for their wording. The football-game prayers in Santa Fe, in contrast, were offered by students, with no restraints on their content. Anthony Griffin, also not surprisingly, cited *Lee* eleven times in his brief for the "Doe" plaintiffs, arguing that Santa Fe school officials had also provided written guidelines that went even beyond those in the *Lee* case, by allowing sectarian prayers at a school-sponsored event. In effect, Sekulow and Griffin were asking the justices to decide which case—*Mergens* or

Lee—they would follow as precedent in *Santa Fe Independent School District v. Doe.*

However much the briefs and arguments in the Santa Fe case would focus on Supreme Court precedent and its application to football-game prayer, there was another powerful factor behind Sekulow's offer to represent the school board. And that factor was politics. Like most advocacy groups, the American Center for Law and Justice had a political agenda, and both Sekulow and the ACLJ's founder, televangelist Pat Robertson, were key figures in conservative Republican circles. But the Santa Fe case became even more partisan when Sekulow agreed to share his thirty minutes of argument with John Cornyn, the Republican attorney general of Texas. State officials, of course, often file briefs and even argue cases that involve their state's interests, and Cornyn, as an evangelical Christian, personally supported football-game prayer. But his request to appear as a "friend of the court" in the Santa Fe case clearly reflected the political ambitions of Texas's governor, George W. Bush, who was then seeking the Republican presidential nomination. Bush and his campaign strategists were keenly aware that evangelical Christians had become a potent voting bloc, and taking a public stand in a prayer case might reap electoral benefits. In an unusual move, Bush signed Cornyn's brief, which governors rarely do. Whether the justices noticed this was less important than the message it sent to an important constituency in the Republican Party.

Jay Sekulow went first at the Court's lectern when oral arguments began on March 29, 2000. Defending the Santa Fe football-game policy, he put his case in one sentence: "It is neutral as to religious or secular speech." In fact, Sekulow repeated the word "neutral" fourteen times in his fifteen minutes of argument, trying his best to avoid the question that Justice Anthony Kennedy finally asked point-blank: "The hard question is, can you give a prayer?" As Sekulow well knew, Kennedy had written for the Court in the *Lee* case, and without his vote it would be difficult to win a majority. Sekulow dodged Kennedy's question, replying that "there is not a majority vote on prayer in this case" and that students would decide whether "to include a secular message or a religious message" in football-game invocations. Justice Sandra Day O'Connor, another crucial "swing vote" in religion cases, kept up the pressure on Sekulow, noting, "There may well be a campaign among students to be chosen." If candidates in the student election promised to deliver prayers, she asked, "then how do you respond to Justice Kennedy's question?" Sticking to his theme, Sekulow replied, "No one knows, whether they campaigned or not, what that high school student might say."

Kennedy virtually telegraphed his vote in his next round of questions. "What we're concerned about is avoiding the schools becoming a forum for religious debates," he told Sekulow. "We are still looking for some mechanism to ensure neutrality, to keep divisiveness out, and I haven't seen what it is in this case. I think the election thing doesn't work." Justice David Souter also cast his vote from the bench, telling Sekulow: "If the student who is given this neutral option chooses to use that option to pray, the school district is forcing children to sit there and participate in this praying ceremony. And it seems to me that's as far as we have to go to decide the case." Experienced lawyers can sense when their case is in trouble, and Sekulow knew, even before he left the lectern, that Kennedy's and O'Connor's critical questions did not bode well for his clients.

When he took the lectern to speak for Governor Bush and Santa Fe school officials, John Cornyn repeated Sekulow's argument that "this policy is constitutional because it is neutral with regard to the message." Justice Ruth Bader Ginsburg cut him off. "That's been repeated by Mr. Sekulow and you," she noted disapprovingly. Her message was clear: Move on to another topic. Justice Stephen Breyer opened that topic with an observation that reflected his reading of the case record, which included the text of Marian Ward's explicitly Christian prayers. "It seems to me that the school district has figured out a way to have a prayer," Breyer said, "and we have schools favoring one religion over another." Cornyn's response that "this is not the government speaking" did not satisfy Justice John Paul Stevens. Supposing the student delivering the football-game prayer "made an appeal to one particular denomination," he asked, could school officials "suggest to him that maybe that had gone overboard a little bit?" Cornyn replied that officials could not "edit or censor the content of the speech, as long as it was on topic." Stevens had a final question: "Even if it's overtly sectarian?" Cornyn stuck to his guns: "As long as it's on topic, that's correct."

Between them, Jay Sekulow and John Cornyn had said nothing about what actually happened in Santa Fe during the conflicts over religion in the town's schools. Neither lawyer, in fact, even mentioned the town of Santa Fe during their arguments. When Anthony Griffin took the lectern, Justice Antonin Scalia gave him just the opening he wanted to tell the justices about Santa Fe. "I don't even know who the plaintiffs are," Scalia said. "Do people have rights to sue anonymously in federal court? I didn't know we could do that." Without mentioning them by name, Griffin brought the Mormon girl in David Wilson's class, the "Doe" children, and the Mason girls into the Court's chamber. He told Scalia that Judge Kent had protected the plaintiffs' identities because "children were intimidated, children were pushed, people who were not plaintiffs had to pull their children out of the school because of protesting the prayer policies that existed in Santa Fe, and that there was an imminent threat" to their safety. "That's the backdrop of this case," Griffin said.

Justice Kennedy's opinion in the *Lee* case had stressed that, although high-school students were not required to attend their graduations, they felt "coerced" by peer pressure to attend the ceremonies, and to sit through prayers they might find offensive. Chief Justice Rehnquist, who had dissented in *Lee*, perhaps inadvertently gave Griffin another opening to talk about Santa Fe. "Am I right in saying that nobody is required to go to a football game?" he asked. Griffin replied that football players, cheerleaders, and band members were all required to attend the games. Justice Scalia opened the door wider: "Is anybody forced to be a cheerleader, or a band member, or a football player?" Griffin's answer prompted a round of laughter in the chamber: "When you're a teenager, yes." In addition, he said, "there's a social pressure that you've got to go to the football game." School officials, Griffin added, should not be allowed to say, "Well, since it's football, let's just let them pray." He con-

cluded by saying that it was naïve "to put our heads in the sand and ignore the culture and the historical phenomenon of what is happening
in Santa Fe, Texas."

In reality, the Santa Fe case had been decided even before Anthony Griffin began his argument. With their critical questions to Jay Sekulow
and John Cornyn, six justices—including the crucial "swing votes" of
Sandra Day O'Connor and Anthony Kennedy—had made their positions clear. Justice John Paul Stevens spoke for this majority in *Santa Fe
Independent School District v. Doe*, in a ruling handed down on June 19,
2000. Stevens rested his opinion firmly on the Court's invalidation of
graduation prayers in the *Lee* case. "Although this case involves student
prayer at a different type of school function," Stevens wrote, "our analysis is properly guided by the principles that we endorsed in *Lee*." He
found no real difference between graduation ceremonies and football
games. The prayers at both, he said, "are authorized by a government
policy and take place on government property at government-sponsored
school-related events."

Stevens also relied on *Lee* in dismissing the argument that Santa Fe
students chose "voluntarily" to attend football games. Noting that cheerleaders, band members, and the players were required to attend, he
added that other students faced "immense social pressure to be involved in the extracurricular event that is American high school football." And for those who do attend the games, "the delivery of a
pre-game prayer has the improper effect of coercing those present to
participate in an act of religious worship." Stevens also rejected the
claim that student "messages" at the games need not be religious in content. "The District asks us to pretend that we do not recognize what
every Santa Fe student understands clearly—that this policy is about
prayer," he wrote. "The district further asks us to accept what is obviously untrue: that these messages are necessary to 'solemnize' a football
game and that this single-student, year-long position is essential to the
protection of student speech. We refuse to turn a blind eye to the context in which this policy arose, and that context quells any doubt that

this policy was implemented with the purpose of endorsing school prayer."

Jay Sekulow had rested his brief and argument on the *Mergens* case, and its distinction between "private" and "official" speech. Stevens replied that delivering prayers "over the school's public address system, by a speaker representing the student body, under the supervision of school faculty, and pursuant to a school policy that explicitly and implicitly encourages public prayer, is not properly characterized as 'private' speech." Finally, Stevens noted that conducting elections, in which candidates were allowed to campaign for the football-game speaker's post, "encourages divisiveness along religious lines in a public school setting, a result at odds with the Establishment Clause." The prospect of elections that might pit Catholic students against Baptists, or "pro-prayer" advocates against "no-prayer" opponents, clearly disturbed the *Santa Fe* majority.

Chief Justice Rehnquist, who had dissented in the *Lee* case, had not changed his views on prayer at school events. Joined by Justices Scalia and Clarence Thomas, Rehnquist wrote a brief but angry dissent from the majority opinion. "The Court distorts existing precedent to conclude that the school district's student-message program is invalid on its face under the Establishment Clause," he began. "But even more disturbing than its holding is the tone of the Court's opinion; it bristles with hostility to all things religious in public life."

Rehnquist first took issue with Stevens on the question of holding elections to choose student speakers. "It is possible that the students might vote not to have a pre-game speaker," he said. "It is also possible that the election might not focus on prayer, but on public speaking ability or social popularity. And if student campaigning did begin to focus on prayer, the school might decide to implement reasonable campaign restrictions." Even if those elected—as Marian Ward had done—delivered prayers at the games, Rehnquist went on, those prayers would be protected by the First Amendment as "private" speech. "The elected student, not the government, would choose what to say," he wrote.

Venting his anger, Rehnquist ventured into what lawyers call a "parade of horribles." The Court's ruling, he wrote, "essentially invalidates all student elections." He used the examples of elections for student-body president or prom kings and queens. "Under the Court's view, the mere grant of power to the students to vote for such offices, in light of the fear that those elected might publicly pray, violates the Establishment Clause." Rehnquist then noted that the National Anthem's final verse—rarely sung at public events—concludes with these words: "And this be our motto, 'In God is our trust.' " "Under the Court's logic, a public school that sponsors the singing of the national anthem before football games violates the Establishment Clause," the chief justice huffed. Stevens responded to Rehnquist in a footnote to his majority opinion: "This is obvious hyperbole." But this rhetorical exchange, part of a long-running duel over religion cases between the Court's two longest-serving members, underscored the depth of feelings in the "cultural war" in which Santa Fe had become the latest battlefield.

————

Back in Santa Fe, the Court's ruling was greeted with mixed emotions. "My initial reaction would be, at this point, to eliminate an invocation or message as crafted," Superintendent Richard Ownby told reporters, adding that the school board would consult its lawyers before making a formal response. Debbie Mason, whose daughters had endured physical abuse for protesting the football-game prayers, was elated. "We should just thank whomever we believe in," she said. "They came out with a strong ruling, so all schools across America would understand that you cannot do this." John Couch was deflated by the ruling: "Is the Supreme Court telling us if you're on public property you're not allowed to express religious speech? If so, I think our First Amendment rights are being trampled on."

But many schools across America, particularly in the Deep South, did keep praying. When the 2000 high-school football season opened in late August, hundreds of games were opened with prayer. After school officials in Batesburg, South Carolina, passed a resolution approving "voluntary" prayer, the student-body president took the microphone in the stadium press box and led fans in prayer. The state's ACLU director promptly vowed to challenge the prayers in court. Open defiance of the *Santa Fe* ruling was the exception, however. In most communities, fans took part in "spontaneous" prayer, gathering outside stadiums or joining them from the stands. ACLU officials took a wait-and-see position on these events, awaiting reports on whether school officials had any part in organizing them. "It seems to me that a planned spontaneous prayer cannot be spontaneous and it violates the Court's ruling," the Mississippi ACLU director said. But Martin Mayne, president of the Houston ACLU chapter, voiced his support for prayers that had no official sanction. "That is exactly the kind of freedom we're fighting for," he said. "The only place we have a concern is if the groups are going to try to get an official place on the program, or use the public address systems. The simple act of any group deciding they want to voice any opinion, that's speech we fight 100 percent of the time to protect."

Reporters flocked again to the first home game of the Santa Fe Indians in September 2000. Organizers of a group called "No Pray, No Play" had predicted that ten thousand Christians from across Texas, double the stadium's capacity, would converge on Santa Fe. "The prayer will be spontaneous," said the Reverend Eugene Easterly, president of Santa Fe's ministerial alliance. "We've talked to the school board, and we believe we will not be in violation of anything." But when the game began, there were few outsiders among the crowd of forty-five hundred, and those who joined in reciting the Lord's Prayer were drowned out by the stadium loudspeakers, announcing the opposing team's arrival on the field. Pastor Dale Toler of Santa Fe's Calvary Crossroads Church told reporters he was pleased. "This was exactly what I anticipated," he said. "It was done in an orderly fashion, we made our statement and we upheld our belief in free speech."

Many of the people at the center of the Santa Fe case have moved away from the town. Richard Ownby resigned as school superintendent and now works for the Texas Education Agency in Fort Worth. After graduating from Santa Fe High, Marian Ward left Texas to attend the University of Arkansas, and her father took a pastorate at another Southern Baptist church. Mike Lopez, the school board member who denounced the Mason family from their church's pulpit, no longer lives in Santa Fe. Jenni Mason now lives in Oregon, where she is active in progressive political causes. Her mother, Debbie, still lives in Santa Fe. "This isn't a bad community," she says. "I'm not moving." But the prayer case took a toll on her good nature. "I still get upset and emotional," she says. "Not for myself but for what I know my daughters went through and what the Doe children went through. This school board will never know the pain they caused these children."

DEBBIE MASON

I was born in Flint, Michigan, in 1956, and lived there until I was eighteen, and then moved to Texas, and I've lived here ever since. I've been married thirty-five years, have four children and six grandchildren. My parents divorced when I was six; it was my mom, my brother and sister, and I; I'm the oldest. My mom was a waitress. I spent a lot of time watching the civil-rights things happening at the time. I remember, when I was in junior high, there was a lot of riots, because a lot of black kids came to our school, and it caused a lot of controversy, fighting and stuff, and I couldn't understand why people were upset because people of a different color were coming to our school. In fact, I brought one girl home for lunch one time, that I had gotten to know very well. And some of our neighbors told my mother not to bring that "n——" back to my house again. I got very, very upset, and my mother got upset, and told them, You don't pay my bills, you don't tell me who she can invite. I just couldn't understand why people would be that way to somebody else.

My maternal grandparents were Catholic and Protestant. That's one reason they came here from Ireland, because in their country it was hard to get married if you were two different religions. My other grandparents, I really don't know what their religion was. My mother just left it up to us, we got to pick whatever church we wanted to go to. So I used to go to church with my one grandmother, and sometimes I'd go to churches with friends. But mostly it was the Baptist Church. And you learned a lot about the Old Testament, the hell and damnation, all the bad things that are going to happen to you. But we were just taught that God loved everybody, and Jesus loved everybody, and there were certain guidelines that you did as a Christian in the world.

I met Dan when he was in high school and I was in junior high; I met him when I was fifteen years old. He was a mechanic for a long time, and then he did paint and body work for a while, and then he became a cement contractor, concrete man, and that's what he did until a year ago, and now he works on the causeway down in Galveston. I was sixteen when we got married. My oldest daughter is Jessica, and she's in her thirties; and then there's Jennifer, in her late twenties; Tiffany is twenty-four, and Danielle is twenty-three. Jenni and Danielle live in Oregon, and Jessica and Tiffany both live here in Santa Fe. They're all married; Jennifer has one little girl, she just turned four, and Tiffany has one little boy, he's three, and Jessica and her husband have four, two are adopted.

We moved down here when it got real bad in Michigan with work; all of the car factories and stuff closed down. My mom and stepfather had bought some land here in Santa Fe, and we used to come down and visit them. They bought the piece of land next door, and so we bought this piece of land. We liked it out here, because it was country; we wanted to raise our girls out in the country. I grew up in a big city, so it was nice to be out in the country. But it's getting too citified out here for me. And that was part of the problem here in Santa Fe, a lot of the controversy, because you were having people with different faiths, different colors, different ethnic groups moving out here, and that was part of the big controversy too.

I really didn't get real involved with the schools until Jennifer started school. I was homeroom mother, taught classes when they needed someone to fill in for an hour or so. At first, it was, Oh, Mrs. Mason, you're wonderful. The teachers were like, We hope we get her children. They all wanted my children because I was very involved in the classroom; whatever the teachers needed I would do; if they needed things in the classroom the school couldn't provide because there was no money—pencils, papers, whatever—we would get it and bring it in; if there was poor children, you'd bring in stuff for them.

But there was a lot of things that I didn't think was right. Such as, if you were poor, you were treated different than the rich kids here in town. We had very few black children here in town, and the ones that were here didn't stay long, they weren't treated good. The teachers were good, it was the other students; and a lot of that, I think, comes from home. It's not the child, because children don't really notice color. It's the adults that do that to them. And I just seen a lot of things in the schools—the rules they had, the laws that govern the schools—that I didn't like. So I'd ask a lot of questions, and lots of times didn't get answers. I had to do a lot of digging, ask for a lot of records. And I'd be at the board meetings, fighting along with the board for the new school, whatever they needed.

So I was very, very involved. If somebody wanted something done, it was, Call Debbie. I had a really good reputation until I got very vocal over the religious issue, and then, as the Bible says, all hell broke loose. Before this, my girls really didn't have no problems. They were happy, they were content, they were very popular. Every Friday night our house was full of kids, all the kids liked to come to our house. The girls were going to church on a regular basis—usually on Sundays they went to the First Baptist Church—and I worked in my garden. The man who picked them up for church, he'd say, Debbie, you need to come to church, you need to come and talk to God. And I'd say, Oh, but what better place than in my flower garden to talk to God? At least this way, it's just Him and I talking. The younger girls started going when they were about three. They really liked going to church, and we would talk about it. My husband and I didn't force them into a religion; we basically let them pick what they wanted to be. They went with their friends; I think they've been to every church in Santa Fe. They'd come home and ask me questions, and I would tell them, Each of us has to interpret it our way.

This whole case didn't start with prayers at the football games. It really started when the girls would come home and start making little comments. This child's being made fun of, because they're Catholic, or they're Mormon, they're not Baptist. And I'd tell them, They shouldn't do that, it's not right. How can you make fun of someone's religion if you don't know nothing about it? It really upset Jennifer. She said, Mom, it's wrong, because I know these kids, and a lot of these kids are not Christian like this community thinks they are. But do you think a child in this town would stand up and say, I'm Buddhist, or I'm Hindu, or God forbid if they said, I'm Muslim? It was bad enough if you were Jehovah's Witness or the Jewish faith.

But what really did it was when Jennifer came home one day with this little red Bible and said men were inside the high school, handing them out to kids. So I went down to the school and I said, There's different kids, different religions in these schools, you can't be doing this. And it was, Oh, Debbie, don't complain, don't complain, you're making waves. I didn't make a big to-do about it, because I figured, Well, they'll take care of it. And then, one day, I was sitting out in my car, waiting to pick up the girls, and they're in front of the doors, handing out Bibles, and the kids didn't have no choice but to go by them. It was so sad, because the kids that took them, you would watch them, they'd walk down the sidewalk and just throw them on the ground or throw them in the trash can. So I walked up to one of the men and said, May I have one of those? And then I went into the school office, and I *slammed* that Bible on the counter, and I says, I want to know what these people are doing out here, handing out Bibles. And the ladies in the office say, We don't know what you're talking about. When I got home, I called Gary Causey, he was the principal. I asked him, Who gave them permission? Well, we sort of did, he says, we didn't think there was any harm in it, they're just Bibles, but we'll check into it. And nothing happened. Jennifer told me they kept coming back and handing out Bibles.

I was so upset I called the ACLU; it took a lot of calling, looking up numbers—I'd never done that in my life. I spoke to Debbie Perkey up in Houston, and she informed me that they had been getting quite a few phone calls; I guess I wasn't the only one calling from here in Santa Fe. From what I understand, it wasn't just parents, it was also staff members that were calling. But they wouldn't say who they were, for fear of what would happen to them. She asked, since so many people had called, if we would like for her to come down and talk to the school board, and explain to them, You can't be doing this, because you're stepping on people's religious rights. I told her that was fine, if that was what other people wanted too. And she came down and addressed the school board, and, oh my God, you would have thought the Devil himself had walked into the Santa Fe school-board meeting. It was one of the scariest moments of my life. People were outraged. How dare she come into our community and tell them what to do! And she was there basically to help the school board, so a lawsuit wouldn't be filed, and they wouldn't get in trouble. She was trying to mend the fence, to keep it calm.

As word got out, more and more people started coming. There were a couple of board meetings that were really ugly. Just the most horrible, horrible things were said. One woman stood up and said that she was Catholic, and I guess their Bible's a little bit different than my Bible is. She says, I don't want my child reading that; if I do, I'll give it to them myself. Some person in the audience said that Catholics weren't Christians, and, oh, she about blew a gasket. And I got up and made a long speech to the school board. That was probably one of the hardest speeches to give, because I knew John Couch, who was the school-board chairman, and Mike Lopez, who went to the same church as my family did. A lot of people who were on the school board at that time went to the First Baptist Church; in fact, some of them taught Bible study to my daughters. When people would stand there and say, "Your children aren't Christian," they should have stood up and said, "Excuse me, her children go to the same church as we do." And none of them did. It was really, really hard.

After the first couple of board meetings, when it was obvious they wouldn't back down on handing out Bibles at the schools, we asked Debbie Perkey if we could have a meeting of everyone who had called, to see if we could try to get it straightened out, because it wasn't going good. She said yes, so we did, maybe twenty people showed up, and she told us the different things we could do. The last resort would be taking it to court, and at that moment nobody wanted to. This is our town, this is our school district, let's try to work it out. We figured we could work with the school board, and the principals. We were trying to keep it very quiet, within our community, we didn't want to raise a stink, but we wanted to let them know: You can't be doing this. There's too many people that have different views than what you have, and it's not fair to the children, because they don't have a choice, they can't get up and say, Adios, I don't like this, I'm going home. Debbie came down, I don't know how many more times, and tried to talk to the school board and get it settled. Some members on the board just decided, Let's go for the whole ball of wax, let's go as high as we can go, and that's exactly what happened.

After we realized the board wasn't going to back down, Debbie contacted Anthony Griffin, a lawyer down in Galveston, and he said he would be happy to come and talk to the school board and see if we could get it straightened out. So he came here a couple of times and spoke to the board, and that didn't go over real good, because, number one, Mr. Griffin isn't white, plus, there were certain people on the board who were bound and determined that they were going to be Christian martyrs. They were going to show all of us, and our community, and this country, and the world, that we were a Christian community, and if we didn't like it, we could leave. If it hadn't been for some of those board members, it may have never went to the Supreme Court. I think, between some of the principals, and the superintendent, and Anthony, and the rest of us, we could have worked it out. But there were some that truly wanted to be martyrs, and to make a statement.

Anthony told us that if anyone wants to file a lawsuit we could say, I want to be anonymous, because the temperament in this community at that time, if some of the people would have known, I think they would have hurt somebody. The feeling in the air terrified me to no end. I'm not saying any of them would have hurt them, but you never know, and it could have been nobody in our community, it could have been outsiders that would come in and do something to them. It had already started hitting the newspapers, and the next thing we know, there was TV cameras, journalists, they were everywhere.

When we met with Anthony, he asked us about what happened in the schools, and we told him about handing out Bibles on the campus, the religious songs that kids were taught in their classes, prayers at lunchtime, prayers at graduation, and things like that. When this case started, the big issue wasn't prayer at football games. I believe it was the school board that decided that football-game prayer would be the issue to take it all the way to the Supreme Court, because in Texas it's football, prayer, and beer, and barbeque. Friday night, it's almost like a war thing, rally around your football team, go out there, support them. What do you have in a community this size? Sports is all there is. You don't have a theater, God forbid if we had a theater in our community. The only thing you really have is church and sports. So that's what they decided to take it to court on, because they decided that was what would make people in this country the maddest: How dare you take prayer away from a football game!

After the lawsuit was filed, we had the hearing before Judge Kent in Galveston, and I had to go testify. Oh my God, I was terrified. There was all this security. And you don't know, some of these people can really hurt you, they can be standing outside with a gun, and you don't know. Before I testified, me and Jesus had a little conversation out in the hallway, and I'm sitting there with my family Bible. I was so upset, so nervous, because I didn't want to be in that position in the first place. I just wanted to be home, taking care of my family. And I sat there, and it's like, God, why am I here? It was so strange, it was like this calmness come over me that I couldn't believe. And I felt like someone touched my shoulder and said, You are here to protect the children, you have to go in and tell the story. And I went in there, and after that it was like smooth sailing.

I'd heard about Judge Kent, that he's a very conservative, right-wing Republican. There was times at the hearing where he would get after people, big-time, scared the living daylights out of me. But with me he was very understanding. Anthony asked me what my religion was, and the school district's lawyers, it was like their chairs almost flew across the room, they couldn't get up fast enough. You can't ask her that! And

Anthony told them, She's willing to tell her religion. And Judge Kent looks at me and says, You don't have to answer that, nobody can ask you what your religion is. And I say, I have no problem saying what my religion is, I'm American Baptist. Judge Kent asked me how I felt, as a Baptist, as a Christian, and I explained to him how I felt and why I felt the way I did.

After this lawsuit was filed, the attitude in the community got really ugly. People were trying to find out who the Does were. I assume the board knew—this is a small town, they probably figured it out amongst themselves; there would be two, maybe three who would be very curious. One of the Does at one time almost did give it out. People in town may know, they may guess; whether they do or not, I don't know. I've been asked if I was a Doe, and I'm like, You think, with me being so vocal, I'd be a Doe? Come on. I told Debbie Perkey, If I decide to join the lawsuit, I will not be a Doe. I was too vocal, I was the main target. But sometimes you have to be a Doe.

Judge Kent was worried about the atmosphere in the community. He made it real clear that you can't "out" the Does, and you can go to jail if you try to find out who they are. So what ended up happening is, instead of the adults doing it, the kids did it. At one time in the high school, Jennifer called me crying one day, Come and get me. And I didn't know what was happening. And when I walked in, they had a petition going around from the churches, with things to fill out: what your religion was, are you a Christian? And if they thought you might be involved in the case, or one of the Does, they'd push you up against lockers, kick you, hit you. My daughters' church was guilty of this. I was so upset over Jennifer, because she was hysterical. What happened then, I complained to the church big-time, I called the school district and complained to them.

When this case was going on, if you came into this town, and you were from a big city like New York or even Houston, I wonder what they would have thought, because all the signs on the churches were "God's with Us," "God's on Our Side." Certain people in the community, they just had it in their heads that they were going to win. There were no ifs, ands, or buts about it. God was on their side, and I guess the Devil was on my side, and the Does', and whoever else felt like that. They had 911 to God, a special number, and this is what they were meant to do. I think that boosted their ego just a little bit more, gave them more of a cause. But what they didn't stop to think about is, maybe they were wrong, and God chose the other side to do His work. They never looked at it that way. They just couldn't see, in their heart, that what they were doing was wrong. And it was wrong to the children. These are children, they're not adults.

I think people were upset with me because I was the most vocal one in the community. A few of the others who were vocal at the beginning got scared when they would go to school-board meetings and see what was going on. There was times when I'd be out someplace and I'd have a car follow me home. We'd get phone calls, people would tell you, Watch your back, watch your kids' backs. We got a phone call from the district attorney down in Galveston that there was going to be a drive-by shooting at one of our meetings, and they had to have security. I had to sit down with my daughters and my husband and explain to them, This could happen if I go to this meeting. And they said, Mom, what are you going to do? And I said, I don't want to leave you kids. And they said, Well, Momma, you got to do what's right. You go, and if something happens to you, it happens to you. But you can't back down from people like that. And I went, and I'll tell you, I was scared to death. Lots of times, when people get involved in cases like this, they'll burn down your house, burn a cross in your yard—that's always a good one. You know, they take a crucifix, which is their religious symbol, and set it on fire. That don't make sense. So I got the word out, very loudly in the community, if they burn a cross in my yard, I'm inviting everybody over for hot dogs and marshmallows. And that stopped them. Because they want you to be scared, they thrive on that. I may be scared, but I'm not going to let them know I'm scared.

There's something interesting about prayers at the football games in Santa Fe. For a long time, we had ministers doing it, we had Catholic ministers a couple of times, but most of the time it was Baptist. No Muslim, no Hindu, no Jehovah's Witness, no Mormon minister getting up there. But after this lawsuit was filed, the school board decided that a student would give the prayer before the game. I went to the game where Marian Ward gave the prayer, after the judge in Houston said she could do it. Jennifer at that time was a photographer—she worked for two newspapers—so she had to go take pictures of the games. Marian wanted to do it from the git-go. She would have done it from the first, she would have raised her hand and said, Oh, can I do it? Can I do it? I give her credit, she got up and she did it, she had to be shaking like a leaf, 'cause when you're in front of that many people it's not easy to begin with. But she also knew that she had the majority on her side, and when you have the majority on your side, who's going to boo you? And they did boo! The press didn't tell the whole truth on it. Oh yes, there was a lot of booing, a lot of people refused to stand. My family, and people who were with us, and all through the stadium you could see people, when she did it, they sat.

That's another thing a lot of people don't understand, when it came to the prayer issue and free speech—because that's what they were trying to use—she has her free speech. If she wants to pray, she can do it by herself, or go outside the gate, like we did when we protested. You can have all the free speech you want, but when you step on someone else's rights, that's when it ends. And the majority cannot step on the minority's rights, and the courts say that over and over, you can't do that.

When the Supreme Court ruled against the school board, oh, they were mortified. I would have loved to been there and seen their faces. When I heard about it, I just started screaming, and I fell to my knees, and I was like, Thank God, thank God. Now I can pray when I want, I can go to church when I want, my church can have its doors open when it wants, the government can't come in and tell them who we have to pray to and when we have to pray.

I lost a lot of my friends, people I've known in the community for a long time that became city-council members, mayors in this community. People you've known for almost forty years all of a sudden don't

talk to you no more, even though they'd come to your house for barbe-
ques, when you'd have your babies they'd call you and congratulate you.
But after this case started, you'd go into the stores, people would be
standing there talking, you'd hear your name being thrown around and
not nice things being said. You know, it's like you have a group of people together and a skunk comes in, everybody just runs, terrified that
you're going to get sprayed. Basically, that's the way it is. People are so
afraid because they don't stop and think, and they just want to believe
what certain people tell them. They made my kids' life hell in school.
For three girls who were still in school, who were popular, who were involved in a lot of activities, having friends over all the time. My children, they lost a lot of their youth because of that, and lot of their
friends. But I never thought of leaving Santa Fe. I used to be told all the
time, We're going to run you out of town. I was like, No, you're not.
Came close a couple of times, because they made it very hard on us fi-
nancially, going from making good money to you don't know if you're
going to have food on the table one day. They make it very hard on you,
because they know how to get you. I had to work at Jack in the Box for
three years, just to put food on the table.

Since the Supreme Court decided this case, things in Santa Fe have
quieted down to a certain degree, unless the case is brought up in the
newspapers. But they're still doing a lot of the things they were doing,
and no one's got the guts to take them to task for it, because they figure
the Supreme Court told them. What people forget is, the courts rule,
Judge Kent ruled, the Fifth Circuit court ruled, the Supreme Court ruled,
but what people don't understand is, they can rule all they want, but
when they break the rules they don't do anything to them. So, basically,
in a way the Does won, and I won, but in a way John Couch and them
won to a certain degree, because who can flex their hand, or say, You
broke the law, you have to go to jail for a week? It's like, This is the way
we ruled, and nothing else is going to happen unless someone else
brings it up again. But Bush figures he's got his people in there now, and
the Supreme Court will change their mind.

When I think about this case, people used to say, Debbie, you've got a lot of guts to stand up against the community. I don't think it's so much guts, it's something in your heart. Because, if you back down, then the next person has to pay the price. It's like I told the school board, and I told kids, and press people, everybody at one time or another is a minority, whether you're a woman, or it's your color, your religion, where you live, what you own—at one time or another, you're a minority. And until you're the minority, you don't know how it feels. But when you become the minority, oh, you know how it feels. And then you look at things a lot differently. It's easy to be a majority, it is so hard to be a minority—one person, or two or three people who speak out and say, Wait a minute, there's something wrong here.

But people like John Couch and Mike Lopez, they seem to forget why we're in this country. Our ancestors came here because they couldn't have the religion of their choosing. If they were the wrong religion, which wasn't the king's at that time, oh my goodness, it was off with your head, you were tortured, the church taxed you. And that's why people came to this country, because you didn't have a choice, you were told what to do. And I don't like being told what to do. My husband can tell me what to do, my kids, my grandbabies tell me what to do all the time. But don't you sit there and tell me that I have to be part of the majority. ❖

JOHN COUCH

I was born in 1954, in Galveston, in St. Mary's Hospital. You hear comments, whether people are BOI?—were you born on the island?—that's a local county saying that you'll hear. My dad's family moved here in the fifties, my mom was born in Galveston and raised in this vicinity; she graduated from high school in La Marque, which is next to Santa Fe. My dad and mom married young; my dad was in the Air Force when I was born; my dad came back and wound up going to work out at Sterling Chemical, which was Monsanto at that time. He worked in operations and manufacturing at the plant out there, that made styrene and other chemicals. I have one sister and one brother; I'm the oldest of the three. My mom and dad are now retired in La Marque, and they help to take care of my grandmother, who's ninety-eight.

When I was five years old, we moved to Santa Fe. It was kind of rural, compared to some of the other surrounding areas. There was a lot of dairy farms out there, and a lot of rice farming in this area. It kind of stays wet, there's a lot of canals. Santa Fe has really grown since then, but I grew up in a small town in neighborhoods, when I was a kid, where you could run around and ride bicycles all over the place, play hide-and-go-seek, and not have to worry about crime or anything else like that. There were very, very strong faith-based people in the community when I was growing up. When I was in the first grade, we learned Psalm 100, "Make a joyful noise unto the Lord," and we recited that for the parents at Thanksgiving. Having prayer at lunchtime was common, nobody thought anything of it. Singing patriotic songs was something we did weekly. Of course, this was in 1961, before the *Engel* case in New York, where they started to ban prayer. When some of these cases started coming out, people at that time just didn't believe they would ever be enforced down here, because it was just so unheard of.

I went through grades one through twelve in Santa Fe; I graduated with honors, in the top ten in my class. I started out wanting to be a doctor, went to the University of Houston. I started out as a biology major. I was big in athletics at the time; I wanted to play basketball, but I didn't wind up playing basketball. I went for three or four years there, but my grades probably weren't high enough to get into medical school, so I dropped out and worked in construction for a few years. Then I got married and went back to school. I probably should have been a lawyer, but I became an engineer. So it was a few years until I started having kids. I've got three kids now: my oldest daughter is at Carnegie Mellon University in Pittsburgh; my son is eighteen, a senior at Santa Fe High School; and my younger daughter is thirteen, in the eighth grade.

After I got my engineering degree, I went to work for a contractor for Dupont, and worked for them for about seven years, and then Dupont wound up hiring me, and I've been working directly for Dupont for the last fifteen years. We make sulfuric acid, and hydrochloric acid, which is highly toxic and highly corrosive, and they ship that to other places where they make the alternative Freons that they put in air conditioning, and they make things like Teflon out of it also. But my job is very important; I try to keep all the chemicals in the pipes and equipment. Dupont is the safest chemical plant: our environmental record is very good, and we do a pretty good job of keeping everything inside. I monitor all the piping and equipment, and make the recommendations for materials and construction.

I got involved in the schools here in Santa Fe when my older daughter was in kindergarten and first grade. I was always concerned about the schools, the quality of education they were getting, the violence and the drug issues in the schools. I was either going to put my kids in private schools, or I was going to get involved and do something about it. Private school is expensive, and I went to school here; I still knew some of the teachers and a lot of the people here. So I ran for school board in 1992. When I started to run, I advertised that I wanted to bring Christian values back to the schools, including hard work, discipline, self-control, that sort of thing.

Immediately after I got on the school board, we ran into a hot-topic issue, and that was abstinence-based sex education. I was really pushing for that, and I had gotten into a debate with the Galveston County health director in the newspapers. It was really interesting, because he was using statistics to make his point, and I was using his same statistics. And, being an engineer, I couldn't be snowed. It was obvious that the sex education that we were using was actually doing more harm than good, the message that we were sending our kids. It took me about four to five years before I got something passed, and we did pass an abstinence-based sex-education program. There was a lot of people that didn't care much about it, but there were other people that were really interested, the people who went to church were really concerned about it. I'd done a lot of research on it, I was citing statistics, and I would use the logic that it's kind of like telling kids that it's okay to drink, and people could identify with that sort of thing. I had a lot of apprehension on some of the board members. I'm always amazed, even with the school board, that people are afraid to implement and do things, because they think that, well, you can't do that, that's against the law. I talked to a lot of the administration people, who said, John, you're probably right, but we just can't do that—I heard a lot of that. Some of them didn't believe we had to do that. The board sets policy, that's the law here in Texas; the administration carries out those policies. But it's gotten to where the administration wants to make those policies also, and I realize a lot of those people have good intentions. So that was a battle I fought early.

I became the lightning rod for a lot of people, because I made several enemies when I was on the board, because I wouldn't push things underneath and hide them, I'd bring them out in the open. I wasn't out to get anybody in trouble, what I was out to do was, if we've got a problem, admit it, and let's work together and see if we can solve it. But there's an inherent nature in school systems that if we've got a problem let's keep it close to the vest, let's don't talk about it, let's try to smooth things over. I'd bring a lot of things up in open session, and shine daylight on it, and when you do that, you're going to ruffle some feathers. But there's an awful lot of people who would sit there and be passive. I had trouble getting things on the agenda, because they didn't want to talk about it, because of the controversy it would stir up. They didn't want to vote on it, because if you vote on it then people are going to see which side of the issue that you're on, and if you do that, then people are going to be upset with you. You'd be surprised how many politicians are like that.

A couple of years into that same term, there was an issue around prayers in the schools. This started with a couple of disgruntled parents; they were always complaining about something in the schools. Debbie Mason and that small group of people that pushed the issue, they had come before the board even before the prayer issues, and complained to the board about some of the problems in the schools. Some of the things they complained about were legitimate, but a lot of them weren't. And, me being president of the board, I even agreed with them from time to time on some of the things we needed to change in the schools. But I really think that some of those people were just out there to show that the school was wrong and push the issue. Most of those people were not educated, they didn't understand the historical nature of the situation; some of the precedents that came through in the last few years have really turned the situation with prayer in the schools upside down, in my opinion.

I was extremely interested in history when I was growing up. At five years of age, I was going to libraries and reading about the Founding Fathers. And that's one of the things that bothers me, that most people don't grasp just how much faith and really a basic Judeo-Christian ethic that the Founding Fathers had, and trying to instill it in American society. You go back and look at the speeches—Washington's Farewell Address that he made about this nation and where we were headed if we didn't adhere to morals and religion. John Adams, Samuel Adams—the list goes on and on, about where this country was going to have to be if it was going to survive. Look at the books by David Barton, of the Wallbuilders group. He just has tons of information. He's even correlated the rise in violence in schools and the drop of grades, the number of kids doing drugs, the high pregnancy rate, since they banned prayer in schools. I'm an engineer, and I understand statistics fairly well, but to me some of the facts are just unbelievable when you start to take a look at what's happened since God was taken out of the classroom and a lot of these problems started to occur.

It took a lot of time for this stuff to migrate down to the local communities, because I remember people telling me they were just devastated, they couldn't get over why some judge would not allow kids to pray in school. After studying it, and going through everything, I am still amazed that we've gravitated to this type of situation. Mainly because I don't think anybody should ever be forced to pray, or coerced, but to limit the majority's free speech to be able to pray, it just amazes me, I can't fathom it. The Constitution talks about inhibiting the freedom of speech, the Free Exercise Clause. The courts have just not seemed to come down on that side as often as they should.

When Debbie Mason and those other parents complained about prayers in the schools, they brought down this ACLU lawyer from

Houston, Debbie Perkey, to meet with the school board. I can tell you this. There was about five board members that were scared stiff, but I wasn't. I was adamant; I knew history, I knew what I thought was right. I sat there and I debated Debbie Perkey on the merits of the issues. It got a little contentious, I'll tell you that, but I think we did the right thing. We didn't back down from the ACLU, and I still believe we're right. There's just no doubt in my mind. I hoped we could get this thing settled without going to court, but I knew in the back of my mind that it would probably be litigated. I wasn't about to let it go. A majority of the board, I believe, felt almost as strongly as I did. There was a gentleman on the board named Mike Lopez, we became famously good friends. He was also very outspoken, as adamant as I was. He used to write a lot of articles to the newspapers. Between Mike and myself, we really pushed the issue pretty hard. Most people on the board, as well as the administration, they shy away from any kind of litigation or legal problems or threats. I found that's a natural tendency for people to stay out of legal problems.

Debbie Mason and those other parents had complained that there was just a broad, sweeping religious overtone in the school that was coercing kids to do this and that, and that just wasn't true. The policy that we had in Santa Fe, to me, was unbelievably fair, in terms of what we tried to implement at graduation and football games. The senior class, at the end of their junior year, would vote whether they wanted to have a message, an invocation, or anything at the football games. And then they would vote who was going to give those. There was no coercion that they had to pray, nobody said who had to do it. It was all seventeen- and eighteen-year-old kids, who I consider young adults, and I just thought it was a pretty good policy.

We had this hearing before Judge Kent down in Galveston. The board's lawyers were from Bracewell and Patterson in Houston. Lisa Brown argued our case in the district court. We had several lawyers, but she was the main one. We beat the pants off the ACLU there. I mean, they really looked ridiculous. To be honest, the ACLU lawyers were just embarrassed, because they just had no case, none whatsoever. The young lady they had in high school came in and said, no, she wasn't affected by any of the prayer at graduation. We had this one parent complaining about kids in the third grade singing the Johnny Appleseed song, which says, "Oh, the Lord's been good to me, I thank the Lord." And the parent went bananas over that. Judge Kent was kind of humorous, he made this comment in court, that I learned the Johnny Appleseed song when I was in school, and there's really nothing wrong with it.

Judge Kent didn't find anything in their favor, with the exception that he warned that we had to give a nonsectarian, nonproselytizing type of prayer at graduation and football games, which myself and Mike Lopez found highly objectionable, because that was telling the students how they had to pray. It was a clear violation of the Free Exercise Clause. You look at the First Amendment, it talks about you can't impose religion, or you can't inhibit the free exercise thereof. In my mind, and in Mike Lopez's mind, they were inhibiting the free exercise by not allowing the students to do whatever the student wanted to do at the time. The way it was told to us was, they couldn't invoke the name of Jesus Christ; they could say "God," but they couldn't say "Jesus Christ." This ought to be left up to the students, this is a message of whatever the students wanted to say. Where do you draw the line? It's the Free Exercise Clause. I think Judge Kent understood it, and he was trying to go as far as he could go, and he was basing his ruling on precedent. That was the *Clear Creek versus Jones* case, from a school district that's just five miles up the road from here. I think the precedent was clearly set wrong to begin with.

After this ruling, we had a football game, the first game of the season in Santa Fe. There was a young lady here, Marian Ward, chosen by the senior class, to give a message before the football game. And I was really aggravated, and I had told the administration at the time, We shouldn't be telling this young lady anything. Between the lawyers and the administration, they were saying that we need to give her some guidelines on what she can and can't say, now that we have the ruling from the Fifth Circuit. My instructions were, we shouldn't be telling her anything. And what happened was, she'd had several teachers and maybe a vice-principal telling her, You can't say this, we don't want you to get certain people in trouble, and they really coerced her, almost to the point of tears, where she was afraid to do anything.

She went and filed a suit in federal district court, saying her rights had been violated, she was being subjected by the administration, her free speech was being violated. I went to the federal court that day; I took off work. When Judge Sim Lake ruled in her favor, there was applause and screaming. I felt a vindication, and when she showed up that evening at the football game, I remember her saying, A real wise judge has given me the right to give a message as I see fit, or a prayer, and I want to take my constitutional right. I remember the stands on both sides stood up and clapped. It was pretty emotional. There was opposition from the ACLU, and maybe a handful of people in all of Santa Fe.

So we still had this ruling that kids could say prayers at graduation and football games, but they had to be nonsectarian and nonproselytizing. The ACLU wasn't happy because they didn't want any prayers, and they were going to appeal. We weren't happy because he was trying to limit what the kids could say. We thought that was unconstitutional. So myself and Mike pushed the board into appealing the case to the Fifth Circuit. If we didn't appeal, I knew the ACLU was going to appeal. It was really amazing. I attacked the ruling in the board meeting when it came up, from a logical standpoint and from a constitutional standpoint. You couldn't inhibit the free speech of the students at the time, and when they get up and decide whatever they want to talk about, that was the spontaneity of the moment, and you just couldn't go in there unless you could prove they were doing harm to the kids somehow. You can't holler "Fire" in a theater—that sort of thing. And Mike attacked it from a Biblical standpoint. It was pretty emotional; I remember the board voting, I think, five to two to send it to the Fifth Circuit.

So we went to the Fifth Circuit in New Orleans, and Lisa Brown argued the case there. I knew we were kind of in trouble, because I looked at the makeup of the three judges. We had a conservative that Reagan had appointed, which I thought was good. We had another guy that I think Jimmy Carter or Clinton had appointed, he was a black judge, and

I figured we were going to lose there. Then we had another guy that Nixon had appointed, but he was Jewish. And the comments around what you could or couldn't say, invoking the name of Jesus Christ, you can kind of guess how he was going to vote. So we lost that case, two to one. So then we appealed it *en banc,* which went to the full Fifth Circuit, and we lost that, they didn't want to hear the case, by a vote of ten to eight, pretty much broken down on ideology, I believe. And so we appealed to the Supreme Court. We knew we had a good chance, even though the Supreme Court only takes about 1 or 2 percent of the cases on appeal. And the reason we thought we had a good chance was because there was this conflict between rulings of the Eleventh Circuit, over in Florida and Alabama. There were several cases that were in conflict.

When we decided to appeal to the Supreme Court, I contacted Jay Sekulow at the American Center for Law and Justice, who's their chief counsel in Washington, D.C. I had started watching Jay on *The 700 Club* from time to time; this was five years before I was on the board. I was just fascinated with his grasp of constitutional law, and he was very good. I had wanted Jay from the start. In between the time we were going between the federal district court and the Fifth Circuit, I made a couple of calls there to see if they were interested, and they weren't interested at the time, they were interested in some other cases, but they were going to closely follow ours. And right after we were granted our appeal to the Supreme Court, we got a call from them, and they were interested in coming to our aid. The lawyers at Bracewell and Patterson were fairly polite about this. They had wanted to argue the case; in fact, they had set up John Cornyn to help argue the case, who was attorney general of Texas at that time. I got a call from the attorney general when I was at work, begging to argue ten minutes of the case. Myself and Mike Lopez had followed Jay Sekulow for a long time; of course, he had more success and argued many more cases before the Supreme Court than Bracewell and Patterson. And that was the logic that we used to convince the rest of the board: This is the guy that we want. He'd won the *Mergens* case, and the *Lamb's Chapel* case, and several others. It just seemed like he was the right guy to argue the case; he had high stature.

I went to the Supreme Court arguments in our case. It was really fascinating. You go in there and there's so much history. It was like a dream come true; I'd studied this stuff, and I was interested in history and politics and where the country was going. And just to be there, I had a sense of unbelievable humility. I remember sitting down and looking around the courtroom, and you see the Ten Commandments there. It just seemed like a huge mistake—having the Ten Commandments there, and here we're arguing about students being able to decide for themselves to have a specific message before a football game or before a graduation ceremony. At the football games, the students were praying for nobody to get hurt, setting an appropriate atmosphere for good sportsmanship. For me, that was a very positive thing, and to think that somebody might feel coerced or have some objection to a prayer at a football game or at graduation was just hard for me to fathom.

I had been studying the Supreme Court for years; I knew all the philosophies of the justices. I knew that, going into this case, there were four big-time liberals, there were two moderates, and there were three conservatives. And we had to get both of the moderates. I remember one of the justices asked Jay, Why would you have the students elect this person? I guess they were driving the point home about minority versus majority. But the example that he gave was, Why wouldn't you have the captain of the football team give the prayer? And I'm sitting there thinking, That's kind of an asinine question. I thought the whole line of questioning was just asinine. Can you not have a message before the game, or possibly a prayer, because one or two students don't want it? I mean, you're kind of inflicting the minority's will over the majority. And the argument the whole time was that kids or young adults are subjected in the school to things that they object to all the time.

I was worried when we left there, because of the responses from Kennedy and O'Connor. I pretty much knew we had the other three, because they're strict constructionists. I knew, the other four, they were from the other end, for sure. If you look at the arguments, the opposite side as well as the Court, the majority opinion focused on the word "benediction." In fact, several experts said that if we'd just had the word "message" in our policy, we'd have been able to win our case. I don't know if I believe that or not. I suggested that to our lawyers, way back when the case was in the district court. I said, You look at the word "benediction," it doesn't have to mean "prayer." Why don't we put the word "message" in there? I thought it was just ridiculous that the judges focused on the word "benediction."

After the Supreme Court ruled against us, on the most part, people in Santa Fe were really disappointed, they were really dejected, they were probably tired of hearing about it for so long. After the decision, *Newsweek* had an article on Santa Fe and had a poll that showed 65 percent of the public supported prayer at the games. Here's the important point that a lot of people don't realize: when people find out it was student-led, and student-initiated, and the kids themselves decided to vote, the numbers go even higher. If the true facts are known, the kids vote on it, they don't have to give a prayer, they can give a message, people start to say, That seems reasonable. There's a really small percentage of the public that thought that was unfair.

I think the real battle now is over the courts. That's what the liberal movement has done now. Obviously, they've lost Congress, they lost the presidency, most of the state legislatures. The only place they have left to fight this, and they learned this a long time ago, is they just litigate, and they'll shop around and find a judge that they want, and they'll push until they win. Conservatives just don't play hardball like the liberals play. I think they did a great job with these last two, Roberts and Alito, where the conservatives kind of woke up and said, We want these guys here. I still don't think they get quite as nasty as the liberals, nothing like they did to some of Bush's nominees—they were just smeared. I think it backfired with Alito; he was a very honorable man.

Looking at the future of the Supreme Court, in my opinion it's always going to boil down to which justices you have on the Court. With Alito going there in place of O'Connor, that's a shift. You've got a solid conservative now, from what I understand, versus what O'Connor was standing for. It's four and four and one now, depending on which side of the road Kennedy's going to stand on. If *Santa Fe versus Doe* went to the Court today, we probably wouldn't win, we'd lose five to four. That's unfortunate. I think the appellate courts have become more conservative, with President Bush's nominations. If we went back to the Fifth Circuit now, we'd probably have a better chance of winning. My big hope is that Bush will get another chance here to name another Supreme Court justice, or perhaps two. Or, in 2008, we get another conservative president. If that happens, there are plenty of schools out there, waiting to litigate this. It's just a matter of time. I kind of doubt that Santa Fe would go down that road; I think there are other schools that would stand in line. We had scores and scores and scores of schools that wrote us and said, We're with you.

But things aren't really going to change unless you have a philosophical change in the Court. Obviously, we went for a couple of hundred years without these kinds of cases reaching the Supreme Court. Some of these cases did reach the Supreme Court; there's precedents saying that God and religion was a big part of our society. We just tend not to look at those, because they're not as recent as some of the other cases. And the overriding thing that really bugs me about these cases in the last fifty years is, why aren't they taking history, and precedent, and court cases early on, why doesn't that play into any of this? And I'm afraid that what it amounts to is whether you have a liberal, activist type mentality, or whether you've got a strict constructionist mentality. Does the Constitution mean what it meant back when the Founding Fathers were there, or does it mean that this is a living, breathing document, and judges can decide what it means today? And I think we're on a very dangerous path if we go down to this idea of a living, breathing document that means what one judge thinks it means. I'm really very fearful. ❖

Chapter 6

"I Am the Lord Thy God"

The Ten Commandments Cases from Kentucky and Texas

Whitley City, Kentucky, is not really a city at all. Just eight miles from the state's southeastern border with Tennessee, it is barely more than a village, with only eleven hundred residents, spread out on both sides of the Norfolk & Southern Railway tracks and Highway 27, a two-lane road that stretches from Miami to the Canadian border in northern Michigan. Despite its small population, Whitley City is the largest town in McCreary County, which itself has only seventeen thousand citizens, most of whom live in hamlets with names like Honeybee and Pine Knot. Whitley City houses the county's government in a two-story brick courthouse on Main Street, topped by a white spire and fronted with an American flag. The county's residents visit the courthouse to pay their property taxes, obtain copies of birth and death records, and perform jury service in cases that rarely generate headlines outside the local newspapers.

Before the fall of 1999, no big-city reporters or television crews had reported anything from McCreary County. But they descended on Whitley City in droves after county officials provoked a six-year legal battle that began in the Main Street courthouse and ended in the chamber of the United States Supreme Court. What began with a simple act—posting a copy of the Ten Commandments on the courthouse wall—produced a decision in June 2005 that upheld lower-court orders to remove the Decalogue from the wall. The McCreary County decision, and the Court's seemingly inconsistent ruling in a companion case from Texas, allowing the display of a Ten Commandments monument on the state-capitol grounds, revealed the continuing judicial debate over the proper role of religion in the public square. But the vast majority of McCreary County residents had no interest in that debate. Eric Williams, who works for the U.S. Forest Service, voiced the prevailing reaction to the decision: "This is the Supreme Court interfering with small-town America's business, where the people were happy with the Ten Commandments."

Visitors to Whitley City pass a billboard on Highway 27 that reflects the deep-rooted beliefs of its people: "WARNING. Jesus is coming. RU ready?" This is hard-shell Baptist country. Some thirty-four hundred of McCreary County's four thousand churchgoers attend services at one of the nine Southern Baptist churches; while another three hundred are Methodists; and most of the rest belong to the Church of God and smaller Pentecostal churches. The county has only one Catholic church, with fifty-five members, and a small Mormon congregation. The nearest Jewish synagogue is more than sixty miles away, across the county's border, in Knoxville, Tennessee.

Not only are most of McCreary County's residents evangelical Protestants, they are unabashedly patriotic and politically conservative. During World War II, more than half of the county's young men volunteered for service; of these 923 soldiers, thirty-two lost their lives in battle. Seven died in the Korean War, another eight in Vietnam. More recently, 162 men and women have served in the conflicts in Afghanistan and Iraq. Members of American Legion Post 115 conduct annual memorial services for those who died in the nation's wars, featuring patriotic speeches and Christian prayer. Not surprisingly, fundamentalist religion and fervent nationalism have combined in McCreary County to make it a conservative Republican stronghold, a political tradition that goes back to the Civil War. Although Kentucky was a slave state, the people in the eastern counties backed the Union and voted for Abraham Lincoln. Virtually all of the region's elected officials are Republicans, and McCreary County voters backed President George W. Bush in 2004 by a three-to-one margin over Senator John Kerry.

McCreary County is also mountain country, and many of its residents proudly trace their ancestry to the settlers who followed Daniel Boone across the Cumberland Mountains in the early nineteenth century. Until the 1960s, the county had a thriving economy, as railroad cars and trucks carried away millions of tons of coal and lumber from the mines and forests in the region. Competition from strip mines, however, along with the federal government's purchase of 70 percent of the county's land for the Daniel Boone National Forest, closed most of the mines and sawmills, leaving the county government and the Forest Service as the leading employers.

Although tourism, spurred by the opening of the Big South Fork River national park in 1974, has created some jobs, McCreary County remains an economic backwater. The per-capita income of the county's residents is less than half the national average; close to half of families with children under eighteen live below the poverty line, rising to 72 percent of those with children under five. More than a third of the county's adults lack high-school diplomas, and the high-school dropout rate is double the state average. With few prospects of well-paying jobs in the county, many of those who do graduate move to more prosperous areas. Those who stay are often unemployed, but they remain loyal to their ancestral home. "If things get terribly bad," one recent visitor wrote, "GMAC takes back the four wheel drive pickup, City Corp gets the television and stereo, and the bank gets the sofa. With replacements from second-hand stores and neighbors or family, burning wood and coal for heat, and keeping a good garden, extended periods of unemployment can be tolerated, though rarely enjoyed."

In short, McCreary County's residents are deeply religious, patriotic, conservative, and resilient. These factors help to explain why Jimmie Greene did not anticipate any objections when he posted the Ten Commandments on the courthouse wall on September 14, 1999. Greene, who headed the county's governing board, the Fiscal Court, had the title of "Judge-Executive," although he performed no judicial functions. The posting ceremony, attended by American Legion members and local pastors, was featured in the local newspaper, the *McCreary County*

Record. Greene was surprised when he received a letter, a few weeks later, from the American Civil Liberties Union office in Louisville. The ACLU's state director, Jeff Vessels, warned Greene that posting the Ten Commandments in the courthouse was unconstitutional, and demanded that the framed copy be removed. Vessels cited a 1980 Supreme Court decision, *Stone v. Graham*, which struck down a Kentucky law requiring public schools to post copies of the Ten Commandments on classroom walls. The national ACLU had recently launched a legal campaign against Ten Commandments displays in schools, parks, and public buildings, and its Kentucky branch had been monitoring the state's newspapers for reports of postings like that in McCreary County.

Jimmie Greene bristled when he received Vessels's letter. Born in 1928, Jimmie had family roots deep in the county's rugged terrain, although he left as a young man to enlist in the Air Force, served in both the Korean and Vietnam wars, and retired after twenty-four years with the rank of master sergeant. When he returned home, Greene became active in Republican politics, and was elected in 1978 to head the county's government. A lifelong Baptist and longtime American Legionnaire, Greene viewed the ACLU's demand as challenging both his faith and his patriotism. "America was based on Christianity," he later said. "I respect other religions, but historically they had nothing to do with the founding of America." Greene noted that he posted the Ten Commandments next to other records of the county's history on the courthouse wall. "I spent twenty-four years of my life defending those documents," he added, "and it hurts me, angers me that we have liberal institutions that are trying to rewrite American history."

Jimmie Greene was not the only Kentucky official who received a letter from Jeff Vessels. The ACLU had collected reports that more than a dozen counties had posted the Ten Commandments on courthouse walls, and warned them of possible lawsuits if they were not removed. Darrell BeShears, whom Greene knew well as Judge-Executive of neighboring Pulaski County, also received Vessels's threat of litigation. The two men did not respond to the letters. But they soon learned that Vessels had not issued an idle threat. On November 18, 1999, the Kentucky

ACLU filed suits in federal court against both McCreary and Pulaski counties, naming Greene and BeShears as defendants.

Greene was surprised to learn that he had been sued for an act of which he was proud. He was even more surprised that one of the two individual plaintiffs in the ACLU suit was his own cousin, Louanne Walker. "I was kind of shocked," Greene told a reporter. "Her mother and father are my aunt and uncle, who happen to be buried in a little plot on the family property. I went out there the other day to visit them, 'cause I thought they might be rolling over in their graves." On her part, Walker confessed that she had expected criticism from family and neighbors. "You know, this is a small county, and I'd say most of the people here are in favor of having the Ten Commandments posted in the courthouse," she said. "I hope they realize this is not a statement about the Ten Commandments. I'm not against the Ten Commandments. I'm just a firm believer in separation of church and state."

Shy with the press, Walker allowed her fellow plaintiff, Dave Howe, to field the media inquiries about the lawsuit. Raised in upstate New York, the son of a Baptist minister, Howe was used to reporters and microphones. A radio disk-jockey, he moved to McCreary County in the 1960s, playing bluegrass and old-time country music on WHAY in Whitley City, whose studio is just down Main Street from the courthouse. Despite his thirty-year residence in the county, Howe said, many people still considered him an outsider and a radical. "I'm not a member of the 12 tribes of McCreary County," he joked. On a more serious note, Howe explained his reasons for challenging the Ten Commandments display. When he saw the Commandments on the courthouse wall, he said, "I felt that they were violating the law." Howe, like Walker, had no quarrel with the Commandments as a moral guide. "Don't take them out of your heart, don't take them out of your home, don't take them out of your church," he said. "But don't put them in my face in the courthouse."

Jimmie Greene, who put the Commandments in the courthouse, pushed back against the ACLU lawsuit. "I think the moral decay of America and the filth we see on television and read in print has reached a degree that folk, whether they believe in the Ten Commandments or not, say we have to put a stop to it," he said. "I'm not going to take them down. It's going to take the big man in the black robe to tell me to take them down." Despite the belligerent tone on both sides, however, the suit did not provoke the kind of community tension and personal animosity that marked similar disputes in other towns. Greene calls Dave Howe "a fine friend" and is a welcome visitor at Howe's home in Parkers Lake, next to the Baptist church that Greene attends every Sunday. Howe says he never faced any hostility during the six-year legal battle over the Commandments. "People down here have been very Christian," he said. "They disagree with my position, but they're tolerant." Greene's cousin, Louanne Walker, adds that "I haven't had any negative feedback" from her role in the case.

———

Before the McCreary and Pulaski cases reached their first courtroom hearing, Jimmie Greene and Darrell BeShears took identical steps that would later prove significant in judicial decisions. Their respective county attorneys, who mostly handled state-law cases that raised no federal constitutional issues, stepped aside in the Commandments cases. On December 8, 1999, Greene and BeShears announced that Ronald D. Ray would represent the counties in federal court. A retired Marine Corps colonel, with Bronze and Silver Stars from Vietnam combat service, and a former deputy assistant secretary of defense during the Reagan administration, Ray was also a vocal supporter of Alabama judge Roy Moore. Known as the "Ten Commandments judge," Moore was then embroiled in controversy over posting the Commandments in his courtroom, and would later be removed as Alabama's chief justice for defying federal court orders to remove a two-ton granite Commandments monument from the state Supreme Court rotunda.

Although Ray believed the Commandments should remain in the courthouses, he advised Greene and BeShears that their displays would more likely survive judicial scrutiny if they were enlarged to include other "historical" documents. Ray knew that ACLU lawyers would rely on the Supreme Court's 1980 decision in the *Stone* case, ruling against display of the Ten Commandments in Kentucky schools. He also knew the Court had ruled in 1984 that officials in Pawtucket, Rhode Island, could allow the Christmastime display of a Nativity crèche in a city park, along with such "secular" symbols of the holiday season as candy canes, reindeer, and Santa Claus. And in 1989, although the Court found unconstitutional a stand-alone crèche in a Pennsylvania courthouse, the justices upheld the nearby display of a Jewish menorah, flanked by a Christmas tree. These were not permanent displays, of course, and reindeer and candy canes did not send the "undeniable" religious message of the Ten Commandments, as the Court had said in its *Stone* decision. But these later cases offered Ray a chance to argue that "expanded" courthouse displays would pass constitutional muster.

Yielding to Ray's advice, Greene and BeShears first persuaded the two counties' governing bodies to adopt identical resolutions, stating that the Ten Commandments were "codified in Kentucky's civil and criminal laws" and that they "agree with the arguments set out by Judge Moore" in defending his courtroom Commandments display, citing "the duty of elected officials to publicly acknowledge God as the source of America's strength and direction." Greene and BeShears then placed eight framed documents on either side of the Commandments in their courthouses. These included excerpts from the Declaration of Independence, the national motto of "In God We Trust," a statement by Abraham Lincoln that "the Bible is the best gift God has ever given to man," and the Mayflower Compact. But these documents, unlike reindeer and candy canes, all contained references to God. They added, in fact, even more courthouse religion to the Commandments displays. Ray, however, assured his clients that the expanded displays were protected by Supreme Court precedent, and promptly filed a motion to dismiss the ACLU lawsuits, arguing that Greene and BeShears had "done nothing wrong" in posting the expanded displays.

The question of whether the county officials had done anything wrong came before federal district judge Jennifer Coffman at a hearing on April 20, 2000. Colonel Ray—the title he insisted on using—would certainly not have picked Coffman to decide the Commandments cases. Named by President Bill Clinton in 1993 as Kentucky's first female federal judge, she was a Democrat and had represented plaintiffs in employment-discrimination cases before joining the bench. Ray also faced a formidable courtroom adversary in David Friedman, who argued for the ACLU's plaintiffs. A partner in a prestigious Louisville firm, Friedman had fifteen years of experience as an ACLU volunteer counsel, defending clients from Republican state officials to Ku Klux Klan members. "My client is the Bill of Rights," Friedman says. Even lawyers who opposed him in other Ten Commandments cases praise Friedman; Francis Manion of the conservative American Center for Law and Justice calls him "everything you want in an honorable adversary."

Ray had a hard row to hoe in the hearing before Judge Coffman, and probably hurt his clients by asking her to consider an eighty-page affidavit from Judge Roy Moore, then campaigning for election as Alabama's chief justice. On his part, Friedman cited the affidavit, and the county resolutions praising Moore, as evidence of the religious motives behind the Commandments displays. "There's no question here why these were put up," he said of the documents that Greene and BeShears had posted along with the Commandments. "The ACLU threw everything but the kitchen sink at Judge Moore, and the Ten Commandments are still on his courthouse wall," Ray replied. "There's no difference between a courtroom in Alabama and a courtroom in Kentucky." Ray also charged the ACLU with "censorship" of the nation's religious history. "The history speaks for itself," he said. "If you stand on history, it's clear we're a Christian nation."

Ray's overtly religious appeal did not impress Judge Coffman. Two weeks after the hearing, on May 5, she handed down an opinion that gave Friedman a hands-down victory, denying Ray's motion to dismiss the cases and ordering McCreary and Pulaski county officials to remove the courthouse documents "immediately" and not erect any "similar displays" in the future. "While a display of some of these documents may not have the effect of endorsing religion in another context," she wrote, "they collectively have the overwhelming effect of endorsing religion in the context of these displays. Each and every document refers to religion. Several have been edited to include only their religious references.

Indeed, the only unifying element among the documents is their reference to God, the Bible, or religion."

Faced with Judge Coffman's order to remove the documents from their courthouses, McCreary and Pulaski county officials had little choice but to comply. "I believe in obeying the rules," said Darrell BeShears, who removed his county's display with no fanfare. Jimmie Greene, however, refused to do the job himself. "I said early on that I would not remove them, and I will not," he told reporters. "I'll go to jail before I take them down. This is one order I will not obey. I'm a law-abiding citizen, but there is a higher power. Could you think of a better reason to go to jail than standing up in defense of the Ten Commandments?" Greene left the unpleasant task to Paul Worthington, commander of Whitley City's American Legion Post, who removed the courthouse display at a ceremony attended by three hundred people, many wearing T-shirts bearing the Ten Commandments. Worthington moved the display to the Legion's building; Greene vowed to appeal Coffman's order to the Supreme Court if necessary. "We're either going to win and America is going to be the winner," he said, "or America is going to hell in a hand basket. We've got to win this."

———

Winning the battle to return the Ten Commandments to the McCreary and Pulaski courthouses seemed a daunting task, considering the firm legal foundation of Judge Coffman's opinion on Supreme Court precedent in Establishment Clause cases. Compounding the problem was the realization by Greene and BeShears that Ronald Ray had virtually handed David Friedman a victory with his "Christian nation" argument. However much they agreed with Ray, federal appellate-court judges were unlikely to give any weight to such an obviously sectarian argument. Ray had, however, filed an appeal with the Sixth Circuit Court of Appeals in Cincinnati, Ohio, which gave Greene and BeShears time to ponder their next move. Out of the blue, they received an offer of help from a Florida lawyer, Mathew Staver.

Like their adversaries in the ACLU and other groups committed to church-state separation, lawyers in Religious Right groups monitor the media for news of cases that fit their agendas. Staver headed Liberty Counsel, the legal group founded by Jerry Falwell, the Baptist preacher and televangelist who gained prominence in the 1980s by creating the Moral Majority, whose evangelical Christian members became a political force in Republican politics. "The idea of separation of church and state," Falwell charged, "was invented by the Devil to keep Christians from running their own country." Mat Staver, who left a successful law practice in 1994 to pursue his Christian goals through Liberty Counsel, has focused most of his efforts on campaigns against gay marriage and abortion. But the Ten Commandments cases struck him as a chance to open another front in the "cultural war" in which he had enlisted as a legal warrior. With a staff of twenty lawyers and an annual budget of $1.4 million, Liberty Counsel could offer Greene and BeShears more clout than Ronald Ray's one-man practice.

Staver also had an idea the Kentucky officials found attractive. He proposed a third courthouse display, in which the Ten Commandments would be flanked, not by religious statements, but with "documents that played a significant role in the foundation of our system of law and government." Greene and BeShears liked the idea, and erected new displays on their courthouse walls, including copies of the Magna Carta, the Declaration of Independence, the Bill of Rights, and all four verses of "The Star-Spangled Banner." Posters next to each courthouse exhibit identified the documents as "Foundations of American Law and Government Display."

After the third displays were in place, Staver dismissed the Sixth Circuit appeal and asked Judge Coffman for a "clarification" of her order, which she denied in September 2000, saying her order "speaks for itself." David Friedman countered with a motion to hold the county officials in contempt of the order barring them from erecting "similar displays" that included the Ten Commandments. Ruling on March 30, 2001, Coffman denied the contempt motion and urged Staver and Friedman to settle the cases by April 30. Basically, she was asking Friedman to agree that the third display conformed to Supreme Court precedent that allowed religious symbols in public places if they were flanked by "secular" items and images. Not surprisingly, Friedman did not agree, reporting that he and Staver could not settle the cases. After hearing arguments from both lawyers, Coffman issued another opinion, on June 22, 2001, ruling that the new displays were a "sham," designed to shield the Commandments behind a façade of supposedly "secular" documents. Rather than shielding the Commandments poster, Coffman explained in her opinion, "placing it among these patriotic and political documents, with no other religious or moral codes, imbues it with a national significance constituting endorsement" of its religious message by county officials.

For a second time in little over a year, the Commandments were removed from the two Kentucky courthouses. David Friedman, who grew up in New York City and is a die-hard Yankees fan, knew that the baseball rule of "three strikes and you're out" does not apply to lawsuits. As he expected, Mat Staver filed a new appeal with the Sixth Circuit in Cincinnati, but the legal equivalent of a rain delay held up arguments in the cases for eighteen months, until December 2002, and another year passed before the three-judge panel issued its ruling on December 18, 2003. Just a month earlier, in what might be seen as an omen, Roy Moore had lost his post as Alabama's chief justice for defying federal court orders to remove the Ten Commandments monument he had placed in the state Supreme Court building.

The long-awaited ruling on the McCreary and Pulaski county cases handed Friedman another victory, this time by a split decision. Judge Eric L. Clay, placed on the bench by President Clinton in 1997, wrote for the two-to-one majority. He upheld Judge Coffman's decision, but focused on an issue her opinion had not addressed. Clay quoted from the poster the counties had placed next to their "Foundations" displays: "The Ten Commandments provide the moral background of the Declaration of Independence and the foundation of our legal tradition," words that Mat Staver had likely composed. Clay found nothing in the display that connected the two documents, and cited historians who asserted that Thomas Jefferson, the Declaration's primary author, did not believe in "the God of the Bible (and thus the Ten Commandments), but the God of Deism." Jefferson "was most inspired by contemporaneous political writings as well as the musings of European philosophers and writers," Clay wrote, finding a "patently religious purpose" behind the "Foundations" display.

The sole dissenter, Judge James L. Ryan, almost sneered at Clay's historical excursions. Named to the bench by President Reagan in 1985, Ryan belonged to the Federalist Society, an influential group of conservative lawyers and judges. Clay's opinion, he wrote, attributed to viewers of the "Foundations" display, and by inference to Clay himself, "an utter lack of common sense, a profound ignorance of American history, and, arguably, an outright hostility to religion in our nation's public life." No courthouse visitor, Ryan continued, "could fail to appreciate what, apparently, my colleague does not: that from the founding of our republic, religion was and always has been, an inherent component of the law and culture of our pluralistic society, and that saying so in the public square *acknowledges* religion, but does not *endorse* it."

On his part, David Friedman exulted in his victory. "The court has rousingly endorsed the principles of religious freedom and rousingly endorsed the requirement that government remain neutral toward religion," he said. "We are delighted with the opinion." Telling reporters "the case is far from over," Mat Staver asked for an *en banc* review of the panel decision by the full court, but the judges turned him down on March 23, 2004. The next step was to petition the Supreme Court for review, normally a long shot, since the justices turn down almost 98 percent of these petitions. But Staver's odds improved dramatically on March 31, when lawyers for Texas governor Rick Perry asked the Court to review a Fifth Circuit decision upholding a Ten Commandments display on the state-capitol grounds in Austin, Texas. Staver filed his petition on June 21, and waited anxiously until the Court granted review in both cases on October 12, setting oral argument for March 2, 2005.

––––

It would be difficult to find any place in the United States more unlike Whitley City, Kentucky, than Austin, the state capital of Texas. For one thing, Austin is six hundred times larger in population, with 657,000 residents, making it the fourth-largest city in Texas and the sixteenth-largest in the nation, circled by a metropolitan area that includes another eight hundred thousand people. Austin's colorful history has shaped its growth from a small town, first settled in the 1830s by what are now called "Anglos," into a diverse and very distinctive city. Originally part of Mexico, Austin became the capital of an independent nation when the Anglos broke away from Mexico and established the independent "Republic of Texas" in 1836. Austin remained the capital after Texas relinquished its independence and was annexed by the United States in 1845. The Civil War made Austin the capital of a Confederate state, after Texas seceded from the Union in 1861. The city's fourth role as a capital came in 1870, when Congress readmitted Texas to the Union.

Austin's shifting relations with Mexico, the Republic of Texas, the Civil War Confederacy, and the reunited American states have all contributed to the city's present composition and culture, and to its status as a liberal enclave in a conservative state. More than a third of Austin's residents are Hispanic, and 10 percent are black; in fact, non-Hispanic whites constitute just 53 percent of the city's population. The biggest institution in Austin, and the major influence on its economy, politics, and culture, is the University of Texas, established in 1883 and now enrolling some forty-nine thousand students. With almost three thousand faculty and seventeen thousand staff members, the UT campus dominates Austin and is the city's largest employer. The university's science and technology programs have attracted high-tech industry to Austin and its suburbs, including Dell, IBM, Apple Computers, and National Instruments. The people who work in these businesses are well educated and affluent; more than half of Austin's white residents have college degrees, and the median family income is fifty-four thousand dollars. Only 9 percent of Austin's families, mostly Hispanic and black, live below the poverty line.

Whitley City and Austin also differ in religion and politics. Catholics, most of them Hispanic, are the largest religious group in Austin, but the city also has more than ten thousand Jewish residents, who attend eleven synagogues, and there are also Buddhist and Hindu temples. Texas, of course, is now a solidly Republican state, and creative gerrymandering has given the GOP control of its legislature and congressional delegation. But Austin remains a Democratic bastion; in the 2004 presidential election, almost 70 percent of its voters supported John Kerry over George W. Bush. In short, unlike those in Whitley City, Austin's residents are diverse in race and ethnicity, affluent and well educated, and liberal in politics. The only link between the big Texas city and the small Kentucky town is that the Supreme Court heard arguments, on the same day in March 2005, over Ten Commandments displays in both places.

———

Every day, thousands of people enter the Texas State Capitol in Austin, a domed edifice that was reputedly the seventh-largest building in the world when it was erected in 1888. Some are legislators, others work in state offices, and many are tourists who gather in the giant rotunda and take guided tours around the building. Many of these people also stroll around the capitol's parklike grounds, which cover twenty-two acres in the city's center. Scattered around the grounds are seventeen monuments and twenty-two historical markers. The monuments, some exceeding thirty feet in height, include statues that celebrate the "Heroes of the Alamo," the fabled Texas Rangers, Confederate soldiers, pioneer women, and Texas cowboys. Somewhat out of place, in this commemoration of Texas history, is a replica of the Statue of Liberty in New York City. Also out of place, in the mind of one frequent visitor to the capitol grounds, is a granite slab, six feet high and three feet wide, shielded by hedges from sight of the surrounding monuments. Carved into the slab is the text of the Ten Commandments, headed by the words "I AM the LORD thy God." The inscription at its base reads, "Presented to the People and Youth of Texas by the Fraternal Order of Eagles of Texas 1961."

Thomas Van Orden is an unusual man, and seemingly an unlikely person to file a lawsuit that wound up in the Supreme Court. He is homeless and jobless, and sleeps in a tent, where he stores his bedding and belongings. Every couple of weeks, he visits the Austin Resource

Center for the Homeless, where he showers and washes his laundry. He gets by, as the Beatles song goes, "with a little help from my friends," who donate food and a little cash. Van Orden, however, is not a stereotypical homeless person, strung out on alcohol or drugs. Until 1999, in fact, he was a member of the Texas State Bar, a 1970 graduate of Southern Methodist University's law school. During 1971 and 1972, he served in Vietnam, first as a helicopter door gunner and later in the Judge Advocate General's corps. After his discharge, Van Orden returned to Texas, got married, and practiced criminal-defense law in Houston and Dallas.

But after Van Orden got divorced and moved to Austin in 1993, things turned bad. He fell into a deep depression and got behind in his legal work. The state bar suspended his license in 1995, charging him with failing to perform work for clients and to pay his bar dues. The bar order also required Van Orden to submit a psychiatric report, certifying that his "current state of mental health does not render him incapable of routine law practice," as a condition of regaining his license. After a three-month suspension, followed by forty-five months of probation, he returned to practice, but was again disciplined in 1999 for failing to report to bar officials who supervised his probation. Van Orden's license was lifted for another forty-five months, until September 2003. But he decided not to return to law practice. "I went through a real hard period and I'm not going back there," he told a reporter, declining to discuss any aspect of his personal life except to say that he had overcome his depression.

Jobless and homeless, Van Orden began spending his days in the Texas State Law Library, housed in the state Supreme Court building, just a few hundred feet from the capitol building. He kept up with legal decisions, especially First Amendment cases. "I'm happy when I get to the library in the morning," he said. "The ordeal of the night is over, and I'm back in a nice environment doing something I enjoy."

Two things happened in the fall of 2001 that gave Van Orden something to enjoy. First, he read a decision in which the Seventh Circuit federal appellate court had ruled unconstitutional a Ten Commandments monument on the Indiana State Capitol grounds. That got him to thinking about the granite slab he passed every time he walked through the capitol grounds to the law library. Van Orden delved into law books, found other cases ruling against Ten Commandments monuments and displays, and decided to file a lawsuit in Austin's federal court. Texas governor Rick Perry, a conservative Republican, headed the list of defendants, along with state officials who administered the capitol grounds. Van Orden filed his suit in February 2002, claiming that the Ten Commandments monument violated the Establishment of Religion Clause of the First Amendment and that he was harmed by having to pass it on his trips to the law library. The district-court clerk waived the filing fee, certifying that Van Orden was a pauper, and he used a four-dollar disposable camera to take pictures of the monument that he attached to his complaint. Raised as a Methodist and later a member of Austin's Unitarian church, Van Orden subsequently explained his motives in bringing the suit. "I didn't sue the Ten Commandments," he said. "I didn't sue Christianity. I sued the state for putting a religious monument on Capitol grounds. It is a message of discrimination. Government has to remain neutral."

Van Orden walked to the federal courthouse for the first hearing on his suit in July 2002, to argue the case himself. The case was assigned to Harry Lee Hudspeth, a senior district judge who had been named to the bench in 1979 by President Jimmy Carter. Although he denied the state's motion to dismiss the case, Hudspeth ruled for the state in his decision, handed down three months later, in October. He applied the three-pronged test established by the 1971 Supreme Court ruling in *Lemon v. Kurtzman*, the decision that struck down public funding for religious schools. The first prong of the *Lemon* test required the state to show a "secular purpose" for erecting the Ten Commandments monument. The state's lawyer referred Judge Hudspeth to a 1961 legislative resolution commending the Eagles for their efforts "to reduce juvenile delinquency." Presumably, young people who viewed the monument would heed its admonitions and behave properly. In his opinion, Hudspeth gave the state a passing grade on this part of the test; the resolution, he wrote, "makes no reference to religion" and showed "a valid secular purpose" in placing the monument on capitol grounds. The second *Lemon* prong bars government actions that have the "primary effect" of promoting religion. Noting that the monument was only one of seventeen on the capitol grounds, Hudspeth ruled that a "reasonable observer" would not "conclude that the state is seeking to advance, endorse, or promote religion by permitting the display." The final *Lemon* prong prohibited "excessive government entanglement" with the monument, which Van Orden conceded it did not.

The Ten Commandments monument passed its first judicial test, and Van Orden would keep passing it while he prepared an appeal to the Fifth Circuit, for a hearing in early 2003. He recruited two University of Texas law students to help with research, and hitched a ride with one for the arguments in New Orleans. The Fifth Circuit was notably conservative, and Van Orden drew a three-judge panel headed by Patrick Higginbotham, named to the court by President Reagan in 1982 and one of its most conservative members. Van Orden knew his Fifth Circuit argument would be a challenge: "It's like I'm appealing to the damn Southern Baptist Convention down there," he said. He was right. Ruling on November 12, 2003, Higginbotham spoke for all three judges in upholding Judge Hudspeth's decision, changing very few of its words. There was nothing in the legislative record, he wrote, "to contradict the secular reasons" for placing the Commandments monument on the capitol grounds to reflect the Eagles' "concern for juvenile delinquency." Higginbotham echoed Hudspeth in concluding that a "reasonable viewer" would look from the monument to the nearby capitol and Supreme Court buildings and recognize its message as "relevant to these law-giving instruments of State government."

Van Orden anticipated this judicial rebuff, but was determined to keep the case going. He returned to the law library and began preparing a petition for Supreme Court review of Higginbotham's decision. The media, even in Austin, had paid little attention to the case before the Fifth Circuit ruling, but word of the "homeless lawyer" drew reporters, who tracked him down in the law library. They treated Van Orden like a sideshow curiosity. A *Los Angeles Times* story set the tone, taking readers into the library. "Inside, a homeless man with tired eyes works at a corner carrel in the basement amid his belongings—a duffel bag with a broken zipper, reading glasses he found in a parking lot, chicken-scratch notes sullied with splashes of instant coffee. His carefully parted hair and striped shirt contrast with his stained teeth and dirty fingernails. Armed with scraps of paper and pens he digs out of the trash, he's been here for two years, trying to define, once and for all, the boundaries of a governmental endorsement of religion."

But the chicken-scratch notes turned into a petition the Supreme Court treated with respect, granting review and giving Van Orden a final shot in his case. He first considered arguing the case himself, but decided to avoid the inevitable "homeless lawyer" stories and seek help from an experienced First Amendment advocate. Out of the blue, he called Erwin Chemerinsky, who then taught constitutional law at the University of Southern California and later moved to Duke University's law school. Chemerinsky, a Harvard Law School graduate, had argued before the Supreme Court and had written more than a hundred law-review articles. Intrigued by Van Orden's case, he readily agreed to help with his brief and argue for him. Initially, the two men communicated by e-mail, between Chemerinsky's office and the public computers in the Texas State Law Library.

In November 2004, a year after Van Orden first called him, Chemerinsky flew to Austin to meet his client in person and view the Commandments monument on the capitol grounds. "I have nothing but the greatest admiration and respect for him," he later said of Van Orden. "He genuinely cares about this issue. He's extremely intelligent and articulate, and I think he did an excellent job of briefing and arguing the case on the trial level and the appellate level." On his part, Van Orden sounded bemused that his chicken scratches had led to the Supreme Court. "You can still do it with a piece of paper, a pen and a law book," he said. "But that will be lost in all the hoopla of the Ten Commandments."

———

There was plenty of hoopla when the Supreme Court met for arguments in the Ten Commandments cases from Kentucky and Texas. Hundreds of people, including five busloads from McCreary and Pulaski counties, braved frigid weather and lined up before dawn for seats in the Court's chamber. "They'll stand out in the cold, and they'll do it gladly," declared Jimmie Greene, who had stepped down as McCreary's judge-executive in 2002 and was accompanied by his successor, Blaine Phillips, and by Darrell BeShears, who still headed Pulaski's government. Of the two McCreary County plaintiffs, only Dave Howe came to Washington for the arguments; Louanne Walker decided to avoid the media frenzy at the Court and stayed home in Whitley City. Fearing that reporters and television crews would swarm around the "homeless lawyer" from Austin, Thomas Van Orden turned down Erwin Chemerinsky's offer of a plane ticket to Washington, and sat on a park bench during arguments in his case.

Only eight justices sat behind the Court's mahogany bench when the session opened. Chief Justice William Rehnquist, suffering from thyroid cancer, remained home to recuperate from radiation treatment. By tradition, the Court's senior associate justice, John Paul Stevens, presided in his place. The Texas case was first on the docket, and Chemerinsky went first, as counsel for the losing party in the lower court. Aware from experience that justices often pounce on lawyers with critical questions after just a few seconds, he began with a forceful statement: "On the grounds of the Texas State Capitol, there is one evident religious statement that conveys a powerful religious message that there is a theistic God and that God has dictated rules for behavior. Of course, the government may put religious symbols on its property, but must do so in a way that does not endorse religion or a particular religion."

Sure enough, Justice Antonin Scalia quickly pounced on Chemerinsky: "I suppose that opening statement suggests that you think that Thanksgiving proclamations are also unconstitutional, which were recommended by the very first Congress, the same Congress that proposed the First Amendment." Chemerinsky gave up just an inch. "I think the Thanksgiving proclamations would be constitutional," he replied. "I think it's very different than this Ten Commandments monument. Here you have a monument that proclaims not only there is a God, but God has dictated rules of behavior for those who follow him or her."

Chemerinsky knew that Scalia would certainly vote against him, and he waited for questions from the Court's "swing" justices, who could tip its narrow balance in either direction. One of these justices, Sandra Day O'Connor, raised a concern that Chemerinsky had anticipated. "How about if they're packaged in a museum-like setting," she asked of the seventeen monuments on the capitol grounds. "Of course, there can be Ten Commandments or any religious works as part of a museum setting," he conceded. "This isn't a museum setting. Every monument on the State Capitol grounds is there because the State legislature wanted to convey a particular message. This is the only religious message anywhere on the Capitol grounds. The Ten Commandments come from sacred texts."

Justice Anthony Kennedy, another swing vote in First Amendment cases, shifted to another issue that Chemerinsky had anticipated. "This is a classic 'avert your eyes,'" Kennedy said. "If an atheist walked by, he can avert his eyes, he can think of something else." Of course, most people would avoid looking at a message only if they already knew what it said. Chemerinsky, however, did not make this point, asking Kennedy instead to "imagine the Muslim or Buddhist who walks into the State Supreme Court to have his or her case heard. That person will see this monument and realize it's not his or her government." Sharpening his point, Chemerinsky noted that the Texas monument was drawn from Christian versions of the Commandments. "A Jewish individual would walk by this Ten Commandments," he said, "and see that the first commandment isn't the Jewish version, 'I am the Lord, thy God, who took you out of Egypt, out of slavery.'" Justice Scalia jumped back into the argument. "When somebody goes by that monument," he retorted, "I don't think they're studying each one of the commandments. It's a symbol of the fact that government derives its authority from God. And that is, it seems to me, an appropriate symbol to be on state grounds."

Justice Stephen Breyer, who normally voted with the Court's liberals on First Amendment issues, hinted that he might view the Kentucky and Texas cases differently. "I come to the conclusion very tentatively," he told Chemerinsky, that "making a practical judgment in these difficult cases" could best be done by looking at "the divisive quality of the individual display case by case. And when I do that, I don't find much divisiveness here. I would love to hear what you think." Aware that he needed Breyer's vote to prevail, Chemerinsky took a bold step, moving outside the Court's hushed chamber. "The Ten Commandments is enormously divisive right now," he replied. "I don't think we can ignore the social reality. The chief justice of the Alabama Supreme Court resigned, there are crowds outside today. I got hate mail messages this week, not because people care about the Ten Commandments as a secular document, but people care about the Ten Commandments because it's a profound religious message." Whether Justice Breyer loved these thoughts when he voted on the case remained to be seen.

From the first to the last sentence of his argument, Chemerinsky stressed that the Commandments sent a "profound religious message" to viewers of the Texas monument. In his countering argument, the state's attorney general, Greg Abbott, stressed the "secular" message of the Commandments. The Commandments, he asserted, "send a secular message to all the people, whether they are believers or not believers, of the important role the Ten Commandments have played in the development of law." Whatever his colleagues thought of this claim, it struck Justice Scalia as heresy. "It's not a secular message," he replied. "I mean, if you're watering it down to say that the only reason it's okay is it sends nothing but a secular message, I can't agree with you. I think the message it sends is that law and our institutions come from God. And if you don't think it conveys that message, I just think you're kidding yourself."

Watering down the religious message of the Commandments was, in fact, exactly what Abbott was trying to do. He knew Scalia would vote to retain the monument, but he also knew the Court's swing justices might be troubled by that message. Justice O'Connor was the most troubled of this group. She had developed a standard in earlier cases, under which governmental "endorsement" of religious practices or symbols violated the Establishment Clause. O'Connor noted that all seventeen monuments on the capitol grounds had been placed there with legislative approval. "Is that not really some kind of endorsement for each one?" she inquired. Abbott tried to duck the question. The state, he replied, "has specifically endorsed nine of those monuments by putting the state seal" on them. "This monument does not have that kind of endorsement on there." This answer must have satisfied O'Connor, who remained silent for the rest of Abbott's argument.

Justice David Souter, however, remained troubled. "Anyone would reasonably assume that the State of Texas approved this message," he observed, "and thought it was appropriate to devote state property to its promulgation." Abbott replied, "There is a very meaningful difference between acknowledging something and endorsing something." Texas, he added, simply wanted to acknowledge the Commandments "as a well-recognized historical symbol of the law. It is not endorsing the religious text of the Ten Commandments." Abbott, who was disabled and delivered his argument from a wheelchair next to the lectern, drew a genial commendation from Justice Stevens "for demonstrating that it's not necessary to stand at the lectern to do a fine job."

Abbott shared his thirty minutes of argument with Paul Clement, the acting solicitor general in the Justice Department, who appeared as a "friend of the court" in both the Texas and Kentucky cases. Politics and religion had both influenced the Bush administration's decision to send Clement to the Supreme Court. President George W. Bush was eager to curry favor with the evangelical Christians whose votes had ensured his re-election in 2004, and for whom the Ten Commandments were a powerful religious symbol. In addition, Bush himself was a "born-again" Christian, and his attorney general, John Ashcroft, belonged to the Assemblies of God church, the nation's largest Pentecostal denomination. Ashcroft had no trouble persuading Bush to back the defenders of the Commandments in Texas and Kentucky.

When he replaced Abbott at the lectern, Clement asserted that Texas was not "endorsing the religious text of the Ten Commandments" by placing the monument on its capitol grounds. But he also, perhaps unwittingly, walked through the door that Erwin Chemerinsky had opened with his reference to Judge Roy Moore. With Mat Staver sitting behind him, minutes away from arguing the Kentucky cases, Clement suggested that it might be unconstitutional to display the Commandments "in a way that it actually looks like a religious sanctuary within the walls of the courthouse." Justice Anthony Kennedy promptly asked Clement whether such a display would "cross the constitutional line" the Court had drawn in earlier cases. Clement conceded that placing the Commandments in a courthouse, at least by themselves, "probably does cross the constitutional line." He quickly stepped back from the courthouse doorway, adding that "a display of the Ten Commandments in some appropriate way in the courthouse certainly wouldn't cross the line that we would have this Court draw."

———

Minutes after Clement sat down, Mat Staver stood at the lectern to defend the McCreary and Pulaski county officials who had first posted the Commandments on their courthouse walls in 1999, without any surrounding documents. Clement's tacit concession that such a display "probably" violated the Establishment Clause put Staver on the defensive with the first question from the bench. The Kentucky cases, Justice Souter noted, "started out with just the Ten Commandments alone," before other documents were added in the second and third displays. Souter did not conceal his skepticism about the motives behind these "expanded" displays. "Everybody knows what's going on," he told Staver. "Everybody knows that the present context is simply litigation dressing and that the object for what is going on was revealed in the first place. What is your response to that?"

Staver knew that defending the initial "stand-alone" Commandments displays was a lost cause. So he took the unusual tack of casting the blame on Jimmie Greene and Darrell BeShears, sitting behind him in the Court's chamber. "They were sued," he told Souter. "They were not jurists schooled in the law. And admittedly they made a mistake." After the Kentucky ACLU sued them, Greene and BeShears "wanted to figure out how to display this particular document." Staver admitted that "they stepped, however, on a land mine" when they added religious documents to the courthouse displays. "Well, they created the land mine," Souter shot back. With his argument in danger of exploding, Staver tried to distance himself from the first and second Commandments displays. "What they have now," he replied, "is the Foundations display, fundamentally different than any previous display." Souter agreed that the Foundations display "includes a lot of legal documents." But he did not let Staver off the hook. "Is there any reason for anyone to believe," he asked, "that display of legal documents or anything else would be there for any other purpose than the display of the Ten Commandments, including the overtly theistic part of the text?" Staver's reply was, at best, disingenuous. "That religious purpose has been buried and has been abandoned," he said. Greene and BeShears, of course, had neither buried nor abandoned their purpose in posting the Commandments, from the first to the last displays.

Justice Souter was clearly skeptical that adding "secular" documents to the courthouse displays had "buried" the religious purpose behind placing the Commandments at their centers. Under the "purpose" prong of the *Lemon* test, such religious motives would cross the constitutional line. Returning to the lectern after Mat Staver sat down, Paul Clement argued that "a focus on purpose is probably not a prudent exercise of judicial resources." In effect, he urged the justices to ignore the first two Commandments displays and focus on the "secular" purpose of the Foundations displays. Justice Souter was not about to ignore reality. "It would be crazy law from this Court," he told Clement, "that said you can engage in religious endorsement, promotions, et cetera, so long as you hide the ball well enough." Clement made no effort to defend the first two displays, suggesting that "bad legal advice or simply frustration at the first lawsuit being filed" led the Kentucky officials into a constitutional minefield. But, he concluded, "municipalities should be rewarded, not punished, for trying to change their conduct to get things right."

When he replaced Clement at the lectern, David Friedman argued that the Kentucky officials had gotten things wrong from the outset. He pointed the justices to two documents in the case record. The first was the resolution adopted by the McCreary and Pulaski county governing bodies right after the ACLU filed its lawsuit in 1999. "In that resolution," Friedman said, "the counties make clear that they relied on and cited approvingly the Kentucky legislature's reference to Jesus Christ as the Prince of Ethics. They made clear that they supported the fight of Alabama Supreme Court justice Roy Moore against the ACLU. They made absolutely clear that they deemed this to be a Christian nation." Friedman noted that the resolution, designed to justify the second displays, with religious documents flanking the Ten Commandments, had not been rescinded or repealed by either county.

Friedman's second document was the framed text that had been placed next to the "secular" Foundations displays. "It asserts that the Ten Commandments, the revealed word of God, provides the moral background of the Declaration of Independence," Friedman said. In his Sixth Circuit opinion, Judge Clay had subjected the Foundations document to historical scrutiny, finding nothing that connected the Commandments and the Declaration. Putting the county resolutions and the Foundations document together, Friedman argued that "the current courthouse display reveals both a purpose and an effect to endorse religion."

Friedman spoke for more than five minutes before he fielded the first question from the bench. Most lawyers who appear before the Court get nervous if they are not quickly interrupted with questions, fearing the justices might be bored by their arguments, or perhaps had all made up their minds about the case. One justice was clearly not bored, although he clearly had made up his mind. Friedman's argument that the Commandments did not provide "the moral background of the Declaration of Independence" drew a sharp retort from Justice Scalia. "That's idiotic," he said. "What the Commandments stand for is the direction of human affairs by God. And to say that that's the basis of the Declaration of Independence and of our institutions is entirely realistic."

Another justice was not bored, and had earlier hinted that he might view the Texas and Kentucky cases differently. Justice Breyer had told Erwin Chemerinsky that "I don't find much divisiveness" over the Texas monument. Friedman opened this issue in the Kentucky cases, noting "the public reaction" to the ACLU lawsuit, "the letters to the editor, the 'Keep the Ten Commandments' signs on yards throughout the county." Breyer seemed receptive to this issue: "It's easy in this area to become far more divisive than you hoped and really end up with something worse than if you stayed out in the first place. In other words, it's a very delicate matter and it's very easy to offend people." Friedman concluded by saying that McCreary and Pulaski county officials were "simply wrapping the Ten Commandments in the flag and, with all due respect, that constitutes endorsement" of religion.

———

Court-watchers in the media and the legal community were divided over whether the Court would uphold or strike down the Commandments displays in the Kentucky and Texas cases. As it turned out, the justices were also divided, handing down conflicting decisions when they ruled on June 27, 2005. By two separate majorities of five to four, the Court banished the Commandments from the McCreary and Pulaski county courthouses, but allowed the monument to remain on the Texas State Capitol grounds in Austin. The divergent outcomes of the two cases reflected the Court's continuing difficulty in defining a consistent judicial standard in Establishment Clause cases. Rather than finding any "bright line" to guide their interpretation, the justices—as they had in earlier cases—looked to the "context" and "setting" of public displays of religious symbols and sentiments.

Ruling in *McCreary County v. ACLU of Kentucky*, the title for the two Kentucky cases, five justices agreed that the "purpose" behind the courthouse displays was to endorse the religious message of the Commandments. Writing for himself and Justices Ginsburg, Breyer, Stevens, and O'Connor, Justice Souter looked to past cases that mandated governmental "neutrality" in religious matters. That principle was violated "when the government's ostensible purpose is to take sides," Souter wrote. It was clear to him that the counties had taken sides by initially posting, by itself, a religious text that rested its prohibitions "on the sanction of the divinity proclaimed at the beginning of the text." It was also clear to Souter that subsequent displays of more secular documents did not erase the clearly religious purpose of the first, which displayed "an unmistakably religious statement dealing with religious obligations and with morality subject to religious sanction." Souter dismissed the revised displays as a "litigating position" adopted by county officials who "were simply reaching for any way to keep a religious document on the walls of courthouses constitutionally required to embody religious neutrality," concluding, "No reasonable observer could swallow the claim that the counties had cast off the objective so unmistakable in the earlier displays."

The Court's "swing" justices in most religion cases, Sandra Day O'Connor and Anthony Kennedy, swung in opposite directions in the Commandments cases. O'Connor joined the *McCreary County* majority with a separate concurring opinion. "It is true that many Americans find the Commandments in accord with their personal beliefs," she wrote, tacitly acknowledging public support for their display. "But we do not count heads before enforcing the First Amendment," she added. The fact that virtually all McCreary and Pulaski county residents were Christians, although O'Connor did not mention this, could not allow that religious majority to proclaim its beliefs on courthouse walls. The Constitution's religious clauses, she concluded, "protect adherents of all religions, as well as those who believe in no religion at all."

Although Chief Justice Rehnquist had not attended the oral arguments because of illness, he read the transcripts and joined Justice Scalia's dissent in the *McCreary County* case, along with Justices Kennedy and Thomas. Reflecting his view that the Establishment Clause did not protect religious minorities or nonbelievers from majoritarian sentiment, Scalia denounced "the demonstrably false principle that the government cannot favor religion over irreligion." He looked to tradition, beginning with the Thanksgiving proclamation of the First Congress, citing "the interest of the overwhelming majority of religious believers in being able to give God thanks and supplication *as a people*." Scalia recognized the "conflict" between adherents of minority religions and nonbelievers, and the majority that believes in the religious commands of the Decalogue. "Our national tradition has resolved that conflict in favor of the majority," Scalia wrote, adding his view that the Establishment Clause "permits this disregard of polytheists and believers in unconcerned deities, just as it permits the disregard of devout atheists." Unlike Justice O'Connor, Scalia counted heads and found more on the side of the Ten Commandments.

The Supreme Court also counts heads when its members vote on cases. The majority coalition in *McCreary County* shifted to the other side in the Texas case, *Van Orden v. Perry*, with Justice Stephen Breyer casting the deciding vote. This case produced seven opinions among the nine justices, another reflection of judicial discord over the place of religion in the public square. Chief Justice Rehnquist, joined by Scalia, Kennedy, and Thomas, wrote a brief plurality opinion that conceded the "religious significance" of the Commandments. But that did not prohibit their public display. "Acknowledgments of the role played by the Ten Commandments in our Nation's heritage are common throughout America," he wrote. "We need only look within our own Courtroom," pointing to a depiction inside the Court's chamber of Moses holding tablets with the Commandments, and to other displays of the Decalogue in federal buildings around the nation's capital. "Simply having religious content or promoting a religious message consistent with a religious doctrine does not run afoul of the Establishment Clause," Rehnquist concluded.

Justice Breyer did not join Rehnquist's opinion, explaining his position in a separate concurrence. "If the relation between government and religion is one of separation, but not of mutual hostility and suspicion, one will inevitably find difficult borderline cases," he wrote. "The case before us is a borderline case." During oral arguments in the Texas case, Breyer suggested that he was looking for a "practical" solution to the Commandments disputes, expressing concern about the "divisiveness" they created. The factor that most influenced Breyer's vote in the Texas case was that the Commandments monument had stood for more than forty years before Thomas Van Orden challenged its display. "That experience helps us understand that as a practical matter of *degree* this display is unlikely to prove divisive. And this matter of degree is, I believe critical in a borderline case such as this one." The Texas monument "has stood apparently uncontested for almost two generations" without provoking any public division, Breyer noted. In contrast, the Kentucky displays had been recently erected, and the *McCreary County* plaintiffs had promptly objected to them.

Breyer knew that hundreds of Commandments monuments stood outside courthouses and city halls, in almost every state. Ruling against the monument in Texas, he wrote, "might well encourage disputes concerning the removal of longstanding depictions of the Ten Commandments from public buildings across the Nation. And it could thereby create the very kind of religiously based divisiveness that the Establishment Clause seeks to avoid."

Among the four dissenters, Justice Souter replied most directly to Breyer's reliance on the forty years that had elapsed before Van Orden challenged the monument he passed when he walked through the capitol grounds in Austin. Breyer seemed to suggest, Souter replied, "that forty years without a challenge shows that the religious expression is too tepid to provoke a serious reaction. I doubt that a slow walk to the courthouse, even one that took forty years, is much evidentiary help in applying the Establishment Clause." Justice Stevens, in his dissenting opinion, decried Rehnquist's "simplistic commentary on the various ways in which religion has played a role in American life," and denounced "the plurality's wholehearted validation of an official state endorsement that there is one, and only one, God." The *Van Orden* majority, he wrote, "would replace Jefferson's 'wall of separation' with a perverse wall of exclusion—Christians inside, non-Christians out." Such a reading of the Establishment Clause, Stevens complained, was "plainly not worthy of a society whose enviable hallmark over the course of two centuries has been the continuing expansion of religious pluralism and tolerance." In the end, Justice Breyer played the role of Solomon in proposing to split the Establishment Clause baby in half, satisfying hardly anyone on either side, whether on the Court or in the American public.

———

Quite predictably, the Court's divided rulings on the Commandments displays sparked divided reactions from those who brought and argued the two cases. On his part, Thomas Van Orden confessed that he was "not happy" about the ruling against him, saying he would spend the day reflecting "on the past three and a half years, including everything I went through." The lawyers who argued the Texas case responded with muted words. Sitting before reporters in front of the capitol-grounds monument in Austin, Greg Abbott said the Court "has made clear that Texas is a model of how governmental bodies across the country can constitutionally display religious symbols." Van Orden's lawyer, Erwin Chemerinsky, pointed to the Kentucky decision as the more significant ruling, calling it "an important victory" for church-and-state separation. "The government is still limited in what it can do with religious symbols on government property," he said.

People in McCreary County reacted with more emotion to the ruling in their case. Jimmie Greene had planned to lead a Fourth of July parade to return the Commandments display from the American Legion hall to the courthouse. "I woke up this morning, just convinced we were going to have a big celebration next week and put the commandments right back in the courthouse," he said. But the Court's decision ruined his plans. "All along through this process I have been optimistic and felt there was no way the Supreme Court could vote against us," Greene told reporters who sought him out in Whitley City. "But after hearing the decision I don't think I have ever felt more depressed in my life. It just broke my heart. I am not ashamed to tell you that I cried." His cousin, Louanne Walker, who sued to remove the Commandments display, had a different reaction. "It was really a wonderful day," she said on learning of the decision. "Surprising, but wonderful." Dave Howe, Greene's friendly adversary in the case, did not hold out an olive branch. "You don't establish a religion," he said. "They were trying to establish Lord Jesus Christ as founder of this country. Jimmie had never denied that. He said he wanted to get God back in the courthouse and that is not acceptable."

David Friedman had some advice for those who still wanted to display the Commandments. "They should do it in their homes, in their religious institutions, on their cars, and not through the government," he said. "The government is all of ours, and it can only be all of ours when it remains neutral." Mat Staver, who had predicted victory in the case he argued, sounded bitter and defiant in defeat. "This battle is far from over," he said. "We're looking to take this case back to the Supreme Court."

————

Staver did not seek a Supreme Court rehearing in the McCreary and Pulaski county cases, but he got a welcome Christmas present on December 20, 2005, when a three-judge panel of Sixth Circuit judges upheld an identical Ten Commandments courthouse display in nearby Mercer County, Kentucky. The story of the Mercer County case offers a graphic illustration of the roll-of-the-dice factor in judicial rulings. The McCreary and Pulaski cases had first been decided by Judge Jennifer Coffman, placed on the bench by President Bill Clinton. In October 2001, while the appeal from her ruling in those cases was pending before the Sixth Circuit, Mercer County officials allowed one resident, Carroll Rousey, to post the Ten Commandments on the courthouse wall, as the centerpiece of a "Foundations of American Law and Government" display. This display, in fact, included the same documents that had been placed in the McCreary and Pulaski courthouses.

Affronted by what he considered an "in-your-face" slap at Judge Coffman's ruling, David Friedman promptly filed another lawsuit for the Kentucky ACLU in November 2001, demanding the removal of the Mercer County display. His opponent in this case was not Mat Staver, but Francis Manion of the American Center for Law and Justice, who headed its Kentucky branch office and had volunteered to defend the Mercer County officials. Unfortunately for Friedman, the case was not assigned to Coffman, but to one of her fellow district judges, Karl S. Forester, named to the bench in 1988 by President Ronald Reagan. The conservative Republican judge ruled that the Mercer County display, unlike those of its neighbors, had not been placed in the courthouse as "a promotion of religious faith," and he dismissed the ACLU's lawsuit. Friedman filed an appeal from Forester's ruling with the Sixth Circuit, which held oral arguments in April 2004, but deferred its decision until the Supreme Court had ruled on the McCreary and Pulaski county cases.

Friedman won those cases by a five-to-four margin in June 2005, and presumed that the Sixth Circuit would feel bound to apply that precedent in the Mercer County case. He was wrong. The judicial crap-shoot in the appellate court had given Friedman a three-judge panel headed by one of the circuit's most conservative judges, Richard Suhrheinrich, placed on the Sixth Circuit in 1990 by President George H. W. Bush. Suhrheinrich looked in the Mercer County case for a detour around the Supreme Court's roadblock to courthouse displays of the Ten Commandments. His opinion, joined by another of President Bush's nominees, Alice Batchelder, wove a circuitous route around the *McCreary County* decision.

Conceding that the Mercer County display was "identical in all material respects" to those in its fellow counties, Suhrheinrich distinguished them on the basis of two factors. First, the posting of the Ten Commandments in the Pulaski County courthouse had been accompanied by the words of a Baptist minister who "testified to the certainty of the existence of God." The Mercer County display, however, showed no evidence "of a ceremony solemnized by a clergyman." Second, the McCreary and Pulaski county displays had been their third efforts to post the Ten Commandments, which the Supreme Court had viewed as a ploy to evade Judge Coffman's ruling against their initial "stand-alone" display. In contrast, Suhrheinrich wrote, Mercer County's display—the first in its courthouse—had not been "tainted" by such a ruse. "The sins of one government should not be revisited on other governments," he concluded.

Suhrheinrich, a member of the conservative Federalist Society of lawyers and judges, could not resist a final slap at the ACLU, adding a swipe at its "tiresome" arguments that the Establishment Clause erected a "wall of separation between church and state." Fuming at this gratuitous judicial insult, and at Suhrheinrich's evasion of the Supreme Court's ruling in the *McCreary County* case, David Friedman asked for an *en banc* review of the panel decision. He lost this bid in April 2006 by a nine-to-five vote. As a consolation prize, Friedman won a blistering opinion from the five dissenters, written by Judge R. Guy Cole, Jr. Notably, all five—including Judge Eric Clay, who had written for the panel that upheld Judge Coffman's order in the *McCreary County* case—had been named to the bench by Presidents Carter and Clinton. Cole found no "constitutional significance" between the Ten Commandments displays in the Kentucky courthouses. "Somehow I doubt that the Mercer County officials were surprised to find out that they had coincidentally erected the same display as their sister counties," he wrote with more than a whiff of sarcasm.

The ACLJ's chief counsel, Jay Sekulow, proclaimed the Mercer County case "an important defeat for the ACLU and other groups that are committed to removing our religious heritage and traditions from the public square." He virtually dared Friedman to ask for Supreme Court review of the Sixth Circuit's ruling. Sekulow had reason to crow, since the replacement of Justice Sandra Day O'Connor by Samuel Alito in January 2006 had most likely provided a fifth and deciding vote on the Supreme Court to uphold Ten Commandments displays. On his part, Friedman confessed to me that he would not "dare" to accept Sekulow's challenge, leaving the Sixth Circuit's *Mercer County* ruling in place.

We do not yet know, of course, how the justices would decide another Ten Commandments case; whether Justice Alito would feel bound to follow the *McCreary County* decision as precedent or feel free to overrule it. On my recent visit to Whitley City, however, I discovered that the Ten Commandments had been returned to the courthouse—not in the lobby, but in the hallway outside the office of Judge-Executive Blaine Phillips. "I think the people here want the Commandments in the courthouse," he told me. This defiance of the Supreme Court's decision reminded me of James Madison's warning that the Bill of Rights might prove no more than a "parchment barrier" against the majority's determination to impose its will on minorities. Louanne Walker and Dave Howe won their case in the Supreme Court, but they may still lose this battle in America's religious wars.

LOUANNE WALKER AND DAVE HOWE

Louanne

I was born in 1947 in McCreary County, and I've lived here basically all my life. My father, Louis, was the postmaster in Parkers Lake, about eight miles up the road from Whitley City. He had a grocery store, and my mother, Nellie, worked there too. My three older brothers were all grown up and away from home when my sister Norma and I were growing up. The Walkers Chapel Baptist Church was right next to our house and the grocery store. We had a back door from our house to the church, front door into the store. It was busy all day long. All the women in the community were in the back door, out the front. That's the way I grew up.

My mother was not from McCreary County originally. She was from Pulaski, which is the county just north of here. Her family were all Democrats, free-living, independent people. She married into a family of Walkers, very close-knit, and all of them Baptists and Republicans. My father was a Republican, and you didn't talk to him about that, not at all. But my mother was a Democrat, a liberal, a strong-minded person. And she instilled her feelings into her children—we got them from her. We just grew up as Democrats and liberals. She was a big supporter of the church, and enjoyed being part of it, but she was also a supporter of separation of church and state, and she brought my sister and me up that way.

The church was a big part of my life when I was growing up. I went to Vacation Bible School every summer, and I was brought up with the Ten Commandments. I remember, when I was eleven or twelve, being baptized in the Cumberland River after a revival meeting, six or seven of us kids all going under the water. Until I was twenty-one, even if I was out on Saturday night, I got up on Sunday morning and went to church. The only thing I enjoyed about church, to tell the truth, was that I loved the gospel music. I still do. If I'm watching TV, sometimes I'll flip over to the gospel-music channel and see if there's a good quartet singing.

I went to a two-room elementary school in Parkers Lake through the eighth grade. Then I went into McCreary County High School, and after I graduated I went to Cumberland College, which is a Baptist school in Williamsburg, about thirty miles from Parkers Lake. I went there off and on, and eventually got my degree in 1973, with a major in sociology and a minor in history.

I got married in 1976. My husband worked for the Department of Transportation, as an inspector. We had two children, both boys. Aaron is now thirty, and Adam is twenty-eight; he's the one we call Dave Junior, after Dave Howe. Dave took him under his wing, and Adam now runs the radio station in the county. I stayed home for ten years, just took care of my children, didn't do anything else. It wasn't a life that I really liked, but I did get to stay home with my children until they were ten or eleven. There came a time, when we were into our divorce, when I had to go to work, didn't really have a choice. So that's when I got a job with the state. I work for Human Resources in family support, and I make determinations for food stamps and Medicaid. I've done that for twenty years now. I had my degree in sociology, and I applied for social services; those are the people who monitor children and home life. That's the original job that I applied for, but someone else applied at the same time and they got that one. I'm glad now that I didn't get it. You go in there and take those kids out of the home; I don't think I would have liked that; it would have been hard. I like my job. It's right here, about two minutes away from my house.

Dave

I was born in 1935 in Pulaski, New York, near the east end of Lake Ontario. We moved from there when I was three, to Oneida, New York. Lived there until I was a teenager, and then we moved again, to Webster, New York, which is outside of Rochester, and I graduated from high school there. My father was a Baptist minister, and my mother's father was a Methodist minister. I went through Sunday school, Wednesday meetings, youth group. I was a PK—a preacher's kid—they're notorious. I haven't met a normal one yet.

I don't know how I wound up the way I am, but, for what it's worth, my parents taught me well. My father was a very liberal minister. He was never what you'd call a preacher, he was more of a pastor. He was seminary-trained, eight years of college. He took me on my first protest march when I was a senior in high school, that would be 1953. We went to New York City for a rally, protesting the blacklisting of radio and television artists. I wrote my senior essay on the subject, which was verboten. The English teacher told us from the get-go that we were not to do anything controversial. Can you believe that? So I wrote on blacklisting. But that was the fifties. I did get a passing grade, though.

After my father passed away, at some point I was talking with my mother, and she admitted that he had lost his faith. He never would tell anyone, or admit to it. He was inclined to believe that there was not a hereafter, and that really bothered him. He felt that he had been operating under a false doctrine for a long time. Really, I think that he wasn't, because he really was more of a pastor, and he lived a life that exemplified what he was preaching. I had no inkling of this when I was growing up. My mother, on the other hand, when her father passed away—I was about fifteen then—I remember asking her what she was feeling, and she admitted to feeling sad, and I said, Well, now you'll see him in heaven. And she said, No, I don't think so, David. There's nothing after you die, it's like going to sleep and never waking up. That's it, end of story. And I said, Mom, how can you believe that? And she said, That's what I believe.

That probably had some influence on me, but then you get to a point where you question a lot of things anyway. If you're going to question your parents' beliefs, and your mother is saying that she doesn't believe in a hereafter, you're naturally going to think that there is, just to be contrary. I tried periodically, over the next few years, to get back into some kind of a religious belief system, but I just couldn't do it. You get to a point of intellectualizing things, analyzing things, and it seems so unnatural, so wrong. Why is there this need for a hereafter? If you don't take care of business while you're here, that's too bad. If you don't believe, you don't believe, and that's basically it.

I started college at the University of Rochester, and didn't like that. Wound up in New York City, working at the Museum of Modern Art, in the basement, in the stockroom. I was taking art classes at the Artists League and sketch classes at the museum, thinking I was going to be an artist. That didn't materialize. Then I went back to Webster, working at Kodak. Got married, as people will do. Decided to go back to New York and try the art world again, wound up working for a photography-supply place. A friend of mine was going to broadcast school, and I joined him, learning to work in radio.

When my wife became pregnant, I decided I didn't want to have a kid in New York City, and wound up getting a radio job in Vermont. Stayed there for a year. I was working for a station on the Canadian border, in northern Vermont, in a town called Derby Line. But I got out of there after the first winter. I was the morning man, and it was an eight-mile drive to the town. Four mornings in a row, it was forty-five degrees below zero on my porch. That was too cold. What really got me was when I'd go down to the post office for the mail and they'd say, Is it cold enough for ya?

After I left Vermont, I went back to central New York, a town called Penn Yan. We lived there for two years, and then I got a job offer in Cincinnati—that was in 1964. I was there for fifteen years. I'd never go back. It's not a bad town, but it's just so conservative. I've got a daughter who lives there, and two grandkids, so I go up there pretty often to be with them, and I have friends up there also. But the politics up there hasn't changed one bit, it's just as bad as ever. And I had a stretch working for the Cincinnati Free Store, which was a nonprofit, devoted to gathering goods that were being thrown out by corporations and grocery stores and distributing them to people that needed them. One of the projects they tackled was doing maintenance for people who couldn't afford maintenance work, and that's what I got involved in, so I learned which end of a screwdriver to use, which turned out pretty handy when we moved down here and found out all of the stuff that had to be done around here. That was a worthwhile experience.

While I was in Cincinnati, I got involved with my present wife,

Carol. We'd been coming down to McCreary County a lot for camping trips. It was Louanne's sister Norma that got us to come down here; she was a bailiff in the court system in Cincinnati, and I got to know her. I met Louanne's mother, who was really wonderful, the one that taught them independence and instilled in them the idea of separation of church and state. Her mother was in her own way a rabble-rouser; she would go and protest coal-mining practices at the courthouse. When Nell passed away, the girls inherited the place their mother owned in Parkers Lake, the old grocery store, with the house behind it. Louanne and Norma convinced us to purchase the place, and Carol and I came up with enough to do it. We turned the store into Carol's pottery shop, which she runs with some help from me.

When we moved down here from Cincinnati, I got a job at the local radio station in Whitley City. They went belly-up, and a friend of mine, an attorney, when the FM license became available, we pursued it, and he and I bought equipment, and he built the station and put me in it. I did that for about twenty years, everything you do in a small radio station: news, weather, morning show, playing all kinds of music. I officially retired a few years ago, but I'm not really retired; I still have a two-hour show on Friday nights, progressive-rock stuff.

Louanne

I actually got involved in the Ten Commandments case through my older son, Aaron. He's very liberal and well educated. Aaron was still living here at home, and we saw this article in the paper about Jimmie putting up the Ten Commandments in the courthouse. And I said, Aaron, can he do that? Aaron said, No, he cannot. And I said, Who can you contact? He said, Probably the ACLU. He e-mailed the ACLU, and David Friedman got right back in contact with him, very quick. So we talked about it, and I said, Aaron, do you really want to do this? And he said, Yup. So he was the initiator, and he was really going to do it. But during that time, he'd been looking for a job, and applied with the Social Security Administration in Iowa, and they called him and offered him a job. He really felt like he couldn't turn the job down, so he had to turn this over to someone else. And he said, Mom, will you do it? I wasn't going to be the one at first, in the spotlight. But I knew that, with him moving, I wasn't just going to let it drop. I knew I was right, so I said, I'll sign the paper. Aaron also gave Dave Howe's name to Dave Friedman. We knew Dave would do it. We've been family for thirty years now.

David Friedman had warned me when it first began that it could get really nasty. I had never thought about it getting bad before he said that, so I was really scared at first, just watching to see if people were going to throw things in the yard or kill my dogs. And I heard it was really bad at one of the meetings about the Ten Commandments. You know, they had rallies. One guy said, We'll have her job. Of course they weren't going to have my job, because I didn't do anything on state time. That was the only threat that I heard. I've walked into the library and different places, and people would say they're with me. They don't want their name out there, although they agree, but they're members of the community, so they don't want to be out there. They're not going to hold that stick up there and say, Take down the Ten Commandments. It's a small place, and you have to live with everybody. I work with the public every day of the week; I'll see two or three hundred of them every month, but I never heard any of them say anything bad.

There wasn't much talk about this in the community, at least that I was aware of. I heard a few comments, but nobody approached me personally. One time, standing in the hall at work, after the Supreme Court ruling, I heard my supervisor say, Well, they can take the Ten Commandments out of our courthouse, but they can't take them off the bumper of my truck. And I thought, No, you want them on the bumper of your truck, fine. That'll work. But the only comments I've had over the years were good ones. People who came into the office, they'd kind of whisper, Good for you, Louanne. I've had so many people call me and tell me, You're my hero. And I say thank you.

I never talked to Jimmie about this. The first I heard from him was through the paper, saying, Oh, I can't believe my cousin is doing this to me. And I thought, Yeah, you should. I love Jimmie, he's family, his mother was my second mother. Jimmie also said that my mother would be rolling over in her grave if she knew what I had done. His mother might be rolling over in her grave, I don't know. But I know my mother's not. I've talked to Jimmie all my life, but not about this. I don't want a religious speech spilled to me, at this point in my life, so there would be no reason to sit down and talk with him. I think he thought it would help his political career.

Dave

Louanne's son Aaron, he's a pistol. I've known him since he was an infant. He alerted me to the fact that Jimmie Greene had posted the Ten Commandments in the courthouse. I didn't have any business in the courthouse, but I went over, and it just ran up me. And I said, How dare he! He knows better than that. And then I got a call from David Friedman, because he'd gotten a letter from Aaron. Aaron had gotten a job in Iowa and moved there, so he couldn't be a participant. He recommended his mother and myself, so when David called I said sure. Which, in retrospect, was probably not the smartest thing to do, because at the time part of my radio show in the morning was a routine called "Cruising the County," covering what's going on in a satirical manner. I had character voices, overdubbed stuff. That would have been a prime candidate for satire, but because I was a party to the lawsuit, I was advised by the owner, who was an attorney, You can't touch it, and if you do, you just made the biggest mistake of your life.

Here's something interesting, which nobody knew at the time, but I don't think I'm telling tales out of school. Right after Jimmie put up the Ten Commandments, the radio-station manager went over to the courthouse and told Jimmie, You know this is wrong. And Jimmie says, It's nothing, nobody will care. He implied that it really didn't matter that much to him, one way or the other. It wasn't until it became a political football that Jimmie started taking up the sword and shield, getting out there and marching for Jesus. He's a religious person, but it really didn't matter to him at the time.

You know, after the Supreme Court ruling in our case, the papers said that Jimmie cried. Jimmie cries easily. Back at a time before this case started, he and I would get into these conversations, slightly inebriated, and he would cry at the drop of a hat. Very maudlin. Nice, likable guy, just absolutely glad-hand you to death. But he's probably one of the most insincere people that you'd ever meet. He'll glad-hand you to your face, you're the salt of the earth, but he'll turn around to the next person and say, That scumbag Dave Howe. Whoever he's talking to, he totally agrees with, 100 percent. He's a consummate politician, I can't argue with that. He's very good at it, but I think his politician days are finished.

Nothing happened to me after we filed the lawsuit. No one made a big fuss about it. Folks down here have been very much Christians about it all. I get along with everybody. I don't think that I represent any kind of a threat. I'm a nonentity; I'm not from around here. I've lived here going on twenty-six years now, but I'm not a member of one of the tribes in McCreary County. And I'm so low-key. Nobody knows what I look like, I've never had my picture in the paper. And I like it like that. I've never been a joiner or participant in things. Pretty much just keep to myself. I don't make public appearances. I told them that when I was hired at the radio station: I don't go out to meet and greet, I just don't do it.

Louanne

I never went to any of the court hearings in this case. I just watched the news and read the paper. I should have, I guess, but we had good old David Friedman fighting the battles, so I didn't know that I even needed to be there. I would have liked to have gone several times, but things came up. I think it's just a TV ploy when you have a lot of people there. You know, I had people one time meeting me at the back door of the office where I work, from the Lexington TV station, and I just told them I didn't really want to make a comment, and I referred them to David Friedman. He's my hero, although I've never met him. Dave Howe and I were invited to some kind of ceremony in Louisville, after the Supreme Court ruling in our favor, to give us an award, but I didn't go. You might call me wimpy, but I don't like to fly, and if I'm going to drive into a city, especially Louisville, someone's got to take me. My son did go, and his wife.

Dave

I went to the Supreme Court for the arguments in our case. Jimmie invited me to go on the buses to Washington, but the ACLU flew me. I'm sure it would have been a hoot, but I actually preferred the leisurely flight, to fly over the barren mountaintops of West Virginia, where they're blowing the tops off of mountains for the strip-mining. We got to the Supreme Court, and it turned out to be the coldest weather they'd had in a long time. So I did not get to go to any of the places I wanted to see. I did walk down to the White House and took a look through the fence, and immediately hustled back to my hotel room; it was so cold, it was bitter.

I was really impressed in the Supreme Court; I had no idea what to expect. It was absolutely awesome. The courtroom is a lot smaller than one would anticipate, very intimate. You're right there, within just a few feet of all the activity. I was in the front section, almost center aisle. Mat Staver, the lawyer from the Liberty Counsel group, went first in our case. I felt sorry for that fellow. I didn't pay much attention to what he said. I so adamantly disagree with that position, I don't want to say I blocked it out, but it's the same routine, over and over and over, and it seems so patently irreconcilable with the truth that I just ignore it. When David Friedman got up, I thought his presentation was absolutely top-notch. He was unflappable. He got hit with some hard questions, and he dealt with them within the blink of an eye. And that was the first time I'd met him; I'd only talked to him on the phone.

Louanne

I just heard yesterday from Dave Howe that they've put new exhibits up in the courthouse lobby, full of quotations about the Bible and Jesus. And the Ten Commandments are back on the courthouse wall, even after the Supreme Court said they have to come down. We can't stand for that! I would be ready to go back to court. And as long as David Friedman and the ACLU will deal with this, we'll be right there backing him. Because, once you have started the fight, why stop? There's a lot more people out there who agree with us, and they just will not stand up with us. They don't want to get their name in it.

In my opinion, politics and religion have gotten too close in this country. That's the scary thing. It scares me when the president starts talking about religion. I think, What do I do now? I don't like that at all. What if eventually it takes over, and the minority, we don't have an option? I've brought my kids up to watch and vote and try to make a difference, but it is scary.

Dave

Looking back on this case, I'd do it again. And I may, now that I know what they're posting down there in the courthouse. But with the Supreme Court the way it is now, with Justice O'Connor gone, it's tipped the other way, and that's kind of discouraging. What really galls me, I think, is this attitude of, Our country, our legal system, was founded on the Ten Commandments. That is not true; it's patently offensive to me that they insist that this is the case. There is absolutely no historical basis for it, and I defy anyone to show me law in any state that tells us we have to worship a God! The prohibitions in the Ten Commandments, like murder, adultery, perjury, theft—that's common law! It's been common law since the get-go; you wouldn't have a civilization without it. Where did they come up with this? And this is ignored by the justices. There's a couple of those guys who really push me the wrong way, and how they got to be Supreme Court justices is beyond me. But as they say, excrement occurs. ❖

JIMMIE GREENE

I was born on May 21 in 1928, in Detroit, Michigan. My mother and father were there at the time, my father looking for work. That wasn't successful, and we moved back to my home in this community, Parkers Lake, Kentucky, when I was two or three months old. My father was Rease Victor Greene, and my mother was Pearl Walker Greene. They were divorced when I was quite young, and my grandpa took us in and raised us, my sister, Bobbie, and I. His name was Pleasant Patrick Walker, but he was known as P.P. or "Tobe." He was born in this county in 1864, just after his father was drafted into the Union Army. He lived to be ninety-eight, and he had sixteen children. Almost everybody around here is a Walker or related to one.

Grandpa had an old country store, and my mother worked in it too. We had approximately twenty families in the little community of Parkers Lake. The store served the surrounding community, twenty miles around. People would bring in their commodities, eggs and chickens and vegetables from their gardens, and Grandpa would trade them their sugar and tobacco and flour and meal, and he sold everything from harness to coffins.

I had a real good country upbringing as a child, very wholesome. Growing up, we went to the creek to go swimming, played ball just about every day when we weren't in school. We played ball down on the highway—you didn't have very much traffic back then—and we did a lot of roaming and exploring in the forest. When I started school, it was a two-room school, the first three grades in one room, and fourth to eighth in the other. So actually you were all there together, and you could learn from each other. If you were observant, you could learn pretty rapidly from the older children. Our teacher would take us to the surrounding communities to play basketball. We just had a lot of playtime, a lot of fun time. This was in the late thirties and early forties, just getting into World War II.

I was brought up in the church, the Walkers Chapel Baptist Church, which was located right next to Grandpa's store and the home I grew up in. The church has always meant very much to me. We're not a church where you show your emotions, but Jimmie does. I'm an emotional person, I get close to God. I'm the only one in our church that stands up and shouts. When the spirit of the Lord hits me, don't sit in your seat,

Jimmie, stand up and praise the Lord. I cry a lot, and I go to the altar an awful lot. If someone goes to the altar, I go with them. You don't go to the altar just because you've got a problem; sometimes you just say, Thank God.

After I graduated from high school in 1946, I worked for a while with a gentleman here who was in the logging business, working in a sawmill. I found that that wasn't to my liking. That's what we had in McCreary County at that time, the timber and the coal business. On February 6 of 1947, I enlisted in the Army Air Corps, as it was known at that time, and spent twenty-four wonderful years in the service. I started out in radio-operator school at Scott Field, Illinois, and that was my specialty in the service, communications. While I was doing my training, I received a congressional appointment to go to West Point. My grandpa arranged that through the congressman who represented McCreary County, who knew him very well. So I was preparing to go to prep school in New York before I went to the academy, and when they gave me my medical examination, I had a couple of molars missing. At that time, you had to have all your teeth to enter one of the military academies, you had to be a perfect specimen. It was a sad day for me when I received word that I wouldn't be going to West Point.

My first tour of duty was in Goose Bay, Labrador; I was up there in '49 and '50. Spent a wonderful year, flying into and out of the Arctic Circle, servicing the weather stations. Came back to Mitchell Field on Long Island, New York, as a radio operator, and I flew some training missions in B-26 light bombers. While I was there, I took the test for pilot training, but I failed it for not having 20/20 vision. I was there for a year when the Korean War started. Ten days later, I found myself in Japan for special training, and I was there for two months, at Nagoya Air Force Base. While I was in training, I had ample time to visit the city and meet people. Like most young men away from home for the first time, my interest in women was quite acute. Most Japanese at that time were very poor, so the girls worked in the Japanese dance halls. The Japanese girls were cute, and I became a frequent visitor to these places. It was in Japan that I acquired a taste for Japanese beer, which was served in large bottles, bigger than a quart, which cost the equivalent of twenty-eight cents in American money, so you could buy quite a few bottles of beer for one dollar.

A few days before General MacArthur made his Inchon landing, I landed in Korea. I spent ten months there, flying cargo aircraft and B-26 bombers on reconnaissance missions. We came under enemy attack one time when I was manning a remote direction-finding station, meaning that aircraft in flight, they would get lost sometimes, and we could steer them into the base. This was on a high mountaintop, and I had some Korean guards with me, and we came under attack. We had prepared foxholes outside of the little shack that we had the radio equipment in, and it was encircled by barbed wire. And when we tumbled out of the shack to jump in the foxholes, I got tangled up in barbed wire and cut my leg pretty badly. I've always considered it hostile fire, but my commanders didn't say, Jimmie, you're entitled to the Purple Heart. The North Koreans didn't do it, you did it.

I had a good ten months in Korea, and then I went back to Japan, to Itazuke Air Force Base in Kyushu. That's where I met Kyoko Yamamoto, who became the mother of my two boys. She was a dance-hall hostess, and I fell madly in love with her. My oldest son, Patrick, was born in 1952, before Kyoko and I were married in 1953. My younger son, Jimmie, was born in 1959; we've always called him Bevo. My eldest son, he went to Vietnam at the age of seventeen, and got fouled up, as many of them do, and got into drugs that just about destroyed him. He's straight now. He lives just across the road from me now. My younger son went into the Air Force and became a sergeant. He lives in Whitley City, and he's the father of my triplet granddaughters; they're two years into college now, and I'm very proud of them.

Kyoko came to the States with me on two occasions, and the third occasion we came back, she decided she didn't want to stay here, and we later got divorced. But she was smart enough to let me bring my two boys with me. She felt, and I've always appreciated that, that I could raise them better here. When I got back home, my mother raised them, just like her own, so they had a good upbringing here.

After the Korean War ended, I was stationed at Air Force bases in California, back to Japan, New York, Okinawa, Kansas, the Philippine Islands, and at various times in Vietnam. I transported the bodies of servicemen who were killed in Vietnam to Clark Air Force Base in the Philippines. And while I was at the Da Nang Air Force Base in Vietnam in 1961, the Viet Cong infiltrated base security and tossed grenades into an officers' tent, right next to the tent I was in. They killed three officers and wounded two others. Those were horrible experiences, and they later sent me to the hospital for psychological treatment.

After Kyoko and I were divorced, I got married again. I was stationed at Clark Air Force Base in the Philippines, and during a weekend trip to Corregidor Island I met Amelia Malixi, on the beautiful white beach across from Corregidor. She was a psychiatrist, and I eventually began to see her professionally due to marital and military psychological problems. She came to the United States in 1968, and we were married at Andrews Air Force Base in Washington, D.C., where I worked in the Presidential Communications Center, which handled all communications with the president while he was flying in Air Force One. That marriage lasted only a very short time, and I became married again, to a beautiful girl, Brenda, who lived in Parkers Lake. Her father was like a brother to me, because we had grown up together in Grandpa Walker's house. Brenda was only nineteen at the time, and I was forty. When her parents found out about us, they were really upset, because we were so closely related and I was also much older than she. But they finally relented, and Brenda and I were married in 1969, although we were later divorced.

I received notification in 1970 that I was going to be sent back to Vietnam. I had already been stationed there and didn't want to leave my young wife, so I decided it was best for me to retire from the Air Force. It was really a sad day when we had our retirement ceremony at Scott Air Force Base, with an effective date of January 1, 1971.

After twenty-four years of service, it was always my desire to come back home to McCreary County, and I became very active in my church and civic affairs. I became the postmaster at Honeybee in 1974 and served there until the post office was closed in 1977. Honeybee is a small community, about eight miles from Parkers Lake, and I live there now with my present wife, Lois, on her family's old place. We had grown up together, and she was my first really true love. I met her again in 1953, when I was home on furlough from March Air Force Base in California. We hit it off just fine, and we dated for the short time I was home. But I was married at the time to Kyoko, who was then in Japan, and told Lois so. I loved Lois and tried to persuade her to go back to March Field with me, but she refused. We were finally married in 1982, and we now have twelve grandchildren and two great-grandchildren, and I'm blessed with my family.

I'm mentioning my service history and these marriages in some detail because it took me a long time to admit that I had serious psychological problems. I would turn to the bottle and to beautiful women to deal with my stress and my guilt. I'm going to jump ahead to the time I realized that I needed help, particularly with my alcohol problem. One day in early 1988, I was at my cabin in the Sawyer Recreation Area, not far from where I live now. I was ready to jump into the gorge and end my life. I stood there with my beloved dog, Hobo, and came to my senses long enough to return to the cabin, telephone our dedicated ambulance service, and ask them to come and take me to the VA hospital in Lexington, where I stayed for three months. I was only in the hospital one day before I realized, Jimmie, you don't have any problems. I discovered this after observing the poor wretched souls around me that were twenty to twenty-five years my junior. Some were in there for alcohol and some for drugs. I really felt sorry for them, and it took me some time to realize that I was no better off than they were. We all had problems, and the majority were Vietnam-related. I finally realized that I was finally back with my own kind. I was back in the military, a military I loved so much. I was the old first sergeant again, and my healing process included walking the hallways and sitting by their bedsides, listening to their stories. This was my therapy.

I'll never forget one time in group therapy when I started crying because I had a guilt complex that so many young men had died in Vietnam and I was still alive. A young Vietnam veteran who had lost a leg in that war jumped from his wheelchair and hobbled over to me and put his arm around me. You know something? That really helped me. Although I did not completely lose that guilt feeling, I did come to grips with it and didn't feel so guilty anymore. Thank God, I have been sober since I got out of the VA hospital.

In 1977, I decided to run for the office of judge-executive in McCreary County. When I was in the Air Force, I was a first sergeant, the enlisted man right below the commander. He takes care of the troops; it's his responsibility for the welfare and morale and everything of the troops. I enjoyed that tremendously. And it helped me here; as I told people in one of my campaign ads, Hey look, being the county judge-executive is just exactly like being a first sergeant in the Air Force: your people are your primary concern.

We had a regime in office at the time that was like the old Tammany Hall, and the people just weren't being taken care of, and I was successful in removing them from office. I had defeated a system that totally despised me. When they left, they took everything. When I first walked into the judge's office in the courthouse in Whitley City, there was an old desk in there that you wouldn't have taken to the dump. There was a nail keg there for a seat; the telephone was jerked from the wall and lying in the corner, trash strewn everywhere, not one record, not one pencil, not one piece of paper. When Mrs. Greene and I walked in, and we had dressed in our finest, we just stood there and cried for a few minutes. Then we came back home and got our work clothes on, went back down and started cleaning up. I served four years as judge and was defeated. Then, eight years later, I came back in 1990 and served until 2003. I was elected four times and served for seventeen years, making me the longest-serving judge in the history of McCreary County, which I'm very proud of.

I got involved in the Ten Commandments issue in 1999, which was during my third term in office. To tell you the truth, it had never entered my mind, but one day a young man came into my office and he said, Judge Greene, you have all of these documents on the walls, but I don't see the Ten Commandments. Well, I'd never thought about it, it never dawned on me that the Ten Commandments is a historical document. So he brought me the Ten Commandments in a big frame. And I said, Well, certainly. Rather than me just going out there and putting it on the wall with the others, I said, This is something that the county government should act on; I don't want to do this alone. So I got the Fiscal Court, the four magistrates, and we voted to post the Ten Commandments, and didn't think any more about it. This was in 1999. And that was our undoing, because we had made it official, and never in my life did I think that somebody would bitch and moan and cry and gripe and holler and scream about the Ten Commandments.

I first found out about the lawsuit when somebody came in and said, Jimmie, do you know that Dave Howe and your cousin, Louanne, have contacted the ACLU and they're going to file a lawsuit against you, and you're going to have to take the Ten Commandments down? Dave I could understand, because he's a northeastern liberal. Dave and his wife, Carol, are dear friends. We differ in philosophies and politics, but we're all God's children, and I love them. Louanne is a first cousin. I have no animosity towards any of them, they're just dear friends.

I think then that we were taken to the district court in London, Kentucky. Our county attorney wouldn't get involved; he just felt, as I recall, that it was out of his jurisdiction. Then I was contacted by Colonel Ronald Ray, who is a lawyer and lives up near Louisville. He had heard about it when it was first in the newspapers, and he called me and says, Jimmie, I'll represent you, and it won't cost you a penny. He got very involved with us. But when we went to court, I think he kind of bungled it, and Judge Coffman ordered us to take down the Ten Commandments.

At this time, they had a Ten Commandments defense fund going on out there. Brother Herschel Walker from a Baptist church in Corbin, David Carr from King of Kings radio in Somerset—they had been organizing all of these gatherings, supporting the Ten Commandments. And they came up with these other historical documents, all the same size, same frame, and they came down, and we put those up again. When Judge Coffman ordered us to take down this display, I personally refused to do that. Being the law-abiding citizen that I am, some people couldn't understand. Well, Jimmie, they said, you're disobeying a lawful order. And when we went before Judge Coffman, the night before, Mrs. Greene packed a bag for me with pajamas and toothbrush, because I felt she was going to find me in contempt and put me in jail. But thank God she didn't find us in contempt. The American Legion, and veterans from all over southeastern Kentucky, and our citizens converged on the courthouse to take them down to prevent me from going to jail.

After that, when our case went to the Sixth Circuit Court of Appeals, we parted ways with Colonel Ray, with no hard feelings, and Mat Staver of Liberty Counsel offered to take the case to the Sixth Circuit, and then to the Supreme Court after we lost that decision. We were very fortunate indeed that he was there to help us out.

When the Supreme Court heard the arguments in our case, we organized five busloads of people to go to Washington and show their support, not only from this county but all over southeastern Kentucky and Tennessee. I did invite Dave Howe to come with us on the buses. Dave has always been a dear friend, and I knew he would be going to Washington, and we had the buses. But he said he would feel uncomfortable, and I can understand. No one would have challenged Dave, I wouldn't have allowed it. We had revivals on those buses, we sang and praised the Lord and testified, had a wonderful time.

Being in the Supreme Court was quite an experience. I was really impressed, sort of felt the historical significance of it, not in the same context with my church, but I felt a feeling of awe. Although, to be honest, I didn't hear any of the arguments. I had failed to bring my hearing aid—I have a hearing problem from the service—and very little did I hear. I was just a spectator. Couldn't even see. I thought that since it was our case we would have been seated closer to our attorney. But I was sitting in the last row, and they had their security walking up and down, very uncomfortable. And we had to sit there through the Texas case, you're talking about two hours. You couldn't stand and stretch, you couldn't do anything. I know I attempted one time, and the guy came over and said, Sit back down.

We figured the vote would go five-to-four in our favor. Justice O'Connor we really felt would be the crutch for us. The arguments were in March of 2005, but we didn't receive the results until the summer, late June. It was quite a shock, especially to know that Justice O'Connor voted against us. I did cry when I heard that we lost. But life goes on.

A lot of people here blame the ACLU for making us take down the Ten Commandments. But I don't hold any animosity toward them, or toward Dave Howe and my cousin Louanne. This is the America that I spent twenty-four years of my life defending. It's an America that I love, and one of our things is our freedom to express ourselves. I just think, on this particular issue, I just don't understand why they would be so opposed.

What disturbs me today, and I grieve about it, I look back on the innocence of my childhood and the principles that were taught me, and I see this eroding here in McCreary County today. We're getting away from how God wanted us to live. I can't imagine living in America twenty-five years from now if we don't get this immigration situation straightened out, if we don't conclude that war in Iraq and Afghanistan. I have a grandson that just came back from Iraq, and he's got problems. I've got another one that just graduated from high school, he'll be going into the Marines next month. They're children, and when they come back they're different; it changes you. We go away, and the American flag and Mom and apple pie, this is what I'm here for; and we come back, and we see all this disunity.

The big thing here is, this case was not about Jimmie Greene. I'm just plain old Jimmie, and people know me as that. It's about the people who believe in something so strongly, and they hang together. It was awe-inspiring to me, to realize that these people, not only do they care about the Ten Commandments, but Jimmie, they care enough about you to keep you from going to jail. It has really been an experience to go through the Ten Commandments case. I have grown stronger in my beliefs and my closeness to the Lord due to this. ❖

Chapter 7

"One Nation, Under God"

The Pledge of Allegiance Case from Elk Grove, California

Elk Grove, California, has several features that distinguish it from similar bedroom suburbs that circle America's big cities. Ten miles south of Sacramento, the Golden State's capital, Elk Grove bills itself as "the first city of the twenty-first century," earning that status with its formal incorporation on July 1, 2000. Having doubled in size over the past two decades, with a current population of 130,000, Elk Grove is now the nation's second-fastest-growing city, topped only by Port St. Lucie, Florida. The farmland around Elk Grove that once produced hops, grapes, and strawberries has given way to housing developments with names like Foxgrove, Wildflower, and Shadow Brook, where home prices begin at three hundred thousand dollars and climb twice that high.

With its close proximity to Sacramento, Elk Grove houses a huge number of government employees; more than 40 percent of its adult residents work in state, federal, and local agencies. The city's largest private employers, led by the Kaiser Permanente health-care system and Apple Computers, also provide well-paid jobs for well-educated workers; family income—close to seventy thousand dollars—almost doubles the national average. Unlike most suburbs, however, Elk Grove is distinguished by its racial and ethnic diversity. Only 54 percent of the city's residents are what the Census Bureau labels as "white, non-Hispanic." Twenty percent are Asian, many of them recent emigrants from Vietnam and China, 14 percent are Hispanic, and 9 percent are African American.

This diversity is accentuated in classrooms within the Elk Grove Unified School District, which includes three adjacent communities. With sixty-one thousand students in more than sixty elementary, middle, and high schools, the district is now the twelfth-largest in California, adding some three thousand students each year. Thirty percent of the district's students are white, 28 percent are Asian, 21 percent are Hispanic, and 20 percent are African American. Between them, the Elk Grove district's students speak eighty languages, with some more fluent in the native tongues of their families than in English.

Perhaps no other district in the nation better reflects what Israel Zangwill, a Jewish immigrant to America, called "the melting pot" in his 1908 play of that name. The "progressive" educators of Zangwill's time designed America's public schools to assimilate the flood of immigrant children into a common culture, undivided by conflicts over ancestry, religion, or class. The vision of "one nation, indivisible, with liberty and justice for all" was expressed in the Pledge of Allegiance to the American flag, composed in 1892 and recited—in those words— over the next sixty years by millions of schoolchildren, including those in Elk Grove's classrooms. Sharing in this daily ritual would foster "the binding tie of cohesive sentiment" that another Jewish immigrant, Supreme Court Justice Felix Frankfurter, viewed as essential in molding children from many nations into citizens of the "one nation" to which they now owed allegiance. Given the increasing racial and religious diversity in Elk Grove's classrooms, it seemed unlikely that any parent would object to his or her child's reciting the inclusive words of the Pledge. And no Elk Grove parent has ever objected to the Pledge in its original form.

One parent did, however, object to recitation of another version of the Pledge in his daughter's kindergarten classroom at the Florence Markofer Elementary School. What prompted Dr. Michael Newdow to file a lawsuit in March 2000 against the Elk Grove school district was not any objection to the Pledge itself but to the inclusion of two words that Congress added in 1954. Acting at the height of the Cold War against "godless" communism, Congress inserted the words "under God" between "one nation" and "indivisible" in the Pledge. The story of New-dow's legal crusade against those two words abounds in both drama and irony. The drama stems from his dogged insistence in pursuing his lawsuit to the chamber of the United States Supreme Court, arguing the case himself and winning plaudits from his adversaries for a "superb" performance. The irony is that the justices ruled against Newdow on grounds that had nothing to do with the case's constitutional merits, but with his "standing" to bring the case on his daughter's behalf. This story, however, did not end with Newdow's defeat in the Supreme Court. Undeterred by his judicial rebuff, he filed another suit against the "under God" words in the Pledge, on behalf of several parents and their children in Elk Grove and neighboring districts, winning an initial victory in 2005 and the prospect of a second argument before the Supreme Court.

———

In many ways, Michael Newdow resembles the "village atheist" of American folklore. Unlike that rustic figure, however, he launched his crusade against the Pledge's reference to God with impressive academic credentials. Born in 1953 in New York City, and raised by nonobservant Jewish parents, Newdow attended high school in Teaneck, New Jersey, and graduated from Brown University in 1974. Four years later, he completed medical school at the University of California at Los Angeles, and then returned to New York for a one-year internship at the Kings County Medical Center in Brooklyn. Newdow went on to practice emergency medicine in hospitals around the country for six years, without staying long in any place; he picked up medical licenses along the way in six states, from California to Florida. "I probably worked in more emergency rooms, conceivably, than anyone else, ever," he later said. His goal was to work "obscene" hours for twenty years and then retire, to pursue his passion for playing the guitar and singing in folk-song clubs.

Along the way, Newdow also picked up a law degree from the University of Michigan in 1988, moonlighting in emergency rooms during his studies. He wanted to reform the medical profession by going after doctors who overprescribed drugs, ordered unnecessary tests, and performed unneeded procedures. But he failed to find a job with a law firm or an advocacy group, and went back to medical practice without taking the bar exam. Newdow moved to California, and resumed a relationship with Sandra Banning, whom he met during his medical studies at UCLA. According to Newdow, they remained "best friends" but never married. In 1994, after Newdow had moved from California to Florida, his daughter was born in Sacramento, and he returned to be closer to her, although he and Banning lived in separate homes. Newdow lived by himself in Sacramento, Banning and their daughter in a house that he owned in Elk Grove. This arrangement stemmed from the oil-and-vinegar mixture of clashing personalities and beliefs. "Life is complicated with Michael," Banning says. "He is intense, and he can be obsessive." On her part, Banning is quiet and private, running a business from her Elk Grove home that provides administrative services to local firms. A self-described "born-again" Christian, she belongs to the Calvary Chapel of Laguna Creek, an evangelical congregation that stresses "the fellowship of believers in the Lordship of Jesus Christ." Newdow, in contrast, is anything but quiet and private, relishing the media spotlight and defending his provocative views at machine-gun speed. "I was born an atheist," he is fond of saying, and has spent almost a decade battling references to God and Christ in the public square.

Banning's relationship with Newdow became even more complicated after he returned to Florida in 1998, to resume a hospital emergency-room job. The next year, he proposed that Banning and their daughter join him in Florida, which they did, along with Banning's son by a marriage that had ended in divorce. However, Banning soon returned to Sacramento, where she filed a petition in family court, winning a temporary order that gave her sole custody of their daughter. Newdow had already, in fact, filed a lawsuit in Florida, claiming that his daughter— who was about to enter kindergarten—would be harmed by reciting those words. But without her presence in Florida, Newdow had no standing to challenge a practice in a school his daughter did not attend, and a federal judge promptly dismissed the case.

Undeterred by this judicial rebuff, Newdow returned to Sacramento in 1999 and prepared another lawsuit, which he filed in the federal district court in March 2000, challenging the Pledge recital in Elk Grove's schools. He listed himself and his daughter—whose name was concealed to protect her from media scrutiny—as plaintiffs, with the U.S. Congress as the first defendant, followed by the school district and its superintendent, David Gordon. Newdow alleged in his complaint that his daughter was injured by being compelled to "watch and listen as her state-employed teacher in her state-run school leads her classmates in a ritual proclaiming that there is a God, and that ours is 'one nation under God.'" By this time, Sandra Banning had become convinced that Newdow was simply using their daughter as a pawn to pursue his legal obsession. "I do believe he loves his daughter, as much as Michael Newdow can love anyone," she later said. "And she loves him. But she's a great vehicle for him to accomplish his other things." Dragging a six-year-old child into a lawsuit struck Banning as a ploy that might place her daughter in the bind of choosing between parents who gave her mixed messages about religion. On his part, Newdow disclaimed any such intention. He professed no objection to his daughter's Christian upbringing in Banning's home and church, but he did object to the state's taking sides in a parental conflict over religion. "I have the right to see that my daughter is not indoctrinated," Newdow said. "Every day in school, by reciting the Pledge, they are telling my daughter that her father is wrong and her mother is right."

———

Newdow had named the Congress as the first defendant in his suit, blaming that body for injecting religion into a Pledge that was initially composed with no reference to God. The historical background of the Pledge reveals its purely secular origins. Back in 1892, the editors of *The Youth's Companion*, the most widely circulated periodical in the country, decided to promote a celebration in America's schools of the four-hundredth anniversary of Columbus's first voyage to the New World. Francis Bellamy, the magazine's assistant editor, drafted a pledge of allegiance that would be recited by students who participated in the Columbian celebration, while they saluted the American flag. Ironically,

Bellamy was also a Baptist minister, but his pledge made no reference to religion: "I pledge allegiance to my Flag and the Republic for which it stands: one Nation indivisible, with Liberty and Justice for all."

The ceremonies that took place on October 21, 1892, were a great success and prompted many schools to make recitation of Bellamy's pledge a part of regular classroom exercises. The flag salute and Pledge first became required by law in New York in 1898, following the American declaration of war on Spain over its occupation of Cuba. Patriotic fervor persuaded other states to follow New York's example, and by the end of World War I, a majority of states required daily flag salutes and recitation of the Pledge in their public schools. After the war, the American Legion and other patriotic groups organized National Flag Conferences, which were held in 1923 and 1924, at which delegates voted to change the Pledge's wording to read: "I pledge allegiance to the flag of the United States of America, and to the republic for which it stands, one nation, indivisible, with liberty and justice for all." Early in World War II, Congress voted to codify that version as the official Pledge of Allegiance, still with no reference to God.

During the Cold War, however, the worldwide struggle with "godless communism" became infused with public religiosity. The outbreak of the Korean War spurred a campaign, launched in 1952 by the Knights of Columbus, a Roman Catholic fraternal group, to add the words "under God" to the Pledge. Two members of Congress, both from Michigan, sponsored bills to achieve this goal. Senator Homer Ferguson appealed to his colleagues with these words: "What better training for our youngsters could there be than to have them, each time they pledge allegiance to Old Glory, reassert their belief in the all-present, all-knowing, all-seeing, all-powerful Creator." Representative Louis Rabaut voiced similar views to the House: "Unless we are willing to affirm our belief in the existence of God, we drop man himself to the significance of a grain of sand and open the floodgates to tyranny and oppression." Both chambers of Congress adopted the bill with no recorded dissent, and President Dwight Eisenhower signed it on June 14, 1954, designated by Congress as Flag Day. God was now part of the official Pledge of Allegiance.

Michael Newdow cited the statements of Senator Ferguson and Representative Rabaut in his lawsuit, as evidence that Congress had been prompted by religious motivations in adding "under God" to the Pledge. Forcing children, including his daughter, to affirm their "belief in the existence of God," he argued, violated the Establishment of Religion Clause of the First Amendment to the Constitution. His arguments, however, initially fell on deaf judicial ears. After a brief hearing, a federal magistrate, Peter Nowinski, recommended that the suit be dismissed, accepting the argument of Elk Grove's lawyers that Newdow had failed to state a claim under the Constitution or federal law. On July 21, 2000, Senior District Judge Milton Schwartz accepted Nowinski's recommendation and entered a judgment of dismissal.

Four months after he filed his suit, Newdow was out of court for a second time. Like all losing parties in federal district courts, he was entitled to seek appellate review of the dismissal, but he faced an uphill battle. Dismissing a case signals to appellate courts that a suit has no legal merit, and most litigants give up at this point. In addition, Newdow was a *pro se* plaintiff: he had filed his suit without a lawyer, since he had never taken a bar exam. Appellate courts generally shy away from *pro se* cases, many filed by cranks who fail to comply with basic judicial rules. Undeterred by these hurdles, Newdow asked the U.S. Court of Appeals for the Ninth Circuit to review his case. Surprisingly, the court agreed to hear the appeal, setting oral arguments for March 14, 2002, in San Francisco. Over the objections of Sandra Banning, a family-court judge allowed Newdow to bring his daughter, then a third-grader, to the arguments. Four lawyers—two from the U.S. Justice Department and two representing the Elk Grove schools—sat across from Newdow in the ornate courtroom.

The case had drawn an interesting panel of three elderly judges. The presiding judge, Alfred Goodwin, an Oregon native and self-professed "cowboy" who owned a sixty-acre timber ranch, was seventy-eight and had been named to the Ninth Circuit bench by Richard Nixon. Stephen Reinhardt, born in Brooklyn and a Yale Law School graduate, was seventy-one and had been appointed by Jimmy Carter. The youngest judge, at sixty-five, Ferdinand Fernandez, was a native Californian who had been placed on the federal district bench by Ronald Reagan, and later on the Ninth Circuit by George H. W. Bush in 1989. Reinhardt was an unabashed judicial liberal, while Fernandez generally voted with the Ninth Circuit's conservatives; Goodwin, befitting his "cowboy" label, was considered a judicial maverick whose votes were unpredictable.

The Pledge case had attracted little press attention in Sacramento, and no reporters attended the oral arguments in San Francisco, which focused on Newdow's standing to bring the suit on his daughter's behalf and Supreme Court precedent in Establishment Clause cases. Newdow, who repeatedly said, "The law is on my side," was perhaps the only person in the courtroom who expected a decision in his favor. The media and the public were caught by surprise when the Ninth Circuit panel issued its decision on June 26, 2002. Writing for himself and Judge Reinhardt, Judge Goodwin ruled that the statement in the Pledge "that the United States is a nation 'under God' is an endorsement of religion" and that its recitation in Elk Grove's classrooms violated the Establishment Clause. "The text of the official Pledge," Goodwin said, "codified in federal law, impermissibly takes a position with respect to the religious question of the existence and identity of God." Quoting from the congressional speeches that Newdow had cited in his brief, Goodwin noted that "the legislative history of the 1954 Act reveals that the Act's *sole* purpose was to advance religion, in order to differentiate the United States from nations under communist rule." By adding "under God" to the Pledge, Goodwin added, Congress had endorsed not only religion in general but "monotheism" in particular. Goodwin turned to the Pledge ritual in Elk Grove's classrooms. "Given the age and impressionability of schoolchildren," he wrote, reciting the words "under God" would convey an impermissible endorsement of "the existence of a monotheistic God."

In his solitary dissent, Judge Fernandez invoked the legal concept of *de minimis,* which means, in plain English, "no harm, no foul." Much like Justice Antonin Scalia on the Supreme Court, Fernandez laced his dissent with scorn and sarcasm. "When all is said and done," he wrote, "the danger that 'under God' in our Pledge of Allegiance will tend to bring about a theocracy or suppress somebody's beliefs is so minuscule as to be de minimis. The danger that the phrase presents to our First Amendment freedoms is picayune at best." Conceding that the words "under God" have religious meaning, Fernandez argued that they could be viewed as violating the Constitution only "in the fevered eye of persons who most fervently would like to drive all tincture of religion out of the public life of our polity." Notably, Fernandez joined the part of Goodwin's opinion that stated, "Newdow has standing as a parent to challenge a practice that interferes with his right to direct the religious education of his daughter."

Even Michael Newdow was surprised by the torrent of outrage that greeted Judge Goodwin's opinion. Speaking for the Elk Grove school board, Chairman William Lugg professed "shock and dismay" at the ruling. "We have a very diverse student population in Elk Grove," Lugg added. "Saying the Pledge of Allegiance draws us together, and helps us celebrate the freedoms that we enjoy in this great country." Politicians of both parties were less restrained in their rhetoric. Speaking to reporters during a trip to Canada, President George W. Bush called the decision "ridiculous." Bush later said, "We need commonsense judges who understand that our rights were derived from God. Those are the kind of judges I intend to put on the bench." Senate Majority Leader Tom Daschle, a South Dakota Democrat, derided the decision as "nuts," and his colleagues promptly adopted a resolution—passed unanimously, with every senator listed as a sponsor—condemning the ruling. Senator Robert Byrd, a West Virginia Democrat and that body's senior member, blasted Goodwin as a "stupid judge" and an "atheist lawyer." Not to be outdone, the House of Representatives voted by a margin of 416 to 3 for a resolution that declared: "The Pledge of Allegiance, including the phrase, 'One Nation, under God,' reflects the historical fact that a belief in God permeated the Founding and development of our Nation." Public-opinion polls showed a solid majority behind the Pledge, with 68 percent agreeing that the words "under God" did not violate the separation of church and state, against 36 percent who disagreed. Clearly, the two-to-one majority on the Ninth Circuit panel did not reflect public senti-ment on the Pledge.

Ironically, many people—few of whom actually read Goodwin's opinion—believed that his ruling had struck down the Pledge in its en-tirety. On his part, Goodwin brushed off the bashing. "I never had much confidence in the attention span of elected officials for any kind of deep thinking about important issues," he said of his congressional critics. "When they pop off after what I call a bumper strip headline, they al-most always give a superficial response." Goodwin was equally dismis-sive of Bush's denunciation: "I'm a little disappointed in our chief executive—who nobody ever accused of being a deep thinker—for pop-ping off." Noting proudly that he won the Combat Infantry Badge in World War II, Goodwin said, "I was supporting the flag then and I still support it."

Nonetheless, what Goodwin called "this wrap-yourself-in-the-flag frenzy" prompted him, two days after his opinion was issued, to order a stay of the ruling until any appeals had been decided, either by the full Ninth Circuit or the Supreme Court. "That was just damage control," he explained of the stay, which was automatic in any event. Its public an-nouncement was designed to counter the mistaken belief—fostered by the media—that schools within the Ninth Circuit would immediately be forced to drop the Pledge ritual. "Their attention span can't handle anything more than a haiku of about four lines," Goodwin said of the media. "The worst thing about it was that some people said we were caving under pressure."

Goodwin did, however, at least bend under pressure from his Ninth Circuit colleagues. Lawyers for the Elk Grove district requested an *en banc* rehearing by a larger panel of eleven judges. Under the court's rules, a majority of the twenty-four sitting judges could grant such re-view. Goodwin himself proposed that his colleagues consider the *en banc* request, although he voted to deny it, over the objections of nine judges, four shy of the necessary thirteen. Six of those dissenters joined an opinion by Judge Diarmuid O'Scannlain, one of the Ninth Circuit's most conservative members. Dismissing Goodwin's original ruling as "wrong, very wrong," O'Scannlain argued that under its reasoning the Gettysburg Address, the Declaration of Independence, and the National Anthem would be consigned "to the chopping block" because they all mention God. Removing the words "under God" from the Pledge, he added, "confers a favored status on atheism in our public life." O'Scannlain referred in his opinion to the public outcry against Goodwin's opinion, prompting Judge Stephen Reinhardt—who had joined that ruling—to denounce any suggestion that the court should reverse itself "by observing the public and political reaction to the decision." Reinhardt answered O'Scannain with these words: "We may not—we must not—allow public sentiment or outcry to guide our decisions. The Bill of Rights is, of course, intended to protect the rights of those in the minority against the temporary passions of the majority."

But the strong feelings of the judicial minority on his court prompted Goodwin to amend his first opinion, removing its holding that Newdow had standing to challenge the 1954 congressional act that added "under God" to the Pledge. As critics noted, that part of Goodwin's ruling effectively made recitation of those words unconstitutional at any public event, a consequence he had not intended. However, the amended opinion, handed down on February 28, 2003, left intact the holdings that public-school recitation of those words violated the Establishment Clause, and that Newdow had standing to challenge the ritual in Elk Grove's schools.

Even with the amended opinion, the Ninth Circuit's denial of *en banc* review made it certain that Elk Grove's lawyers would ask the Supreme Court to hear its appeal from that decision. Although Judge Goodwin's first opinion had dismissed the U.S. Congress as a defendant, the federal government placed its weight behind the school district. John Ashcroft, who then served as attorney general in the Bush administration, told reporters that the Justice Department "will spare no effort to preserve the rights of all our citizens to pledge allegiance to the American flag." Michael Newdow was eager to make his case before the Supreme Court justices. "I think they'll rule in my favor, and it would be nice to get this settled and get all this religious dogma out of our government as the Establishment Clause requires," he said. "I wouldn't be surprised if this case was nine–zero." Newdow, of course, was anticipating a unanimous ruling in his favor. Many observers, however, considered it more likely that—if the Court took the case—the justices would rule nine to zero against him. But laying bets on the outcome of Supreme Court cases is risky, with too many judicial wild cards in the deck.

Newdow got his chance to argue before the Court when the justices granted, on October 14, 2003, Elk Grove's petition to review the case, setting oral argument for March 24, 2004. The justices set out two questions for both sides to address in their briefs: first, whether Newdow had standing to challenge the Pledge recitation in his daughter's school; and, second, whether recitation of the Pledge, with the words "under God," violated the Establishment Clause. The Court set a deadline of December 19, 2003, for the Elk Grove district, and groups supporting its position, to file their briefs, with those from Newdow and his backers due on February 13, 2004. With the clock ticking, lawyers on both sides began working feverishly on their briefs.

Every high-profile Supreme Court case draws friend-of-the-court briefs from interest groups that want to present their positions to the justices. Most have some institutional or ideological ax to grind, on issues from abortion to zoning. The case of *Elk Grove Unified School District v. Newdow* generated almost fifty briefs, twenty-seven supporting the district and twenty backing Newdow. Few of these briefs, on either side, had anything distinctive to add to those of the parties they supported; they mostly cited the same cases as precedent and restated the same arguments.

Predictably, conservative politicians and Religious Right groups lined up behind the Elk Grove school district and the Pledge. Members of the U.S. Senate and the House of Representatives filed separate briefs for the district, along with all fifty state attorneys general. Pat Robertson's legal arm, the American Center for Law and Justice, headed the Religious Right groups, which included Liberty Counsel, the Alliance Defense Fund, and the Christian Legal Society. The American Legion and the Knights of Columbus also backed the district, as did the National Education Association and the National School Boards Association. Between them, these groups represented millions of members and influential political figures.

Newdow's supporters had many fewer members and much less political clout. Only the American Civil Liberties Union and Americans United for Separation of Church and State, which filed a joint brief, had any real influence, with some 460,000 members between them. Seven atheist groups, most with only a handful of members, filed briefs for Newdow. Not surprisingly, not a single elected official risked political suicide by urging the Court to strike down "under God" in the Pledge. Even groups like the American Jewish Congress and People for the American Way, fearful of being tarred as "atheist" fronts, backed out of agreements to join the ACLU and Americans United brief.

Both the ACLU and the AU, in fact, viewed the Pledge case as a potential disaster, especially since 2004 was a presidential election year. Conceding that Newdow was "clearly correct on the issue," Steven Shapiro, the ACLU's legal director, nonetheless hoped the Court would "avoid turning this case into a major battleground in the cultural wars at the height of a presidential election campaign." The best outcome, Shapiro felt, would be for the Court to duck the constitutional issues by ruling that Newdow lacked standing to bring his suit. On its part, Americans United asked the Court in September 2003 to "defer consideration" of the case until Newdow's custody battles over his daughter had been finally decided by California's family courts.

Another factor behind the apprehension of ACLU and AU lawyers was their fear that Newdow could not handle the stress of Supreme Court argument. The justices had granted his request to argue his own case, but he was highly emotional about the custody issue. "It's hard to concentrate" on the Pledge issue, he admitted. "This thing has shattered my life." The prospect of Newdow's blowing up at the arguments terrified the ACLU and AU lawyers. "They're afraid that here's this guy taking on this important case, and they think he's a lunatic," he said. "They may be right." To ward off such a disaster, the AU's lawyers asked the

Court to give them fifteen minutes of Newdow's half-hour of argument, but he opposed that request, and the justices denied the motion for divided time.

The ACLU and AU lawyers were also concerned that Newdow's brief would antagonize the justices. The Court's rules limited both parties to fifty pages, with strict limits on type size and margins. Newdow's first drafts ran close to a hundred pages, and were little more than diatribes about the persecution of atheists like himself. His drafts also included sarcastic references to every justice then on the Court, and even derogatory comments about former chief justice Earl Warren. I volunteered to help Newdow edit his unwieldy brief, along with my former Harvard Law School classmate Erwin Chemerinsky, the noted constitutional-law professor at the University of Southern California, and later at Duke University. Initially resistant to our electronic blue pencils, Newdow grudgingly removed the most offensive language and trimmed his brief to the fifty-page limit. His final brief, Chemerinsky and I agreed, was polished and professional, although still forceful in tone.

Newdow also prepared for his argument by taking part in a dozen moot-court sessions, facing off with law professors in practice arguments at a dozen law schools, including Berkeley, Stanford, Yale, and Georgetown. He impressed his audiences with total command of Supreme Court precedent and lightning-fast responses to probing and often hostile questions. Newdow also practiced in his Sacramento home, pasting photographs of the Supreme Court justices on the wall, anticipating questions from each, and ready with quotations from their earlier opinions in church-state cases. Above his desk was a framed picture of his daughter, smiling broadly. The Pledge case took a back seat to his daughter. "I'd give up the case in a second to be with my kid," he said, but the family-court judge in Sacramento denied his request to bring her to Washington and witness his argument before the Supreme Court. Newdow was determined, however, to bring her into the chamber, even without her presence.

Sandra Banning did come to Washington to hear the Pledge-case arguments. She had accepted the offer of Kenneth Starr, a former solicitor general and nemesis of Bill Clinton as the Whitewater special prosecutor, to file an *amicus* brief on her behalf, arguing that Newdow lacked standing to represent their daughter. Starr, now a partner in a prestigious law firm, noted in his brief that Banning and her daughter were Christians and had no objection to the words "under God" in the Pledge. Despite her personal differences with Newdow, Banning admired his tenacity in the Pledge case. "He can be very easily sidetracked," she told a reporter. "But I don't know, he might just surprise us. He's got it this far."

———

Michael Newdow sat alone at the counsel table in the Supreme Court's ornate chamber on the morning of March 24, 2004. Fifty years old, slight of build, and sharp-featured, with thinning brown hair, he opened the loose-leaf binder on the table. Two words were printed in large type on the first page: "TALK SLOW." Newdow normally spoke at a machine-gun pace, full of the argument he had spent months preparing, in a case that challenged another two words, printed in much larger type on dozens of placards carried by demonstrators who crowded the sidewalks outside the Court.

Newdow sat alone at the counsel table because he was supremely confident that he would prevail. "I'll win because I've got the Constitution on my side," he told a reporter before the arguments began. "No one knows this case better than I do." Newdow had some reason to feel confident as he waited for the arguments to begin. It would take a ruling by five Supreme Court justices, out of eight who heard the arguments, to reverse the Ninth Circuit decision in his favor. Justice Antonin Scalia, who would have certainly voted to uphold the words "under God" in the Pledge, had recused himself from the case after Newdow challenged his criticism of the Ninth Circuit ruling in a speech to a religious group. Of the remaining eight justices, only Chief Justice William Rehnquist and Justice Clarence Thomas were sure votes to uphold the Pledge. And the Court's recent decisions in school-prayer cases, written by Justice Anthony Kennedy, had struck down prayers at public-school graduation ceremonies and football games. Newdow had directly aimed his Supreme Court brief at Kennedy, who held the key vote in the Pledge case. If Kennedy agreed that the words "under God" in the Pledge constituted a "religious exercise" that was similar to prayer, Newdow had an excellent chance of winning his case. But if Kennedy disagreed, and distinguished references to God in prayers from "under God" in the Pledge, he had little chance of prevailing.

How far Newdow could get in his argument without being sidetracked on the standing issue, and whether he would lose his composure, depended in large part on the arguments of his legal adversaries, who sat across from him in the Court's chamber. As the winning party in the lower court, Newdow would speak last, with the advantage of hearing their arguments and responses to questions from the justices. The lawyers who had come to defend the words "under God" in the Pledge of Allegiance were a mismatched pair. Terrence Cassidy would argue first, defending the Elk Grove school district. A partner in a Sacramento law firm, Cassidy's practice centered on defending builders in "construction defect" cases. Although he had represented several local school districts in employment cases, and had won an earlier Supreme Court case, Cassidy had no prior experience in First Amendment cases, and his brief failed to cite the Court's most important Establishment Clause decision, the *Everson* case of 1947, holding that government must remain "a neutral" in disputes over religion. Newdow had certainly provoked a dispute over religion in challenging the Pledge, but Cassidy argued in his brief that the words "under God" had no religious meaning and were simply "ceremonial" in nature. This was hardly an argument designed to convince skeptical justices, especially Justice Kennedy, whose school-prayer opinions had cited *Everson* for authority. Cassidy's brief, in fact, rested almost entirely on the claim that Newdow lacked standing to bring his suit against the Pledge.

Cassidy shared his counsel table with a far more experienced lawyer, Solicitor General Theodore Olson, representing the federal government as the nation's counsel in the Supreme Court. A close friend of Kenneth Starr and a fellow stalwart in conservative legal groups, Olson had argued more than twenty cases before the Court, both as a private lawyer and for the government. Olson's brief far outweighed Cassidy's in polish and style, but it also ignored both the *Everson* case and its "neutrality" doctrine, dismissing Kennedy's school-prayer opinions as inapplicable to the purely "ceremonial" Pledge.

On this chilly Wednesday morning, every seat in the Court's chamber was occupied. The Pledge case attracted one of the biggest crowds in years. Well before midnight, people camped out at the foot of the marble steps leading to the Court's huge bronze doors. Many were wrapped in blankets and sleeping bags, for protection against the near-freezing chill. Others sat in deck chairs, chatting with neighbors or reading by flashlight. Around the corner, on the Court's west side, members of the Supreme Court bar stood in line at their special entrance, sharing coffee from thermos jugs. Many of the lawyers represented friend-of-the-court groups on both sides. The "lawyers' line" began at three in the morning, and I was the second to arrive, at four. The line had grown so long by seven-thirty, when the Supreme Court's clerk opened the door, that several dozen bar members did not make the cut. One disappointed lawyer returned to the public line and bought a pass to the chamber for one hundred dollars, from someone willing to trade a seat for cash.

On this morning, Chief Justice Rehnquist called the first of the two cases scheduled for argument that day, which involved a municipal licensing ordinance from the town of Littleton, Colorado. Hardly anyone in the chamber, aside from the contending lawyers, had come to hear these arguments, but they soldiered on for an hour, undoubtedly conscious that the audience was impatiently waiting for them to relinquish the lectern to the lawyers who sat behind them. Before the Littleton lawyers took their seats, Justice Scalia quietly left the chamber, leaving just eight justices to hear the next case.

Without any reference to Scalia's departure, Rehnquist announced, "We'll hear argument next in Number 02-1624, the Elk Grove Unified School District and David W. Gordon versus Michael A. Newdow." Terrence Cassidy had agreed with Solicitor General Olson to divide their thirty minutes equally; Cassidy would address the standing issues in the case, with Olson using his time to discuss the constitutional questions. Cassidy began his argument by claiming that Newdow had no standing to challenge the words "under God" in the Pledge, because Sandra Banning had been granted custody of their daughter. The Ninth Circuit judges, Cassidy argued, had mistakenly ruled that Newdow had standing as a parent to influence his daughter's views on religion without state interference, and had disregarded California state law on parental control on this issue. But just minutes into his argument, Justice Sandra Day O'Connor leaned forward in her seat and said, "Normally, I guess, we defer to the courts of appeals in deciding issues of state law." Cassidy struggled to recover from this judicial rebuke, reciting passages from his brief, but the justices seemed eager for Cassidy to sit down and relinquish the lectern to Solicitor General Olson. After ten minutes, Cassidy asked to reserve his remaining five minutes for rebuttal to Newdow's argument. He seemed relieved to end the grilling from the bench.

Dressed in the traditional swallowtail suit that his predecessors as solicitor general had adopted more than a century earlier, Olson began with an effort to rescue Cassidy on the standing question. But he seemed to lack any real interest in the issue, simply repeating Cassidy's argument during his first several minutes at the lectern. Eager to drop the standing question, Olson shifted course. "If I might turn to the merits," he said, "this Court has repeatedly held that the Pledge of Allegiance is a ceremonial, patriotic exercise." He got no further before Justice John Paul Stevens, the Court's most senior member in both service and age, interrupted with a question: "Do you mean repeatedly held or repeatedly said?" Stevens had read the claim in Olson's brief that decisions in earlier cases had distinguished the Pledge of Allegiance from school prayers and other "religious exercises" the Court had struck down as violations of the Establishment Clause. But the references to the Pledge in these opinions were "dicta," the legal term for statements that were not necessary to the Court's decisions. Olson conceded that earlier opinions had "said" that the words "under God" in the Pledge might be constitutional, but argued that these statements were "more than dicta." Fourteen different justices, in cases decided over the past four decades,

Olson continued, "have indicated that the Pledge of Allegiance is not a religious exercise, it is something different, of a ceremonial nature."

Olson then faced a question from Justice Ruth Bader Ginsburg, the Court's most active questioner, along with the absent Scalia. "Forget all that dicta," she told Olson. "Do you think that the words, 'under God,' have the same meaning today as when they were first inserted in the Pledge" in 1954? Olson provoked laughter in the chamber with his answer. "Yes and no," he replied. But he returned to his claim that "numerous decisions of this Court have indicated in dicta" that the amended Pledge is "an acknowledgment of the religious basis of the Framers of the Constitution." Olson concluded with the claim that the Pledge "is not what the Court has said the Establishment Clause protects against, that is to say, state-sponsored prayers, religious rituals or ceremonies."

————

When Olson sat down, it was finally Michael Newdow's chance to argue the case he had doggedly pursued for more than four years. Chief Justice Rehnquist welcomed him to the lectern: "Mr. Newdow, we'll hear from you. Please proceed." All those present in the chamber leaned forward in their seats, waiting to hear his first words. And they were words never before spoken in the Supreme Court. Turning to face the American flag on his right, Newdow began: "I am an atheist. I don't believe in God. And every school morning my child is asked to stand up, face the flag, put her hand over her heart, and say that her father is wrong."

No lawyer speaking on Newdow's behalf could have begun with such a direct, personal statement. Many people in the chamber reacted with an involuntary gasp of surprise. Newdow's reference to his daughter prompted an equally personal question about the impact of his controversial case on her. "Your daughter is the one that bears the blame for this," Justice Kennedy said. "She's going to face the public outcry, the public outrage" at her father's attack on the Pledge. But Newdow did not agree with Kennedy. "I'm not convinced that there are going to be adverse consequences to my daughter," he replied. "My daughter's going to be able to walk around and say that my father helped uphold the Constitution of the United States."

Newdow's friends and supporters in the chamber were relieved when the questions turned from the standing issue to the religious content of the Pledge, and the Court's earlier rulings against school prayer. Chief Justice Rehnquist, who had consistently dissented from those rulings, reminded Newdow that Olson had portrayed the Pledge as simply "descriptive" of the nation's ideal of "one nation under God, with liberty and justice for all," with no requirement that children who recited the Pledge affirm their belief in these ideals. Newdow firmly disputed Olson's claim. "It's an affirmation of belief," he replied. "It says under God. That's as purely religious as you can get." Olson had argued that children who recited the Pledge should be aware that it merely "acknowledged" the religious beliefs of the Constitution's framers. Newdow responded, "It would be an amazing child to suddenly come up with this knowledge of the history of our society and what our nation was founded on." He continued: "All of this has to do with religion, and to say this is not religious seems to me to be somewhat bizarre. To suggest that this is merely historical or patriotic seems to me to be somewhat disingenuous."

Justice Stephen Breyer, the Court's junior member and a former Harvard Law School professor, posed a question that echoed the amazing claim in Kenneth Starr's brief for Sandra Banning that even atheists like Newdow could be "comfortable" with the words "under God" in the Pledge. "Do you think God is so generic in this context that it could be that inclusive?" Breyer asked. "And if it is, then does your objection disappear?" Newdow responded with seeming incredulity. "I don't think I can include under God to mean no God, which is exactly what I think," he replied. "I deny the existence of God, and for someone to tell me that 'under God' should mean some broad thing that even encompasses my religious beliefs seems like the government is imposing what it wants me to think in terms of religion, which it may not do. Government needs to stay out of this business altogether."

From the opposite end of the bench, Justice David Souter followed Breyer's lead. Was the reference to God in the Pledge, he asked, "so tepid, so diluted, so far from a compulsory prayer that it should be, in effect, beneath the constitutional radar?" Newdow responded with his closest approach to anger in the entire argument. "That is a view that you may choose to take and that a majority of Americans may choose to take," he replied in heated words, "but when I see the flag and I think of pledging allegiance, it's like I'm getting slapped in the face every time, bam, you know, this is a nation under God, your religious belief system is wrong."

Newdow answered Souter's suggestion that the words "under God" in the Pledge were "beneath the constitutional radar" by noting the "divisive" response to the Ninth Circuit's ruling in his favor. "The country went berserk because people were so upset that God was going to be taken out of the Pledge of Allegiance." Chief Justice Rehnquist leaned forward in his chair. Like a good prosecutor, he asked Newdow a question to which he already knew the answer. "Do we know what the vote was in Congress, apropos of divisiveness, to adopt the under God phrase?" Newdow looked surprised at the question, but answered honestly, like a good witness. "It was apparently unanimous," he replied. "There was no objection." Rehnquist leaned back, a smile on his face and his point made. "Well, that doesn't sound divisive," he said, as the audience chuckled in appreciation of his debater's skill. Newdow's quick response prompted a different audience reaction. "That's only because no atheist can get elected to public office," he retorted. At that point, the public section of the chamber erupted in applause, rewarding Newdow for his riposte. Rehnquist looked shocked. Laughter was fine, and often filled the chamber, but applause was a breach of the Court's decorum. "The courtroom will be cleared if there's any more clapping," he growled. The deputy marshals who stood around the chamber shot stern looks at the spectators, who remained quiet during the rest of the arguments.

Justice Ginsburg posed another question. Were the words "under God" in the Pledge, she asked, more like the words "In God we Trust" on the nation's currency, "which nobody really cares very much about anymore." Newdow replied that the public reaction to the Ninth Circuit ruling in his case showed that people really cared about retaining those words in the Pledge. "I would merely note," he said, that every senator had voted for a resolution supporting the Pledge, and that "it was on the front page of every newspaper. This is supposed to be one of the major cases of this Court's term. I think clearly it has enormous significance to the American public and that's why this is important." Newdow then reminded the justices of the "neutrality" doctrine their cases had affirmed since the *Everson* decision in 1947. He included the absent Justice Scalia in his calculation. "Seven members of this Court," he said, "six sitting today, have said that we need neutrality, and here we have the quintessential religious question, does there exist a God? And government comes in, yes, there exists a God. That is not neutrality by any means." When a lawyer has five minutes left of argument time, a white light flashes on the lectern, and when the time has expired, a red light goes on. As Newdow's thirty minutes came near its end, he beat the red light with seconds to spare. "There's a principle here," he concluded, "and I'm hoping the Court will uphold this principle so that we can finally go back and have every American want to stand up, face the flag, place their hand over their heart and pledge to one nation, indivisible, not divided by religion, with liberty and justice for all." With those words, Newdow closed his binder and returned to his seat at the counsel table.

The arguments were not quite over. Cassidy had reserved five minutes for rebuttal, and he took the lectern to repeat his claim that Newdow lacked standing in the case, because "it is his daughter who is affected by the Pledge" and because Sandra Banning had no objection to her participation in the Pledge ceremony. Cassidy then argued that the Pledge had no "religious purpose" and simply fostered "national unity and citizenship of our young students." Justice Stevens interrupted Cassidy. "I hate to take your rebuttal time," he said, "but one of the amicus briefs filed in this case has this sentence in it." Stevens then read from the brief filed by a group of Christian ministers, supporting Newdow's position. "If the religious portion of the Pledge is not intended as a serious affirmation of faith," Stevens read, "then every day government asks millions of school children to take the name of the Lord in vain." Stevens leaned forward in his seat. "Would you comment on that argument?"

Cassidy had clearly not expected this question, and he took several seconds before replying. "I would disagree," he finally told Stevens, "because we feel that the use of the term, 'one nation under God,' reflects the political philosophy of our country, as set forth in the Declaration of Independence, that ours is one of a limited government, and that's the philosophy that's now more enhanced, more reflected in the 1954 act" that added the words "under God" to the Pledge. By reciting the Pledge, Cassidy argued, children "are learning about our country's nationalism and civic unity at a very early stage. They don't say the Pledge of Allegiance and go home." When the red light flashed, Cassidy had begun another sentence. "Likewise, I would submit that the Pledge of——." But he was abruptly cut off by Chief Justice Rehnquist. "Thank you, Mr. Cassidy. The case is submitted." At promptly three minutes past noon, the justices rose from their seats and filed out from the chamber, disappearing behind the velvet curtain. The arguments were over, and the waiting for the Court's decision had begun.

As the marshals escorted spectators from the chamber, Newdow's friends and supporters headed for his counsel table, shaking his hand and praising his performance. Into this gathering, another lawyer approached from the first row of the lawyers' section, offering his hand and a warm smile. Kenneth Starr, whose brief for Sandra Banning had defended the Pledge with evangelical zeal, shook Newdow's hand and said, "Mike, I just want you to know that you made a superb argument."

Newdow certainly won the day with the reporters who covered the arguments. National Public Radio's veteran Supreme Court commentator, Nina Totenberg, praised his "virtuoso" performance. Another veteran, Linda Greenhouse of the *New York Times*, almost gushed in her account: "No one who managed to get a seat in the courtroom is likely ever to forget his spell-binding performance." Even Sandra Banning offered a backhanded compliment: "Michael did very well. He showed as much passion in front of the Supreme Court today as he shows in family court." It remained to be seen whether Newdow had won the day with the justices.

———

Whether by design or not, the Court handed down its decision on Flag Day, June 14, 2004, fifty years to the day after President Eisenhower signed the bill adding "under God" to the Pledge of Allegiance. Michael Newdow had not won his day with the justices. Five of the eight who heard the arguments joined the brief opinion that Justice Stevens wrote for the Court. "In our view," he said, "it is improper for the federal courts to entertain a claim by a plaintiff whose standing to sue is founded on family law rights that are in dispute when prosecution of the lawsuit may have an adverse effect on the person who is the source of the plaintiff's claimed standing." Stevens did not, however, explain what "adverse" consequences of ruling on the Pledge's constitutionality might have on Newdow's daughter. "When hard questions of domestic relations are sure to affect the outcome," Stevens continued, "the prudent course is for the federal court to stay its hand rather than reach out to resolve a weighty question of federal constitutional law." The notion of judicial prudence, as legal scholars have noted, offers judges an easy out from deciding questions they would prefer to duck. And ducking the Pledge case during an election year might have seemed the better course for Stevens, whose questions during oral argument clearly signaled his agreement with Newdow on the constitutional issues.

Three justices, however, declined to duck those issues. In her concurring opinion, Sandra Day O'Connor conceded that the case raised a "close question" under the Establishment Clause. "There are no *de minimis* violations of the Constitution," she agreed, "no constitutional harms so slight that the courts are obliged to ignore them." But she viewed the words "under God" in the Pledge as a permissible form of "ceremonial deism" that should be "properly understood as employing the idiom for essentially secular purposes," much like the national motto and "The Star-Spangled Banner." Their references to God, O'Connor wrote, "are not minor trespasses upon the Establishment Clause to which I turn a blind eye. Instead, their history, character, and context prevent them from being constitutional violations at all." O'Connor also joined the concurring opinion of Chief Justice Rehnquist, who argued that Newdow should not be given a "veto power" over his daughter's participation in "a commendable patriotic observance" that reflected the "democratic choices" of Congress, the California legislature, and Elk Grove's school officials.

Clarence Thomas was the only justice willing to confront the constitutional issues that his colleagues had ducked. "I conclude that, as a matter of our precedent, the Pledge policy is unconstitutional," he bluntly stated. The cases to which Thomas referred, including *Lee v. Weisman* in 1992 and *Santa Fe Independent School District v. Doe* in 2000, held that even voluntary prayer in public schools violated the Establishment Clause. But these cases had been "wrongly decided" and had "no basis in law or reason," Thomas argued. Alone on the Court, he believed that the Establishment Clause applied only to acts of Congress, and that states were free to promote religion or even to establish official state churches. No other justice shared this idiosyncratic view, but Thomas seemed clearly right that *Lee* and *Santa Fe*, had they been applied as precedent, would have required his colleagues to uphold the Ninth Circuit's ruling in the Pledge case, which had cited those cases as binding authority. We can only speculate, of course, on the case's outcome if Newdow and Banning had not been locked in a custody battle over their daughter, or if 2004 had not been an election year.

As the justices certainly recognized, their ruling did not end the Pledge dispute. Another case, with plaintiffs whose standing could not be challenged, was likely to reach the Court within a few years. And Michael Newdow was determined to continue his legal crusade. "There's no problem in bringing the case right back," he told reporters after his defeat. Newdow took and passed the California bar exam, allowing him to represent clients in state and federal courts. Armed with his law license, Newdow quickly found willing plaintiffs in Elk Grove and neighboring school districts, parents and their children whose identities were concealed as "Does" and "Roes" in the complaint he filed in Sacramento's federal court in January 2005. Newdow also found a sympathetic federal judge for his new lawsuit, Lawrence Karlton, placed on the bench in 1979 by President Jimmy Carter. Ruling on September 14, 2005, Karlton denied the district's motion to dismiss the case. The Supreme Court, Karlton noted in his opinion, had not reversed the Ninth Circuit's holding that the words "under God" in the Pledge violated the Establishment Clause. It was therefore his "duty as the judge of a subordinate court" to apply the "binding precedent" of that decision to the new Pledge case.

Writing as a senior judge, with twenty-six years of service on the bench, Karlton felt free to chastise the Supreme Court for its lack of guidance in Establishment Clause cases. After all, only three months earlier, in June 2005, the justices had split in deciding challenges to displays of the Ten Commandments in public places, ruling against displays in two Kentucky courthouses and upholding one on the Texas State Capitol grounds. The Court's "recently articulated distinction between those governmental activities which endorse religion, and are thus prohibited, and those which acknowledge the Nation's asserted religious heritage, and thus are permitted," Karlton complained, was "utterly standardless, leaving those of us who work in the vineyard without guidance."

Judge Karlton seemed glad to leave the job of defining those boundaries to higher courts, but he could not resist taking a final swing at the Pledge. "As preposterous as it might seem," he wrote, "given the lack of boundaries, a case could be made for substituting 'under Christ' for 'under God' in the Pledge, thus marginalizing not only atheists and agnostics, as the present form of the Pledge does, but also Jews, Muslims, Buddhists, Confucians, Sikhs, Hindus, and other religious adherents who, not only are citizens of this nation, but in fact reside in this judicial district."

Karlton's decision sent the Pledge case back to the Ninth Circuit for a second time. But it returned with another set of lawyers to join Michael Newdow and Terrence Cassidy. Karlton had granted the motion of the Becket Fund for Religious Liberty to represent ten parents and their children as "intervenors" in the case, along with almost two million members of the Knights of Columbus, the group that launched the campaign to add "under God" to the Pledge. The Becket Fund, one of the smaller but better-financed of the Religious Right legal groups, vowed to oppose Newdow's "ideologically bankrupt" attack on the Pledge. But its presence in the case signaled an escalation of the ideological "cultural wars" in which the Pledge has become a battleground.

However the Ninth Circuit rules on Karlton's decision, which is still undecided at this writing, the Supreme Court will certainly be asked to revisit the Pledge case, and Michael Newdow might once again face the justices as an outspoken atheist. But in the meantime, children in Elk Grove's schools will continue to pledge their allegiance to "one nation, under God."

MIKE NEWDOW

I was born in 1953 at Bronx Hospital in Bronx, New York. I had an older brother, and then got a younger sister. We lived in the Bronx until I was seven, and then we moved to Teaneck, New Jersey. My father was an electrical engineer who worked for what are called job shops, like temporary employment agencies—somebody would have a job, and he'd work on that and then go somewhere else. He eventually decided to make more money doing that than being an electrical engineer, so he started his own shop. My mother was his partner in doing that, which was nice because they worked out of the house.

We were Jewish, culturally. We must have gone to temple once or twice, but I don't remember if we did. My mother, she doesn't remember telling me this, we didn't discuss this stuff much, but I remember her telling me she believed in God, and I knew my father didn't. She just told me that because she wanted me to get a balance, which was a good idea. I always thought she did, but it turned out she doesn't. We really never discussed it that much. It wasn't until after the Pledge case came up and I talked to her and she said, No, I don't believe in God. My parents did ask if I wanted to go through Bar Mitzvah, but I said, No, thank you. Religion always seemed to me like mass delusions; I never gave it any credence. If there's one thing that I think defines me, I've always challenged everything. My father used to say "black," and I'd say "white." Whatever he'd say, I'd say just the opposite.

School wasn't hard for me. My first-grade teacher at PS 95, in the Bronx, kind of pushed the class, and there was only myself and this one girl who could actually keep up with what she was doing; she had us spelling "encyclopedia" and "dictionary." And so, when I went to New Jersey, I had already had in first grade everything they were doing in second grade. The story is—I don't remember, but my parents say— that I started really doing badly in school, so they tested me. Turned out I was bored, because I had already done it, so they put me up in third grade. I went all the way through high school in Teaneck, did the standard high-school stuff. I did a lot of sports—track, football at the beginning, but that was because I didn't want to be on the soccer team with my brother, who was really good. But I got on the soccer team, and I had a great record. I was the goalie, and we had a guy on our team who was from Scotland and was incredible on offense. I only gave up three goals in the first fifteen games, and one of those goals was because I was standing on the midfield line, because this guy always had the ball down there, and somebody kicked it over my head.

I wound up at Brown University, I think, because of soccer, because I had this great record. That was the only college I applied to, and I got an early decision. I wanted something that was not too big, and somebody said, How about Brown? And I didn't know anything about it. In retrospect, I think I was wrong. I was there from 1970 to '74. I worked a lot to put myself through school, worked in the cafeteria, stuff like that. I was pre-med, took mostly science courses, and got a B.S. in biology. I wanted to take the other things, but I just couldn't stand it. You had to take two semesters of English; one of the courses in English was set design, so I took that. And my other course was an introductory English course, and I remember hearing all this nonsense these people were discussing, I was just watching everybody say nothing. Like, there was a dog in the class that somebody brought, and they'd say, Does the dog know more than us? So my final paper was called "The Bullshit of English 101." It was a great paper, but the professor gave me a B-plus. She was really insulted—you could see her comments—because I kept track of all the nonsensical discussions they had. The fact that I got a B-plus was actually pretty good, because it was an A paper.

When I applied to medical school, there's a lot of competition, so I applied to about seventeen schools—you just check the schools on a form, it's like twenty-five bucks each. And I wound up at UCLA, which was a state school and cheap. I loved med school, although I made one big mistake. I went to one class in genetics, an introductory class when school started, and the professor said, It's really important to come to class; I hadn't been going to many classes. I was called in to see the dean once for not going to classes. If you spent your time just reading the books, you'd do much better; lectures don't do anything. I decided at the beginning, you don't really learn the stuff you need in class, it's like you're just putting in time. You can get a lot out of it if you put a lot into it, but you can also get a lot out of it without putting a lot into it. Like anatomy lab; there is nothing more inefficient than anatomy lab. You have four people sitting around doing nothing, while one person is going through this very slow motion of dissecting, to do what? Oh, there's a muscle. Give me a picture, I could see it in two seconds. But the way to learn it, I just don't think you need all the classes and lectures. You really learn it after you get out.

They had this thing at UCLA where you could only be away from school for two months out of four years. But they had this list of clerkships that counted as being at UCLA even though they weren't. One was up near Yosemite, doing family medicine in a clinic, so I did that. And the other one was up in Kotzebue, Alaska, just over the Arctic Circle, with the Indian Health Service. That was incredible, it was great. There were all these little towns, mostly Native Alaskans, maybe fifty houses, with no medical care, maybe just a nurse who wasn't that experienced. So they'd call in to us in Kotzebue for something that required some expertise, not that I had much. They'd send these bush pilots to come get you, and they stayed like twenty feet over the tundra, and you can't see, because it's always misty. And these guys would just go by the compass, and they'd get to where they think they're close to the town, and the people on the ground would radio to the pilot and say, We hear you, you're a little east—until they find the place. And you'd get out of the plane, and everybody would think you're this big physician; you don't tell them you're just a med student. But it was great experience, because in med school you don't learn anything about working with patients.

I did my internship at Kings County Hospital in Brooklyn. I decided I wanted to do emergency medicine, and public hospitals had plenty of patients, and you get to learn to be a doctor. I think the reason I picked emergency medicine was that I wanted to know that if something ever happened to somebody when I was there, I'd know what to do. So the ER gives that, plus it's instant gratification: you fix people right away. When you get out of med school, you have no idea how to take care of a patient. You're really frightened, and these people are trusting you. But in these big county hospitals, you're doing surgery, as much as I wanted. The residents aren't even doing that in teaching hospitals. And in the ER, you get gunshot wounds and stuff like that all the time, as opposed to some nice facility in the suburbs, where you hardly ever see one.

My plan was to do an internship at Kings County and then go to a real academic place for my residency, because I'd have all the experience and then do some learning. But it turned out that 1979 was the year that emergency medicine became a formal specialty, and they didn't want all these docs who'd been working for years having to go back and do a residency, so they grandfathered you in and you'd get board-certified. So I never did a residency. There are still places where they won't take me because I didn't do a residency, even though I've been board-certified for twenty-five years, like that would make a difference.

So, after I finished at Kings County Hospital, I went all over the country, doing what's called *locum tenens*, *locum* meaning "place" and *tenens* meaning "temporary." Back then, ER was a new specialty, and board-certified docs could pretty much get a job anytime. The nice thing was that I could just take off if something else came up; I liked that freedom. I had like fifteen licenses, because you had to get licensed in every state. I mostly worked in the states—Michigan, Florida, New Jersey, North Carolina—but I also worked in Guam, and I worked on Ascension Island, which is between Africa and South America.

I decided to go to law school in 1985, while I was working in hospitals around Ann Arbor, Michigan. I didn't like the way medicine was being practiced, and I still don't. Doctors order tests that are totally unindicated, it just makes no sense. So my goal was to stop physicians from doing needless stuff, and I thought going through the law would be the way to change that. The thing I remember most about law school—and it was ten years after medical school, so I don't know if society had changed or the difference was between law and medicine—but in medicine nobody ever thought about money or talked about money; it wasn't even an issue. We were really there to learn this material. I never heard, in my entire four years in med school, anybody talking about, You can make a lot of money. It just never entered into the discussion. And the first day in law school, all I heard was, Do you know about this firm, they've got this great bonus. That was really significant. I don't know if it was the different fields, or just the ten years. But there was this tremendous emphasis on making money.

In law school, as opposed to med school, you can really get by with doing nothing. I remember my first essay exam in tort law. I always thought tort law was this ridiculous system, it just makes no sense. There's no relationship between the negligence and the injury. People who are negligent get off scot-free, and people who are really hurt don't get compensated. I thought, There's a much better way to do this. So, on the tort final, the professor gave us this case, you're a judge, and X, Y, and Z happens, how would you rule? I wrote one sentence: Because the law is this, I'd go this way. However, given the opportunity to pontificate on this, I wrote this five-page essay on how I thought the tort-law system should be handled. It was a really good essay, too, but she gave me a C-plus. That was one of the great things about being in that position: I didn't care how I did.

After I finished in 1988, I didn't take the bar exam, because I didn't know if I was going to practice law. I sent out a bunch of résumés, saying I'm a physician-attorney, and I didn't get a single answer. I don't recall anyone even saying, No, we don't want you. Maybe they thought I'd be too expensive, I'd want too much—I don't know. So I just kept doing my medicine and didn't think about it. I kept moving around for another ten years.

The way I wound up in Sacramento was that my daughter's mother, Sandy Banning, was raised around here. I'd first met her when I was doing my med-school clerkship up near Yosemite, but then we drifted apart, and we didn't get back together until several years later. She had been married before I met her, and had a son, and then got divorced. Sandy had lived with me in North Carolina, but she decided she was lonely for her family and moved back, and she had a job here. My daughter was born in Sacramento in 1994. At that time, my parents had a place in Florida, a condominium in Fort Lauderdale that they went to a couple of times a year, four weeks total per year, and the rest of the time it was empty. And I had taken Sandy and her son to Florida a number of times, along with my daughter.

This whole lawsuit thing started with going to a store in Chicago to buy soap. My daughter and I would travel together sometimes, just the two of us. So one time, this was in '97, she and I went to Chicago, to visit my friends Larry Marshall and his wife, who are both lawyers. Larry was teaching then at Northwestern's law school, and he's now at Stanford. My daughter and I were staying with them, and they had a shower, but they never had regular bar soap in their house, just this liquid stuff, and it drove me crazy. So I went to the store and bought them like a hundred bars of soap, so I could take a shower when I'm visiting. And while I was in the store, waiting in line, I just happened to look at all my coins and currency, and it struck me for the first time that it's on everything, "In God We Trust." It was on a one-dollar bill, and a five, and a twenty, and all the coins. And I thought, Holy smoke, I remember something from law school—this can't be constitutional!

So I decided I was going to bring this case against "In God We Trust." I didn't know how you file a lawsuit—they didn't teach you this in law school—and what I knew was ten years old. I had never worked in a law firm. In a way, I wish I hadn't even gone to law school and wasted those three years. Because, it's incredible, any person with a computer and a printer can take a case and challenge and uphold the Constitution. I mean, you don't need anything. What a country!

So I filed the "In God We Trust" case in Florida—this was in '98. Then I realized the Pledge of Allegiance case was stronger, and my daughter was just about to start kindergarten. Considering everything that happened later, it's important to know that Sandy knew about this from the beginning, back in Sacramento in '97. In the house that I live in now, we were sitting at the dining-room table, Sandy was there, and one day I was working on this stuff and I turned to my daughter and recited the Pledge of Allegiance without "under God." This was while she was in pre-school; she hadn't been in kindergarten yet. I didn't even know she'd ever heard the Pledge of Allegiance. And I go, "One nation, indivisible, with liberty and justice for all." And as soon as I hit the word "all" she goes "under God." She had picked up that it was missing. I thought, Look at what this does to a four-year-old kid; I didn't even know she knew the thing, and she immediately knew this. Sandy was right there when it happened, and we discussed it. So she was fully aware the whole time. In her initial pleading in the custody case in 1999, to keep me from being a parent to my kid, Sandy said, He's trying to use our daughter to get "under God" out of the Pledge of Allegiance. She said, I didn't know about it, I was only vaguely aware.

Anyway, I'm doing research for the "In God We Trust" case—every night I'm doing this, I'm really into it—and I'm learning more and more and more. And I keep seeing opinions talking about the Pledge of Allegiance, and "under God" in the Pledge. And I'm thinking, That's a better case! Because "In God We Trust" is the national motto, and nobody has to recite it, although it's still unconstitutional. But in the

Pledge, we had a Pledge of Allegiance that was working fine, and Congress passed a law that did nothing, except put in these two words that are clearly religious. So I said to myself, I'm doing the wrong case, I should have done the Pledge of Allegiance. And my daughter's about to start school. But I'd already filed the "In God We Trust" case, and the U.S. attorney had sixty days to reply to my complaint. And then they called me when their brief came due and said, Can we have another sixty days? So I took that as a sign from above, and I changed my case. In the federal courts, Rule 15 says, as of right, you can amend your complaint once, and I amended it to challenge "under God" in the Pledge of Allegiance.

I lost in the district court—the judge said it was a frivolous case. No district-court judge is ever going to say the Pledge of Allegiance is unconstitutional. So I took it to the court of appeals in the Eleventh Circuit. While the case was in the process of appeal, Sandy said she's not going to stay in Florida, so we moved back to California. I wrote to the Eleventh Circuit and said, I'm no longer going to be here, I'm going to California with my kid, so they dismissed the case as moot. So I had to file over again in California, which was great, because now I know what I'm doing, I've done it once. Now I've had a practice run, and I know exactly what the U.S. attorney's arguments are going to be.

So I filed the Pledge of Allegiance case with the district court in Sacramento in 2000; my daughter was then in first grade in Elk Grove. After I filed the suit, I went to one of the Elk Grove school-board meetings. I went to ask them: What are you doing here? You're supposed to be protecting all the students, all the parents. Why are you fighting this case? You're saying something that offends the religious views of certain people; your job is to protect everybody; why are you taking this on? I still don't understand. It was interesting at that meeting. There's a tremendous amount of diversity in Elk Grove, and they had just been given awards for minority programs, and they made this big thing about how we're a diverse society. And I said, You guys are talking about diversity, and here you are, going on about diversity; how can you do this? They would not accept it. That's what religion does to you.

The district judge dismissed the case, and I appealed to the Ninth Circuit. In the Ninth Circuit, again, I had no idea what I was doing. I called my friend Larry Marshall, and I asked him, What happens in an oral argument? I didn't even know who goes first. But I knew I was going to win, there was no question in my mind. I'd looked up the three judges on my panel, opinions they'd written before, and I knew Judge Reinhardt was on my side. And then Judge Goodwin, in the middle of the oral argument he says, You know, I remember when they put "under God" in the Pledge, back in 1954; I don't know how they were allowed to do that. So I knew I had Goodwin and Reinhardt. The third judge, Fernandez, didn't ask many questions, but I knew he wouldn't make any difference even if he voted against me, which he did.

And so, a month before it came out—you don't know when it's coming out—I figured people were going to call and complain about the decision. My phone is not in my name, but I got another line and put it in my name for this occasion. And what I planned to do was to have a computerized message that would say, Hi, this is Mike Newdow: for comments, press one; for questions, press two; for criticisms, press three; and for threats, press four. The software for the phone arrived the day the opinion came out, but I never got to install it.

When the Ninth Circuit decision did come out, in June of 2002, there wasn't any issue about my standing to bring the case. Judge Goodwin agreed that I had standing, both as a parent and as a taxpayer. Sandy came out with the standing thing; nobody had focused on that before. That wasn't her idea, that was clearly the Religious Right. The week after the Ninth Circuit decision came out, they flew her back to Washington on a private jet, twenty-five thousand dollars round-trip, just to go on television and further their agenda. They didn't have anything to do with this case, but they turned this into Newdow versus Banning, when she had nothing to do with this case. There was nothing in family law that had to do with this case; it was really my case, and my daughter was not a party in it. But the Religious Right made standing the issue, focusing on the custody case that Sandy had filed, to keep me from sharing our daughter, and they did a great job.

When my case was scheduled for oral argument before the Supreme Court, in March of 2004, I'd already done eleven moot courts at law schools around the country, because it was a high-profile case, so everybody agreed to fly me to their school. I'd never done moot court in law school; I didn't even know what a moot court was. All I knew was that people walked around in ties and jackets. But after all these moot courts in law schools, I felt fairly confident about being able to talk.

Everyone said I should go and see a case or two beforehand in the Supreme Court. My case was on a Wednesday, so I went earlier, on Monday, to see a case, and I literally fell asleep. The guard came up and said, Hey, you can't sleep here! I think I heard four cases, and three were really boring. But there was one interesting case, where this guy, I think it was in Utah, was standing outside his pickup truck and a cop asked for his ID, and he wouldn't give it to him, so he got arrested. Then I went to the Capitol, across from the Supreme Court. It was a beautiful sunny day, and I lay down on the Capitol grounds, and a guard came over and asked for my ID, and I said, I was just in the Supreme Court, I'm not sure I have to give this to you. But I decided I didn't want to get my name in the paper, so I did give it to him. As it turned out, the guy in the pickup truck lost his case, so I guess I did the right thing.

When I got to the Supreme Court for the argument, they prep all the lawyers, tell them what's going to happen and what the rules are, which you already know. I think it's just to get the lawyers calmed down and not so nervous. I remember them telling us that we could keep these quill pens that are on the lawyers' tables in the courtroom. Big deal! You can get these pens for fifty cents, down at the gift shop, and they don't even work. What a disappointment.

When my argument began, I thought I would be nervous, but I wasn't. The first five seconds, your heart starts pounding, but then it went away and I never felt it again. The other side, the school-board lawyer and the solicitor general, went first, and they focused on the standing issue, I think because I had them cold on the Establishment Clause and the religious nature of "under God" in the Pledge. And after I started my argument, Justice Kennedy picked up on this in his questions to me. He was buying into this: You're using your kid, this is a family-law issue.

My feeling was that the standing argument was their out, that nothing I was going to say on standing would make a difference. If they don't want to hear this case, they're going to use that as their excuse. And when the decision came down, it was based on this notion of "prudential standing." Somehow, it wouldn't be "prudent" for the Court to decide this case on the constitutional issues. I don't think "prudential standing" was ever mentioned until the decision. The other side didn't say anything about prudential reasons; I thought this was all Article III, and that's how I argued the whole thing. Justice Stevens, who was my hero up until that moment, wrote that decision. He had this whole thing in his earlier opinions, about how you shouldn't use standing to keep people out. But they obviously wanted to duck the case in an election year. Great testimonial for our judicial system!

As soon as I lost, I said, I'll be back. I won't give up. This whole thing on standing is just ridiculous. First of all, I think they're wrong. Anybody has standing not to have a national Pledge of Allegiance that goes against their religion. A bunch of people in the Sacramento area were interested in a new lawsuit, people that I knew or had contacted me. So I filed a new case, with myself as a plaintiff and with parents in other school districts around Sacramento. I had three plaintiffs drop out before I even filed the case. One person said, I'll lose my job if they find out I'm an atheist. Another had a kid whose teacher said, Stand up, or get out of this fucking country! That's pretty traumatic for a kid in school. This is a real thing. This isn't even a close case. These people are going to lose their jobs if they stand up for their religious rights. What kind of America is this? It should be changed. And I think I'm better at it now; every day that goes by, I read more and I learn more.

I was dismissed in the case, because my daughter was now in middle school in Elk Grove, and they don't recite the Pledge in her school, although I think that decision was wrong. But the district judge left in the parents from the school district in Rio Linda, which is just north of

Sacramento, and ruled in our favor. The Rio Linda school board has appealed that decision, and it's now back in the Ninth Circuit.

Not too long ago, I went to Alabama—some Baptist church invited me to speak. And I said, I'll go, but you've got to get me Roy Moore to talk to, so they did. So Roy Moore and I sat for about an hour and just discussed the issues, with about twenty or thirty people around. And afterward, people came up to me and said, You know, you're right. This was a Baptist-church audience, and I'd gone to church with these people, and they understand the issue. People have a very mistaken idea; they think this is against God. And it's not; it's not a case of those who believe in God versus those who don't. It's those who believe in equality versus those who don't. And people need to understand that.

They come out with these polls, that 90 percent of the population wants God in the Pledge of Allegiance. And that's why we have an Establishment Clause; that was predicted by the framers of the First Amendment. But if you ask people the right question—Do you think government should treat all religious views with the same respect?—I think you'll have 95 percent or 100 percent for that. Once people understand that no one's religious views are being threatened here, they understand the issues. Go out in the public square, get on your knees, worship Jesus, have your revivals—no one stops you. That's an absolute right you have. You just don't have the right to have government join you, that's all. I love the idea that people have other views. It's a much more interesting world to me. ❖

BILL LUGG

I was born here in Sacramento on June 27 of 1928. It's kind of unique, because I was born in a house rather than a hospital. My dad was a staunch Christian Scientist, and they didn't believe in doctors. My mother, although she had been brought up in the Methodist religion, just followed along with that, so she had me at home. She swore up and down it would never happen again, because there weren't any doctors to help, any of the things they do for you in hospitals. And I was exceptionally large; I weighed ten pounds, two ounces, and that's a whopper for kids. When my brother came along, she went to the hospital. I grew up here in Sacramento, spent all of my memorable youth in the southwest portion of the city.

My dad was born in Sacramento in 1877. His dad came from England; he was an inside finish painter. He contracted tuberculosis and died when my dad was nine years old, so he had to go out and go to work to help support the family. He did not graduate from any kind of school. He worked for the California State Library, worked there for forty-three years. He was supervisor of library crafts, and that entailed bookbinding, gilding the books, all kinds of photographic work, and he supervised the printing operation. In 1935, Talking Books for the Blind came out, and he took that over. My dad would spend time in the stacks, reading books to improve his education.

My mother was born in Live Oak, California, up in Sutter County. Her family came originally from Scotland, and they migrated to Quebec, then to Michigan, and came from Michigan out to California. My great-grandfather had a ranch in Live Oak. My mother went to school in Live Oak, and then high school in Marysville. She had a high-school diploma, which was something in those days. From there, she got a job in the state library, and that's where she met my dad, in the blind department. Once they got married, she was a homemaker from there on.

I was raised in the Christian Science Church. They really didn't have any programs for youth; it was more of a religion for older folks. I got sort of disenchanted with some of the things they believed, and when I got married, my wife and I went with my folks to the Christian Science church, but we were kind of getting lukewarm on it; there were holes that I could see in it. For a while, we went to a United Brethren church, after my dad passed away, until they went together with the Methodists and became the United Methodists, and their whole doctrine changed then, became much more liberal. It just wasn't for us, and we didn't do anything about church for quite a while. It wasn't until my first grandson was born, in 1985, that we started going to Grace Evangelical Free

Church here in Elk Grove, and that's where we go today. It's a real Bible-believing church, and it's totally based on the truth of the Scriptures.

I went to the schools in Sacramento City Unified. The education we got then was a lot different than what it is now. It didn't cover such a broad span of things, but what it did cover it covered pretty thoroughly. I had a good knowledge of geography, a good knowledge of American history, up to that point, and math and English, although English was never a strong subject for me, but math I enjoyed. It was a different kind of an education than kids get today. I don't think there were more than two or three African Americans in the school where I went. The area that I lived in was all white, lower-to-middle-class folks.

I was in high school during World War II, and I can remember some incidents growing up. I went down with my folks to Santa Cruz, on the boardwalk, and they had one of those Skee-Ball games, where you roll the ball up into the holes. My dad tried that, and he got a prize, a little paper flowerpot. And he turned it over and it said, Made in Japan. I can see him to this day; he just threw that thing to the floor and stomped it into a pulp. There was a lot of animosity towards Japan; they had marched into Manchuria, did terrible things over in China. They were expanding, and we were shipping iron over to them as fast as we could ship it. My dad had been involved in the Republican Party; he was a conservative guy. He was never very happy with President Roosevelt, but I'll say this: never in my household, in my life, did I ever hear anybody refer to him in a derogatory manner. He was the president, and we were taught to respect that, even if we may not have liked what he was doing. And I don't see that today in a lot of homes. I don't even see it in the media today; I think it's a shame.

I remember the evacuation of the Japanese Americans after Pearl Harbor. I was in junior high at the time. In my school there was only one Japanese girl, and one day she wasn't there, and I don't think any of us knew what happened to her. It didn't cross my mind at the time that there was anything wrong with the evacuation. Much later, I realized that the Japanese Americans were very loyal and patriotic citizens. I got to know Al and Mary Tsukamoto, who lived over in Florin, which is part of the Elk Grove district. Al's family ran a strawberry and grape farm, and he graduated from Elk Grove High School before he was sent to an evacuation camp in Arkansas. Al was a great guy, and his wife, Mary, was a wonderful, sweet person. She was very active in the schools before she passed away, and there's now an elementary school in Elk Grove named after her.

My family was always very patriotic. We never missed a parade. My dad always wore a hat; the flag never went by without that hat coming off. Today, I see kids watching the flag go by, and they just watch it and don't make any kind of salute. That bothers me, but, nevertheless, you have to recognize that times have changed. That's the way things are in some families. I don't condemn them; I think the problem is that today, if you want to have many of the material things that people have, both people have to work, and the kids get short-changed on that kind of thing. The parents get through work, they come home, they're tired, and if Mom has to fix something to eat, that just adds more to the work. And everybody has to pitch in and clean house and wash clothes. I don't think the kids get the kind of quality time that we had when we were young and growing up, where Mom stayed home and did all the work during the day and was always there when we got home.

I graduated from high school in 1946. At that time, what is now Sacramento City College was then a junior college and was part of the city unified district, so it's actually a K–14 district. I just progressed right on through that. I started off in junior college intending to become an electrical engineer. I got through a year and a half, and I was really struggling with integral calculus. And I really thought that I wanted to work with my hands; I like to do things physically. So I changed my major and went into electronic technician, and I graduated in January of 1950 with an A.A. degree. I started trying to find a job in that area, and jobs were not to be had for people with a theoretical background; they wanted folks that had practical experience, and that didn't work.

So I went to work for the state in various positions. I started in the Department of Motor Vehicles for a time, and then went to the Department of Water Resources, and then back to the DMV for about two years. And from 1952 to 1954 I worked in the state prison in Folsom. I had taken the clerical test, and I passed the test for senior clerk. A job came open up there, and I thought, It's not that far from home, and I decided to go do it. Really didn't have any idea about what it was. I was notary public at Folsom; every other week, I'd go down to the prison yard and notarize for these guys, and they notarized everything that they'd ever written or thought of writing. Some of them were going through the court system, and if they'd get thrown out of the Supreme Court, they'd come back and start over again. A lot of them spent a tremendous amount of time in the law library which was there for them. I don't regret that time at all; it was a chance to see how the other half lives, and I got a real education. Not many of us get that opportunity.

I was never in the Army, because I had poor eyesight and had to wear glasses. I was never a good sports person; I didn't like gym, I'd be glad if they never had it. Nobody wanted me on their team, because I couldn't see well enough to do anything. So, when I got to high school, I went into the ROTC, and I really liked it, and I served there for three years. I was out for about a year after I finished school, but I really missed being in the military, so I went into the California National Guard, and I served there for almost ten years. That was along with these other jobs that I had. I was on active duty with the Guard for three years, here in Sacramento. And for a time I was at Aberdeen Proving Ground in Maryland, for about four months. I spent every weekend out, looking at historical things. Since my maternal grandfather was in the Civil War, I kept looking to find out where he might have been; he had been wounded and discharged early in the war. I spent at least three weeks at Gettysburg, going all through that area, spent time at Valley Forge, went to Baltimore to Fort McHenry, every place I could go, because I loved history. I really had a great time doing those things.

After I left the job at Folsom Prison, I went from there to the electronics industry, working in sales, and was industrial sales manager for Sacramento Electronic Supply for a number of years, and then, for a short period, was a part owner of a business, and then I went back to the electronic-supply company. This was a family-run business, and I finally realized that I'd gone as far as I was ever going to go with it. The pay wasn't bad, but it didn't go up with inflation. And I got a chance in 1974 to take a test for buyer for the North Sacramento school district. So I said, I'll try it, and I passed, and I was chosen for the job. There was a lady in charge of the office who was an accountant. I was there for about two years, and I got promoted to purchasing agent. Not long after that, the gentleman who was in charge of support services came to me and said, You know, this lady is going to quit, and if you want that job you have to learn something about accounting to do it. So I went home and talked to my wife, and we signed up to go to night school in accounting. She stopped before we got into the class on governmental accounting, but I took that also, and I did well in it. So, when the time came, I got that job as office manager and accountant.

My wife, when my son got into junior high school, she found work as a yard supervisor at Rutter Middle School, here in Elk Grove, and then she went on to be an aide, and had various jobs in the Elk Grove district. So I got to be familiar with many of the folks that were here. In 1983, the lady that was on the school board from our area in the district decided not to run again. Before that time, I had never even thought about getting on the school board. I got approached by one of the guys that knew my wife, and he said, Why don't you run for school board? So I thought, What the heck, why not? I liked working with kids, I liked working with the schools, and so I ran, and I won, by about a hundred votes. Although we have to run from the area where we live, we're elected at large, so therefore we're not beholden to one small group. It's been a joyful time ever since, and I've enjoyed every minute of it. Sometimes we have trouble, but it's so far overshadowed by the chance to be out there with kids. There's a lady on the board with me, Jeannette Amavisca, who's been on the board since 1981, two years longer than I have. Every year we dress up like Dr. Seuss; she puts on the Cat in the Hat suit, and we go out and read to the kids, and those little kids just love that. In all the years that I was in school, we never saw a board member or the superintendent. And in this district the board people are out in the schools, the superintendent is out; they're not strangers to these people.

When I started on the board, we had around fourteen thousand kids in the Elk Grove district. We had two high schools, and two middle schools. Now we have over sixty thousand kids; it's grown by leaps and bounds. We were just talking the other night about high school and middle school number 10. The district covers a third of Sacramento County; it's 320 square miles. And what's happened is that development has come in and just filled up a lot of empty spaces. There's talk of putting up another twenty-thousand-home development out to the east.

Elk Grove is now a very ethnically diverse district, but when I first came on the board, the largest population was here in Elk Grove, and they were all folks that had been here for a long time, a very conservative kind of a group. One of our problems was that, when the district began to diversify, Elk Grove High School didn't follow that diversification. We were concerned that these kids that we were sending out of Elk Grove High weren't really going to know too much about how to live with folks from other cultures. It wasn't happening, but it's changed now. At one point we had eighty foreign languages spoken in the district. We've got Hmong, we've got Russians, everything you can think of.

I guess the first time when we heard anything about the Pledge of Allegiance case was when Dr. Newdow came to a school-board meeting, this was back in 2000. We have a place on the agenda for people to speak to us on items that are not on the agenda. He just showed up one night and gave us a talk. He made a speech about the Pledge, and we all just kind of sat there and said, Well, okay, so what? Then he filed suit, and after that took place and we were notified that he had done that, we of course got counsel, Terry Cassidy, from a firm in Sacramento, and we responded to the suit. And I remember Dr. Newdow coming before us, and he sounded like he was on the verge of tears. He couldn't understand why we would respond to his lawsuit! And the superintendent, Dave Gordon, said, You filed the lawsuit; we have to respond. That was always one that amazed me. I thought, Here's this guy, he's an attorney, he's a medical doctor, and he doesn't know why we responded to this.

But I've never had any conversation with him. He came to more than one board meeting. One night he came, and it was a hot night, and he was sitting in the audience with what looked like an Army field jacket on, and he just sat there and slept through the whole meeting. We sort of wondered why he was there. And then, for a long time, we didn't see him anymore, and of course the case wound its way through the courts.

My impression of Dr. Newdow is that he's obviously a very intelligent man, but I'm just not sure I understand where he's coming from. One of the things that has always been a puzzle to me is, these people that are avowed atheists spend their life trying to prove there is no God. It seems to me that if you already believe there isn't any, why are you spending all this time trying to prove it? It says to me that you're not really sure of the ground you're standing on. From that standpoint, I've always kind of wondered, just what do you hope to prove? The other problem I have with it all is that it almost sounds like the tail trying to wag the dog. I don't know why the majority should have to bend to the will of a few. I don't know what the atheist population is in the United States, but I doubt that it's very large, when compared to whatever kind of religious group you want to talk about.

On the school board, we didn't spend a lot of time discussing the Pledge case. The only times that I remember we officially talked about it were in closed sessions where the lawyers came and presented information to us and sought our decisions on what to do. There were a lot of people in the community who were really fed up with this, and you could tell that because, during the time of our flag salute at board meetings, that phrase was accentuated in loud voices coming from the audience. So we could tell we were on solid ground.

When the Ninth Circuit came down with their decision that the Pledge was unconstitutional, that was really a shock and a surprise, that they would do what they did. I was dismayed, because we knew that we were presented with, well, you can stop here or go on, and none of us were willing to stop, so we went on. Once that happened, then all of us became interested in this Ninth Circuit court and what was going on, and it soon became apparent that that's not unusual for them. It's a very liberal court. I think in one year they had twenty-three cases reversed by the Supreme Court out of the twenty-four they heard, which doesn't say much for their ability.

I wasn't able to go to the Supreme Court hearings, but some of our people were, and from what I understand, they all said Dr. Newdow presented a great case, but he didn't have any standing, because of the custody issue over his daughter. The Court just threw it out. And now that he's filed another suit, he doesn't have standing again as far as our district's concerned, because his daughter's in middle school now, and they don't salute the flag. We have other patriotic kinds of things that they do, but they don't salute the flag every morning like they do in the elementary schools.

In my opinion, the words "under God" in the Pledge don't refer to any specific religion. They don't conflict with what the First Amendment says, as far as I can see, and I'm no lawyer. But just reading that amendment, Congress certainly didn't say that we have to follow any specific religion. I think you have to recognize that the "under God" words were placed there because this country was founded basically on Judeo-Christian principles. Let's face it: our laws are based on the Ten Commandments. There are a number of books about this; I just got one recently through a group called American Vision, which is headed by Gary DeMar, who is a pastor down in Atlanta, Georgia. This book talks about the Founding Fathers and what motivated them to do the kinds of things they did.

I know that some people say the Pledge doesn't contribute anything to our civic education in the schools, that it's just a kind of ritual. I think in the lower grades it probably doesn't mean much to kids, but I think in high school it becomes a good teaching point in U.S. history and current events. And it really helps to instill a sense of patriotism. When I first came on the school board, I had a real struggle, because the way kids are brought up today is totally different than the way it was in my home. I guess the height of the patriotism came when the Second World War started. I think the difference today is that then we were fighting a country, we could focus our attention on Japan, or Germany, or Italy;

today, we're fighting an ideology that's throughout the world. It's not the same; we're not fighting a country anymore, we're fighting an ideology, and that's a hard thing to fight. You may be my enemy, but I don't know that; I look at you, and you're a good guy. You're finding these people everywhere.

We need to bring patriotism back, and I think it is. What really brought it to a head was 9/11; that seemed to provoke a lot of it. I see more people walking around with American flags in their lapels, like this thing I'm wearing. Now it's kind of dying off, because we're moving away from that period in time. I think folks over here feel reasonably safe because of all the things we've put in place to make it so, but I think there's some countries in this world that we'd better be taking good notice of, with the advent of these long-range ballistic missiles, and we've got a couple of rogue regimes that are not above using something like that to gain their ends, whatever they may be.

Looking back on this whole Pledge case, to me, this is an issue of majority rule, which is what the Constitution is based on. Obviously, if what the majority wants to do is not legal, then certainly something should happen to stop it. But in this case, it's not illegal, it doesn't violate the Constitution, as far as I understand it. And because it doesn't, and because the majority of folks want it, I don't think the minority should be able to say, Well, no, you can't have it. I respect their views, and their right to express them, but if the majority can't rule on things like acknowledging God in the Pledge, then we're ruled by the few instead of the many. We need to think about that. ❖

Chapter 8

"In the Beginning"

The "Intelligent Design" Case from Dover, Pennsylvania

On the surface, the township of Dover, Pennsylvania, has little in common with the small town of Dayton, Tennessee. Eight hundred miles apart, the two communities are separated by more than geography. Founded in 1753, Dover is still dominated by the ancestry and religion of its original settlers, drawn by the rich farmland in southeastern Pennsylvania. Close to half of the township's eighteen thousand residents have German roots, and Lutherans remain the largest denomination, followed by Methodists and Catholics. Until recent decades, services in many of the area's Lutheran churches were conducted in German, and the white spire of Calvary Lutheran Church towers over Dover's main square. Pushed by the expanding populations of Pennsylvania's capital of Harrisburg, twenty miles to the north, and the industrial city of York, eight miles south, Dover is rapidly losing its rural character and becoming a suburb of its neighbors. Dover's residents exceed the national average in family income, and fewer than one in twenty families lives below the poverty line.

In contrast, Dayton—although first settled in the 1820s—was not incorporated until 1895. With just over six thousand residents, the town has remained almost stable in population for decades, with few jobs to attract newcomers. Thirty miles from Tennessee's border with Georgia, Dayton reflects the political and religious conservatism of the "Bible Belt" region. Like most rural towns in Tennessee and neighboring states, Dayton is a Southern Baptist stronghold, with nine Baptist churches in the town and dozens more in outlying areas, along with many Pentecostal and "Holiness" churches. Family income is barely half the national average, and more than one in five of Dayton's residents fall under the poverty line.

In short, Dover has become increasingly affluent, urban, and religiously diverse, while Dayton remains poor, rural, and fundamentalist. Despite these differences, however, the two communities share one thing. Eighty years apart, they both drew national attention over the determined efforts of self-proclaimed "creationists" to combat the Darwinian theory of evolution in high-school biology classes. In 1925, reporters flocked to Dayton to witness the famous "monkey trial," which featured a dramatic courtroom duel between two of the nation's most eminent lawyers, Clarence Darrow and William Jennings Bryan. Late-night television still features the classic 1960 movie *Inherit the Wind*, a thinly disguised recounting of the Dayton trial, with Spencer Tracy winning an Academy Award nomination for his portrayal of the character based on Darrow. In both the trial and the film's climactic scene, Darrow drew from Bryan—who took the stand as an expert on the Bible—confessions that he could not explain how Joshua made the sun stand still, or where Cain found his wife. Audiences were expected to view Bryan—and most probably did—as a Bible-thumping yahoo, feebly defending the Genesis account of creation that modern geologists and biologists had demolished and discredited.

The actual defendant in the 1925 trial was almost lost among the courtroom bombast. John T. Scopes, a young science teacher at Dayton's high school, had volunteered to challenge a newly enacted Tennessee statute that made it "unlawful for any teacher to teach any theory that denies the story of Divine Creation as taught in the Bible, and to teach instead that man has descended from a lower order of animal." Scopes had responded to a notice placed in the nearby Chattanooga newspaper by the American Civil Liberties Union: "We are looking for a Tennessee teacher who is willing to accept our services in testing this law in the courts. Distinguished counsel have volunteered their services. All we need now is a willing client." Scopes became the client, and Darrow headed the ACLU legal team that defended him. Bryan, who had lost three presidential elections as the Democratic candidate but still retained wide popularity and recognition, entered the case on behalf of the World's Christian Fundamentals Association, an evangelical group founded in 1919 and the origin of the "fundamentalist" label that its adherents first accepted and later tried to shed. First among the WCFA's "fundamentals" was belief in Biblical inerrancy, beginning with the Genesis account of creation, based on six twenty-four-hour days, some eight to ten thousand years ago.

Relegated to a minor role in both his trial and the later movie, Scopes freely admitted in his brief testimony that he had violated the Tennessee law by using a widely adopted text, *A Civic Biology*, featuring the Darwinian theory of evolution. After the presiding judge, John T. Raulston, excluded all but one of the expert witnesses Darrow had recruited to explain the scientific evidence for evolution, the jury promptly convicted Scopes, and Raulston then imposed a hundred dollar fine on him. Darrow had expected to lose in Dayton: "We think we will save our point and take it to a higher court and settle whether the law is good," he told the jury in his summation. But his plan was derailed at its first stop, when the Tennessee Supreme Court reversed the conviction because the law required the jury, not Judge Raulston, to impose the fine. This "technical" flaw, which the state judges could easily have disregarded, achieved their obvious purpose in blocking the Scopes case from completing the journey Darrow had planned to the United States Supreme Court.

It is tempting to look back on the "monkey trial" as the last gasp of Biblical creationists, with their champion "beaten and beaten badly" on the witness stand, as the *New York Times* almost gloated at the time. The Scopes trial was, in fact, Bryan's last gasp. The "Great Commoner" died in Dayton, five days after the trial concluded, although his name lives in the town through Bryan College, committed to "unequivocal acceptance of the inerrancy and authority of the Scriptures."

There are several reasons, however, to resist that temptation. One is that Bryan College is far from the only institution whose faculty and students accept Biblical inerrancy and creationist teaching. Several hundred thousand students currently attend Christian private schools, from elementary grades through colleges and universities, and most receive creationist teachings in biology classes. The American Association of Christian Schools has one thousand members, and the Council for Christian Colleges and Universities represents 105 "Bible-based" institutions, including Bob Jones University in South Carolina, at which President George W. Bush spoke during his 2000 campaign. The federal Department of Education also estimated in 1999 that more than 850,000 children are being home-schooled, many by parents who object to evolution in public-school classes, and who use such texts as *Biology Through the Eyes of Faith*. Altogether, probably two million of the nation's fifty million elementary and high-school students, and a half-million college students, are taught to accept Biblical creationism and to reject Darwinian evolution as contrary to "God's word."

Even in the public schools, many students are raised by parents who reject evolution, and whose children sit in biology classes with their beliefs already set. A recent national poll, conducted in November 2005, showed that 45 percent of those surveyed accept the Genesis account of creation, a figure that has not changed since 1982. The recent poll also reported that 37 percent of the public—and 45 percent of those who supported President Bush in 2004—agree that creationism should replace evolution in public schools. Even more revealing, a 1997 survey of public-school teachers in Pennsylvania showed 39 percent agreement that creationism should be given "equal time" with evolution in science classes, with comparable results from other states. The National Center for Science Education direly concluded from these surveys that "many teachers do not teach evolution, and many teach it inaccurately." Clearly, belief in creationism did not die with William Jennings Bryan in Dayton, Tennessee.

———

Against this backdrop, the road from Dayton to Dover is shorter than maps and calendars would suggest, and reflects the almost unique structure of American public education. In most other countries, from England to Japan, teachers in every subject follow an identical curricu-

lum and assign the same textbooks, designed and chosen by a central-
ized educational bureaucracy. Students in every school, from small
towns to big cities, read the same books and take standardized national
exams. Those in Dover, England, for example, take the same "Eleven-
Plus" exams before graduation as students in London. These "top-down"
systems give local officials little control over what is taught in their
schools, and give teachers little control over their lesson plans.

In contrast, American public schools are governed by some fifteen
thousand autonomous school boards, most of whose ninety-five thousand
members are elected by local residents. Decisions on hiring superinten-
dents, approving school budgets, setting tax rates, and choosing textbooks rest in most communities with local school-board members. Over
the past century, however, state officials have imposed broadly worded
"standards" for public-school curricula, and many states—prodded by
federal laws—now administer standardized tests by which local schools
are graded and which determine levels of state and federal funding. But
the American tradition of "local control" of education has, thus far, not
yielded to pressures for national curricular uniformity. Consequently,
students in Dover, Pennsylvania, are not required to read the same biology textbooks as their counterparts in a dozen other Dovers, from
Maine to Oregon.

The events that later catapulted the Pennsylvania township into national headlines began with no publicity on January 9, 2002. Richard
Nilsen, superintendent of the Dover Area School District, had arranged
an evening "retreat" at the Shady Grove Elementary School. A former
social-studies teacher, Nilsen had earned a doctorate in educational administration from Temple University in Philadelphia, and had just replaced the former Dover superintendent after three years as his
assistant. He wanted to begin his new job with an informal meeting at
which Dover's school administrators and board members could share
their plans for the coming year. Over a dinner prepared by the school's
cafeteria staff, Nilsen asked the nine board members to outline their
priorities. His notes from the meeting reflected such perennials as bud-
getary concerns, discipline, and building plans. Like most districts with

expanding populations, Dover needed more buildings for its thirty-five hundred students, but its residents had recently elected several board members who campaigned on a "no-new-taxes" platform, creating tensions with incumbents who pushed for new schools and programs such as full-day kindergartens.

One new board member, however, voiced a priority that apparently drew no comment from his colleagues. Nilsen's notes simply recorded that Alan Bonsell had mentioned "creationism" as his primary concern for the Dover schools. Bonsell owned a local auto-repair shop, and his father, Donald, had earlier served on the board. Elected as a fiscal conservative, Bonsell had not raised any religious issues during his campaign, although a fellow candidate, Jeff Brown, later said that Bonsell told him he did not believe in evolution and wanted to return "creationism" to Dover's biology classes. Bonsell belonged to the Church of the Open Door in nearby Shiloh, whose statement of belief proclaims that "the Bible is the very Word of God and is the only infallible rule of faith and practice," and that "all persons are lost apart from regeneration and are condemned to eternal punishment, while the saved even now possess eternal life."

During his first year on the board, Bonsell did not push to insert creationism in Dover High's biology classes, a required course for all ninth-grade students. Under the Pennsylvania "academic standards" for biology, students in all the state's public schools would be tested on their ability "to describe the mechanisms in the theory of evolution" and to explain "how natural selection is impacted by alterations in the environment." Alan Bonsell had told Jeff Brown that he wanted to serve on the board's Curriculum Committee, and was named in the fall of 2002 to chair this four-member group. Although Bonsell did not bring up creationism at board meetings that year, he raised his "concerns" about evolution with Michael Baksa, the district's newly appointed assistant superintendent, whose duties included curriculum design. Bonsell had reviewed the ninth-grade biology text, and complained to Baksa that "Darwin was presented as a fact, not a theory." Baksa assured Bonsell that he would raise these concerns with the school's biology teachers, but they apparently remained unaware of Bonsell's objections to evolution for several months after his discussions with Baksa.

In March 2003, Superintendent Nilsen convened another board retreat, at which Bonsell argued that creationism "belonged in biology class alongside evolution." Shortly after this meeting, Mike Baksa stopped by the Dover High classroom of Bertha Spahr. Known to everyone as "Bert," she had taught chemistry at the school for almost forty years and now chaired the science department. Baksa wanted to give her "a heads up that there is a member of the school board who is interested in having creationism share equal time with evolution," Spahr recalled. When she asked, "Which board member are you referring to," Baksa "told me it was Alan Bonsell."

The next day, April 1, Spahr went to see Dover High's principal, Trudy Peterman, telling her that Baksa had reported that Bonsell was looking "for a 50/50 split with Darwin and some alternative" to evolution in biology classes. "I asked her what direction she would give both me and the department concerning this issue," Spahr later said. "The only direction she gave me was to tell the biology teachers that we will teach evolution as directed by the state standards. We could, in fact, mention that there was another theory and then direct the students to either contact their families or their pastors if they wished to investigate that further."

Right after this conversation, Peterman recounted its substance in a memo to Spahr and Baksa, with a copy to Superintendent Nilsen, stating that an unnamed board member "wanted fifty percent of the topic of evolution to involve the teaching of Creationism." Although Peterman's memo simply recounted her conversation with Bert Spahr, and did not propose any response, Nilsen viewed it as stepping on Mike Baksa's toes, since Peterman's duties as Dover High's principal did not include curriculum matters. Nilsen had repeatedly clashed with Peterman over school issues, and seized on the memo to justify a "negative" evaluation of Peterman's job performance. "I had the belief that Dr. Peterman exaggerated constantly," Nilsen later said, "and this reflected another exaggeration." When he later testified in court about this memo, with its clear warning that creationism might become a divisive issue in Dover's schools, Nilsen conceded that he never asked Baksa or Spahr whether Peterman had misstated or exaggerated anything in the memo. After board members received Nilsen's critical evaluation of her performance, Peterman resigned as Dover High's principal, the first casualty in the town's battle over Darwin. She wound up with a new job as superintendent of another Pennsylvania district, happy to escape the cross-fire in Dover.

Dover High's science teachers, however, were not happy to find themselves in Alan Bonsell's sights. Shortly before the 2003 school year began, Mike Baksa arranged a meeting of the two sides. Jennifer Miller, known as Jen, had taught biology at the school for eleven years and guided the discussion for her junior colleagues, Rob Eshbach, Rob Linker, and Leslie Prall. Before the meeting, Baksa met briefly with the teachers and told them Bonsell was a "young-earth creationist" who believed "that the earth is somewhere around 10,000 years old." Bonsell's major question for the teachers was "how we taught evolution," Miller later said. She explained, "We teach the origin of species, not necessarily the origin of life. His concern was definitely with the teaching of the origin of life." It seems clear, however, that Bonsell—who lacked any science training—misunderstood the distinction between the two concepts, although the teachers may have missed his confusion. What Bonsell apparently understood as the "origin of life" was the question of human origins. Based on his literal reading of Genesis, he objected to any teaching that mankind had descended from lower orders of animals. But Jen Miller's assurance that she and her colleagues did not teach the "origin of life" satisfied Bonsell. What scientists call the "origin of life," however, is the highly debated and still-unresolved question of how living organisms emerged from inanimate matter, billions of years ago.

Recalling this meeting, Bonsell said the teachers addressed the "origin of species" through the concept of "adaptation over time, or micro-evolution, and I remember one of the examples they talked about was the peppered moth and how it changed colors over time." Most creationists accept the concept of microevolution, limited to adaptive changes within distinct species, but they firmly reject the concept of macro-evolution, the process by which separate species emerge. Whether anyone at the meeting realized Bonsell's mistaken reversal of the two concepts—almost like confusing left and right—is hard to say. The biology text used by the teachers did, in fact, address the "origin of species" and stated, as a basic principle of evolutionary theory, that "living things have been evolving on Earth for millions of years." Nonetheless, Bonsell left the session pleased. "There were no arguments," he later said. "It was a nice, cordial meeting."

Despite the surface cordiality, the teachers were not pleased. Bonsell was most concerned, Jen Miller later said, "that we would convey something to the students that was in opposition to what their parents were conveying to them at home," and that students would conclude that "somebody is lying, basically." In truth, Miller and her colleagues were greatly disturbed after meeting with Bonsell. They perhaps feared that he might go over the biology text with a fine-tooth comb and discover its statement that "monkeys, apes, and humans" shared a common ancestor, based on fossil records that went back some 4.5 million years. Although they skirted the topic of human origins in their classes, a "young-earth creationist" like Bonsell might return with further questions about their text and teaching methods.

Jen Miller and Rob Linker, in fact, quickly dropped methods they had used in teaching about evolution. Miller stopped taking her students into the hallway with long strips of paper on which they marked out stages in evolutionary development, from early single-celled life forms to primates, to illustrate the recent emergence of complex species, including humans. Linker ended his practice of drawing a line on the blackboard and writing "evolution" on one side and "creationism" on the other. He recalled telling his students that "creationism was based on Bibles, religion, Biblical writings. And I remember saying that we're not going to cover this side because it's illegal for me to talk about that side in a public school." After the meeting with Bonsell, he said, "I just felt there was some controversy, because I had to tell how I taught a particular subject. I didn't know if I was doing something wrong with writing creationism on the board, so I just figured I would stick to the book."

———

Sticking to the book, as the teachers soon learned, did not satisfy Bonsell. Their biology text, in fact, became hostage to the school board's creationists. At the board's first meeting in January 2004, Bonsell was elected president, and named a new board member, William Buckingham, to chair the curriculum committee. Buckingham, a retired prison supervisor, shared Bonsell's creationist beliefs and his opposition to evolution. He belonged to the Harmony Grove Community Church in Dover, whose members agree that "the Bible is the verbally inspired, infallible, and inerrant Word of God," and that "hell is a place of eternal conscious punishment for those who have rejected Christ." Dover's science teachers quickly discovered that Buckingham was even more committed than Bonsell to adding creationism to the biology curriculum.

Back in June 2003, the board had approved funds to purchase new copies of the biology text. Buckingham, however, had gone through the book with an even finer comb than had Bonsell, making notes that listed every reference to Darwin. Buckingham brought his notes to the board's public meeting on June 7, 2004. The board's agenda included approval for the purchase of several science textbooks, but not for the biology text. Board meetings always began with a "public comment" period, and Barrie Callahan wasted no time in questioning the omission of the biology text from the agenda. Callahan was a former board member and a longtime critic of policies she considered wasteful or tainted with politics. She demanded to know why the board was holding up approval of new biology texts. Speaking as the curriculum committee chair, Bill Buckingham replied that the book was "laced with Darwinism," and that he wanted to find a text that presented a balance between evolution and creationism. Alan Bonsell agreed with Buckingham, saying there were only two theories that could be taught, creationism and evolution, and the district would face no problems if both were presented. Buckingham, outspoken and short-tempered, grew testy after

Barrie Callahan argued that Dover's biology teachers needed new books before fall classes began. "It is inexcusable to have a book that says man descended from apes with nothing to counterbalance it," Buckingham shot back.

In most towns, school-board meetings rarely draw crowds or generate newspaper headlines. Dover's meetings were covered by freelance reporters from the two competing daily papers in nearby York, Joe Maldonado for the *Daily Record* and Heidi Bernhard-Bubb for the *Dispatch*. The verbal sparring of Barrie Callahan and Bill Buckingham, and his repeated mentions of creationism, alerted both reporters to the front-page potential of their stories, and they both descended on Buckingham after the meeting ended. Maldonado scribbled down another quote from Buckingham, which appeared in his account of the June 7 meeting: " 'This country wasn't founded on Muslim beliefs or evolution. This country was founded on Christianity and our students should be taught as such.' "

Many of Dover's residents read one or both of the York newspapers, and their reports on the school board's June 7 meeting drew a crowd of more than a hundred people to its next session, a week later. Once again, the biology text and creationism dominated the meeting, beginning with the public-comment period. Bill Buckingham's wife, Charlotte, stood up first, a Bible in her hand. For more than ten minutes, she quoted from Genesis, demanded to know "how we can allow anything else to be taught in our schools," argued that "evolution tells nothing but lies," and recited Gospel verses that promised hellfire and damnation for those who refused to become "born-again" Christians. Bill Buckingham, who punctuated his wife's remarks with "Amens" from his seat at the board's table, followed with these words to the audience: "I challenge you to trace your roots to the monkey you came from." Still in a lather, Buckingham argued that "nowhere in the Constitution does it call for a separation of church and state," and denounced "liberals in black robes" who he claimed were "taking away the rights of Christians." He ended with this appeal: "Two thousand years ago, someone died on a cross. Can't someone take a stand for him?"

Not surprisingly, the June 14 board meeting prompted even larger headlines in the York newspapers. "Church/State Issue Divides, Creationism Draws 100 to Dover Meeting," read the caption over Heidi Bernhard-Bubb's report in the *Dispatch*. Warnings of possible lawsuits over teaching creationism also stirred comment in Dover. Following the June 7 meeting, Bernhard-Bubb had called Rob Boston, who handled press relations at the Washington, D.C., headquarters of Americans United for Separation of Church and State. After recounting the references to "creationism" at the board meetings, she reported his group's threat of litigation against the Dover board. She also reported Bill Buckingham's retort that "he did not believe the members of AU know what it means to be an American." Paula Knudson, a staff attorney in the Harrisburg office of the American Civil Liberties Union, also told Bernhard-Bubb that ACLU lawyers would challenge any move to inject creationism into Dover's biology classes.

News of Dover's battle over evolution quickly spread beyond the township, drawing the attention of a young lawyer in Seattle. Shortly after the June 2004 board meetings, Seth Cooper received an e-mailed article from one of the York papers about the conflict. Cooper worked for the Discovery Institute, a conservative think-tank dedicated to propagating the concept of "intelligent design" as an alternative to Darwinism. Known by the shorthand label of ID, this concept—as defined by the Institute—"simply holds that certain aspects of the universe and living things can best be explained as the result of an intelligent cause rather than merely material and purposeless processes like natural selection." What supposedly distinguished ID from Biblical creationism were its proponents' claims that this "intelligent cause" did not require belief in God as the "designer" of the universe and living things, and that ID was a valid scientific theory, capable of being tested by rigorous scientific methods. Critics of ID scoffed at both claims, pointing to the openly expressed Christian beliefs of its leading advocates, and noting that ID violated the first principle of scientific methodology, that any theory must be capable of "falsifiability" through observation or experimentation. When Dover's evolution battle reached the courtroom in

September 2005, scientists on both sides argued at length about ID's claims. But in June 2004, Seth Cooper was primarily concerned that Bill Buckingham needed a lesson in legal reality.

Most likely, Buckingham had never heard the term "intelligent design" before he received a phone call from Cooper, out of the blue. "I told him that his Board would run afoul of the First Amendment of the Constitution should it choose to require students to learn about creationism or to censor the teaching of the contemporary version of Darwin's theory," Cooper later wrote. He knew the Supreme Court had struck down in 1968 an Arkansas law that banned teaching "the theory or doctrine that mankind ascended or descended from a lower order of animals." Cooper was also familiar with the Court's 1987 ruling that Louisiana could not require "balanced treatment" in biology classes of "creation-science" and evolution. Whether Cooper mentioned these cases to Buckingham is unknown, but he tried to warn Buckingham against "leading the Dover Board on any unconstitutional and unwise course of action concerning the teaching of evolution."

In reality, Cooper's effort to dissuade Buckingham from adding "intelligent design" to the Dover biology curriculum reflected the Discovery Institute's attempts to distance itself from connection with "creationism" of any variety. Publicly committed to a "we don't know" position on who or what the intelligent designer might be, the DI feared that any school board with avowed creationist members, such as Buckingham, would be sitting ducks for lawsuits filed by the ACLU or other pro-evolution groups. As Cooper knew, the DI's long-range goal of getting "intelligent design" into biology classes as a "scientific" alternative to evolution could be set back, or even derailed, by people like Buckingham. Institutional self-interest, more than qualms about creationism— the DI fellows included several "young-earth" creationists and many more of the "old-earth" variety—prompted Cooper's "back-off" advice to Buckingham.

Although Cooper had consistently denied that he ever encouraged Buckingham to push for ID in Dover's schools, the two men have different recollections of their conversations. Buckingham later claimed that

Cooper had been initially supportive of his efforts. "He'd call me to see if we were going forward," he told a reporter. But news accounts of the ACLU's litigation threats prompted Cooper himself to back off. "He was afraid we were going to lose the case," Buckingham said. "And he thought, if we did lose the case, it was going to set intelligent design back for years. He just didn't think we were the proper people to be pushing this at this time. I think they thought we jumped their gun, so to speak."

In fact, Cooper unwittingly pushed the Dover board closer to a legal showdown with Americans United and the ACLU by sending Buckingham a Discovery Institute video called *Icons of Evolution*, based on a book with the same title, written by one of the Institute's fellows, Jonathan Wells. Like most of the Institute's forty-eight fellows, whose research and writings it funded, Wells had impressive academic credentials, having earned doctorates in religious studies from Yale and biology from the University of California at Berkeley. Neither his book nor the Institute's video, however, disclosed Wells's membership in the Unification Church, headed by the Reverend Sun Myung Moon, whose devotees called him "Father" and who claimed equal status with Jesus as the Messiah. "Father's words, my studies, and my prayers convinced me that I should devote my life to destroying Darwinism," Wells wrote in 1996.

Equally committed to this goal, Bill Buckingham arranged, through Mike Baksa, for Dover's biology teachers to view the *Icons of Evolution* video, which purported to explore numerous "flaws" and "fallacies" in Darwinian theories of evolution. Wary of Buckingham's threat to hold up purchase of new textbooks, the teachers watched the video but turned thumbs down on showing it to their students. Undeterred by Seth Cooper's warning that teaching any version of creationism, even under the mask of "intelligent design," would precipitate a lawsuit, Buckingham nonetheless decided that ID offered a defensible cover for his creationist beliefs. What he needed, since the teachers had rejected the *Icons* video, was another ID source, preferably a biology textbook he could use as a bargaining tool with the recalcitrant teachers. Buckingham also wanted to find a legal group that would defend the Dover school board against the lawsuit that Cooper had predicted, and that the Discovery Institute was unwilling to enter.

Surfing the Internet on his computer in July 2004, Buckingham found the answer to both questions at the same Web site. He picked up his telephone and called Richard Thompson in Ann Arbor, Michigan. Thompson, president and chief counsel of the Thomas More Law Center, was more than happy to provide the legal support that Cooper had declined to offer Buckingham. During their conversation, Thompson also told Buckingham about a book called *Of Pandas and People: The Central Question of Biological Origins*, recommending that he obtain a copy, which he promptly ordered from an Internet site. The *Pandas* book was just what Buckingham had been looking for, and became his bargaining chip with the science teachers. Its publisher, a Texas-based group called the Foundation for Thought and Ethics, was devoted to "promoting and publishing textbooks from a Christian perspective," and advertised *Pandas* as "a supplement to the high school biology textbooks presenting the scientific rationale for intelligent design as an alternative to Darwinism."

The book's authors stated their central thesis in this sentence: "Intelligent design means that various forms of life began abruptly through an intelligent agency, with their distinctive features already intact—fish with fins and scales, birds with feathers, beaks, and wings, etc." In other words, all species—including mankind—had been created in their present forms, without "common descent" from earlier forms. This claim had drawn a scathing review in 1999 by Kenneth R. Miller, a Brown University biologist and co-author of the text used in Dover's biology classes. Miller panned the *Pandas* book as "a collection of half-truths, distortions, and outright falsehoods that attempts to misrepresent biology and mislead students as to the scientific status of evolutionary biology." Six years later, Miller became the lead-off witness in the trial over Buckingham's campaign to put ID and *Pandas* into the biology curriculum.

But when Buckingham received his copy of *Pandas* in July 2004, he didn't bother to check any reviews; in fact, as he later conceded, he hadn't read the book and had no idea what "intelligent design" meant, except that it was an "alternative" to Darwinism. That was all he wanted, however, and *Pandas* fit the bill.

Buckingham played his *Pandas* chip when he discovered that Dover's biology teachers wanted the school board to purchase a new edition of Miller's textbook, just published in 2004. The board had scheduled a meeting on August 2 to consider this request. Tempers flared over Buckingham's demand that the board purchase both books as a package deal. With one of nine members absent, the board first split four to four on a motion to approve the Miller text; under board rules, the motion failed. At this point, Buckingham spoke for the four "no" voters: "If we don't get our book, you don't get yours." Jeff Brown, who sat on the board with his wife, Casey, promptly accused Buckingham of "blackmailing the board and holding the students hostage." With the meeting on the verge of chaos, one of the board's members, Angie Yingling, suddenly switched her vote, providing a five-to-three majority for purchasing the Miller text. When the meeting ended, Joe Maldonado of the *York Daily Record* approached Buckingham, who lashed out at Yingling: "I can't believe you did that, do you know what you've done?" Speaking of her fellow board members, she replied, "I feel you were blackmailing them. I just want the kids to have their books."

Maldonado's story on the contentious meeting, under the headline "Biology Book Squeaked By," alarmed the school district's lawyer, Stephen Russell, already concerned about potential lawsuits. He called Richard Thompson at the Thomas More Law Center, reporting their conversation to Superintendent Nilsen through an e-mail on August 26. "They refer to the creationism issue as 'intelligent design,'" Russell wrote. Referring to the *Pandas* book, he added, "I guess my main concern at the moment, is that even if use of the text is purely voluntary, this may still make it very difficult to win a case." Although Nilsen shared Russell's message with the Curriculum Committee members, Buckingham was still determined to put the *Pandas* book in Dover's biology classrooms.

Buckingham finally exacted his quid pro quo from the science teachers at a meeting on August 30. Bert Spahr still rankled from his earlier demands to know if students were taught that "man comes from a monkey." Responding in "utter frustration," she later recalled, "I looked at Mr. Buckingham and I said, 'if you say man and monkey one more time in the same sentence, I'm going to scream.'" Spahr objected to using *Pandas* in any way, but Jen Miller had grown tired of conflict. She countered Buckingham's insistence that the biology teachers use *Pandas* as a "companion" to the Miller text with a compromise offer to place it in classrooms as a "reference" book, later explaining her hope that "maybe this will go away again."

Satisfied with this compromise—just short of capitulation—by the teachers, Buckingham still faced an obstacle. Barrie Callahan, the board's most insistent critic, had warned of legal consequences if copies of *Pandas* were purchased with public funds. Buckingham had an inspiration. Before one of the September services at the Harmony Grove Community Church, he stood up and made a plea for donations to buy the books, collecting $850 in cash and checks. Buckingham deposited the funds in his personal bank account, and then wrote a check for that amount, made out to Donald Bonsell, the father of the board president, Alan Bonsell. He then gave the check, with the notation "Of Pandas and People," to Alan, who passed it to his father, who in turn put the check in his account and ordered sixty copies of *Pandas*. When a former board member, Larry Snook, later inquired about the source of the funds, Buckingham and Bonsell professed ignorance. And when Bert Spahr received the books, she discovered a catalogue from the publisher listing *Pandas* under the heading "Creation Science."

September 2004 was also a busy month for Mike Baksa, the assistant superintendent. At the board's direction, he drafted a change in the biology curriculum: "Students will be made aware of gaps in Darwin's theory and of other theories of evolution." Reluctantly, the science teachers agreed to support Baksa's language as the best they could make of a bad situation. Alan Bonsell took Baksa's draft to the Curriculum Committee, on which he served as an ex-officio member. At a meeting on October 7, with no teachers present, Bonsell pushed through his revision, which read: "Students will be made aware of gaps/problems in Darwin's theory and of other theories of evolution, including but not limited to intelligent design. Note: Origins of Life is not taught." The statement also cited *Pandas* as a reference text. Baksa then sent both versions to the full board for consideration at its meeting on October 18.

Tempers flared once again as the board debated the competing statements. Noel Wenrich, although a professed creationist, offered several motions to defer a decision until the science teachers could respond to Bonsell's revision of Baksa's proposed resolution, but only Casey and Jeff Brown sided with him. Bonsell and Buckingham had their votes lined up, and prevailed by a final margin of six to three. Casey Brown then asked for the floor and read her resignation statement, ending ten years of board service. "There has been a slow but steady marginalization of some board members," she told the hushed audience. "Our opinions are no longer valued or listened to. Our contributions have been minimized or not acknowledged at all." She looked directly at Bonsell and Buckingham. "I myself have been twice asked within the past year if I was 'born again.' No one has, nor should have, the right to ask that of a fellow board member. An individual's religious beliefs should have no impact on his or her ability to serve as a school board director, nor should a person's beliefs be used as a yardstick to measure the value of that service. However, it has become increasingly evident that it is the direction the board has now chosen to go, holding a certain religious belief is of paramount importance." When she finished, Jeff Brown tersely announced his own resignation, leaving two empty chairs as the meeting ended.

Bill Buckingham, who sat quietly while Casey Brown read her statement, seemed eager after the meeting to take on a lawsuit. Joe Maldonado asked him about the potential costs in legal fees if the board lost a courtroom battle over the ID policy. "My response to that is what price is freedom?" Buckingham replied. "Sometimes you have to take a stand." Superintendent Nilsen took a more pragmatic view. "No administrator wants to be involved in a costly lawsuit," he said. But a costly lawsuit now seemed inevitable. The board's approval of the biology curriculum change made Dover the nation's first district to mandate the teaching of "intelligent design," and dissenting parents had already contacted the Pennsylvania ACLU to volunteer as plaintiffs against the district.

The resignations of Jeff and Casey Brown, and later of Noel Wenrich, opened three seats on the board, which the incumbents filled with ID supporters. One of the new members, Ed Rowand, was the minister of a local Assemblies of God church, an evangelical denomination that rejects evolution. Rowand was an avowed "young-earth" creationist, but he supported the ID policy and voted to give Mike Baksa the unenviable task of drafting a statement the teachers would read to students before they began the evolution unit. Baksa's initial draft described evolution as the "dominant scientific theory" of biological development, and stated that "there are gaps in Darwin's theory for which there is yet no evidence." The board, however, cut the first term from the statement and snipped the word "yet" from the second.

The final version, adopted in November 2004, contained four paragraphs, with several key sentences. The first informed students they were studying evolution only because the state required them "to learn about Darwin's Theory of Evolution and eventually to take a standardized test of which evolution is a part." The message was clear: Teaching about evolution wasn't our idea. Next, students were advised to be skeptical of evolution: "Because Darwin's Theory is a theory, it continues to be tested as new evidence is discovered. The Theory is not a fact. Gaps in the Theory exist for which there is no evidence." Third, students were pointed—without any skeptical words—to a theory and a book their teachers had rejected: "Intelligent Design is an explanation of the origin of life that differs from Darwin's view. The reference book, Of Pandas and People, is available for students who might be interested in gaining an understanding of what Intelligent Design actually involves." Finally, students were instructed not to ask their teachers about what the *Pandas* subtitle called the "central question" of biology: "The school leaves the discussion of the Origins of Life to individual students and their families."

Alan Bonsell had started his campaign to add "creationism" to Dover's biology classes in January 2002, pushing for a "fifty-fifty split" with evolution. Almost three years later, he settled for a ten-sentence statement that promoted "intelligent design" as an "alternative" to Darwinism, wearing down the science teachers through what Bert Spahr called a "long and tiresome" process. The final product of this process, which Bonsell and Bill Buckingham both seemed to welcome, was the lawsuit filed by the Pennsylvania ACLU and Americans United on December 14, 2004, in the federal district court in Harrisburg.

The ACLU recruited a team of volunteer lawyers from a prestigious Philadelphia firm, Pepper Hamilton, headed by Eric Rothschild, who also served on the legal advisory council of the National Center for Science Education, a pro-evolution group that had closely monitored the developments in Dover. "I've been waiting for this for fifteen years," Rothschild told the NCSE's director, Eugenie Scott. Tammy Kitzmiller, whose daughters, Megan and Jessica, attended Dover High School, headed the suit's eleven plaintiffs. The complaint Rothschild drafted in *Kitzmiller v. Dover Area School District* alleged that the board's ID policy would "compel public school science teachers to present to their students in biology class information that is inherently religious, not scientific, in nature," and "was added to the curriculum precisely because of its religious contents and nature," violating the First Amendment's Establishment of Religion Clause.

Ironically, the group that first mentioned "intelligent design" to Bill Buckingham, the Discovery Institute, tried hard to head off the ACLU's lawsuit. Seth Cooper, the Institute lawyer who sent Buckingham the *Icons of Evolution* video, feared a legal defeat that would cripple the Institute's long-range plans for building a solid base of ID research before pushing for its inclusion in public-school biology classes. "We do believe a lawsuit is certain in your situation," Cooper warned Alan Bonsell on December 10, 2004. "We strongly recommend some corrective action be taken." Four days later, Rothschild filed the ACLU's suit, but Cooper made one last effort to end the case before it went to trial, flying from Seattle to meet with Bonsell and Buckingham. "I implored the Board

Members in direct terms to withdraw or significantly alter their ID policy," Cooper later wrote. However, "the Dover Board chose to completely disregard our legal and policy recommendations." Beneath the surface, Cooper viewed Richard Thompson as a publicity-seeking legal zealot who would damage the ID cause. As the case progressed, the private dispute between the Institute and the More Center flared into a public squabble, damaging both groups.

Two events in January 2005 put Thompson in a deep legal hole, with Rothschild supplying the shovel. First, Dover school officials demanded that biology teachers read the board's ten-sentence ID statement to their students. The teachers responded with their own statement, refusing to comply. "I believe that if I as the classroom teacher read the required statement, my students will inevitably *(and understandably)* believe that Intelligent Design is a valid scientific theory, perhaps on a par with the theory of evolution," they informed Richard Nilsen. "That is not true. To refer the students to 'Of Pandas and People' as if it is a scientific resource breaches my ethical obligation to provide them with scientific knowledge that is supported by recognized scientific proof or theory." The teachers put their position in capital letters: "INTELLIGENT DESIGN IS NOT SCIENCE. INTELLIGENT DESIGN IS NOT BIOLOGY. INTELLIGENT DESIGN IS NOT AN ACCEPTED SCIENTIFIC THEORY." Confronted with this revolt, Nilsen and Mike Baksa read the board's statement to biology classes while the teachers stood outside their classrooms in silent protest.

Rothschild and his Pepper Hamilton partner, Steve Harvey, also put Bonsell and Buckingham under oath in pre-trial depositions, which can be used at trial to "impeach" the veracity of a witness's courtroom testimony. Rothschild and Harvey wanted first to establish that both men's creationist beliefs lay behind the board's ID policy. Harvey went first with Buckingham: "Do you believe in a literal reading of the book of Genesis as it relates to the story of creation?" Buckingham agreed: "That's one of the foundations of my faith." Armed with the newspaper articles by Joe Maldonado and Heidi Bernhard-Bubb, Harvey then asked if Buckingham had ever mentioned creationism at board meetings. "Never said that," he replied. Harvey moved to the source of the money that had been used to purchase copies of the *Pandas* book: "Do you know where that came from, who donated them?" Buckingham professed ignorance: "No, I don't." Harvey pressed him: "Did you ask where it came from?" "Didn't want to know," Buckingham replied.

Rothschild conducted Bonsell's deposition, encountering the same denial that creationism had ever been discussed or even mentioned at board meetings. Asked to define the differences between Darwinism and intelligent design, Bonsell replied, "Darwinism is everything basically happened by chance, where intelligent design says that it didn't happen that way." Pressed to expand his answer, Bonsell said, "Life is much too complex to have happened strictly by chance. It is complex and somehow was designed." "By who?" Rothschild asked. "I don't know," Bonsell replied. When Rothschild turned to the source of the funds to purchase copies of the *Pandas* book, Bonsell replied, "I don't know." Pressed in more than thirty questions to recall the source of the money, Bonsell repeated, "I don't know," to each inquiry.

During these depositions, Harvey and Rothschild engaged in what lawyers call "fishing expeditions," asking questions to which they do not know the answers from records in their possession. Months later, they hooked two big fish, after Superintendent Nilsen turned over his notes of the board retreats in 2002 and 2003, recording Bonsell's references to "creationism," and Richard Thompson produced a copy of the $850 check that Buckingham had given to Bonsell, with the inscription "Of Pandas and People." Nilsen's notes and Buckingham's check later became prime exhibits at the *Kitzmiller* trial, and the depositions returned to haunt Bonsell and Buckingham as impeachment of their trial testimony. Richard Thompson's clients did him no favors in their denials, under oath, of any mentions of creationism and their professions of ignorance about the source of the *Pandas* money.

———

The *Kitzmiller* trial finally began on September 26, 2005, in the Harrisburg courtroom of District Judge John E. Jones III, who conducted a "bench" trial, without a jury. In effect, Jones was the only person whose opinion would decide the case. Named to the federal court by President

George W. Bush in 2002, the fifty-year-old Jones had an impeccable Republican background, having worked in the party for years, including an unsuccessful congressional race in 1994. He was a Lutheran, a former Boy Scout leader, and an avid golfer—in short, the model of a conventional lawyer and judge. But he had also worked as a part-time county public defender, once drawing criticism for defending a man accused—and later convicted—of murdering a twelve-year-old boy. Jones took credit for convincing the jury to spare his client from the death penalty, a task many lawyers would have shunned.

In the Dover case, Jones presided over what became two separate trials, although lawyers on both sides called witnesses in no particular order. In one, he conducted what became almost a graduate-school seminar, in which nine expert witnesses—six for the plaintiffs and three for the defendants—covered the fields of biology, history, theology, education, and philosophy. Sandwiched among the experts, Eric Rothschild and his ACLU colleagues put Dover High's science teachers, headed by Jen Miller and Bert Spahr, on the witness stand to explain their objections to the board's ID policy and the *Pandas* book, along with Dover parents, and former board members Casey and Jeff Brown. On the other side, Richard Thompson and his Thomas More team called Alan Bonsell to defend the board's policy, along with Richard Nilsen and Mike Baksa from the district's administration. During twenty-one days of testimony from thirty-three witnesses, Jones gave lawyers and witnesses great latitude in asking and answering questions. "We're going to be here for a while," he said at the trial's outset, "and we have plenty of time to try this case." At its conclusion, the testimony covered almost six thousand pages, with hundreds more in exhibits and depositions.

In the first courtroom battle over intelligent design, each side presented a scientific "star" witness, Kenneth Miller for the ACLU and Michael Behe for the More Center. In many ways, they looked alike, both with salt-and-pepper beards, and had matching credentials. Miller earned a Ph.D. in biology from the University of Colorado, taught at Harvard for six years, and moved to Brown University as a professor in 1980, where he conducted research in cellular biology. Behe, who earned his Ph.D. in biochemistry from the University of Pennsylvania, had taught at Lehigh University in Bethlehem, Pennsylvania, for twenty-three years, and focused his research on bacterial structures. Both men had written widely read books on evolution: Miller's was titled *Finding Darwin's God: A Scientist's Search for Common Ground Between God and Evolution*, and Behe's had the title *Darwin's Black Box: The Biochemical Challenge to Evolution*. Miller and Behe shared another feature: both were practicing Roman Catholics.

Ken Miller almost bounded to the stand as the trial's lead-off witness, examined by the Pennsylvania ACLU's legal director, Witold Walczak. "Dr. Miller," he began, "I want to ask you five questions to elicit your opinions about the big issues in this case." Posing his questions like a catechism lesson, Walczak first elicited Miller's agreement that "evolution is an eminently testable theory and that it is broadly and generally accepted by the scientific community." Miller next agreed that "intelligent design is not a testable theory in any sense, and that as such, it is not generally accepted by the scientific community." Third, Miller gave his opinion that "intelligent design is not science, and therefore it cannot be construed as a scientific theory in any sense whatsoever." He also stated his belief that "intelligent design is inherently religious and is a form of creationism. It is a classic form of creationism known as special creationism." Finally, he said that the Dover board's ten-sentence statement about evolution and intelligent design "falsely undermines the scientific status of the theory of evolution, certainly does not promote student understanding or even critical thinking, and does a great disservice to science education in Dover."

"Let's now explore the basis for your opinions," Walczak continued. "What is science?" With that broad question, Miller laid out two basic rules for scientific inquiry. First, he said, "science tries to provide natural explanations for natural phenomena. So one of the most basic rules is that practitioners of science seek their explanations in the world around us, in things we can test, we can observe, and we can verify." Second, he added, "scientific inquiry must be open, it must be subject to duplication, replication, test and examination by other scientists." Miller then explained: "If you invoke a non-natural cause, a spirit force or something like that in your research and I decide to test it, I have no way to test it. I can't order that from a biological supply house, I can't grow it in my laboratory. And that means that your explanations in that respect, even if they were correct, were not something I could test or replicate, and therefore they really wouldn't be part of science."

Miller, an avid Boston Red Sox fan, drew a smile from Judge Jones with a reference to the previous year's American League playoffs: "One might say the reason the Red Sox were able to come back from three games down against the New York Yankees was because God was tired of George Steinbrenner and wanted to see the Red Sox win. In my part of the country, you'd be surprised how many people think that's a perfectly respectable explanation for what happened last year. And you know what, it might be true, but it certainly is not science."

On a more serious note, Walczak moved to the claim—repeatedly made by Alan Bonsell and Bill Buckingham—that evolution was not a "fact" but simply a "theory" that was little more than speculation. "So is evolution a theory or a fact?" he asked Miller. "We often use the word 'evolution' to refer to the fact that life has changed over time," Miller replied. "Evolution is as much a fact as anything else that we know about the natural history of this planet. However, the use of 'evolution' as a theory is basically used to describe the mechanisms by which those changes took place. And in that respect, evolution is, indeed, a theory because it is a powerful, useful, and predictive explanation of a whole range of scientific facts."

Miller explained to Judge Jones his objections to Dover's ID policy. "By holding this up as an alternative to evolution, students will get the message in a flash. And the message is, you got your God-consistent theory, your theistic theory, your Bible-friendly theory, and over on the other side, you got your atheist theory, which is evolution. It produces a false duality. And this statement tells them, I think, quite explicitly, choose God on the side of intelligent design or choose atheism on the side of science." Miller brought his own religious beliefs into the court-room. "I say that as a person of faith who was blessed with two daughters, who raised both of my daughters in the church, and had they been given an education in which they were explicitly or implicitly forced to choose between God and science, I would have been furious, because I want my children to keep their religious faith."

His passion cooled, Miller then took on Behe's argument, the basis of his book, *Darwin's Black Box*, that some biological systems are "irreducibly complex," in that removing one component would render the system incapable of functioning. In Behe's view, this showed evidence of an "intelligent designer" behind the system, and negated the possibility that it could have evolved from less complex organisms. Miller first treated Judge Jones to a slide show, projected on a large screen in the courtroom, depicting organisms—including Behe's favorite example, the bacterial "flagellum" that looks something like an outboard motor to propel bacteria—that Behe claimed were "irreducibly complex." In slide after slide, Miller pointed to organisms that, he claimed, functioned perfectly well without such supposedly necessary mechanisms, including the blood-clotting systems of whales, another of Behe's favorite examples. Despite Miller's use of highly technical terms, such as the "Type III secretory system," Jones seemed enthralled by a "show-and-tell" lecture that lasted several hours. At one point, Miller admitted that even "my mother" might have difficulty following him, to which Jones replied, "Or me!"

Noting that he and Behe had frequently debated these issues, Miller said of his scientific adversary that he makes "a large number of claims regarding irreducible complexity, regarding the biochemical argument from design that have been repeatedly falsified by experiments, by observations in nature, and that's the point that I try to make in these debates, that these claims have been examined, considered by the scientific community, and generally falsified. I'm sure that he disagrees with me, but of course, he'll get a chance to say that himself. Perhaps he'll get up here in a couple days and say, you know, I listened to everything Dr. Miller said and, by God, he's got it exactly right." Judge Jones seemed amused: "We'd have a real story then, wouldn't we?"

Actually, three weeks passed before Michael Behe took the stand to answer Ken Miller's attacks on his concept of intelligent design. Not surprisingly, he disagreed that Miller had been "exactly right" in his criticisms. Robert Muise of the More Center's legal team opened the questioning: "Sir, what is intelligent design?" Behe offered this one-sentence definition: "Intelligent design is a scientific theory that proposes that some aspects of life are best explained as the result of design, and that the strong appearance of design in life is real and not just apparent." Muise then quoted Miller's definition of ID as " 'the proposition that some aspects of living things are too complex to have been evolved and, therefore, must have been produced by an outside creative force acting outside the laws of nature.' " Behe accused Miller of a "mischaracterization" of his views. "Professor Miller is viewing intelligent design from the perspective of his own views and sees it simply as an attack on Darwinian theory," Behe said. Having sat through Miller's testimony, Behe knew that his adversary had tried to link ID with creationism. "Intelligent design is a scientific theory, based entirely on observable, empirical, physical evidence from nature plus logical inferences," Behe stated. "Creationism is a religious, theological idea."

Behe explained the process of inference that led him to embrace the ID concept, reading from a slide on the screen that faced Judge Jones. "We infer design when we see that parts appear to be arranged for a purpose," he began. "The more parts that are arranged, and the more intricately they interact, the stronger is our confidence in design. Since nothing else than an intelligent cause has been demonstrated to be able to yield such a strong appearance of design, the conclusion that the design in life is real design is rationally justified." Muise then gave Behe the opening to discuss his favorite organism, the bacterial flagellum, which popped up on his next slide. "This is really only a little illustration, a kind of a cartoon drawing of the flagellum," he told Jones. "And it's really much more complex than this." Behe first explained that the bacterial flagellum "is quite literally an outboard motor that bacteria use to swim. And in order to accomplish that function, it has a number of parts ordered to that effect." He pointed to the drawing on the screen.

"The motor is actually a rotary motor," he began. "This part here is the propeller. The propeller is attached to something called the drive shaft by another part which is called the hook region which acts as a universal joint, to transmit the rotary motion from the drive shaft itself through the propeller." Behe concluded his lecture: "Most people who see this and have the function explained to them quickly realized that these parts are ordered for a purpose and, therefore, bespeak design."

Outboard motors can't work without a propeller or drive shaft. Behe used this mechanical analogy to explain his concept of "irreducible complexity." Removing any part of the bacterial flagellum would render it useless, he said. And evolution could not explain how any of the flagellum's parts might have begun in other forms as "precursors" to the completed organism. Only in their present form, created by an "intelligent cause," could their shape and function have been designed, Behe argued. But he was careful to limit the concept of "irreducible complexity" to the level of biological cells, "systems whose active molecular components we can elucidate," he explained. "When you go beyond a cell, then you're necessarily talking about a system, an organ or an animal or any such thing, that is so complex we really don't know what we're dealing with, so the term irreducible complexity is confined to molecular examples."

Behe knew that other ID advocates, including the creationist authors of the *Pandas* book, had pushed his concept of irreducible complexity much higher up the biological ladder, as far up as giraffes. "Even though most people commonly think of large organisms" as being so complex they must have been designed in those forms, Behe said of ID's most fervent proponents, "irreducible complexity focuses on the cell and systems smaller, because we have to elucidate all the parts," of which giraffes and other animals simply have too many to isolate in the laboratory. But he stuck with his "inference" from cellular organisms that "intelligent design" was a better explanation of biological complexity than evolution.

The "central question" of biological origins and change, of course, was that of identifying the "intelligent designer" of organisms from bacterial flagella to giraffes. Eric Rothschild waited for two days, while Behe showed Judge Jones dozens of slides in what Muise called his "Biology 101" lectures, before Muise turned his client over for cross-examination. Brandishing his "dog-eared" copy of Behe's book, *Darwin's Black Box*, Rothschild flashed page 193 on the courtroom screen. He asked Behe to read three sentences: " 'To a person who does not feel obligated to restrict his search to unintelligent causes, the straightforward conclusion is that many biochemical systems were designed. They were designed not by the laws of nature, not by chance and necessity; rather, they were planned. The designer knew what the systems would look like when they were completed, then took steps to bring the systems about.' " This designer—who planned these systems, knew what they would look like, and took steps to put all their parts in working order—sounded a lot like God, Rothschild suggested. Behe replied that he took no position on who or what the designer might have been. Rothschild reminded Behe of his testimony that "you personally believe the designer is God." "Yes," he agreed. Rothschild then put on the screen an article Behe had written about ID in a philosophy journal. "What if the existence of God is in dispute or is denied?" Behe had asked. "Is the plausibility of the argument from design affected? As a matter of my own experience the answer is clearly yes, the argument is less plausible to those for whom God's existence is in question, and is much less plausible for those who deny God's existence." Rothschild turned from the screen to the witness stand: "It's a God-friendly theory, isn't it, Professor Behe?" he asked. Behe declined to give a "yes" or "no" answer to Rothschild's question. "I've argued a number of places," he replied, "that it's the proper role of a scientist to leave aside those other considerations as much as possible and focus simply on the scientific data."

Over five days of testimony between them, Kenneth Miller and Michael Behe—both devout Catholics and trained biologists—seemed more alike than different. Although Behe hedged his answers with numerous qualifications, they agreed that God had created the universe, which operated by "natural" laws; that our planet is billions of years old; and that Darwin's theory of evolution best explains the progressive development of life forms above the cellular level. And they both re-jected any form of "creationism" based on the Bible. Where they dif-fered, it seemed, was simply over whether the features of cells at the molecular level had evolved from simpler forms or had been designed by an intelligent creator. Dover's ninth-grade biology students were un-likely to hear the term "irreducible complexity" in their classes, which Judge Jones heard dozens of times in the "Biology 101" course that Miller and Behe conducted in his courtroom. More important to Jones, however, were the questions of whether Dover's ID statement and *Pandas* belonged in the township's high school. Miller and Behe had clashed over these questions, but it would take other witnesses to give the judge the evidence he needed to decide them.

———

As it turned out, the witness on whose testimony Jones relied most heavily in deciding the Dover case was one the More Center lawyers tried hard to keep off the stand. Barbara Forrest, a philosophy professor at Southeastern Louisiana University, had written a book entitled *Creationism's Trojan Horse: The Wedge of Intelligent Design*, published in 2004. The ACLU legal team called Forrest as an expert witness to docu-ment the religious roots of the ID movement. Richard Thompson, the More Center's chief counsel, argued heatedly to Judge Jones that Forrest lacked any credentials in either science or religion, and was thus un-qualified to testify about ID's scientific claims or its theological under-pinnings. Thompson lost this skirmish, and Eric Rothschild got right to the point when Forrest took the stand: "Do you have an opinion about whether intelligent design is religious in nature?" Forrest agreed that ID "is essentially religious" and is "a form of creationism." The ID move-ment's leaders, she added, rejected evolution "in favor of a supernatural intervention in the process of nature and in favor of special creation of life forms."

Forrest buttressed her testimony with a raft of quotations from ID advocates, projected on the courtroom monitor. She began with Phillip Johnson, whose 1991 book, *Darwin on Trial*, had launched the move-ment as an intellectual force and hit the best-seller lists. Johnson, a retired law professor at the University of California, Berkeley, with no training in science, had launched a crusade against evolution after a sudden conversion to evangelical Christianity. He put his credo into words that Forrest read to Judge Jones: " 'My colleagues and I speak of theistic realism, or sometimes mere creation, as the defining concept of our movement. This means that we affirm that God is objectively real as creator, and that the reality of God is tangibly recorded in evidence accessible to science, particularly in biology.' "

The colleagues to whom Johnson referred were clustered in the Discovery Institute, which adopted his book as its bible. A self-professed intellectual revolutionary, Johnson advised his disciples to seek "nothing less than the overthrow of materialism and its cultural legacies," which he traced to the influence of Darwin, Marx, and Freud. To achieve this ambitious goal, Johnson proposed a long-term "wedge strategy" to promote intelligent design. Adopting his title, the Institute circulated a document, headed "The Wedge Strategy," as a fund-raising pitch to wealthy conservatives. "If we view the predominant materialistic science as a giant tree," it stated, "our strategy is intended to function as a 'wedge' that, while relatively small, can split the trunk when applied to its weakest point." Johnson envisioned intelligent design as the sharp end of this wedge. "Design theory promises to reverse the stifling dominance of the materialist worldview, and to replace it with a science consonant with Christian and theistic convictions," the "Wedge" document proposed, citing Michael Behe's *Darwin's Black Box* as a "positive scientific alternative" to Darwinism.

Behe's roles as a fellow of the Discovery Institute, and as the Dover school board's lead-off expert witness, offered Forrest an opening to link the religious underpinning of the "wedge strategy" to the board's ID policy. She also exploited Behe's connection to the *Pandas* book, to which he had contributed a section. Over the strenuous objections of the More Center's lawyers, Judge Jones allowed Forrest to read excerpts from two versions of the book. The first, drafted in 1986 and never published, included these sentences: "Creation means that the various forms of life began abruptly through the agency of an intelligent creator with their distinctive features already intact. Fish with fins and scales, birds with feathers, beaks, and wings, etc." This version had been changed, however, after the Supreme Court struck down, in 1987, the Louisiana law that mandated "balanced treatment" in biology classes of "creation-science" and evolution. The second *Pandas* version changed the first sentence to read: "Intelligent design means that various forms of life began abruptly through an intelligent agency, with their distinctive features already intact."

Pointing to a graph on the courtroom monitor, Forrest noted that the words "creation" and "creationism" in the first version had been replaced more than 150 times with "intelligent design" in the second. What had been designed as a creationist book, she concluded, had been camouflaged as ID, solely to circumvent the Supreme Court's ruling against teaching creationism. In his cross-examination of Forrest, Richard Thompson stressed that the first *Pandas* version had never been published and that no member of the Dover school board had ever seen it. But the damaging testimony remained on the record. Ironically, Thompson himself had first told Bill Buckingham about the *Pandas* book, unwittingly setting the trap that Forrest had now sprung. Equally ironically, her effective use of the "Wedge" document followed the Discovery Institute's unavailing arguments to the Dover school board that its ID policy would fail a legal challenge.

Two weeks after Barbara Forrest completed her testimony, Richard Thompson engaged in a public squabble with one of the Institute's lawyers, Mark Ryland. Speaking in Washington, D.C., at a forum sponsored by a conservative think-tank, the American Enterprise Institute, Ryland complained that his group had "gotten sucked into" the Dover case after the More Center rejected its advice that defending the school board's ID policy was "risky." Thompson retorted by asking Ryland "exactly where was the heart of the Discovery Institute," adding, "As soon as there's a controversy, they back off with a compromise." Ken Miller, who sat on the panel with Ryland and Thompson, relished this intramural spat. "I'm *really* enjoying this," he interjected. "This is the most fascinating discussion I've heard all day!"

With the trial still in progress, Thompson was not likely to enjoy the battle he faced in Harrisburg, knowing that his ACLU adversaries had prepared a courtroom ambush for his two most vulnerable witnesses, Bill Buckingham and Alan Bonsell. Thompson, in fact, had not planned to put Buckingham on the stand, fearing that his pre-trial deposition would give the ACLU lawyers ammunition to impeach his testimony. In that deposition, Buckingham had repeatedly denied ever using the word "creationism" at board meetings, and had also denied any knowledge of the funds used to purchase the *Pandas* book. Knowing what was in store, the More Center lawyers could only sit and grit their teeth when Steve Harvey called Buckingham as a "hostile" witness for the plaintiffs. Harvey wasted no time, handing Buckingham a copy of his deposition. "It's your testimony that creationism was never said by any board member, including you, at any board meeting?" Harvey asked. "That's true," Buckingham replied. "And is it your testimony that creationism was never said to any reporters after any board meeting?" Harvey continued. "That's true," Buckingham insisted. Harvey then flipped a switch, projecting on the courtroom monitor a videotape of Buckingham speaking with a television reporter after the board meeting on June 7, 2004. "My opinion," he said, "it's okay to teach Darwin, but you have to balance it with something else, such as creationism." Did he stand by his testimony? Harvey demanded. "I misspoke," Buckingham conceded.

Harvey returned to the deposition, reading from the transcript of Buckingham's interrogation about the *Pandas* money: "Question: Were you curious to know where it came from? Answer: Didn't want to know." Harvey then handed Buckingham the $850 check from his account, with the notation "Of Pandas and People." Visibly shaken, Buckingham looked at the check. "Mr. Buckingham, you lied to me at your deposition," Harvey said. "Isn't that true?" With the witness on the ropes, Judge Jones ended his battering. "Mr. Harvey, why don't you move to the next area," he suggested. "I get the point, and you've made the point very effectively." Harvey knew when to stop. "Your honor, I'm done."

Jones may have ended Buckingham's ordeal because he knew the former board member's addiction to prescription painkillers may have clouded his memory. But he showed no sympathy for Alan Bonsell, who denied any recollection of having received the *Pandas* check from Buckingham. After Bonsell responded with "I don't know" to more than thirty questions from Steve Harvey, the judge demanded to see a copy of his deposition by Eric Rothschild. "We're going to go through it," Jones told Bonsell. "I apologize if it's lengthy, but I think it's important." One by one, he read Rothschild's questions about the *Pandas* money, and Bonsell's denials that he knew its source. Visibly angry, Jones turned to Bonsell: "You didn't mention anything to Mr. Rothschild about getting a check from Mr. Buckingham for $850, did you?" Bonsell stammered his reply: "I didn't receive—that I didn't receive a check from Mr. Buckingham? No, I already said, I haven't—I did not tell him about receiving a check from Mr. Buckingham. But I still, you know, don't believe I misspoke." Jones clearly did not believe Bonsell, who left the stand with a cloud of perjury over his head.

The *Kitzmiller* trial ended on November 4, 2005, with its decision in the hands of Judge Jones. Four days later, Dover's voters made their own decision, in an election that pitted eight of the school board's members against a slate of challengers who opposed the ID policy. A week before the election, the heated campaign had taken a nasty turn when the incumbents sent voters a mass mailing, prepared by Alan Bonsell, attacking their opponents as tools of the ACLU. Bonsell's letter claimed the ACLU defended groups that "put out information on how adults can lure young children into having sex with them," and backed "special rights" for terrorists. "I think the ACLU is a very terrible organization," he told reporters. Another board member, Ron Short, was even more emphatic. "I fear the ACLU more than I fear al-Qaida," he said. What most voters feared, however, was the prospect of further conflict over an issue that had divided the community into hostile camps. On November 8, Bonsell came in next to last at the polls, as voters ousted all eight incumbents on the ballot, sparing only one member whose term had not expired.

Bonsell ducked reporters after his defeat, but televangelist Pat Robertson was not equally reticent. "I'd like to say to the good citizens of Dover," he told his *700 Club* viewers, "if there is a disaster in your area, don't turn to God, you just rejected him from your city. Don't ask for his help, because he might not be there." The media uproar over his comments prompted Robertson to back down, but only a little. "God is tolerant and loving," he conceded in a press release, "but we can't keep sticking our finger in his eye forever. If they have future problems in Dover, I recommend they call on Charles Darwin. Maybe he can help them."

On December 20, six weeks after the voters rebuked Bonsell and his board colleagues, Judge Jones issued his own rebuke in a detailed, 139-page opinion, with hundreds of citations to the trial transcript, exhibits, and depositions. Jones first addressed the question of whether intelligent design qualified as a legitimate scientific theory. "While answering this question compels us to revisit evidence that is entirely complex, if not obtuse," he wrote, "after a six-week trial that spanned twenty-one days and countless hours of detailed expert witness presentations, the Court is confident that no other tribunal in the United States is in a better position than are we to traipse into this controversial area."

Relying heavily on Ken Miller's testimony, Jones concluded that "ID fails on three different levels, any one of which is sufficient to preclude a determination that ID is science." First, he wrote, "ID violates the centuries-old ground rules of science by invoking and permitting supernatural causation" of biological changes. Jones then rejected Michael Behe's defense of intelligent design: "The argument of irreducible complexity, central to ID, employs the same flawed and illogical contrived dualism that doomed creation science in the 1980's." Finally, he stated, "ID's negative attacks on evolution have been refuted by the scientific community."

Having concluded that ID lacked scientific merit, Jones then explored its religious roots, with copious citations to Barbara Forrest's testimony. He singled out a statement by ID's intellectual godfather, Phillip Johnson, that the "Darwinian theory of evolution contradicts not just the

Book of Genesis, but every word in the Bible from beginning to end. It contradicts the idea that we are here because a creator brought about our existence for a purpose." The Discovery Institute's "Wedge Strategy" document, Jones noted, provided compelling evidence that ID's proponents were, in fact, latter-day creationists who cloaked their religious motivations behind the mask of science. Because ID "is grounded in theology, not science," he concluded, it "has utterly no place in a science curriculum."

Judge Jones could easily have ended his opinion, and shortened it considerably, with his ruling that Dover's ID policy constituted "a strong endorsement of a religious view" and violated Supreme Court precedent against teaching creationism in public schools. He felt compelled, however, to chastise the board members who voted for this policy for their "striking ignorance" of the ID theory. "Conspicuously," he wrote, "board members who voted for the curriculum change testified at trial that they had utterly no grasp of ID." Jones directed particular scorn at Alan Bonsell and Bill Buckingham, whom he accused of coercing their ignorant colleagues into voting for the ID policy, despite their own admitted lack of knowledge about ID.

Ignorance did not spare Bonsell and Buckingham from a judicial tongue-lashing. Six times in his opinion, Jones accused them of lying under oath, both in their depositions and at the trial. First, he found it "incredible that Bonsell disclaimed any interest in creationism during his testimony. Simply put, Bonsell repeatedly failed to testify in a truthful manner about this and other subjects." Jones then cited the testimony of ten witnesses that Bonsell and Buckingham had both talked about creationism at board meetings in June 2004. This record showed, Jones concluded, that both men "either testified inconsistently, or lied outright under oath on several occasions, and are accordingly not credible on these points." Jones moved to their repeated denials that either man knew the source of the money used to purchase the *Pandas* book. "The inescapable truth is that both Bonsell and Buckingham lied" about these funds in their depositions, Jones wrote. "This mendacity was a clear and deliberate attempt to hide the source of the donations," he added. Jones was particularly incensed that school-board members "who so staunchly and proudly touted their religious convictions in public, would time and again lie to cover their tracks and disguise the real purpose behind the ID Policy."

Jones made clear that he did not question "that many of the leading advocates of ID have bona fide and deeply held beliefs which drive their scholarly endeavors. Nor do we controvert that ID should continue to be studied, debated, and discussed." His ruling was limited, Jones wrote, to holding that "it is unconstitutional to teach ID as an alternative to evolution in a public school science classroom."

Judge Jones anticipated the criticism he knew his opinion would trigger from the Religious Right, and replied with his own rebuttal. "Those who disagree with our holding will likely mark it as the product of an activist judge," he wrote. "If so, they will have erred as this is manifestly not an activist Court. Rather, this case came to us as the result of the activism of an ill-informed faction on a school board, aided by a national public interest law firm eager to find a constitutional test case on ID, who in combination drove the board to adopt an imprudent and ultimately unconstitutional policy." Jones summed up his feelings in this final sentence: "The students, parents, and teachers of the Dover Area School District deserved better than to be dragged into this legal maelstrom, with its resulting utter waste of monetary and personal resources."

Sure enough, his opinion provoked the reaction that Jones had predicted. "The Dover decision is an attempt by an activist federal judge to stop the spread of a scientific idea and even to prevent criticism of Darwinian evolution through government-imposed censorship rather than open debate, and it won't work," replied John West of the Discovery Institute. Richard Thompson, who headed the Thomas More Law Center's legal team at the Dover trial, looked forward to a more conservative Supreme Court. "Unfortunately," he said, "until the Supreme Court adopts a more coherent and historically sound jurisprudence, school districts like Dover will be at risk of costly lawsuits by the ACLU for adopting such modest curriculum changes such as the one at issue."

The new Dover school board, however, had no stomach for the costly lawsuit that its former members had forced on the district's taxpayers. At its first meeting, in January 2006, the board voted to forgo an appeal of Judge Jones's decision, and to rescind the ID policy that had sparked the lawsuit. But the debate over evolution did not end in Dover, Pennsylvania, just as it did not end in Dayton, Tennessee, eighty years earlier.

Opponents of Darwinism have not given up their goal of persuading local and state school boards to "balance" the teaching of evolution with a watered-down form of creationism in the guise of "intelligent design." However, Judge Jones's opinion in the Dover case was clearly a major setback to the "Wedge Strategy" of the Discovery Institute, despite the DI's claim that his ruling had no legal force beyond that Pennsylvania district.

In reality, the impact of that ruling has already been felt as far from Dover as Kansas; in August 2006, voters in that state's Republican primary election ousted two anti-evolution incumbents on the state board of education, returning control to a pro-evolution majority. Ostensibly nonpartisan, the Discovery Institute had effectively campaigned for the incumbents with a barrage of radio ads, narrated by Jonathan Wells, one of the DI's fellows. After this defeat, the DI complained that "the Darwinian faction scared Kansas educators with the prospect of being sued on the basis" of the Dover decision, adding that evolution supporters "triumphed in Kansas and further victories elsewhere may be expected." Despite their gloomy legal prospects in the wake of Judge Jones's ruling, the DI and its anti-evolution allies pin their hopes of ultimate victory for the "Wedge Strategy" on a future case before the Supreme Court's new conservative majority. Of course, that majority might shift, depending on the outcome of future presidential and senatorial elections, in which religion and politics have become increasingly intertwined. Keeping in mind that the Kansas voters who supported the pro-evolution candidates were all Republicans, in a heavily conservative state, the political tide seems to be receding for Darwin's opponents.

Meanwhile, Jen Miller's ninth-grade biology students at Dover High will once again trace the Earth's evolutionary timeline in the hallway. "That would definitely be something that I'd put back in," she said, after the school board voted to take intelligent design out of her classroom.

CASEY AND JEFF BROWN

Casey

My nickname is Casey, that's what most people call me, although my family still calls me by my given name, which is Carol. I was born in 1947. My father was career Army, a demolitions expert in World War II, served in the Pacific, European theater, Korean conflict. I was raised in the service; we lived primarily in the Pacific and the Orient, Guam, the Philippines, Taiwan, Thailand, Japan. I was born here, because my mother wanted me to be born in the continental United States. She had this thing about American soil. She had me here, in York, because her family lived in York County, had been here since 1687.

On my mother's side of the family, they're mostly German. Her family came over prior to the American Revolution, to escape religious persecution, and they basically walked across Europe to Rotterdam, because it was the only port where they could get passage to America. They became the Plain People, the Amish, the Mennonites, the Brethren. I have Amish cousins, even now, who don't have electricity in the house. My father's family came over as indentured servants from Scotland. My grandfather was a butler for the Firestone family, and my grandmother was an upstairs maid.

I was brought up in two churches. When we visited or stayed with my mother's parents, we went to my grandmother's church, which was Brethren. They have the more basic values, not like the fundamentalists today. You didn't wear your faith on your sleeve, you lived it. On my father's side, they're Episcopalian. My grandfather was raised in the Church of England, and he joined the Episcopal Church after becoming an American. My mother decided to join that church, and I'm now an Episcopalian. Being raised in both churches, though, was good for me. I was actually confirmed in both. There were differences, but they're both very clear that you make your own decisions on matters of belief. You do not have to accept the virgin birth, you're not asked to accept creationist stories as an article of faith. You didn't just learn a bunch of things by rote. We were always encouraged to ask questions, to search for answers. I was taught very early that no one has a lock on the truth, that their way is the only way. That upbringing opened me to faith, and Jeff and I both did that with our kids. We each have a child from a previous marriage, but we were both custodial parents, and we had a kind of blended family. We would answer their questions; we've got books on every religion. Even today, we talk about religion.

I went to school all over, mostly base schools. When my dad went to Korea, we came back and mostly stayed with my mother's family. I went to high school in York—that's where I finished. Then I went to Millersville State College, which was then a teacher-training school. I quit college after two years, because I didn't really want to teach. I wanted to do pre-Columbian archaeology, but women didn't do that. I grew up in a time when women were raised, if you went to college, to find a husband, live in the suburbs, and raise children. I was unhappy, so I left college, went out on my own, and then decided that I did want to teach after all. I finished college and went into teaching, but I couldn't make a living at it, and began running with an ambulance, working as a paramedic, and found out I really liked that too. I did that for a while, and was also working on the side as a newspaper reporter, because I loved to write. I started with the *Lancaster Sunday News*, which became the *York Dispatch*. They used to run a series called "I Know a Story," and I had submitted several, mostly about family in the old days. That was how I got started there, and when I began working full-time, I did sports, covered fires, school-board meetings, you name it.

Jeff

I was born in Dover Township in 1950, grew up in Washington Township, right next door in York County. I grew up in the middle of nowhere, virtually a frontier, not in the literal sense, but the mentality of Washington Township was very much that of a frontier. I was raised to feel that Dover, a town of two thousand people, was cosmopolitan. And if you saw where I was raised, you would understand why. I went to a one-room school, with an outhouse, which was no big deal, because our house had an outhouse. We didn't have a telephone until 1955, because they had not run the telephone lines out that far. It was pretty primitive.

Washington Township is part of the Dover school district, and I graduated from Dover High School. I went all the way through school here, graduated, no further education. I spent two hours in a college classroom as a guest instructor—that's my entire higher education. When I finished high school, I grew my hair down to my shoulders and hitchhiked around the country. I went to New York, the East Village, then to Boston, went to California. I married a woman I met in Hollywood, at the corner of Sunset and Vine. We came back here, got married, had a kid, and got divorced. I had all kinds of jobs, whatever I could find. I worked in a flour mill, I worked in factories—the money was good, and I could leave the job at the door. I liked that. Now I'm working by myself as an electrician, the first thing I really loved doing.

I went to Lutheran churches when I was growing up, but I never bought into "the Bible is literally true" stuff. That's a bunch of baloney. You know, the Ark had two of everything on the face of the earth in one boat? It's impossible, it couldn't happen. The Tower of Babel? If you can't reach heaven with structural steel, you ain't going to reach it with a stone building. Forget that one too. It's a nice story, but it's malarkey. I love the story of Adam and Eve—it's a great parable, a great understanding of what makes people different from animals—but it's nothing remotely resembling science.

Casey

I ran for the Dover school board in 1995 because of my daughter's special needs. Julie was born in 1970. She was twenty-three days early, and she didn't breathe when she was born. So she was a special-needs child, and she's a special-needs adult. As recently as ten years ago, parents of special children, whether physical, mental, or emotional, got short shrift. You really had to fight. And if you didn't know where to go, or who to ask, they'd flat-out lie to you. And there was a stigma. I had to fight every step of the way to get Julie properly classified. Ultimately, she left the Dover district, because we did not have the classes she needed. In this area, one district has one type of class, another has a different one, and you have an exchange of services. So Julie graduated from Central York High School, because they had the learning-support classes she needed.

At that time, I'm reporting on other school districts and what they're doing, and they're so incredibly dedicated, and it hit me, It's time you put your money where your mouth is. So Jeff and I talked about it, there was an election coming up in 1995, there were a number of openings, and I ran a write-in campaign. There were several seats with no candidates—seats were going begging. I was running as the parent of a special-needs child, and to represent other parents of special-needs children, because they didn't have an advocate on the board. I spent ten dollars, on pens and copies of instructions on casting write-in votes. There were eight write-in candidates, and I came out on top.

When I joined the board, I was unpopular from day one, because I did not accept blanket answers. I wanted to know the whys, wherefores, and everything. The superintendent when I went on was used to a board that said yes to whatever he wanted. I didn't play ball, because I just wouldn't accept what he told us, I wanted to know what was going on. Most board members were go-along types. They put me on the Policy Committee, which was their biggest mistake. If you're going to do the job, you do your homework. I knew the Pennsylvania school code inside and out, and I'm not boasting; it's a fact. We had policies that hadn't been reviewed in over a decade. Now they're all up-to-date. More than that, I could say, No, the school code says we can't do that. And I caused major headaches. I reversed the district's lawyer on one issue because I knew the code—she was wrong and I proved her wrong.

Jeff

Casey was on the board for five years before I decided to run. What prompted me was the way they treated her. I was getting increasingly frustrated by the stories that were coming home, and finally I decided I was going to run. I was nervous running, thinking voters might not like a husband-and-wife team on the board, but usually you couldn't even get candidates for the bloody school board, and there were only five candidates for five seats. What really pushed me was that Noel Wenrich filed for the board also. We didn't even know if it was a man or a woman, with a name like Noel. But that made it six people running for five seats, so I wouldn't automatically get elected. And I ran against the board. This is a little town, and not much happens here normally. So reporters would call me up and ask for quotes. Everybody else would blow them off. Not me. I just loved it. So I'm just blasting the school board up one side and down the other—never any individuals, just the board itself. On Election Day, I whomped 'em. Noel Wenrich also got on, bumping off the person the president had hand-picked to replace her, who came in last.

Casey

The religion thing started when we had a school-board retreat in January 2002. I had just been sworn in as board president, and the retreat was my idea. Rich Nilsen had just become the superintendent, after his predecessor took early retirement. We needed to mend a lot of fences. Alan Bonsell was new to the board, and we knew him slightly, but not too well. We ran together for the board. As the board president, I appointed Alan as chair of the Curriculum Committee. I kept an eye on it, but I also gave him a free hand. And he was questioning, and that was fine, as long as he was staying within the white lines.

Jeff

Dr. Nilsen went around the board and asked all the members what their major areas of concern were. Alan's major concern was that creationism should have some sort of place in the biology curriculum. My reaction was that Alan had freshman fever. New board members think they can change the world. I remember having a discussion with Alan in private, and his religious views were very well known to me. Alan was of the opinion that there was an awful lot wrong with evolution; in his opinion, the Bible was literally true, and anywhere that science conflicted with the Bible, there had to be some mistake on the part of scientists.

But I didn't care. It was all a matter to me of, What's he doing between the white lines? And he wasn't pushing creationism on the board during his first year.

Here's an interesting thing about a board like this, how one person can change the whole tenor of the board. Bill Buckingham was appointed to the board in 2003, to fill the seat of someone who had resigned. At first, he was okay. In fact, he agreed with us on most issues. But he left for a while, to go into rehab for addiction to painkillers he'd been taking after several operations on his back. After Bill came back, I noticed a dramatic change in him. He was bitter, vicious, judgmental, and that's when things started going really wrong. He and Alan were both young-earth creationists, but Alan was pretty easygoing and didn't make it a big issue when he chaired the Curriculum Committee. When Alan became board president, in 2004, he named Bill to chair the committee, and Bill turned creationism into a personal crusade. He had a very forceful personality, and some of the other board members just looked to him for how to vote.

I have a vivid memory of the board meeting on June 7, 2004. Bill had reviewed the ninth-grade biology textbook, the Miller and Levine book. And at this public meeting, he said the book was "laced with Darwinism" and that we needed to find a companion text that would balance evolution with creationism. My initial reaction was, Oh God, do we have a PR problem! This guy just said something incredibly stupid, and there were two reporters sitting there, writing furiously. We are in trouble. And these stories in the York newspapers got out on the wire services. Prior to our next meeting, on June 14, we had an executive session. Bill was all excited, like a little kid. He said, I've been getting calls and letters from all over the United States, because it went wire service. He was especially proud of the Discovery Institute having contacted him. Now, Bill later testified that at both of those board meetings he was talking about intelligent design, and that the Discovery Institute had explained it to him. I can tell you for a fact, Bill knew squat about ID at that point. He didn't even know the bloody term. In the June meetings, Bill used the term "creationism" constantly. He never talked about anything else.

There's another reason this lawsuit would never have happened without Bill Buckingham. And that's the *Pandas* book he got from the Thomas More Law Center. Bill said at the trial that he contacted the More Center first, that he'd found them on the computer, looking for material on intelligent design. But that's not what he told me. He told me that they called him, he didn't call them, which makes a lot more sense. Their Web site didn't even mention intelligent design. And Bill's computer-illiterate, to be honest. Anyway, we got a copy of the *Pandas* book three days before Bill wanted a vote to buy the bloody thing. Casey's on the Curriculum Committee; she should have had a copy of that book instantly.

Casey

I found out about the *Pandas* book from Mike Baksa, the assistant superintendent. He called me, and I told Jeff, and Jeff got a copy of the book. We took turns reading it through the weekend. Reading that book, number one, a lot of the terminology was not understandable for a ninth-grader. Number two, some of the diagrams were totally inaccurate, made no sense. I'm looking at them, and I'm going back to the encyclopedias—wait a minute! There were errors. Number three, I'm thinking to myself, I could substitute "creationism" for "intelligent design" in this book, and it would make more sense. That was long before we knew there were earlier drafts that used the terms "creation" or "creationism." And it turns out that's exactly what they did, taking out "creationism" and replacing it with "intelligent design."

Jeff

I also remember the board meeting in August 2004, when we were scheduled to vote on buying the Miller and Levine biology textbook. There were only eight members present, since one was in Florida. I walked in there, knowing that Alan, Noel, Casey, and I were going to vote for it. And there was one other name, Bill Buckingham. He had promised Casey he would vote to buy the Miller and Levine book. And then he voted no, which made it four to four, and the motion to buy the books failed. I was stunned. The whole deal was an extortion setup. He was going to hold the biology book hostage unless we agreed to buy the *Pandas* book. And I said, Suppose we read this *Pandas* book and decide it isn't worth the taxpayers' money? Bill looked me right in the eye and said, Either I get my book or you don't get yours! That's when I blew a gasket. I was ready to come across the table—I wanted a piece of that man, and I wanted it bad! Angie Yingling, who was sitting next to me, later said she thought I was in danger of having a heart attack. Only one person in that meeting was in any danger, and it wasn't me. Angie was so scared that she changed her vote, and gave us the fifth vote to buy the Miller and Levine textbook.

Bill still didn't give up on the *Pandas* book. The next board meeting, in September, we were in executive session, and Bill said that he was soliciting people in the district to buy the *Pandas* book privately and donate them to the school. That shouldn't be a problem, I said, we have a standing policy for donations to our library. And he said: I'm not asking people to fork over their hard-earned money for a book going into the library. I want it in the classroom, as a supplemental text. I said, That could be a problem, because we can't use texts that aren't on the approved curriculum list. But he wasn't backing down. And then both Alan Bonsell and Jane Cleaver said, Put me down for a donation. Now, I did not see them hand him the money, but they both volunteered to donate. Very shortly thereafter, it was announced that this donation had been made, anonymously. When the *Pandas* books arrived, Dr. Nilsen assured me they'd be placed in the back of the classroom, they'd gather dust, be stuck in a closet and forgotten about, and this was just to keep Bill happy. Nilsen later testified that the books were never in the classroom, they went right to the library, but I know that wasn't true.

By October of 2004, it was pretty clear to me and Casey that the board would get sued if they adopted the policy that would require teachers to mention intelligent design in biology classes. I thought the board would have second thoughts and back off. But I didn't realize the extent of the influence the Thomas More Law Center had on these clowns. They are the ones, I've referred to them constantly as carpetbaggers, who came into the district and assured these rather naïve and undereducated individuals that, as long as you have a lawyer in your hip pocket, the laws really don't mean that much. We tried, we really tried, we pushed the money angle hard, because we figured that they're not going to put the taxpayers' money at risk on this ridiculous scheme. But they said, "Thomas More won't cost us anything, they'll defend us for free." "Not if you lose!" "We're not going to lose! The More Center is not going to lose! We're going to win." Bill Buckingham said several times, "We'll fight this all the way to the Supreme Court." And I said, "Bill, you are mighty brave with other people's money. The taxpayers did not sign on for this."

But the board went ahead with the ID policy, and it was set for a final vote on October 18. Our twentieth wedding anniversary was October 16, and we were going out that night, but we never made it, because Casey let slip that she had been seriously considering resigning. And I said, You're kidding—because I had been thinking the same thing. Neither one of us had discussed it with the other, because we didn't want to influence each other. But both of us were so fed up with the direction the board was taking, and the fact that we were being increasingly ostracized by our former friends, because we didn't believe the right things religiously. And that's what it boiled down to. We didn't go to the right church, we didn't believe in the six-day creation, and therefore our opinions were viewed as worthless. We were both fed up, and we both wanted out. Casey had already prepared her resignation letter, but I was just going to say something informally.

We got to the executive session before the meeting, and Dr. Nilsen handed out two different versions of the statement for the board to vote on. We'd only found out about this three hours earlier. One statement was from the Curriculum Committee, although Casey was on that committee and hadn't been consulted about it. Alan Bonsell had drafted that statement, which said that Darwin's theory of evolution had "gaps" and "problems" and that intelligent design was an alternative theory that students should know about. It also said the *Pandas* book was available as a reference for students who wanted to learn more about ID. The other version, which the teachers had approved, was basically the same, but it didn't mention ID or the *Pandas* book. The teachers would have accepted *anything* that did not mention ID, but the board was adamant that ID be in there.

Noel Wenrich proposed I have no idea how many motions, but motions he could live with, and the teachers agreed they could live with, but they didn't include the words "ID." That was the deal-breaker for both sides. The board insisted that ID be in there, and the teachers insisted it not be in there. That was it in a nutshell: it had to promote ID or they weren't going to vote for it. We went through all the parliamentary motions, the teachers addressed the board, I addressed the board, Noel addressed the board. Casey didn't say much; she was pretty fed up.

Finally, we reached the point where it was like, What's the point, let's put this to bed, and they voted it through, six to three. It was a done deal, it was going to happen. Alan Bonsell and Bill Buckingham had their votes all lined up. I can tell you for a fact that Sheila Harkins, Heather Geesey, Jane Cleaver, and Angie Yingling didn't have a clue about what ID was. Alan and Bill had told them how to vote, and they just went along. They walked in there, they'd gotten their marching orders ahead of time. Right after the vote, Casey immediately asked for the floor, and read her letter of resignation. Angie looked at me and said, Is Casey resigning? And I said, Yeah, and she's not the only one. She got this sad, hurt look on her face, and I said, Angie, if you had spoken up, and gotten Heather or Jane with you, the motion would have failed.

Casey

After the meeting, Noel went up to Bill and said, I hope you're happy, you just caused us to lose the two best board members the district has ever seen. And Bill told him, Well, Casey is an atheist. Alan later accused us, me specifically, of destroying the board. He impugned my faith, and the faith of everyone who agreed with me, and told me directly that I was going to hell.

If there's one thing Jeff and I learned from this experience, it's the difference between people like Noel Wenrich and Bill Buckingham.

They're both young-earth creationists, very firm in their religious beliefs. But Noel recognized that he was elected to represent all the people in the district, not just those who share his beliefs. Bill came on the board with a religious agenda, and pushed it so hard that he ultimately cost the taxpayers a huge amount in legal fees. Whatever his personal or physical problems, and I can understand them, he should not have bullied the board into forcing his religious beliefs into the Dover schools. As I said, no one has a lock on the truth, and I think that's a lesson we need to remember. ❖

THE REVEREND ED ROWAND

I was born on Long Island, New York, in 1961. My dad worked as a machinist for the Grumman aircraft company. My parents were older when I was born, and they retired and moved to Pennsylvania, a tiny little town called Smethport. It's in the northwest part of the state, close to the New York border, about seventy miles south of Buffalo. I'm the youngest of four boys. We were all raised to be Christians, in the Assemblies of God church. My brothers all do very well. One is an air-traffic controller, one works for the Federal Aviation Administration in management, and one with the Quaker State oil company. Having good jobs, they have lots of toys—four-wheel drives, boats, guns. I kind of felt, all through high school, that I did not want to be a minister. I didn't know any ministers that had all the things my brothers have. That was a real problem for me, because I like toys, and hunting and fishing, so I didn't think too much about the ministry.

I decided to pursue a career in engineering, and I went to the University of Pittsburgh for a couple of years. But I was fighting the call to the ministry, and I didn't have peace. I struggled with that, but knowing what you're called to do, and running from that, bothered me. It came to a point where I couldn't fight it anymore. So I talked to my pastor, and talked to my parents, and made the decision to transfer to Valley Forge Christian College, which is an Assemblies of God school in Pennsylvania. I started there in 1981, and that's where I met my wife. I did an internship at a church on Long Island, came back from New York and graduated from Valley Forge in 1984, and was ordained in the ministry.

I thought I'd go back to New York, but the door didn't open that way, and you go where there's a job. So we ended up in Ohio, across the river from Pittsburgh, as an associate pastor. I was two years there. The senior pastor at that church, who was from Indiana, was going back there. We could have gone with him, and continued to be an associate pastor, but we didn't want to go further from our parents, who were from Pennsylvania. So when he left, we came back to Pennsylvania. I was at a church in Bloomsburg for five years, and then we moved to Wilmington, Delaware, and I was an associate pastor there.

In 1995, I got a call from a church in Dover. I thought it was Dover, Delaware, but it was Dover, Pennsylvania, which I'd never heard of. The churches in the Assemblies of God are sovereign, they can hire whoever they want. Most of the time, they will go through the hierarchy in the denomination—Hey, our pastor's left, we're looking for another pastor—they'd have some résumés of people who are looking for a church, send them to the church, and they'd pick one. My superintendent had recommended me; he said, There's a great guy. They called and asked if I would come.

So, eleven years ago, we came to Dover. Wilmington is a city, and I like the country. Coming here into woods and farmland—I absolutely loved it. We have three kids now. Joshua was in first grade when we moved here, and Jessica and Justin were born here. We've lived in both the city and the country; there's not as much anxiety for a parent, raising a child here, as compared to New York or even Delaware.

After our kids started school here, my wife and I were doing mostly volunteer things in the schools, if they needed chaperones for field trips. In ministry, if I'm not in the office doing Bible study, or visitation, or sermon prep, I could go with the kids and get that done later. In the evening, there's less phone calls and interruption, and you can be more productive in less time anyway. So I was free to volunteer and help out—not a lot—my wife did more. But with the younger ones, before they started school, she was home. A lot of times, field trips and stuff, they'd ask for a man. There'd be some boys in the class who were rough, and having a man would keep them in line. Also, we have a traveling sound system for the church. If the school would have a fun day outside, I'd bring it; we could have music and announcements. Having access to this stuff endeared me to the school and the leadership there.

The volunteering is what got me involved in the school district, because the principals knew me. You ask any one of them. What would you say about Ed Rowand? Well, first thing, I'm a minister. Is he a religious zealot, trying to push his beliefs on kids? Has he ever come in and tried to proselytize? Has he ever been out of line? No, that guy's here, and he'll help me. That guy cares about our kids. He'll bring in this program, and speakers that will motivate the kids and deal with some of the issues and problems we have in school. I think that's what they would say.

So, in 2004, when there was a vacancy on the school board, they encouraged me to apply. You're here, you volunteer, you care about this district—why don't you consider running? And some people from my church who are involved in politics on a local level also encouraged me. So I submitted a résumé, and the board chose me to replace a member who had resigned. There were actually five new board members in a very short time in the fall of 2004. Three people had moved from Dover—Bill Buckingham, Jane Cleaver, and Noel Wenrich. This thing with intelligent design came up almost at the same time, and with that the husband and wife resigned from the board, Jeff and Casey Brown.

I joined the board after it adopted the intelligent-design policy in October of 2004, but I was on the board when the ACLU lawsuit was filed that December. And I was a defendant in the case, at least in a technical sense, as a board member, up through the trial in the fall of 2005. Right after the trial ended in November, I was defeated in the school-board elections, along with the other seven members who were on the board then. The voters had their say, and I don't have any regrets or hard feelings. But I don't think my personal views on creationism or intelligent design played any role in that election; it was really about decisions the board had made before I became a member.

That being said, I did support the intelligent-design policy. But there are some misconceptions that need to be cleared up. First of all, I personally believe in creationism. You read Genesis. God created Adam out of the dust on the ground and breathed into him the breath of life, and Adam became a living soul. How did that happen? Did some amoeba climb out of the primordial slime, and that amoeba evolved into a man? You want to believe that? Okay. I think that takes a greater measure of faith than: God did it, and, boom, here it is. And that comes from my belief that everything in the Bible is the Word of God. If you rip out the first page of Genesis, you have to rip out every other page. It all stands together, or else nothing stands. However, I don't believe we should teach the Bible in school. Some would disagree with me. A lot of people really push that. I don't think we should teach creationism in school. And I've never hidden that from anybody.

A second misconception is that Alan Bonsell and Bill Buckingham were talking about creationism at the board meetings in June of 2004. I was there at the meetings, and that's not how I remember it. I'm pretty sure that Alan did not say that. As a minister, I think if that word had been said by Alan, as president of the school board, I would have heard it. If he had said "creationism," bam, my ears would have perked up like a Doberman, and I would have been focused on what he was saying. Bill Buckingham may have said that. Bill said a lot of things off the cuff; some of that was insulting, some of that he apologized for; but in some of that he was goaded. Here's a lady, Barrie Callahan, a former board member, who's at every meeting and makes comments at every meeting, and develops a reputation as a pain in the neck. And then, one time, two times, three times, a board member says something off the cuff, he's frustrated with her, that's reported. Look what he said at the meeting! And he was pretty forceful: Look, this is what I think, and I'm going to do what I think is right. If you don't like it, don't elect me next time. Pretty blunt, pretty straightforward, but he wasn't hiding it, he wasn't being two-faced about it.

We want to label all these people as religious zealots who are trying to get their religious agenda into the school, and are using ID as the means to get creationism discussed, and that's the problem. Nobody on that school board had any intention whatsoever of forcing their religion on the schools, though the plaintiffs clearly feel like that was at issue here, and Buckingham didn't help, because of some of the comments he made off the cuff, and became a pain. People would take a shot at him: Look at what this Christian guy said! Well, did you hear what the other side said, how they goaded him into making these comments? But the papers kept hammering. This is not right, they're wrong. They're crucifying Bill Buckingham.

Third, it seems to me that the problem in Dover came about because people said we were teaching intelligent design in biology classes. If that was true, I believe we would have a debate. But it wasn't. They were *not* teaching intelligent design. There was no explanation as to what intelligent design was in the classroom. But it was spoken of regularly in the media, and in the lawsuit, like, Should we be teaching intelligent design or not? That would be a great debate, if indeed we were teaching ID, but we weren't. The idea in the Dover school district, as I saw it, was that the law in Pennsylvania required that Darwin's theory be taught. And the teachers will teach biology. There are some various different views of the origin of life, one of which is Biblical creation. We are not here to talk about the Bible, or creation, we're here to talk about Darwin's theory. From this point on, the teacher would say, we're not talking about creation, we're talking about Darwin's theory of evolution. That wasn't a problem. That was the practice in Dover. That's what the state standards say, and that's what we were conforming to.

The idea is education. What we tried to do with the one-minute statement was to let the kids know there are other theories. We're not teaching them, because by law we are required to teach Darwin's theory—this is what you're required to know on a standardized test, so that's what we're teaching. We do want you to do well on the test. But we would encourage you to check out these other books and learn, and you and your pastors and your families talk about this. Is that not good?

I think the lawsuit was more about the *Pandas* book than mentioning intelligent design in the one-minute statement the board adopted. I did not read the whole book, but I did look at it. Having said that, if this is not a required reading, in order for me to study evolution, do I have to agree with it all? Or do I just have to know this is what Darwin said? I'm being tested on it—do I have to agree with it, do I have to believe it? Intelligent design? This is what they're saying. Okay. I know the view, I know the contrary, I know where it contradicts the Bible. Are we telling the kids what to believe? If you are a student in biology, if you have a textbook, and you have a reference book, one of which is required, one of which is optional, with all of your other studying, what are you going to do? What's the chance you're going to crack that reference book, or skip it? And so there was an agreement with the teachers that *Pandas* will be a reference in the library. If the kids want to look at it, great! There's enough of them that anybody who wants one can get one.

I sat through almost every day of the trial. I missed one or two, but not very much. Those who were bringing the lawsuit put their expert witnesses on the stand. Ken Miller, who wrote the biology textbook that's used in the Dover schools, said that presenting intelligent design as an alternative to Darwin's theory is not good teaching. There is, in his words, quote, only one view, Darwin's view. There is no other view. And it's not a theory, it's a fact. I was there, I heard him say it. And he prefaced this by saying, I do believe in God. Ken Miller teaches biology at Brown University. In his biology class, he discusses ID, gives his students literature or handouts on ID. And as a part of his teaching, it is discussed, pros, cons, whatever. Is that not good education? Well, obviously, if it wasn't, he wouldn't do it. And yet in high school we can't even so much as mention that there is another view, or that there may be other views: this is the only view.

The expert witnesses for the plaintiffs made a case for *Pandas* being a problem because there's some things in there that look like creationism, but it uses the words "intelligent design." They kept saying, over and over and over again, do you mean to tell me that this intelligent designer created fish with scales, and birds with feathers? Now, that's a creationistic view. I believe that. Did the intelligent designer do that, does that fit within ID? I'll leave that for the experts to argue. I don't have a problem with that. But somehow that is so foreign, that is so contrary to what Darwin would say or teach or believe, that we're teaching the worst kind of lie, the worst kind of education, providing that for our kids with this book—we simply cannot have that in the library. That book should be burned!

Barbara Forrest testified for the plaintiffs that intelligent design was just another form of creationism. She is a secular humanist. She has a belief system; it is not a religious belief system in that sense. But she does have a belief system that anybody that would believe anything religious, you know, there's something wrong with that. We should protect the minds of our young kids and keep that religious stuff from coming to them, because it's fanaticism, was the word; "superstition" was another word that she used. And so, on cross-examination, one of our lawyers asked, What do you mean by that? And how do you feel about these religious leaders today in America? And she commented about ministers, about Focus on the Family, James Dobson, He's an extremist. One of our senators here in Pennsylvania, Rick Santorum, is Catholic and has said that he thinks ID is a good thing to add to the education of students. How do you feel about him? He's an extremist. These were her statements. And when she said that, I thought to myself, Lady, you're the extreme one here. But that was my opinion. She did not convince me at all or have much influence on me, but she seemed to have a lot of influence on Judge Jones. Evidently, her testimony affected him, yes.

There were days you went to court, you felt beat up. They bring in this expert, that expert, they took that one-minute statement and they said, This is the stupidest thing, whoever wrote this? The superintendent, in coordination with the teachers, wrote this thing. The teachers approved it, and then they get on the stand and it's, Look what the administration did, they wrote the most ignorant thing. And they had their experts, word by word, phrase by phrase, destroy it, and beat them up. These expert witnesses, Ken Miller and Barbara Forrest and the others, gave the idea that our kids shouldn't be taught this unscientific, super-stitious notion of intelligent design, that somehow we're going to mess up their heads. Well, that was not our intention, to mess the kids up.

I have no outstanding impressions of Judge Jones—he was doing his job. The plaintiffs made a very good case, and the judge has ruled their way. After the trial, he wrote his decision, and I disagree with him on some of the things he wrote. There were some areas where I think he went beyond what he needed to give his decision, with characteriza-tions of some of the people who served on the school board and their motives. I think he was unfair to them. That didn't in any way affect his decision on whether the board's ID policy was legal. But all this other stuff, saying that board members lied on the stand, I don't believe it really needed to be said.

I am not in favor of teaching religion in school; I am not in favor of teaching creationism. I would not want that mandated for school. First of all, I don't know that the teachers would know enough about it. Sec-ond of all, I don't know if they would believe it. And that opens the door, you would think, to someone coming in with yet another view, and another view. And where does it stop? Do I necessarily want the Buddhists to come in, and as a part of biology class to say, Here's what we believe? It's religion. But I don't agree that ID is religion, and there-fore should not be allowed in the biology classroom, that it's just an-other name for creationism.

Some of Darwin's stuff I have a problem with. Do I not want my son to be exposed to that, because somehow that's going to mess him up? No. I think my wife and I have done a good job helping all of our kids to learn and instructing them, what is the truth. Scripture says, Raise up a child when he is young, and when he is old he will not depart from it. I think Joshua and all my children have a proper education. I am not wor-ried that somehow the school district is going to mess them up. So you want to expose them to that—fine. My job is to talk to them about crea-tionism. My job as a father is to instruct them in the home; my job as a pastor is to instruct them in the church.

My son Joshua probably said it best to *Newsweek* magazine. They asked him, Do you have a problem with hearing about evolution, being a minister's son? And my son said, You know, I'm called to the ministry too, and I'm going to be a missionary. If the class on biology, on evolution, so disturbs my faith, destroys my faith, how strong is my faith? Joshua's pretty straightforward in what he professes. He is the Bible-club president in the school, and he encourages other kids: How are you guys doing? We'll have a devotional in the Bible club. Anybody not feeling well? We'll pray for you. Isn't that a great thing?

There's another interesting thing about this case that most people don't realize. From the trial, and the news reports, it seemed like all the teachers opposed ID because it's bad science. That's what they said, but that's not the way it happened. Two of the biology teachers are preachers' kids. My son was in biology class, and he asked the question: "Now that you're done teaching Darwin's theory, do you believe it?" "Now, Joshua, I'm a minister's child, just like you are." "You didn't answer the question," he said. "Are there any other theories?" "Yes, there are." "What would they be?" "Creation would be one." "Do you believe that?" "Yeah, I do believe that, because I'm a preacher's kid." So here's my minister, my dad, telling me we were created. And here's my science teacher telling me we evolved. Who's lying? Is my minister lying? Because what he's telling me from the Bible does not coincide with what my science teacher's telling me. And what my science teacher's telling me, does that coincide with what my minister's telling me? And the students are put in this position—is somebody lying? That's a dilemma. Part of this is, can we reconcile this? Why does somebody have to be lying? Because the two theories definitely have their differences. And to admit that, is that good education? To me, that's great education. Are we not all about learning? Would that not cause learning to take place?

Is there something to ID? I don't know enough about it to really make an expert opinion. Prior to this past year, I didn't know much about ID at all. They go into principles, the clotting of blood and the creation of the eye and all of these irreducible complexities, and sometimes I'm like, It's dry, it's deep, and I'm like, Oh, man. But on the surface, looking at it, and I heard a lot more at the trial, listening to the experts, the fact that there are the arrangement of parts looks as though someone designed it. Is that going to destroy somebody's view? Can that not be positive for the overall education of our students? Intelligent design, Darwin's view—put them together, make your decisions, learn more about them, balance them off? Is that not good? Some people think it's not.

You can have a great debate on whether the majority of people in a community should be able to decide what's taught in their schools. For the most part, people in Dover agreed with the school board's ID policy. Channel 21, WHB in Harrisburg, did an unofficial poll, randomly called people, and 65 percent of the people said they thought what we were doing was right, and they had no problem with the presentation in the biology class. That really shook those that were plaintiffs. We have to convince a significant majority that this is evil, this is wrong. And they got some clergy, and they got some teachers, and they made a pretty strong effort to convince people that this is wrong, and we are corrupting our students, and this is not the place for it, other than what we already have. And I think they pretty much succeeded, with the election that replaced every school-board member who was up for another term. Straight across the board. I guess it's possible to see that as saying that what we were doing was not for the best interests of the students. And if that's your premise, then maybe this was embarrassing for Dover.

Looking back on this experience, for me, I learned a lot. As I said, I don't believe we should teach religion in the schools. But I also don't believe that intelligent design is religion, contrary to what the plaintiffs' experts testified and how Judge Jones ruled. I don't know that I buy into all of ID, I don't know that I buy into all that Darwin has to say either. But I'm also quite confident in what I believe. I'm a simple person, and I like keeping things simple. It's simple to believe in Scripture. I know what the Bible says, and that's simple. God did it, bam! ❖

Conclusion

Our journey to battlefields in America's religious wars has taken us across the nation, from California to Pennsylvania, with stops along the way in Texas, Kentucky, and Washington, D.C. We have met and talked with people who are atheists, Jews, and many kinds of Christians, from both mainstream and evangelical denominations. They differ in age, gender, income, politics, and occupation. They live in small towns, suburbs, and big cities. They reflect the tremendous—and growing—religious diversity in American society. What they have in common—and what sets them apart from most other Americans—is that each has played a role in recent legal battles over religious symbols and practices in the public square, some as willing volunteers and others as reluctant conscripts.

What can we learn from this journey, and from the stories of the people with whom I talked in visiting their communities? Before I offer my own thoughts on these questions, let me return to the words of Oliver Wendell Holmes, quoted in this book's preface: "We live by symbols." There is a little story here, worth telling for the light it sheds on the pages between that preface and these concluding remarks. I first read those words in my constitutional-law casebook at Harvard Law School in 1977. They were quoted, without citation, in the excerpts from a 1940 Supreme Court opinion by Justice Felix Frankfurter, upholding the expulsion in 1935 of a twelve-year-old girl, Lillian Gobitis, from the junior high school in Minersville, Pennsylvania. Lillian, a Jehovah's Witness in an overwhelmingly Catholic town, had refused on religious grounds to join the daily salute to the American flag and recital of the Pledge of Allegiance.

Portraying the flag as "the symbol of our national unity," Frankfurter warned in *Minersville School District v. Gobitis* that Lillian's refusal to join the salute and the Pledge "might cast doubts in the minds" of her classmates and weaken their loyalty to America. Frankfurter's opinion struck me as callous and cruel, and I was relieved to discover, in my casebook's next excerpt, that it had been overruled three years later, in an opinion by Justice Robert Jackson, striking down the expulsion of Jehovah's Witnesses from public schools in West Virginia. Writing in *West Virginia Board of Education v. Barnette*, Jackson agreed with Frankfurter on the power of symbols like the flag. "Symbolism is a primitive but effective way of communicating ideas," he stated. But every person, Jackson added, "gets from a symbol the meaning he puts into it, and what is one man's comfort and inspiration is another's jest and scorn." Lillian Gobitis had not scorned the flag by refusing to join the salute and Pledge, but she had defied the orders of Minersville's elected school-board members, who had voted to authorize her expulsion for this "act of insubordination."

Justice Jackson put this local conflict into a broader context. "The very purpose of a Bill of Rights," he wrote, was to place its protections "beyond the reach of majorities and officials and to establish them as legal principles to be applied by the courts." The rights of religious and political minorities, he wrote, "may not be submitted to vote; they depend on the outcome of no election." Jackson put his final rebuke to Frankfurter in this resonant sentence: "If there is any fixed star in our constitutional constellation, it is that no official, high or petty, can prescribe what shall be orthodox in politics, nationalism, religion, or other matters of opinion or force citizens to confess by word or act their faith therein."

Ten years after I first read these opinions, I sat down with Lillian— then in her sixties and now in her eighties—and recorded her story for my book *The Courage of Their Convictions*, heading the chapter on her case with the title "We Live by Symbols." Between the time I quoted

Holmes's words in this book's preface and my writing of its conclusion, I decided to track down their source, which I found in a speech he delivered in 1901 at a celebration of the life of Chief Justice John Marshall. Holmes's four words began a sentence that Frankfurter did not complete, but that deserves quotation here: "We live by symbols, and what shall be symbolized by any image of the sight depends on the mind of him who sees it."

This brief story of the flag-salute cases and Holmes's words illustrates several themes that run through this book, and that offer some insight into America's growing religious wars. First, virtually everyone—from militant atheists to evangelical Christians—recognizes the religious "ideas" that are communicated by such symbols as the Latin cross and the Mosaic tablets of the Ten Commandments. Similarly, hardly anyone disputes the religious nature of the Biblical account of creation or references to God in prayer and the Pledge of Allegiance. Second, what is in the mind of each person who sees a religious symbol—the feeling it evokes—reflects that person's values and beliefs. These are shaped by the widening circle of institutions that begin with the family and end with the complex network of the broader culture in which we all live, a culture that is parochial for some, and national and even global for others.

Most people, as common sense tells us and social scientists have confirmed in countless studies, adopt the values and beliefs of their parents in religion and politics. The children of Baptists tend to be Baptists, those raised in Catholic families are likely to be Catholic. Generations of Republicans are matched by generations of Democrats. More than a century ago, Gilbert and Sullivan noted in one of their operettas, "Every boy and every gal who's born into this world alive, is either a little Liberal or else a little Conservative." There are many examples of this general rule, illustrated by the personal stories in this book. John Couch, the school-board chairman in Santa Fe, Texas, who defended the prayers at the high school's football games, was raised in a Southern Baptist family, and his children follow that faith. Ed Rowand, another school-board member in Dover, Pennsylvania, was raised in the evangelical Assemblies of God church, joined its ministry, and has a son who intends to become a missionary in that denomination. But there are many exceptions to the rule. For example, Jay Sekulow was raised in a liberal Jewish family and became an evangelical Christian. Phil Paulson, who challenged the Mount Soledad cross in San Diego, was confirmed in the Lutheran Church and became an atheist. Louanne Walker and Jimmie Greene, who took opposite sides in the Ten Commandments case in Kentucky, are first cousins, attended the same schools, and belonged to the same Baptist church. My point here is simply that each person's values and beliefs, whatever their source and however changeable, affect their differing perceptions of a religious symbol or practice, and their feelings about whether it belongs in the public square.

By themselves, values and beliefs are confined to the interior recesses of each person's mind. What makes them meaningful is their intensity, which can range from apathy to zealotry, from resignation to resolve. Imagine two couples, each standing in the lobby of the McCreary County Courthouse in Whitley City, Kentucky, and looking at the Ten Commandments display on its wall. One member of the first couple says to the other, "I don't think the Commandments should be here, but the county board voted to put them up, and that's what most people want." The other says, "I don't think they should be here either, and I'm going to call the ACLU and see if they'll help us get them down." One member of the second couple says to her companion, "I think it's great to have the Commandments here, but if a judge says we have to take them down, that's the law and we have to obey it." The other replies, "I don't care what some activist judge says. Those are God's laws up there, and I'd go to jail before I'd take them down."

This is what actually happened in McCreary County. Louanne Walker did call the ACLU in Louisville, and her cousin Jimmie Greene, who had placed the Ten Commandments on the courthouse wall, did vow that he would go to jail rather than take them down. In Santa Fe, Texas, Debbie Mason called the ACLU in Houston to seek help in ending prayers at her daughters' schools, and John Couch, the school-board chairman, vowed that he would go to jail rather than obey a court order to end the prayers. Several parents in Dover, Pennsylvania, called the

ACLU in Philadelphia to block the school board's decision to force high-school biology teachers to read a statement endorsing "intelligent design" in their classes on evolution. Faced with a costly lawsuit, the board's president, Alan Bonsell—an evangelical Christian and professed creationist—vowed to pursue the case to the Supreme Court. In San Diego, California, a Vietnam veteran, Phil Paulson—who called himself an "atheist in a foxhole"—filed a lawsuit to remove a Latin cross from the Mount Soledad park; in response, city officials vowed to "save" the cross in the face of judicial orders to remove it. And in Elk Grove, California, another atheist, Dr. Michael Newdow, pursued to the Supreme Court his challenge to the words "under God" in the Pledge of Allegiance, confronted by school-board members who vowed to defend the Pledge ritual to a final judicial decision.

In all these cases, both the challengers and defenders of religious symbols and practices matched their divergent values and beliefs with great intensity. The same intensity of commitment to their cause fueled the efforts of lawyers like Eric Rothschild and Richard Thompson, who battled each other in the "intelligent design" case, and David Friedman and Mathew Staver, who argued before the Supreme Court in the Ten Commandments case from McCreary County. Behind these lawyers are organizations like the ACLU and Americans United on the Separationist side, and the ACLJ and Liberty Counsel on the Religious Right, with more than a million supporters between them, demonstrating their intensity of commitment with dues, donations, and petitions. But these dedicated activists, the backbone of any cause—civil rights, feminism, gay-and-lesbian rights, or protection of the spotted owl—make up just a small fraction of the American public. Political scientists estimate that no more than 3 to 5 percent of the public takes an active role in issue politics, with the vast majority on the sidelines, some cheering for one side or the other on the playing field, but most not even showing up for the game. Close to half of eligible voters don't even cast ballots in presidential and congressional elections, and races for local school-board and city-council seats often draw less than 10 percent of registered voters. To switch metaphors, issue activists drive the locomotives

of politics, pulling behind them a long train of coaches filled with doz-
ing passengers.

Depending on the issue, from protecting Social Security benefits to
funding stem-cell research, many of these passengers can be jolted
awake and will respond to appeals to sign petitions or send letters to
elected officials, from city councils to the Congress. But even the dues-
paying members of interest groups often ignore such appeals. For example, when Jay Sekulow urged his ACLJ supporters in 2006 to sign
an online petition asking President Bush to "save" the Mount Soledad
cross by taking the park site under the federal government's eminent
domain power, only 170,000 people on Sekulow's e-mail list of eight
hundred thousand members clicked a computer button to join the petition campaign.

Given these figures, we might well conclude that America's religious
wars are more akin to Civil War re-enactments, fought with blanks and
wooden bayonets. One respected political scientist, Morris Fiorina of
the Hoover Institution at Stanford University, disparaged the notion of
a deeply divided electorate in his 2005 book, *Culture War? The Myth
of a Polarized America.* Citing a slew of public-opinion polls and voting
studies, Fiorina made this emphatic point: "The simple truth is that
there is no culture war in the United States—no battle for the soul of
America rages, at least none that most Americans are aware of. Certainly, one can find a few warriors who engage in noisy skirmishes.
Many of the activists in the political parties and the various cause
groups do, in fact, hate each other and regard themselves as combatants
in a war. But those hatreds and battles are not shared by the great mass
of the American people . . . who are for the most part moderate in their
views and tolerant in their manner."

Fiorina makes a compelling argument that Americans, in general,
have become more tolerant in recent years on such issues as civil rights
and gay-and-lesbian rights. He notes that older people—less tolerant on
these issues—are "dying off" and "being replaced by more tolerant
younger cohorts" in the population. The ranks of cultural warriors on
these issues, Fiorina concludes, "are being thinned by mortality." But he

makes a significant concession on the issues raised in this book: "Has religiosity become a more important correlate of American voting behavior than it was in past decades? The available data indicate that the answer is yes." The best predictor of conservative voting is not age, gender, or party affiliation; rather, it is church attendance. In the 2004 presidential election, six out of seven of those who attended church services every week supported President George W. Bush over Senator John Kerry.

As fellow political scientists, Fiorina and I agree that religion has become a significant factor in American politics. Wearing my lawyer's hat, however, I take issue with his contention that the broader "culture war" is largely the invention of sensation-seeking journalists, "driven by the need to make the dull and everyday appear exciting and unprecedented." Journalists do flock to the Supreme Court's steps to record the reactions of Barry Lynn and Jay Sekulow to the arguments in religion cases, but the media do not invent these cases. There are hundreds of Whitley Citys across the country, and hundreds of people like Louanne Walker and Dave Howe, willing to call the ACLU or Americans United to challenge religious symbols or practices in their towns. Over the past decade, there have been lawsuits—or threats of suits—over issues like school prayer, Nativity scenes, and the Ten Commandments in every state, in places such as Humansville, Missouri. Many of these cases are resolved without litigation; others are settled after a suit is filed, like the Ten Commandments case I handled for Carrie Roat in Humansville; and a handful reach the Supreme Court and draw national media coverage.

It may be true, as Fiorina argues, that the nation's Carrie Roats belong to "small, unrepresentative minorities," and that vastly larger majorities—whatever their views on issues like the Ten Commandments on schoolroom or courthouse walls—simply do not have the intensity of commitment to file lawsuits and endure the hostility of their town's majority. In dismissing the notion of a "polarized" electorate, Fiorina is himself in the minority of those who write about America's culture wars. Most agree that the war is real, and is growing in intensity as the combatants on both sides struggle for "the soul of America," as

Pat Buchanan declared at the 1992 Republican national convention. Buchanan, in fact, most likely borrowed the "culture war" term from the 1991 book *Culture Wars: The Struggle to Define America*, written by James Davison Hunter, a noted sociologist at the University of Virginia. Dividing Americans into culturally "orthodox" and "progressive" camps, Hunter looked closely and perceptively at the widening gap between the values and beliefs of these two groups over the spectrum of social and political issues, from abortion to foreign policy.

In his follow-up book, *Before the Shooting Begins: Searching for Democracy in America's Culture War*, Hunter wrote in 1994, "When cultural impulses this momentous vie against each other to dominate public life, tension, conflict, and perhaps even violence are inevitable." Certainly in conflicts over abortion, which Harvard law professor Laurence Tribe has aptly described as "the clash of absolutes" between its most fervent defenders and opponents, Hunter's prediction of violence has proved accurate, by the murders of doctors who performed abortions.

Hunter's books, although overtaken since their publication by significant political and legal developments, still provide a refreshing balance of scholarship and journalism. Two more recent books deserve mention here, because they both—in very different ways—illustrate the perils of an unbalanced approach to conflicts over religion in the public square. Noah Feldman, a law professor at New York University, takes what I call the Pollyanna position in his 2005 book, *Divided by God: America's Church-State Problem—and What We Should Do About It*. Labeling the contending sides in America's religious wars as "values evangelicals" and "legal secularists," Feldman correctly notes that the "deep divide" between them "is not primarily over religious belief or affiliation—it is over the role that belief should play in the business of politics and religion." Feldman calls on the church-state combatants to lay down their arms and surrender hard-earned territory to their opponents. Legal secularists—basically this book's Separationists—should give up their objections to religious symbols and practices, such as public display of the Ten Commandments and school prayer. Feldman's prescription is "to allow public religion where it is inclusive, not exclusive, and to allow religious displays and prayers so long as they accommodate and honor religious diversity." Feldman does not address the problem of how to accomplish this without some kind of religious police, making sure that school prayers, for example, are either bland and generic—like the Regents' prayer in the *Engel* case—or that they balance references to Jesus with equal time for Muhammad or Buddha.

In return for this concession by legal secularists, Feldman urges values evangelicals—basically the Religious Right—to abandon their quest for government funding for religion, such as school vouchers and "faith-based" social programs. He puts his formula for solving the church-state issue into five words: "no coercion and no money." Largely a product of law-library research, Feldman's book shows no evidence that he talked with anyone on either side of America's religious wars. It is almost comical to imagine Barry Lynn and Jay Sekulow—whom Feldman does not mention—sitting down to sign a peace treaty based on his surrender terms.

Michelle Goldberg, on the other hand, talked with dozens of people for her 2006 book, *Kingdom Coming: The Rise of Christian Nationalism*. A journalist for the online *Salon* magazine, Goldberg takes what I call the Chicken Little approach, focusing on the outer fringes of the Religious Right, particularly the Christian Reconstructionist movement. Goldberg correctly notes that advocates of a "Christian nation" have gained a foothold in the Republican Party, with their greatest strength in Southern and Midwestern states. But she incorrectly exaggerates the influence of Reconstructionists in the party. An offshoot of old-fashioned Calvinism, Reconstructionism is based on "dominion" theology, which in turn is rooted in a "post-millennialist" reading of the Bible. In contrast to "pre-millennialists," who look forward to the imminent return of Christ to rule for a thousand years before the final victory over Satan's earthly forces, "post-millennialists" assert that Christians must rule over civil society for a thousand years before Christ returns.

This doctrinal dispute may seem esoteric to those not steeped in Calvinist theology. Boiled down, however, the Reconstructionist program calls for a return to the Mosaic legal code of the New England

Puritans, imposing the death penalty for such crimes as homosexuality, blasphemy, and cursing one's parents, with stoning as the preferred punishment. "Why stoning?" asks Gary North, the Reconstructionists' most outspoken leader. "There are many reasons. First, the implements of execution are available to everyone at virtually no cost." In addition, he writes, "executions are community projects—not with spectators who watch a professional executioner do his duty, but rather with actual participants." Not a single Republican leader, of course, endorses North's gruesome proposals, but Goldberg weaves occasional contacts between Reconstructionists and GOP leaders—largely at meetings with open invitations—into a conspiratorial web that stretches to the Capitol Building and the White House administration of President George W. Bush.

To be fair, Goldberg steps back from her frequent equation of Christian nationalism with fascism, buttressed by numerous citations to Hannah Arendt's classic 1951 book, *The Origins of Totalitarianism*. "Fascism isn't imminent in America," Goldberg concedes. "But its language and aesthetics are distressingly common among Christian nationalists," she nonetheless warns. Goldberg, it bears noting, is only the latest in a string of latter-day Jeremiahs, beginning with Sinclair Lewis, whose ironically titled 1935 novel, *It Can't Happen Here*, explored the Depression-fueled rise—and eventual fall—of an American fascist movement. There were real fascists and Nazis back then, but they never posed a serious threat to American democracy. Despite Goldberg's warnings, the Christian Reconstructionist movement today, more theocratic than fascist in its ideology, poses no more of a threat to impose "God-based" laws on the nation.

Despite their substantial differences about the sources of today's religious wars—Feldman thinks secularists are bent on shoving evangelicals out of the public square, while Goldberg views the Religious Right as determined to turn non-Christians into second-class citizens—they both recognize that the primary battlefield in these conflicts has become the federal judiciary, with control of the Supreme Court as the prize. On this crucial front, the outcome depends very largely on political developments, with the 2008 presidential election as the battle for which the contending sides have already begun rallying their forces. Barring the death or retirement of current justices before that election, President Bush's successor will almost certainly have at least two or three Supreme Court seats to fill during his or her first term. The most likely vacancies would come from the Court's liberal wing: Justice John Paul Stevens was born in 1920, and Ruth Bader Ginsburg in 1933. Neither of them would voluntarily leave the Court while Bush remains in office, but the election of a Democratic president would almost certainly prompt their retirements. Needless to say, all these speculations are hedged with qualifiers; no one can read any justice's mind, and they all have life tenure on the bench.

Assuming, however, that the Court retains its current membership until the presidential inauguration in January 2009, one thing is certain: both sides in America's religious wars will throw all their resources into the Senate confirmation battles over the next Court nominee. With the replacement of Justice Sandra Day O'Connor by Samuel Alito in 2006, the Court's precarious balance in religion cases now hinges on the decisive vote of Justice Anthony Kennedy. Consistently opposed to school prayer for the "coercion" it imposes on captive audiences of impressionable students, he also voted to uphold the Ten Commandments displays in both Kentucky and Texas as permissible "acknowledgments" of the nation's religious heritage and traditions. Given his divided votes on challenges to religious symbols and practices, Kennedy's future colleagues will likely decide whether he retains or relinquishes his role as the swing vote in Establishment Clause cases, and whether the Court's "hopeless disarray" in these cases will be resolved in the coming years.

————

Concluding this book with a focus on one Supreme Court justice, or the outcome of one presidential election, would leave the misleading impression that a single person or event can shape the future course of America's religious wars. From colonial days until the present, Americans have been—as they will remain—divided over the proper role of religion in the public square. Today, roughly equal numbers stand on the opposite sides of Jefferson's metaphorical "wall of separation" between church and state. Only a small fraction, however, have enlisted as combatants in the contending forces of the Separationist and Religious Right groups that battle over religious symbols and practices. Driven by deeply held values and beliefs, partisans in both camps provide the foot soldiers who contribute money, sign petitions, and show up at campaign rallies for candidates who support their causes. American politics has always been dominated by committed activists, but religion adds to the intensity of many partisans.

I returned from my recent visits to the towns and cities whose local conflicts over religion are recounted in this book with a renewed appreciation for the willingness of ordinary Americans to take a stand for their beliefs. Some of the people I talked with, like Louanne Walker in McCreary County, Kentucky, are soft-spoken and shy away from the media spotlight. Others, like her cousin Jimmie Greene, run for office and seek out cameras and microphones. Some, like Debbie Mason in Santa Fe, Texas, never finished high school; others, like John Couch, their town's school-board chairman, have college degrees. What all the people I talked with share, and what most impressed me about them, is their basic commitment to American democracy and the rule of law. After some four centuries of religious conflict, America's religious wars continue, but they are now fought in courtrooms, and not in inquisitions that end with banishment, prison, or the hangman's noose. But as we celebrate our Constitution's dual guarantees—freedom from established religion, and freedom to exercise our religious beliefs—we should not forget the sacrifices of people like Anne Hutchinson, Joseph Weatherford, and Mary Dyer. It was their sacrifices that led to our cherished liberties.

SOURCES AND SUGGESTED READINGS

This book is a blend of journalism and scholarship, both mine and that of many others who have written about the cases and issues it covers. More than any of my previous books, it relies heavily on material from Internet sources, largely newspapers and organizational Web sites. Rather than burden readers with several thousand footnotes, I list below for each chapter the primary sources from which these accounts are drawn, with references to the local and regional newspapers that reported the cases I have recounted, the judicial proceedings and opinions in them, and books that deal with these issues. Readers who wish to locate the sources of any quoted material can find them with a few keywords on search engines like Google or Yahoo. I would be glad to provide sources and can be reached by e-mail at pirons@ucsd.edu.

In the Preface, I refer to two books on the "wars" over religion in the public square: David Limbaugh, *Persecution: How Liberals Are Waging War Against Christianity* (Regnery Publishing, 2003), and Clint Willis, *Jesus Is Not a Republican: Right-Wing Movements and Political Power in the United States* (Thunder's Mouth Press, 2005).

For Chapter One, a useful background source is my own book *A People's History of the Supreme Court* (Penguin, revised and updated edition, 2006). There are also four good books that deal with the Establishment Clause and debates over its "original intent" and judicial interpretation. On the "Separationist" side are Leonard Levy, *The Establishment Clause* (University of North Carolina Press, 2nd revised edition, 1994), and Isaac Kramnick and R. Laurence Moore, *The Godless Constitution: A Moral Defense of the Secular State* (W. W. Norton, updated edition, 2005). On the "accommodationist" side are Daniel Dreisbach, *Thomas Jefferson and the Wall of Separation Between Church and State* (New York University Press, 2002), and Robert L. Cord, *Separation of Church and State: Historical Fact and Current Fiction* (Baker Publishing Group, 1988).

In Chapter Two, all of the Supreme Court cases I discuss are recounted briefly in my *People's History of the Supreme Court*. The full text of the opinions in these cases can be found on the Web at findlaw.com, by entering the case name, and also in the volumes of *United States Reports*, available in most big-city and university libraries. Cases are cited by volume, beginning page number, and year of decision. For example, the first case discussed in Chapter Two, *Gitlow v. New York*, can be found at 268 U.S. 625 (1925). The remaining cases in this chapter, in order, are: *Cantwell v. Connecticut*, 310 U.S. 296 (1940); *Everson v. Ewing Township*, 330 U.S. 1 (1947); *McCollum v. Board of Education*, 333 U.S. 203 (1948); *Zorach v. Clauson*, 343 U.S. 306 (1952); *Engel v. Vitale*, 370

U.S. 421 (1962); *Abington Township v. Schempp*, 374 U.S. 203 (1963); *Lemon v. Kurtzman*, 403 U.S. 602 (1971); *Lynch v. Donnelly*, 465 U.S. 668 (1984); *Allegheny County v. ACLU*, 492 U.S. 573 (1989); *Epperson v. Arkansas*, 393 U.S. 97 (1968); *Edwards v. Aguillard*, 482 U.S. 578 (1987); *Wallace v. Jaffree*, 472 U.S. 38 (1985); and *Lee v. Weisman*, 505 U.S. 577 (1992).

An invaluable background source for Chapter Three, and by far the most comprehensive book on the Religious Right, is William Martin, *With God on Our Side: The Rise of the Religious Right in America* (Broadway Books, 1996). Other useful books on this topic include Sara Diamond, *Roads to Dominion: Right-Wing Movements and Political Power in the United States* (Guilford Press, 1995); Sara Diamond, *Not by Politics Alone: The Enduring Influence of the Christian Right* (Guilford Press, 2000); Frederick Clarkson, *Eternal Hostility: The Struggle Between Theocracy and Democracy* (Common Courage Press, 1997); and Kevin Phillips, *American Theocracy: The Perils and Politics of Radical Religion, Oil, and Borrowed Money in the 21st Century* (Viking, 2006).

There are no books on the Separationist movement, but readers might want to consult, for background, Susan Jacoby, *Freethinkers: A History of American Secularism* (Metropolitan Books, 2004). George Barna's polling data can be found at his group's Web site, barnagroup.com. Each of the Separationist and Religious Right legal groups has voluminous, and regularly updated, material at their respective Web sites: the American Civil Liberties Union (aclu.org); Americans United for Separation of Church and State (au.org); American Center for Law and Justice (aclj.org); Liberty Counsel (libertycounsel.org); Thomas More Law Center (thomasmore.org); and Alliance Defense Fund (alliancedefensefund.org).

For Chapter Four, on the Mount Soledad cross case, much of the news coverage came from articles in the *San Diego Union-Tribune*, and can be accessed through the Internet on that paper's Web site. I have also drawn on my own files on that case, as Philip Paulson's lawyer from 1989 to 1998. Judge Thompson's initial opinion in this case can be found at *Murphy v. Bilbray*, 782 Federal Supplement 1420 (S.D. Cal. 1991); and the subsequent Ninth Circuit opinions at *Ellis v. City of La Mesa*, 990 Federal Reporter 2d (9th Cir. 1993), and *Paulson v. City of San Diego*, 294 Federal Reporter 3d (9th Cir. 2002).

Chapter Five, on the Santa Fe, Texas, football-game prayer case, draws on news reporting in the *Houston Chronicle* and the *Galveston Daily News*. Judge Kent's initial ruling in 1995 was not printed in official court reporters, but is quoted in the Fifth Circuit opinion upholding that ruling, *Santa Fe Independent School District v. Doe*, 168 Federal Reporter 3d (5th Cir. 1999). The transcript of the Supreme Court oral arguments in this case can be found on the Internet at oyez.org under the case name. The Court's opinions are at 530 U.S. 290 (2000), and can also be accessed at findlaw.com.

Chapter Six, on the Ten Commandments cases, draws on news reporting in the *Louisville Courier-Journal*, the *Lexington Herald-Leader*, and the *McCreary County Record*. The Sixth Circuit opinion in the Kentucky cases is at *McCreary County v. ACLU of Kentucky*, 354 Federal Reporter 3d 438 (6th Cir. 2004). The Supreme Court oral-argument transcripts in this case can be found on the Internet at supremecourtus.gov/oral_arguments/argument_transcripts.html (03-1693), and the Court's opinions, which are not yet printed in United States Reports, under the case name at findlaw.com. The Fifth Circuit's opinion in the Texas case, *Van Orden v. Perry*, is at 351 Federal Reporter 3d 173 (5th Cir. 2003), the Supreme Court oral-argument transcripts at supremecourtus.gov/oral_arguments/argument_transcripts.html (03-1500), and the Court's opinions at findlaw.com.

Chapter Seven, on the Pledge of Allegiance case from Elk Grove, California, draws on reporting in the *Sacramento Bee* and the *Elk Grove Citizen*. The Ninth Circuit opinion in this case, under the caption *Newdow v. U.S. Congress*, is at 328 Federal Reporter 3d 466 (9th Cir. 2003). The Supreme Court oral-argument transcripts are at supremecourtus.gov/oral_arguments/argument_transcripts/02-1624, and the Court's opinions at 542 U.S. 1 (2004).

Chapter Eight, on the "intelligent design" case from Dover, Pennsylvania, draws on reporting in the *York Dispatch* and the *York Daily Record*. The entire trial transcript, some six thousand pages in length, and Judge Jones's opinion, can be found on the Internet at talkorigins.com, under the keyword "Dover." There are two Web sites, that of the Discovery Institute (discovery.org) and that of the National Center for Science Education (natcenscied.org), that have much useful material on the "intelligent design" issue. Readers might also want to consult the following books: Edward J. Larson, *Trial and Error: The American Controversy over Creation and Evolution* (Oxford University Press, 3rd edition, 2003); Kenneth R. Miller, *Finding Darwin's God: A Scientist's Search for Common Ground Between God and Evolution* (HarperCollins, 1999); Michael Behe, *Darwin's Black Box: The Biochemical Challenge to Evolution* (Free Press, 2nd revised edition, 2006); Phillip E. Johnson, *Darwin on Trial* (InterVarsity Press, 2nd edition, 1993); and Barbara Forrest and Paul R. Gross, *Creationism's Trojan Horse: The Wedge of Intelligent Design* (Oxford University Press, 2004).

In the Conclusion, I have quoted from the Supreme Court opinions in the Jehovah's Witnesses flag-salute cases, *Minersville School District v. Gobitis*, 310 U.S. 586 (1940) and *West Virginia Board of Education v. Barnette*, 319 U.S. 624 (1943). I also quoted from and discussed the following books: James Davison Hunter, *Culture Wars: The Struggle to Define America* (Basic Books, 1992); Morris P. Fiorina, *Culture War? The Myth of a Polarized America* (Longman Publishing, 2nd edition, 2005); Noah Feldman, *Divided by God: America's Church-State Problem—and What We Should Do About It* (Farrar, Straus, and Giroux, 2005); and Michelle Goldberg, *Kingdom Coming: The Rise of Christian Nationalism* (W. W. Norton, 2006).

INDEX

Culture War? (Fiorina), 344–45
Culture Wars (Hunter), 346

Darrow, Clarence, 282–83
Darwin, Sir Charles, 47, 282
Darwin on Trial (Johnson), 310
Darwin's Black Box (Behe), 304, 306, 309, 311
Dayton, Tenn., 37–38, 281–84
Declaration of Independence, 7–8, 188, 191, 192, 206, 244, 256
Dees, Morris, 95
Democratic Party, 21, 84, 102, 115, 189, 349
Discovery Institute, 292, 294–95, 300–301, 311–12, 316–18
Divided by God (Feldman), 346–47
Dobson, James, 61
Doerr, Edd, 56
Douglas, William O., 22, 26–27
Dover, Pa., *see Kitzmiller v. Dover Area School District*
Dustin, Carl, 99–100
Dyer, Mary, 6–7, 350

Eagle Forum, 58, 59
Eagles, Fraternal Order of, 195, 197, 198
Easter Cross, *see* Mount Soledad (Easter) cross; *Paulson v. San Diego*
Edwards v. Aguillard, 38–39, 40
Eisenhower, Dwight, 239, 257
elections, U.S.:
 of 1928, 21
 of 1960, 46
 of 2004, 49, 101, 183, 195, 203, 246, 258, 345
 of 2008, 349
Elk Grove Unified School District v. Newdow, 54, 59, 61, 234–80
 author's interviews with participants in, 260–80
 author's involvement in, 247
 background to, 234–36
 legal history of, 235–60
Engel v. Vitale, 28–30, 31, 32, 347
Epperson v. Arkansas, 38, 42
Establishment Clause, U.S. Constitution:
 adoption of, 14–15
 original intent and, ix, 1, 9–10, 23
 other Supreme Court rulings on, xiv–xv, 16–43, 143, 145, 190
 religious conflict leading up to, 2–7
 tax support for religious schools and, 21

 text of, ix, xiv, 14–15
 see also specific cases
evangelical Christians, 2–3, 5, 46, 47, 48–52, 58, 60, 94, 203, 283, 346–47
Everson v. Ewing Township, 21–24, 27, 29, 33, 42, 249–50, 255
evolutionary theory court cases, xii, 38–39, 47, 281–338

Faith and Values Coalition, 59
Falwell, Jerry, xvi, 50, 55, 56, 59, 61, 191
Federalist Society, 193, 213
Feldman, Noah, 346–47
Ferguson, Homer, 239–40
Fernandez, Ferdinand, 98, 241–42
Fifth Amendment, U.S. Constitution, xv, 17
Finding Darwin's God (Miller), 304
Fiorina, Morris, 344–45
First Amendment, U.S. Constitution, 16, 23, 196, 199, 293
 due process and, xv, 17
 first clause of, *see* Establishment Clause, U.S. Constitution
 Free Speech and Free Press clauses of, 17–18
First Unitarian Church, 92
flag, U.S.:
 as symbol, ix, 340
 see also Pledge of Allegiance
Flag Day, 239, 257
Florence Markofer Elementary School, 235
Focus on the Family, 61
football games, prayers at, *see Santa Fe Independent School District v. Doe*
Forrest, Barbara, 310–12, 315
Foundation for Thought and Ethics, 295
"Foundations of American Law and Government Display," 191–93, 206, 212
Fourteenth Amendment, xv, 17–19, 43
Frankfurter, Felix, 22, 24, 27–28, 29, 235, 339–41
Freedom From Religion Foundation, 96
Friedman, David, 54, 189–93, 205–6, 211–14, 343
Frye, Donna, 110
fundamentalists, 47–48, 283

Genesis, Book of, x, 38, 48, 282–84, 288, 291, 301, 316

A People's History of the Supreme Court
The Men and Women Whose Cases and Decisions
Have Shaped Our Constitution
In the tradition of Howard Zinn's classic *A People's History of the United States*, Peter Irons chronicles the decisions that have influenced virtually every aspect of our society, from the debates over judicial power to controversial rulings in the past regarding slavery, racial segregation, and abortion, as well as more current cases about school prayer, the Bush/Gore election results, and "enemy combatants." A comprehensive history of the people and cases that have changed history, this is the definitive account of the nation's highest court.

ISBN 978-0-14-303738-5

Jim Crow's Children
The Broken Promise of the *Brown* Decision
In 1954 the U.S. Supreme Court sounded the death knell for school segregation with its decision in *Brown v. Board of Education of Topeka*. So goes the conventional wisdom. Weaving together vivid portraits of lawyers and such judges as Thurgood Marshall and Earl Warren, sketches of numerous black children throughout history whose parents joined lawsuits against Jim Crow schools, and gripping courtroom drama scenes, Irons shows how the erosion of the *Brown* decision—especially by the Court's rulings over the past three decades—has led to the "resegregation" of public education in America.

ISBN 978-0-14-200375-6

The Courage of Their Convictions
Sixteen Americans Who Fought Their Way to the Supreme Court
They are carpenters, bartenders, doctors, lawyers, students, teachers; they are male, female, black, white, Asian, Hispanic; they are heterosexual, gay. They pursued their beliefs, and their constitutional rights, all the way to the Supreme Court. In *The Courage of Their Convictions*, Peter Irons goes beyond the faceless names referred to in court decisions, bringing us the voices of the actual people who fought for their rights, as he insightfully conveys the human side of the workings of our constitutional system.

ISBN 978-0-14-012810-9